The Prodigal Husband

Justice Denied: The Law versus Donald Marshall, 1986
Unholy Orders: Tragedy at Mount Cashel, 1990
Rare Ambition: The Crosbies of Newfoundland, 1992

The Prodigal Husband

The Tragedy of
Helmuth and Hanna Buxbaum

Michael Harris

Canadian Cataloguing in Publication Data

Harris, Michael, 1948–
The prodigal husband: the tragedy of Helmuth and
Hanna Buxbaum

ISBN 0-7710-3956-5

1. Buxbaum, Helmuth, 1939–   . 2. Buxbaum, Hanna,
1936-1984. 3. Trials (Murder) – Ontario – St. Catharines.
4. Murder – Ontario – Strathroy Region. 5. Criminals –
Ontario – Biography. I. Title.

HV6535.C33S82 1994   364.1'523'092   C94-931544-3

The publishers acknowledge the support of the Canada Council,
the Ontario Ministry of Culture, Tourism and Recreation, and the
Ontario Arts Council for their publishing program.

Typesetting by M&S, Toronto
Printed and bound in Canada.
The paper used in this book is acid-free.

McClelland & Stewart Inc.
The Canadian Publishers
481 University Avenue
Toronto, Ontario
M5G 2E9

1 2 3 4 5   98 97 96 95 94

For Hanna

"There's two people to Helmuth Buxbaum. You don't even know the other side of Helmuth Buxbaum, Mr. Greenspan. There's no possible way you could know. I have seen it." – Robert Barrett, co-accused in the Hanna Buxbaum murder, October 23, 1985

"The situation that arose in the Buxbaum case is one which in my experience can occur where an accused person refuses to raise insanity as a defence. . . . In these cases when counsel follows the instructions of their client and the Crown does not raise the defence and the trial judge does not leave the defence to the jury, there is a real risk that a person who was insane at the time of the commission of the offence will be convicted." – Neuropsychiatrist Dr. Andrew Malcolm

"The heart is deceitful above all things and desperately wicked: who can know it?" – Jeremiah 17:9

Contents

Preface

When Clayton Ruby came to me in the spring of 1990 with a proposal from one of his clients to reinvestigate the man's conviction for murdering his wife, I was reminded of an old truth; for better or worse, we are all captives of our past.

As the author of two books on famous miscarriages of justice, I have gained a reputation as something of a literary ghostbuster, the person to call when a spook is loose in the halls of justice and the usual exorcisms have failed. The reality is far less exalted: I am better described as a slow hound with a good nose – traits that have proven useful in running to ground that most elusive of game, the truth. As Clayton Ruby probably knew before he called, my work on the Donald Marshall and Mount Cashel cases had left its mark on me: having seen firsthand that *everything* can and does go horribly wrong in a system nobly designed to produce justice, I will always bring an open mind to the claims of desperate men – an open mind and a critical one.

Ruby came straight to the point: despite unsuccessful appeals all the way to the Supreme Court of Canada, it was his belief that there had been a tragic miscarriage of justice in the sensational case of Helmuth Buxbaum, the wealthy nursing home owner who in 1986 had been convicted of arranging his wife's death. He said that Buxbaum was an even sorrier victim of injustice than Donald Marshall, albeit for different reasons. No one was in a better position to make that comparison than Clayton Ruby. He had personally represented Marshall at the royal commission that indicted the Nova Scotia justice system in 1990 for having sent an innocent man to prison for eleven years. I was intrigued by Ruby's comparison. One of Canada's great criminal lawyers was telling me that the Buxbaum case was even worse in its own way than the country's most notorious miscarriage of justice. Before deciding whether to get involved, I needed to find out why.

Ruby explained that the courts had violated one of the fundamental principles of Canadian law by trying and convicting a mentally incompetent man, despite indisputable *physical* evidence of serious brain damage and insanity. For purely legal reasons, the substantial body of medical evidence that Ruby believed established Helmuth Buxbaum's insanity had never been examined in court. To leave him in prison, Ruby said, was like beating an animal that would never understand why it was being punished.

I took the next step; communicating directly with Helmuth Buxbaum. He, too, linked his case to Donald Marshall's, but to my surprise, this time the comparison was direct. Buxbaum claimed to be innocent of any involvement in his wife's murder. There was no mention of insanity. In fact, during later meetings at Kingston Penitentiary, he adamantly denied any mental incompetence: "My lawyer knows that I'm innocent," Buxbaum told me. "If you agree to look into my case, you will soon see that I had nothing to do with Hanna's death."

Noting the discrepancy between Ruby's and Buxbaum's claims, I conducted preliminary investigations that persuaded me that the full story of this tangled affair had yet to be told. I agreed to a commission to reinvestigate the bizarre circumstances surrounding the murder of Hanna Buxbaum. My basic condition in subsequent negotiations was unwaveringly clear and forcefully presented on my behalf by Edward Roberts, now minister of justice for Newfoundland. I would not be entering the fray as Buxbaum's champion, the way a lawyer does when he accepts a case, but rather as an independent investigator. My fundamental task would be to test the assertions of the convicted man and his counsel against the facts as I found them. To do that, I required access to all information in the possession of Buxbaum's many lawyers and complete editorial control over its use. Over the years, I have followed the principle that the truth is found in the facts, not in a writer's opinion of them. If, at the end of the day, the facts supported Helmuth Buxbaum's protestations of innocence, or Clayton Ruby's claim that his client was insane, my investigation would reflect that: but if a different story emerged, that is the one I would tell. Helmuth Buxbaum and his lawyers agreed.

Four long, difficult, and fascinating years later, I had worked through the most complex case I have ever been associated with. The trail led through daunting legal and medical thickets, the heartbreaking wreckage of a once vibrant family, and a police investigation that was nothing short of staggering in its scope and intensity. The book that is the product of that odyssey, *The Prodigal Husband*, contains no author-simulated dialogue, no unattributed information, or changed names. Every quote comes verbatim from personal interviews, police records, court testimony, private correspondence, or medical records. The book contains the most intimate of information, including something that is usually not found in works of this kind – detailed quotes from the victim, Hanna Buxbaum, taken from a life story she taped with a friend a few years before her murder. Together with scores of love letters between Helmuth and Hanna, which have been translated from German, that life story has allowed me to create a portrait of the Buxbaums that is surprisingly complete. From their early days in the refugee camps of Europe, I follow them through their dizzying business success in North America to the ominous beginnings of the tragedy that by 1986 had so completely overtaken them. It is not often that a fundamentalist Christian multimillionaire stands in the dock, charged with his wife's murder, while his children watch from the public gallery. As Helmuth Buxbaum's remarkable trial would show, rarely has the attainment of the American Dream ended in such tatters.

Joseph Conrad once wrote that particular voyages sometimes stand as an illustration of life: the same can be said of certain dread crimes. You are about to be immersed in such a murder. It is a tale that begins in faraway places where dreams were kept alive in the chaos of war and later realized in that land of milk and honey called Canada. It is an epic of faith and blind toil, piety and love, that ultimately turned to drugs, betrayal, and murder. A decade later, it still fascinates and repels, a judicial chestnut wrapped in a medical controversy. The tragedy of Helmuth and Hanna Buxbaum is, as Conrad says, an illustration of life – a dark tale of what there is to fear in the human condition and what there is to pity.

Whether the story has a final, as yet unwritten, chapter will be for others to decide.

Michael Harris
Lunenburg, Nova Scotia
July 5, 1994

Acknowledgements

In a work of this magnitude, an author is indebted to many, many people. Here are a few whose assistance was particularly important:

Mr. Justice Harry J. Keenan, an old friend, eminent legal scholar and fine judge who helped with difficult points of the law; Mr. Justice John O'Driscoll, the judge who presided at the trial of Helmuth Buxbaum and who graciously shared remembrances of the celebrated case; the Honourable Edward M. Roberts, justice minister of Newfoundland, and his director of public prosecutions, Colin Flynn, who also advised on matters of the law; Mr. Justice Michael Martin, who prosecuted the Buxbaum case, and his assistants, Alisdair MacDonald and Brendan Evans, who were kind enough to discuss the Crown's case; OPP officers Mel Getty and Paul Edwards, who shared their personal recollections of the Hanna Buxbaum murder investigation; Deputy-Commissioner Ron Piers, the lead investigator of the Buxbaum murder case, a superb policeman, and the person the author is most indebted to for his unfailing assistance in making clear the inner workings of one of Canada's most comprehensive murder investigations; Clayton Ruby, the criminal lawyer who handled Helmuth Buxbaum's various appeals, and who shared his exhaustive knowledge of the case and the law in an ever helpful way; Greg Richards, Helmuth Buxbaum's civil lawyer, who always made himself available to the author in ways that greatly aided the project; Dr. Ruth Bray and Dr. Andrew Malcolm, who were good enough to assist the author in his portrayal of the medical issues by discussing the psychological and psychiatric evidence; Dr. Graham Turrell, whose personal recollections of his psychological examination of Buxbaum deepened the author's understanding of the medical evidence; medical illustrator David Aldrich, whose drawings based on CAT-scan evidence provided the first graphic protrayal of the extent of Helmuth Buxbaum's brain damage; Ella Agnew, another of Buxbaum's civil lawyers, whose timely interventions moved the project out of the inevitable ruts it fell into from time to time; Ernst Achenback and Crystal Savory-Lohnes, German scholars who translated extensive family records and correspondence that was essential to the recreation of the early history of the Buxbaums; Helmuth Buxbaum, who waived all solicitor-client privilege in this matter and extended to the author his time and most intimate personal records so that details of this case never before revealed could be written about; and Phillip Buxbaum, one of Helmuth Buxbaum's sons, who greatly assisted the author with certain family details and insights into his father.

The author regrets that the man who directed Helmuth Buxbaum's defence, Edward Greenspan, declined to be interviewed for the book. Every effort was made to portray accurately this eminent lawyer's participation in the case.

Of course, there would be no book without McClelland & Stewart, and the author's deepest appreciation goes to Avie Bennett, the economic engine that drives Canada's premier publishing house, and to Doug Gibson, a great publisher and an old acquaintance. The author's appreciation also goes out to senior editor Dinah Forbes, whose deft editorial touch helped streamline a very large manuscript. Dinah also saved the author from some of his excesses, which, as anyone who knows him can confirm, is a little like making it across the bridge without the troll getting you.

Finally, to Lynda Harris, the author's indispensable partner in crime, what is there to say? This is not the first roller-coaster ride she has shared with him, and he trusts it will not be the last. The author only hopes that the good times outweighed the bad, as they did for him, because of her sunny spirit and pure heart. There is no one finer.

JULY 4, 1984

That night, Robert Barrett and his drunken bodyguard injected more drugs than their female companions thought possible. At one point in the marathon coke-fest, Barrett made a game of tossing syringes into the walls of their suite in Toronto's Westbury Hotel. As the man known as "Squirrel" in the bars and strip joints of London shot cocaine to get high and dropped Valium to bring himself down again, one of the girls realized how he'd gotten his nickname. Up and down, up and down — "just like a goddamn squirrel."

But Robert Barrett didn't particularly care about the spectacle he was making of himself. He was just happy to be in Toronto. It wasn't Florida, but it was a lot better than London. Until July 5 had come and gone, anywhere was better than London.

Only a week ago Barrett and another London-area addict and petty criminal, Pat Allen, had collided over the collection of a drug debt and ended up negotiating the fine points of a contract killing. Allen, or "Speedo" as he was known for his epic addiction to amphetamines, had at first promised to find someone interested in accepting $10,000 to kill the wife of a wealthy local businessman; on reflection, he had decided to do the hit himself.

With Barrett establishing his alibi at a raucous Toronto drug party, Allen made his way to a London tavern to fortify himself for the work ahead. Before going in, he opened the trunk of the blue Chevy Nova rental car he was driving and worked on the sluggish trigger action of the Harrington & Richardson .32-calibre revolver he had stashed there earlier in the day. Satisfied that it was in working order, he went inside for a drink. He had everything he needed for the imminent murder except for some helpers, a detail that was taken care of when local toughs Gary Foshay and Terry Armes walked into the bar.

After hours of drinking, Allen, Armes, and Foshay drove to East London where they bought an eighth of an ounce of amphetamines for the wholesale price of $150. With his companions racing along on the Superman high of speed, it was the perfect moment for Allen to make his pitch.

"Do you want to make $3,000?" he asked Foshay.

"How?"

"I can't talk in front of Terry," Allen said.

"Terry is my partner," Foshay replied.

After considering his position for a moment, Allen decided to proceed.

"I have a job to do – killing somebody – and I need help."

"I'm interested," Foshay said.

"Good," Allen said.

Back at the tavern, the three men drank and danced until closing time. On their way out, Allen presented Foshay with his choice of weapons:

"I have a .32 or you can use a machine gun."

"I would like to have the machine gun," Foshay replied.

With his supporting cast in place, Allen drove to the London apartment of a girlfriend to pick up the KK9 he had been storing there for the past month. After shooting more speed, the men hid the loaded gun in the trunk of the Nova and drove through the dark countryside to the spot on Highway 402 where the ambush was to take place – a steep embankment overgrown with wild wheat and reeds. At the bottom was a covered storm sewer feeding into a stream that ran through a heavily wooded ravine.

Feeling the pleasant rush of being in charge, Speedo pulled over and explained how the hit would go down. Looking down at the drain cover he had removed earlier that afternoon, he completed his instructions.

"We will kill her in the gully and throw her in the drain," Allen said.

"That's fine," Foshay said.

Terry Armes enjoyed a private laugh. He had known a lot of rounders in London who became one-man crime waves after too much booze and speed. Gary Foshay was "gung-ho" about Allen's plan, but Armes merely nodded his approval, pretty sure that his friends were talking "pure bullshit." It was agreed they would return to the scene of the execution at 7:45 A.M. to prepare for the delivery of their victim by the man none of them had ever met – Helmuth Buxbaum.

Until then, there was nothing to do but lie low until sunrise.

✦ ✦ ✦

While the highwaymen were making their plans, and her husband was shooting cocaine in the privacy of his elaborate fallout shelter, Hanna Buxbaum was sleeping soundly in her Komoka dream house. Just the day before, they had returned from a two-week European vacation and she was still exhausted from the transatlantic flight and the long drive back to their southwestern Ontario home from the airport in Buffalo.

For the past several months, Hanna's twenty-three-year marriage had been beset by strange and dreadful events, the worst being her husband's stubborn addiction to cocaine. But with Helmuth's promise to seek help for his drug abuse and his application for admission to a Christian psychiatric hospital folded neatly in the bottom of her purse, she felt that the solution to their heartbreaking problems was finally in sight.

She thought back to their happy vacation in Europe. The highlight for her had been the Passion Play performed at Oberammergau, Germany, in the Bavarian Alps. Its theme of sin and atonement had been good for her husband, a refresher course in the Christian morality that had once been the centre of his life. But the ancient play had also offered dark prophecy. As the tenor soloist on Oberammergau's mountainside stage had sung just before Christ was betrayed to his executioners by one of his own disciples:

The most terrible of deeds
Is soon done,
Today, this very night . . .

I

HELMUTH

"I considered getting run over by a train or jumping off a bridge, but then I would usually think about how it would hurt my mother and I would discard my suicidal musings until the next violin lesson."

— *Helmuth Buxbaum on his youth in post-war Austria*

Spring 1945 — a season of human scarecrows stirring amidst the rubble-heap of Europe. Emerging from one form of internment or another, an army of refugees rode cattle-cars back to their native cities, where life was little better than it had been in the camps. Surrounded by poverty, disease, and starvation, they sifted through the ruins of war for what remained of their families, a grim but necessary accounting before the work of rebuilding could begin.

Like many European couples, Otto and Luise Buxbaum had been separated by war. Ethnic Germans, they had met and married in Siberia in the wake of the First World War. Otto, who had converted to Protestantism and become a preacher in a Russian prison camp, was well suited to his staunchly religious wife, Luise. They eventually settled in Melk, Austria, and later in Labiau, East Prussia.

There, on March 19, 1939, the Buxbaums' nine children — Maria, Friedrich, Otto Jr., Gottlieb, Elizabeth, Isbrandt, Esther, Lydia, and Hildegunde — were joined by a tenth, Helmuth. The last child was given a middle name that symbolized the family's piety — "Treugott," which means God is faithful. Within a few months of Helmuth's birth, war uprooted the Buxbaums for a second time, sending them tumbling across the battle-scarred terrain of Europe and Russia.

Otto and his eldest sons were drafted, but only after Nazi authorities closely examined the family tree for any taint of Jewish blood. Friedrich went into the infantry, Gottlieb into the anti-aircraft defences, and young Otto into the U-boat service that would bring Hitler's war to North America. Fluent in six languages, Otto senior, a veteran of the Kaiser's army, became a translator. When his train pulled out of the railway station, neither Otto nor Luise knew that it would be five long years before they would be reunited in a world that had changed terribly.

As if a harbinger of the bitter days ahead, their twelve-year-old daughter, Elizabeth, died of a ruptured appendix on September 24, 1940. Then death came calling from the same heavens that the Buxbaums so often importuned in prayer. When, late in the war, Allied planes began the deadly carpet bombing that reduced cities like Dresden to rubble, the German high command began to move the civilian population away from the hottest war zones. Luise and the remaining six children, including young Helmuth, were evacuated to Saxony in western Germany in 1944. They were part of a human tide of refugees from East Prussia and Silesia who fled west in the face of the approaching Russian Army. Luise, then forty-four, felt like "Lot's wife" as she stood on the railway platform beside her children and the few belongings they could carry, wondering if the family would ever be together again.

Towards the end of the war, Luise worked as a Red Cross nurse in an auxiliary hospital helping refugees to cope with the misery of Germany's final agony. Everywhere the caravan of dispossessed humanity went the bombers seemed to follow. Luise and the children were constantly shifted from camp to camp, searching for a safe haven that no longer existed. To young Helmuth, the chaos was exciting: "Seeing people huddled around open fires to warm themselves and riding on cattle trains was interesting and inspiring for my young eyes," he later recalled.

Luise had taught her family not to steal, but the Lord also helped those who helped themselves – especially when they were starving. During their stay in Saxony in a single attic room, her son Isbrandt made nocturnal forays for freshly planted seed potatoes, fleeing the scene of his compromised religious beliefs when the farmer chased him away with oaths and a wooden club. He became a hero to Helmuth when he returned one night with a delicious treat for the family table – a dead cat.

On Christmas Day 1944, six months after the Allies had established a beach-head at Normandy, Luise placed an undecorated evergreen tree in a flower pot, and celebrated Christmas with her six children. It was a far cry from her childhood memories of Christmas in the Crimea, where she was born, when the whole village had gathered in front of a magnificent tree bedecked with candles to sing, recite poetry and perform the nativity play. But even though her children were hungry and there were no presents to give, they could still sing the praises of the Lord who had so far spared them from the worst ravages of war.

Luise celebrated her twenty-fifth wedding anniversary on July 4, 1945, still not knowing whether her husband and older sons were alive. Believing her only chance of learning their fate was to return to Melk in Austria, where Otto's parents lived, she appealed to the mayor of Saxony, who helped her to purchase train tickets to Passau, Austria.

For three mind-numbing weeks, Luise and the children slept on the floor of the railway station waiting room, "squeezed in like sardines." Ill-fed and unable to wash, the Buxbaums prayed and patiently waited for the Red Army troops that were blocking travellers at the Saxony-Bavarian border to lift their siege. Finally, two transport trains loaded with iron pipes, on top of which perched a thousand Austrian soldiers and 250 women and children, pulled out of the Vogtland station. But their joy at being sent back to Austria quickly disappeared. No sooner had the whistle signalled their departure than whispers began that everyone was being deported to Siberia. For Luise, who had travelled halfway around the world to escape Russian persecution, the irony was overwhelming.

Just before it reached its destination, the train collided head-on with another locomotive. The engine and first two cars were demolished, and several other cars were thrown down a steep embankment. But the third car, in which the Buxbaums were riding, remained on the tracks unscathed. The children were in shock. Little Helmuth was mesmerized by the macabre sight of Austrian soldiers impaled by the train's cargo of pipes, which on impact had become deadly spears.

The survivors were taken to Frankfurt, where Russian soldiers herded Luise and the children behind the barbed wire of a refugee camp that had housed Red Army soldiers captured by the Germans. Infested with bedbugs and lice, the filthy barracks soon spawned outbreaks of typhoid fever, malaria, and dysentery. The prisoners, mostly women and children, were soon reduced to living skeletons. The Russians finally decided that the best way of dealing with these harmless casualties of war was to ship them back to Austria.

In Melk, Austria, Otto Buxbaum and his older sons sat amidst the ruins of their former life. After years on the Russian front, Otto had made his way back home. Soon afterwards, his conscripted sons also returned, pale ghosts emerging from a five-year nightmare. With the exception of

Friedrich, who had lost a leg in combat, the rest of the Buxbaum men returned physically intact.

Otto was sitting at the dinner table one evening in the fall of 1945 when he looked out the window and saw a little girl who reminded him of his daughter Hildegunde. When the emaciated child stretched out her arms towards him and croaked the single word "Papa," Otto realized that his family had been restored to him. The Buxbaums had lost their village to the Russians, but what was Labiau compared to their family, their God, and the miraculous opportunity to begin yet again?

The Buxbaums were better off than the thousands of other displaced people in that they had a temporary sanctuary with Otto's parents in Melk. Otto found a job as a registrar for the City of Melk, but the pay was modest and he relied once again on his language skills to supplement his income, translating identity forms for the Russian troops occupying lower Austria. But the family remained poor. When the Buxbaums finally moved into a place of their own, it was an apartment shared with a retired school teacher. The family of eleven shared one bedroom, a living room, and a small, cold kitchen.

Six-year-old Helmuth soon learned to respect and fear the pious autocrat who was his father. To toughen his children, Otto sent them to school barefooted and drummed into them his belief that hard work was an indispensable element of Christian virtue. Although he didn't spend a lot of time with his youngest son, Otto wanted Helmuth to study not only the Bible, but the works of Homer, Shakespeare, and Tolstoy – a tall order even for as bright a child as Helmuth. The boy was also encouraged to draw more of his pencil sketches of castles, monasteries, old houses, and human faces, drawings that his father believed showed real promise.

To Helmuth, it was as if there were two people inside his father: the sensitive and interesting teacher who nurtured his talents and the religious martinet who brooked no departure from his rigid edicts. More than once, Otto paddled Helmuth with a wooden spoon, a far cry from the treatment he had been used to from the doting mother who had cradled him in cellars during air raids. The rootlessness of life during the war had left Helmuth a sissified child who lived in terror of many things; his family's reunion had added another: being spanked by his father. Elementary school provided little relief from the tensions of his strict home life. Poor and Protestant, the little boy who had been raised with his sisters was mercilessly teased by his predominantly Roman Catholic schoolmates in Melk.

His only childhood companion was Hubert Mueller, another weakling who was also tormented by his peers. The two boys commiserated with one another over their harsh lot, which they tried to ease by listening to Hubert's radio in the Muellers' basement apartment or by spying on Helmuth's sisters in Helmuth's fourth-storey walk-up.

Sexual speculation was one of their pet subjects. Hubert was fairly convinced that he had entered the world through his mother's navel, but Helmuth, who approached the subject with a mixture of fear and fascination, had his doubts. He had known for a long time that his parents were "up to something" in their room when they sent him to the kitchen window on Sunday afternoons with instructions to count the leaves on the trees. But it wasn't until he was awakened by their love-making (as the youngest member of the large family, he shared Otto and Luise's double bed) that he knew exactly what. "The whole thing terrified me," he later recalled.

Timid as he was, Helmuth carried out little rebellions. Even though Otto strongly disapproved of Hubert because the boy's family drank and smoked, Helmuth persisted in the friendship. He would also slink off to a field and smoke weeds rolled up in newspaper. When Helmuth was caught stealing cherries from a neighbour's tree, Otto dispatched him to seek forgiveness and offer compensation to the aggrieved party. The walk to the neighbour's backyard was the longest of his young life, but, afterwards, Helmuth was struck by the healing power of forgiveness. "That day my father taught me a lesson for life," he remembered later.

Aiming to recreate the cultured life the family had left behind in Labiau, Otto pressed each of his children to learn a musical instrument. While his luckier siblings were taught to play the piano or flute, Helmuth was selected to study the violin. His teacher, Herod, was a nasty curmudgeon with a fondness for twisting his pupils' ears and shouting in their faces. Whenever Helmuth got his lessons wrong, Herod struck him across the fingers with a violin bow. The sensitive child often broke down during these tirades and dreamed of escape. "I considered getting run over by a train or jumping off a bridge, but then I would usually think about how it would hurt my mother and I would discard my suicidal musings until the next violin lesson."

As the youngest child, Helmuth resented being bullied and manipulated by his siblings. He took particular offence to his older brother, Otto

Jr., whose bicycle he washed to make a few extra schillings. When it came to collect, Otto Jr. told his younger brother to "mark it in his book." Despite the younger child's careful bookkeeping, pay day never arrived. Although his sisters exhibited no outright cruelty, they were often cold to him, the result, he later concluded, of having been made to hand-wash his soiled diapers when he was a baby.

Helmuth turned to his mother for the love he needed. He admired Luise for keeping the family together during the war, a feat he attributed to her rock-solid faith in God. Later, he would marvel at her sheer capacity for work, raising ten children without a sewing machine, a washer, or a refrigerator. Whatever she faced – homelessness, poverty, or the incessant demands of her church – Luise Buxbaum had a way of coming through. It was a lesson in uncomplaining diligence that Helmuth would not forgot.

Luise's indefatigable nature was also noticed by officials of the Austrian Lutheran Church. Helmuth resented the demands the church made on his overworked mother, but it was thanks to her "volunteer" fundraising for the Lutheran Home Mission Board that she was often sent on other canvassing trips around Europe. Accompanying her on a jaunt to Switzerland, which had remained neutral during the war, Helmuth got his first glimpse of the happier side of life. The average Swiss looked like a swaggering millionaire compared to Helmuth's Austrian countrymen who had been beggared by Hitler's war. In Switzerland he got his first taste of fresh fruit, chocolate, and fancy cheeses – dazzling commodities to a child who had spent the first six years of life amidst sudden death and starvation. "People there smoked good-smelling cigars, were well dressed, and they smiled," he recalled later. The young boy secretly dreamed of returning to be part of the good life; his stern father, however, had other plans.

Helmuth was just thirteen when Otto got him his first job. Melk's undertaker needed a boy to lead funeral processions to the local cemetery and Otto, believing that the moral development of youth was better served by funerals than festivals, volunteered his youngest son. With a heavy, wooden cross slotted into a pouch in his sturdy leather belt, Helmuth led Protestant processions fifty feet up the hill to the side-entrance of Melk's cemetery. There, he fought back tears as he absorbed the dread lesson of human mortality.

While burying the badly disfigured victim of a motorcycle accident, Helmuth suffered his first migraine headache, a condition he shared with his father and that would afflict him for the rest of his life. Happily for

Helmuth, the drug Caffergot he was prescribed made him so sick that he missed many days at school. It also won him reprieves from the "nerve-racking" Sunday morning services that Otto Buxbaum led at the local public school. Otto was frequently so overwrought by the Bible stories he taught that he could not get through the Scripture without breaking into tears, a spectacle that made Helmuth uneasy and embarrassed.

Religion remained Otto Buxbaum's abiding passion. There were heated debates around the Buxbaum table between Otto and a variety of Baptist, Mennonite, and Lutheran ministers over the subtleties of Calvin-ism and Arminianism. This theological mudwrestling convinced Hel-muth that God's divine intervention, not human reason, was the only path to real faith. Once again, it was his simple and pious mother who showed the way to true religion.

Luise Buxbaum got some unexpected help in that direction from North America. Billy Graham, the new high priest of the mass evange-lism then sweeping the United States, became her husband's hero. It wasn't long before the whole family was swept along in Otto's enthusiasm for the man whose services became a lightning rod for the Lord's personal intervention in troubled lives. Just before his fourteenth birthday, Hel-muth became a born-again Christian. Now he too belted out the Ameri-can hymns along with his father, thinking how strange it must have sounded to their neighbours to hear the Buxbaums singing in English so soon after Germany had lost the war.

In 1952, Otto Buxbaum decided that his clever, youngest son should be sent to boarding school in nearby Krems to study architectural engi-neering, a practical outlet, he thought, for Helmuth's gift for drawing. If successful, Helmuth would become a construction technician, the Aus-trian equivalent of an engineer. With so much to rebuild in a shattered world, it seemed like a profession with a future. And who knew, perhaps Helmuth would even match the accomplishments of his namesake, the Helmuth Buchsbaum who was one of the architects of St. Stephen's Dome in Vienna.

The years at Krems were miserable and lonely for Helmuth. Once again, as the school's only Protestant, he was ostracized by his Roman Catholic schoolmates. Only one boy made friends with the unpopular outsider, who looked so funny in the hand-me-downs he received from the Mennonite Relief Committee. The school was staffed by former German soldiers, who took out the bitterness of their country's defeat on the boys under their control, and was run more like a prison camp than a place of learning. There was little to vary the institution's austere routine of bad food, long hours, and enforced study. One of the few diversions was a mandatory dancing course that gave the boys access to the opposite sex. "I was extremely shy," Helmuth remembered. "The girls were all extremely shy. We would put our sweaty hands together and dance. The dancing was awkward, but still, it was something to look forward to. This was really the only contact I had with girls from the time I was fourteen until I was eighteen."

But there was surprising flint in the callow outcast. Helmuth knew that if he was ever going to smoke the kind of cigars whose aroma still drifted through his memories of Switzerland, getting his *matura* or diploma was the necessary first step, no matter how unpleasant that might prove to be. With the example of his mother's awesome work ethic in mind, and a private vow never to subject the children he one day hoped to have to the humiliation of poverty, he put his head down and bulled through the academic thickets of Krems.

The year 1957 brought dramatic changes to the young man's life. Towards the end of his time at Krems, Helmuth fell in love with his friend's cousin, Helga Kummer, who was four years his senior and willing to have sex with Helmuth. Despite opposition from his parents, Helmuth longed to marry his sexual tutor. His dream edged closer to reality after he graduated from Krems and landed a job with the Zwettler company in Vienna, one of Austria's most prestigious construction firms. As the middle man between the company's superintendent and its chief engineer, he received a healthy salary of 2,000 schillings a month. He lived cheaply in his brother Gottlieb's Vienna apartment and squirrelled away most of his earnings to setting up house with Helga. But his dream was shattered the day that he read in Helga's diary her blissful account of relationships with two other men.

Helmuth was heartbroken, but there was no turning to his mother for comfort. Earlier that year, Luise and Otto had emigrated to Canada, where they hoped to retire in peace far from the continent that had caused them so much suffering.

But shortly after the couple, then in their late fifties, arrived in Canada, they lost their life savings trying to help one of their sons establish a wholesale livestock business. Facing a future every bit as dismal as anything they had encountered in post-war Austria, with the added depression of cultural isolation, they turned to their youngest son for help. Helmuth, feeling devastated over Helga's betrayal, driven by duty, and fearful of being drafted into the Austrian army, answered their call on December 18, 1958.

When he left Vienna, Helga Kummer accompanied him to the train, handing him a book of poetry as a going-away present. A few miles out of the station, Helmuth opened his compartment window and threw it away. Whatever his future might hold, it would not include the faithless lover who had broken his heart.

Canada was a cool stepmother to Helmuth Treugott Buxbaum. The standard chest x-ray required before authorities would issue immigration papers revealed that he was missing part of a rib in his back, the result of treatment for severe pleurisy as a child. The rib had been removed to insert a tube into the then four-year-old's chest cavity to drain his lungs. Anxious to avoid Europe's post-war outbreak of tuberculosis, Canadian immigration officers were rejecting all applicants who suffered from chest ailments; Helmuth was one of the unlucky applicants caught in the regulatory net.

Desperate to reach his floundering parents, he reapplied. This time Helmuth drew an official who was less interested in the prominent scar on his back than in the fact that the young Prussian had acquired some English – for Helmuth this was a sign of providence, since he'd received his crude grounding in the language largely through church activities. It may have been a man who issued his visa at the Canadian Embassy in Vienna, but it was God who had made the bureaucratic waters part.

Helmuth's destination was Kitchener-Waterloo, a preferred locale for immigrants of German descent. He found his disillusioned parents frightened for their future and yearning to return to Austria to continue their work with the Lutheran Church. Helmuth realized that the only way he could help them was to find a job as quickly as possible. He landed a position in Northern Ontario at the Stanleigh Uranium Mines in Elliot Lake, but the construction technician who had been a year and a half away from becoming an engineer in Austria was relegated to the role of a miner's helper. As the lowest man on the totem pole, the DP who spoke tortured English was fair game for the practical jokes of his co-workers. "One time they sent me for a sky hook. I went running around like a dummy looking for a sky hook," Helmuth remembers. "I asked everyone where I could find a sky hook. They just laughed at me. Eventually, somebody explained the joke to me."

Life down the mine was a daily ordeal. The diesel fumes that choked the tunnels triggered Helmuth's debilitating migraines, and not a single shift passed without him becoming sick to his stomach. During what he later described as the worst period in his life, he served as an underground warehouseman, a dynamite delivery man, and a geiger-counter operator.

Although his life was as lonely as the desolate landscapes of Elliot Lake, the darkhaired immigrant with the expressive green eyes found other uses for his time. He shut himself in his quarters at night and watched television to improve his English, consoling himself with the idea that if he could only make a success of himself, there would be plenty of time later to enjoy the fruits of his labours. Realizing that he would have to educate himself all over again if he were to make his way in his new country, Helmuth worked feverishly to improve his position and to save money.

In just two years, he had literally worked his way into the light by earning a promotion to assistant plant engineer – his first job above ground since arriving in Canada. He accomplished this by taking correspondence courses in mine surveying from a school in Scranton, Pennsylvania. After more correspondence courses, he wrote a few Grade 13 exams so that he could one day enrol in a Canadian medical school. Helmuth had been seized with a new and dizzying ambition: "I saw very quickly that a man of diligence, thrift, and determination could become financially successful. I thought that I could conceivably become a millionaire by the time I was thirty years old."

Hardworking and iron-willed, Helmuth's every financial decision was dominated by a mania for thrift. When his company offered houses to its employees for only $500 down, he quickly bought one. He lived in his modest bungalow with sixteen other people, including his parents, sister Hilde, brother Isbrandt, various children, and a French family – a veritable "ant hill" as he would later describe it. He was ready to sacrifice all creature comforts, including simple privacy, in order to pay off his investment and to get ahead. Like many European immigrants, Helmuth Buxbaum intended to make the most of the opportunities Canada offered.

One by one, he overcame the obstacles in his path. He was able to help his parents financially and even arranged for his brother Otto Jr. to come to Canada from Austria to join the family in Elliot Lake, overcrowding the small house to the breaking point. Helmuth's mother and father marvelled at their youngest son's staggering industry. Luise Buxbaum happily cooked for the miners who boarded in Helmuth's house, but privately worried that her model son was working too hard. What he needed was a good wife to look after him and she had the perfect candidate in mind.

2

HANNA

"I really and sincerely love you, dear Hanna . . . There may
be bad times waiting for us, but with our Lord Jesus Christ
we will stand them . . . I kiss you softly a thousand times."
– *Helmuth Buxbaum to Hanna Schmidt, August 1960*

At first glance, Hanna Schmidt seemed an unlikely match for Luise Buxbaum's brilliant and ambitious son. Hanna was almost three years older
than Helmuth, and her formal education had ended at Grade 4. She had
spent most of her teenage years working on the sausage line in the J. M.
Schneider meat-packing plant in Kitchener. A devout Mennonite, she
lived an almost cloistered life, sharing a bed with her mother into her
twenties and spending her recreational time reading in the family garden
in the summer and skating in Kitchener's Victoria Park in the winter. At
age twenty-three, Hanna Schmidt was still a virgin. But Hanna did have
one thing in common with Helmuth – her background.

Hanna's parents were ethnic Germans who, before the war, owned a
small farm in Laschingen, Poland, an agricultural town near the Russian
border. There, they brought up their three children, Martha, Henry, and
baby Hanna according to the gentle tenets of Menno Simons, the six-
teenth-century Dutch Anabaptist, after whom the Mennonites were
named. Hanna remembered life there as idyllic. Albert Schmidt tended
his sheep, cows, and pigs and worked the land, while Ottilie ran the
household and raised the children. In winter, the children wore the
hooked shoes she made them that were hung by the hearth each night to
dry; in summer, they switched to the wooden clogs carved by their father.

The family kept bees which Albert would call back to the hive by
banging a heavy bell, and Ottilie made strudel from the apples, pears, and

sweet and sour cherries in the orchard. From their earliest years, the children were expected to share in the work according to their physical capabilities; Hanna's first job was to milk the gentler cows and help her mother make butter and sourdough bread.

There was still time for fun. Hanna loved playing in the hayloft, jumping through a small hole into the flaxen stacks of hay piled on the barn floor below. Although she was afraid of horses, she enjoyed the sleigh rides to cut the family Christmas tree and to visit her aunt and cousins who lived three hours away.

On winter evenings, the Schmidts held devotions around their large kitchen stove. Encircled by his children, Albert read from the Bible as Ottilie sat at her spinning wheel. Although singing Christian songs was encouraged, folk music and dancing were frowned on as too worldly. The effervescent Hanna, who loved to sing and whistle, had to be reminded more than once that the polka was a sin. But for all her high-spiritedness, Hanna took her parents' moral instructions to heart. When a photographer came to take a family portrait, Hanna became angry when the birdie she was told to watch for never appeared. Her mother and father had taught her always to tell the truth, so why should she tolerate an adult who told tales?

Even after the start of the Second World War, the Schmidts continued to live in relative peace. But then Hitler, having secretly signed a non-aggression pact with Stalin, proceeded to carve up Poland like a geopolitical roast. The Mennonite family suddenly found itself in the Soviet controlled sector. The world, with all its woes, was irresistibly closing in on their rural retreat.

By 1941, Hitler had turned against his former ally. Despite their ethnic origins, the deeply religious Schmidts disapproved of Germany driving the Russians back behind their old borders and relegating Polish nationals to the status of slaves. On bitter winter nights, Albert Schmidt would sneak out of the family farm and bring back Polish road crews, who were forced to keep the highways cleared of snow by their Nazi masters. Ottilie fed the men mashed potatoes, sauerkraut, and hot tea, and invited them to warm their frozen feet by the fire.

More than once, Ottilie returned from a shopping trip to town in tears over the treatment meted out to Polish Jews by their German conquerors. Their houses and farms were seized, their goods sold, and the smallest transgression against the rules of occupation brought swift and deadly punishment. In the privacy of their farmhouse, Albert Schmidt quoted

Scripture to his wife to make his point that a country that perpetrated such atrocities against the Jews would never be victorious: "Who touches my people, touches the apple of my eye," he gravely repeated.

By the end of 1942, the myth of German invincibility came to an end in the frozen killing fields of Russia. The day that eight-year-old Hanna saw Red Army soldiers marching up her laneway through the snow, she ran into the house and hid under her bed. But there was no hiding from the Russians who had rolled into Poland to reclaim territory lost to the Germans in 1941. Two weeks after the Russian occupation began, soldiers dragged her from her hiding spot and snatched away the doll she was clutching. To her astonishment, some of the soldiers were rolling cigarettes from the onion paper torn out of Bibles they had stolen along the way. Others began carrying off the household articles that had comprised her universe ever since she could remember.

The Schmidts were forced off their farm at gunpoint. After finding stacks of papers in Martha's bedroom, the illiterate soldiers wanted to execute the Schmidts as spies. In fact, Hanna's older sister had been studying on the side while working in a bank in a nearby city – an explanation Albert Schmidt was finally able to make with the fortuitous arrival of an educated officer who was able to read the allegedly damning documents. (Martha herself was able to avoid the fate that overtook her family by hiding out in various attics and eventually escaping to western Germany in the back of a vegetable truck.)

Ottilie dressed Henry and Hanna in as many suits of clothes as they could wear without making it impossible for them to walk. Hanna marched away from her beloved farm wearing seven dresses. Heading down her laneway for the last time, Hanna looked over the white picket-fence to the fields where she had so often played in the snow, wondering when they would be allowed to come home again.

The Schmidts and many of their neighbours were forced to march three miles to a nearby village, the column growing a little longer at every farm lane where the German former owners joined the ranks of the dispossessed. When they reached their destination, they were herded into a large hall, where males over the age of sixteen were separated from the women and younger children and loaded aboard wagons for the long trek back to Russia. Albert Schmidt was one of the first to go.

"On the twenty-ninth of January [1944], my father was taken away on a wagon. I remember he was crying; very sad and crying. The only thing he was able to say was goodbye to my mother. And to us, he waved. And he said, 'Children, be good to your mother.' . . . He had a Bible in his hand, that's the only thing the Russians didn't take away, and he said, 'Tillie, you have the children, you have the Bible. You need the Bible for the children.' All my mother could do was just grab the Bible and the wagon was gone."

For the next five years, Ottilie and her children were slaves toiling for no more than the food that kept them alive for another day in the fields or factory. Henry was assigned to another farm, leaving Hanna and her mother to work for a Polish farmer in their former village. They soon found out how lucky they were. Stories of unspeakable cruelty began to filter back from families who had been sent out of their districts to work for strangers. It was easier, it seemed, to abuse people you didn't know.

While Ottilie laboured in the fields, it was Hanna's job to watch the cows, making sure that they grazed constantly. "'Henka,' my mistress would shout, using my Polish name, 'the cow is lying down again. Get it up, get it up!'" Although Hanna's Polish taskmasters were generally kind, they occasionally forgot to feed her, prompting the child to help herself to a few eggs which she would pierce with a needle and suck dry. Hard as they were worked on the farm, mother and daughter came to no harm.

It was a different story in the towns where Red Army commandants now ruled. Speaking German was outlawed and all ethnic Germans had to go by Polish names. Ottilie was careful to call her daughter Henka in public, but she remained Hanna in the privacy of their spartan farm quarters, where they whispered in their native tongue. Once a week, the commandant rounded up German women for ritual beatings, which were administered in front of City Hall by local Polish children. Ottilie's farmer, who liked her, gave the commandant a bottle of vodka to spare her the lash. On those occasions when the bribe didn't work, Ottilie came home with deep, blue bruises all over her body.

During the long, cool nights Hanna and her mother would nestle into the warm coat Ottilie had managed to spirit away from their farm. Ottilie spoke constantly about a wonderful place called Canada, where she hoped to begin life afresh when the war was over. Her sister had emigrated to Edmonton in 1936, and her letters spoke glowingly of the place where there was plenty of food, and best of all, no war. Hanna was enthralled: "Such a desire came into my heart, as a nine year-old child, to live in that country some day. That was our main thing, our main hope, to get out of Poland, get into West Germany and get to Canada," she remembered.

✦ ✦ ✦

In the fall of 1946, Poland's Russian masters rethought their policy of assigning ethnic Germans to work on local farms. The Germans were rounded up a second time and transported to a prison camp near Gdansk. There, Ottilie was assigned to the laundry and eleven year-old Hanna was assigned to look after the younger male children. Henry was immediately separated from his family, but housed in the same compound. Impressing their Polish overseers with their diligence, the Schmidts avoided the beatings that were meted out to less industrious inmates.

In the spring of 1948, their situation took a turn for the worse. The Schmidts were loaded into a cattle-car with other prisoners and informed that they were being shipped to East Germany. In fact, their destination was a far stricter camp in central Poland, near Bombeig. On arrival, they were stripped and deloused. Hanna was humiliated and terrified, although she was one of the lucky ones who was able to keep her thick hair after authorities failed to find any offending eggs in it. The inmates' clothes were then sterilized in an oven, and mothers were taken from their children so that prison administrators could put them to work.

Suffering from painfully swollen legs and feet, which made operating a treadle impossible, Ottilie was given a job hand sewing buttons and buttonholes on Polish army uniforms. Ottilie saw her daughter only on Sunday afternoons, when they were allowed to whisper through a fence for fifteen minutes if she had made her quota of uniforms. She became frantic when dysentery swept through the camp and Hanna fell ill. Luckily, there were doctors of German descent in the prison and the child was nursed back to health.

Life was very hard for the lonely teenager cut off from her mother's love. Every morning a Polish matron awakened the girls and supervised them as they swept and washed their quarters. Afterwards, rain or shine, they were led outside, where, dressed in uniforms with their names embroidered on the breast pocket, they marched to Polish songs. After a spartan lunch consisting of a single slice of bread (a notoriously slow eater during her farm service, Hanna quickly changed her ways in the camps), they were led into an auditorium where they watched propaganda films, whose theme was how badly the Germans had treated the Polish people during the war.

After dinner, the thirty-five girls in Hanna's dormitory neatly folded their uniforms and laid them over chairs in the centre of the room. Hanna, who mothered the younger children assigned to her unit, lined up the girls' shoes for the morning inspection. If the commandant found a crumpled uniform or a single shoe out of place, he would throw the uniforms on the floor and order the girls to clean them up. To avoid his rage, Hanna would make a perfect crease in her uniform and slip it under her mattress overnight so that it would look crisp for the morning inspection.

Ottilie finally convinced the camp commandant to allow Hanna to move into her dormitory. After a month of sewing buttons on uniforms, Hanna was asked by the commandant to run messages. The new position had its fringe benefits. Some of the guards who sent Hanna to the canteen for cigarettes allowed her to keep the change, which she hoarded until she could buy sausage which she shared with her mother and brother. "Those were our special treats," she later recalled. "We were happy for the little bit that we were able to have."

With a ribbon pinned to her left sleeve, Hanna was allowed to carry messages beyond the prison compound, a dizzying treat for a child who had been incarcerated for nearly three years. But with her mother and brother behind barbed wire, the idea of escape was unthinkable. "We knew we were in God's hands and that freedom would come some day – for all of us," she said.

By the spring of 1949, the Polish government had grown weary of feeding the thousands of ethnic Germans still in its prison camps and cast around for a less expensive policy. After protracted negotiations, East Germany agreed to take some of the inmates, starting with mothers who had small children. Hanna watched in envy as the first shipment of 200 souls was marched out of the prison to the train station. Somehow, she thought, the Schmidts had to find a way to join them.

During her work as a messenger, Hanna had been given free and regular access to the prison offices, where she had come to know the clerical workers in charge of processing the inmates bound for East Germany. They encouraged her to apply to one of the camp's two commandants – one harsh, the other more compassionate – who had the final word on who could go. One morning as Hanna delivered her messages in the office, one of the secretaries, who knew that the "good commandant" was on duty, squeezed her hand and said softly in German, "Try today."

Hanna assembled her mother, brother, and an elderly former neighbour who begged not to be left behind and told them to follow her. Trembling, she pinned on her messenger's ribbon and told them to walk a few paces behind her, hoping to create the impression that she had been asked to bring them to the office. The petrified group got through the first guard post, but were challenged at the second. Glancing casually over her shoulder, Hanna explained that she had been summoned by the commandant. Assuming that they had all been summoned, the guard let them pass.

The commandant interviewed each of them before making his decision. The only hitch came when Ottilie was told that she couldn't leave because Poland needed sewing-machine operators. Hanna quickly pointed out her mother's grossly swollen feet and legs and explained that she couldn't operate the heavy sewing machines. One look at Ottilie's specially cut shoes persuaded the commandant that the young girl was telling the truth. Permission was granted for all to leave. "I could have jumped for joy," Hanna remembered, "but we had to contain our feelings and even look sad."

Two weeks later the group answered the roll call for the last time and then marched for two hours to the train station. Before the train left, an old man tapped on the wooden slats of each cattle-car with a stick and asked the occupants if anyone wanted to stay in Poland. "Mother said, 'I'm born German, and I will die German.'"

Just when the Schmidts thought that they would never get underway, the train pulled slowly out of the station headed for Communist East Germany, a huge step closer to the freedom they had been dreaming about for years. Three days later, they rattled over a bridge high above the Oder River and arrived in Frankfurt.

After disembarking, the first thing Hanna heard was the sound of people freely speaking German, a simple act that had been a serious crime in the world she had known for nearly half her life. The family was given spending money and passports and were allowed to wander the city until they were assigned a new home. It was the first time Hanna had ever seen shops, and she marvelled at their well-stocked windows. After reuniting their elderly neighbour with her relatives, they set out for their new home, a large collective farm where the Schmidts were given a room of their own. For the first time in five years, they were able to close a door on the outside world.

While Hanna and Henry attended school, Ottilie laboured in the fields for potatoes and small amounts of cash, which she used to buy the children their first new clothes and shoes since they had been put off their farm. As a bonus for her diligence, Ottilie was allowed to glean the fields after the regular harvest. Working after school until dark, and on

Saturdays, they managed to harvest fifty-four sacks of wheat. They sold some for cash and made the rest into the bread and cake they would soon be carrying with them on their break for freedom.

They were caught on their first attempt. After riding a train to the border of East and West Germany, they set out on foot in the company of five other people to cross at a place where a river formed a natural divide between the two sectors. They were within 300 feet of the border when they heard dogs barking and voices in Russian ordering them to stop or be shot. Ottilie urged the children to run, but Henry tugged on his mother's coat until she stopped in her tracks. Everyone was arrested.

Back at the detention centre, the Russian commander asked why they wanted to go to the West. Ottilie, whose older daughter Martha had already escaped to the West, explained that she had another child on the other side and wanted to reunite her family. Suddenly, Hanna began to wail uncontrollably.

"Why is your daughter crying?" the officer asked.

"She wanted to see her sister so badly, and now you caught us," Ottilie replied.

She was told to take her children and return to the farm. Instead, she found a man who, for a fee, promised to show them a safe route to the West through his own property.

Just two mornings after their first attempt, they crossed the river on a raft made of "six fat trees." Remembering what they had been told by their guide, they kept moving as fast as they could; if the Russians saw them, they wouldn't be the first escapees to be forcibly returned to the eastern sector or summarily shot. There was even no guarantee that the German police on the other side wouldn't send them back after they had safely negotiated the quarter-mile of no man's land. When a West German border guard emerged out of the mist with his machine gun slung casually over his shoulder, there was a moment of almost unbearable tension before he finally spoke. "Good morning," he said. "You made it."

Feeling like Gideon in the Promised Land, the Schmidts thanked the Lord for his ultimate blessing. "It was a miracle," Hanna declared. "It was just like a real heavy stone was lifted from our heart and mind. To be free!"

Almost as soon as they arrived in West Germany, Ottilie applied to emigrate to Canada. Three months later, she received a telegram from the Canadian embassy to report to a Mennonite camp where prospective immigrants were being screened. They were questioned by an immigration officer, who explained that Canada was only accepting "displaced persons" who didn't have a nationality. After extensive medical examinations, the Schmidts could hardly believe it when they became one of the first refugee families holding West German passports to be accepted into Canada. The Mennonite Central Committee gave the family money and new clothes for their journey.

A few days later, they set out from the port city of Bremen aboard a former troop ship bound for Quebec City. The children bounced on the clean sheets in their private cabin and marvelled at the ship's indoor washrooms. Despite the joy of being free, they felt a moment of sadness when the vessel slipped its lines and edged away from the country and continent that, however roughly, had nurtured them.

"I remember when the boat started to move, it was a rejoicing day and it was a little bit sad. Although Germany wasn't our birthplace, it was our homeland. We didn't know what our future was or what would happen to us or who we would meet. We just had to put our hope into our faith. Whatever God will bring our way, we would accept it," Hanna said.

For six and a half days, there was nothing but ocean and heaven and thoughts of being reunited with their older sister, Martha. Hanna gorged on the delicious food they were given, gaining seven pounds during the crossing primarily as a result of her love affair with a new treat, cornflakes. As the ship approached Quebec City, there was a terrible storm, but that didn't stop the Schmidts from peering through the porthole for their first glimpse of Canada.

The Red Cross had told Ottilie before they left Europe that her husband, Albert, had died of kidney failure a month after he was sent to Siberia, and now Ottilie said a prayer for the man who hadn't lived to share this day. Hanna was overcome at the first sight of land, a grey cliff that loomed up out of the mist. "The feeling of seeing land as we were approaching Quebec was really tremendous."

As soon as they cleared customs and immigration, the Schmidts boarded a train for Jordan Station, a tiny agricultural community on the Niagara Peninsula. After travelling all night and the rest of the next day, they arrived at their destination, where they were met by the Griebrecht family, Russian Mennonites who had emigrated to Canada in 1926 and established a fruit farm. Mrs. Griebrecht and her son drove them to the farm in the back of a truck.

At 6 A.M. the next day, bone-tired from their journey, they were awakened to pick cherries. Although their new life began much as their old one had ended – with backbreaking work for low pay – there was a major difference; in a year, they would be free.

Three months later, a young woman visited one Sunday afternoon. It was Martha Schmidt, who hadn't seen her family in six years.

For twenty minutes, the tears poured down everyone's cheeks. When it came time for Hanna to speak to her sister, everything she had endured was reduced to a single memory of the day her childhood had ended: "They took my doll, Martha," she sobbed. "They took my doll."

Ottilie Schmidt began saving her salary of forty dollars a month for a single purpose: to put the Schmidt family under one roof again. Everyone worked to the same end, including Hanna, who got a job as a house-keeper for two dollars and fifty cents a week. Henry found work in Kitchener's General Spring Factory, which made car seats for General Motors. After an arduous year on the farm Ottilie paid off her passage to the Griebrechts. She then went to work as a cleaner in a hospital, where she was eventually joined by Hanna. To qualify for the job, the young girl pinned up her waist-length braids to look older than her fourteen years. By Christmas 1950, the Schmidts were in their own apartment in Kitchener. "After moving to Kitchener, we knew that we would never go back to Germany. Things were really looking up. The Lord was blessing us," Hanna later recalled.

A further year of penny-pinching enabled the family to put together a $2,000 down payment on a house. Hanna and Martha were now working at Schneider's meat packers, one of the better-paying companies in Kitchener, for eighty cents an hour. For the mortgage Ottilie borrowed from an elderly German who occasionally lent money to his former country-men. Their dream was finally realized: Martha, Henry, Hanna, and "Mutti" (Ottilie) finally owned their own house. "It was just like heaven on earth," Hanna remembered.

After Martha got married and moved out on her own, the family organized its social life around the church. The Schmidts attended the Mennonite Brethren Church, where Hanna was baptised in 1951 after an emotional born-again experience the year before, and they never missed an opportunity to put their Christian principles to work. Ottilie took particular interest in a Prussian couple who arrived in her city and workplace in 1957. Anxious to help fellow Europeans down on their luck, she invited Otto and Luise Buxbaum to lunch; with so much in common, a friendship developed. After Helmuth joined his parents in Canada in 1958, his mother told him about the generous Mrs. Schmidt and her lovely daughter, Hanna. "She said, 'If you are thinking of marriage, she would be a very good wife,'" Helmuth recalled later.

Helmuth gently resisted his mother's well-intentioned match-making, saying that he was too young to tie the knot, but Luise Buxbaum quietly persisted. Even after the Buxbaums followed their son to Elliot Lake, they kept in touch with the Schmidts, secretly hoping that Helmuth and Hanna would get together.

A year later they got their wish. During a visit to Kitchener, Helmuth finally spoke to Hanna on the telephone and arranged to visit the Schmidts. Ottilie led the young man into the garden, where Hanna was reading under a lilac tree. Her first impressions of Helmuth were far less restrained than their initial telephone conversation in which they had addressed one another in German as thee and thou: "He was tall and slender and *handsome*! I thought to myself, 'Oh boy, this young man won't even look at me.'"

Hanna was wrong. Helmuth engaged Hanna in a long and emotional conversation about their European families and war-scarred childhoods. They were delighted by how much they had in common, including the fact that they both taught Sunday school. By the end of the weekend, Helmuth was very much the importuning suitor. Could he write to her, see her again, would she visit him in Elliot Lake?

Hanna was attracted, but behaved with rigid propriety. She suggested that he visit *her* at Keswick Camp, a Baptist retreat in Muskoka where she planned to holiday during the first week of August. Helmuth eagerly agreed, and the Bible-struck immigrants indulged in a whirlwind romance.

During their two days at Keswick Camp they were inseparable. Helmuth took Hanna on a boat ride, "And you know," she said later, "we never came back!" Even though it was only the second time they had ever seen each other, Helmuth proposed. Flattered by the young man's impetuousness, Hanna was nevertheless taken aback. Her practical side told her that things were moving too fast. "I said, 'Wait a minute Helmuth, you don't know me and I don't know you.'"

Hanna explained her reservations. For one thing, she was older than he was; for another, she had little formal education compared to Helmuth's professional training in Vienna. The anxious young man dismissed both quibbles, pointing out that his brothers had all married older women and that his education was more a credit to his parents, who had scraped together the money to pay for it, than to him. He confessed to Hanna that his mother's fondest wish was that they would some day marry. Hanna bent but didn't break. She told Helmuth he would get his answer in a month, after she had had a chance to pray for guidance and to discuss the proposed match with her mother.

After Helmuth returned to Elliot Lake, he and Hanna began a weekly correspondence in German. While his sister Hilde played cards with Papa Otto in the cramped kitchen, Helmuth wrote letters to the woman he had fallen in love with to the delight of his doting mother. After he was elected president of the local Baptist Parish youth group, he wrote to her expressing his dismay about what had happened at his first official meeting: "I did not like the dancing, smoking, and record playing, which I do not approve of." He repeatedly complained to Hanna of crude colleagues who embarrassed him with their dirty jokes and drinking. Even worse was the sinful pride of his immediate superior who, he felt, constantly placed himself above God's judgement: "How blind people are," Helmuth wrote.

Hanna patiently responded to Helmuth's missives, quoting Scriptures that might help him with his problems and invariably presenting the picture of a pious young woman who carried out her duty to God with stunning dedication.

"Now I would like to tell you something about my wonderful vacation which God gave me," Hanna wrote. "We have gone on a boat nearly every day. How lovely is the nature which the Lord sent us with His great love! We climbed a mountain on Wednesday night and saw how the sun sets. It was a magnificent picture. It is no wonder that David called out in his Psalms, 'Lord, how great are Your works!' The next morning we all got up early to see the sunrise. It was again a picture that I cannot describe. Then we had a short prayer session. On the path to the mountains, important Bible verses were written on the rocks. One of the verses has become very important to me . . . 'In all thy ways acknowledge Him and He shall direct thy paths.'"

A week before Hanna was to give him her answer, Helmuth finished a gruelling shift in the mine and made the eight-hour drive to Kitchener. He found the Schmidt household, with its German conversations and religious zeal, a welcoming oasis in a new and hostile culture. Helmuth was impressed by Hanna's extensive collection of religious books and records and her obvious deep faith. He also admired her dedication to her job at Schneider's, although he was anxious to get her out of the meat-packing plant. When she offered to work in order to put him through university, he wrote, "I would not want to be supported by my wife . . . You have worked long enough in the stench and cold and I want you to relax when we are married."

As the weekend passed, he became more and more convinced that they were made for each other. They shared a common ethnic background, a similar religion, and a grim history of religious persecution and grinding poverty. In many ways, Hanna reminded Helmuth of his mother, a woman who exhibited a pure spirit and a buoyant personality despite life's disappointments. But after a weekend of family suppers and church services, Hanna still hadn't given him an answer.

The big moment finally came on Labour Day weekend, 1960. Hanna sensed his low spirits over her long-delayed reply and couldn't wait to tell him as they sat in the Schmidt's garden that Ottilie had already given her blessing to the match. Hanna recalled, "When we were alone, he looked at me and he took my hand and he said . . . 'What is your answer?' I said, 'Helmuth, if I wouldn't be serious, I wouldn't have let you come on this trip. I would say, Stay where you are, I think the Lord doesn't want us to be together.' You should have seen the lightening of his spirit!"

Helmuth wanted to get married at Christmas, but Hanna thought such haste unseemly and wanted to hold off until the following June so that people wouldn't get the idea that she was pregnant. In any case, she needed time to arrange the wedding, put her affairs in order, and look into the question of where they would live. Although part of her was still uneasy over how quickly their love affair had progressed, she was convinced that she had chosen the right man. "Can you imagine taking such a chance?" she later asked a friend. "But it was the Lord's will."

Romantic ecstacy flooded their almost daily letters. "Today is a cloudy day without sun . . . but my heart is so bright with sunshine and totally without clouds when I think of you and of the two beautiful days with you. Oh Hanna, I am so in love with you . . . I send you a rose from our bush . . . Let it also be a symbol that I love you very much."

Hanna handled the unaccustomed passion in her life with a mixture of awkwardness and joy. She was both embarrassed and proud when her engagement ring caused such a stir at the factory. After receiving one of his more ardent letters, she had cut herself twice at work because, as she wrote, "my thoughts were with you." But if her emotions were unusually turbulent, her heart was steadfast. She wrote, "Yes, my dear Helmuth, you are the man whom I can and do love from the bottom of my heart. When I think of our future together, it greatly pleases me that we will go the way of the pilgrim together. But we must not let ourselves forget, dear Helmuth, Christ will rule first in our lives. Then everything will be good."

Every weekend now, Helmuth drove to Kitchener to spend a few days with his fiancée. He took comfort in the spiritual realm they inhabited, a place so different from the austerity of Elliot Lake and the often godless society of North America. "The way things are today inspires the Devil, and he looks for people who do not give any time to God," Helmuth wrote. "Man is distracted and the devil is more excited and busier than before . . . Who reads the Bible in the evenings now, or early in the day?"

In a decision that eerily paralleled his father's conversion to Protestant-ism in Russia, he exchanged his Lutheran faith for the credo of the Men-nonite Brethren, signing an oath not to smoke, drink, or watch movies. Helmuth also decided to make a clean breast of his limited experiences with Helga Kummer in Europe. Hanna forgave him, but not before mak-ing it clear that it had been sinful of Helmuth to engage in sex outside of marriage.

Forgiveness wasn't the only thing on the young man's mind. Helmuth began sending Hanna Scriptures that offered a model of the proper rela-tionship between man and wife. "I have found a very interesting point in Genesis 3 which I had not noticed before: And thy desire shall be to thy husband, and he shall rule over thee."

Helmuth mildly chastised Hanna for taking a religious junket to the United States in the company of another man. "That step was a little thoughtless of you . . . So far as I know you, Hanna, you are a very pure girl and I know that you will be faithful as we are engaged. But think what other people will say who know that you are engaged when you go away for the weekend with another man."

When trouble erupted between Otto Jr. and his wife, Elfriede, over their unhappy emigration to Canada, Helmuth turned it into a parable for Hanna. He depicted his brother as working diligently to learn Morse code so he could get a job with the railway as a telegraph operator, while a discordant "Elfie" brought "hatred and strife" into their Christian house by opposing him. "You will be a good little wife and listen to your hus-band when he is with his family, which appears to be Elfie's main short-coming," Helmuth wrote.

Ever accommodating, Hanna replied, "I would not say anything against your plans, my sweetheart, that you believe correct . . . I would like to be a wife who will obey her husband." The patriarchy Otto Buxbaum had maintained in Melk was being re-created in North America by the son who so feared and admired him.

In the autumn of 1960, the Schmidts and Buxbaums held a European-style engagement party for the couple that featured so many religious rituals it resembled a wedding ceremony. The highlight of the evening came when Helmuth and Hanna exchanged rings, observing the old country custom of wearing them on their right hands until their wedding day. Helmuth's father concluded the event by reading passages from the Bible and blessing the new couple. Although she had shared a bed with her mother since emigrating to Canada, Hanna now followed European etiquette for an engaged woman, sleeping alone (on the living-room couch) until her wedding night.

The wedding very nearly didn't take place. Just after his engagement party, Helmuth was involved in a serious car accident in Elliot Lake, crashing through the windshield of his car and breaking his leg and kneecap. While visiting him, Hanna decided that she would rather begin her married life anywhere but the northern mining town that had nearly claimed Helmuth's life.

She got her wish. Once he was better, Helmuth visited Kitchener's Water Commission to inquire about job openings. As luck would have it, the commission had been looking for a skilled draftsman to draw plans for a new water system for the city. With his construction technician's certificate from Krems and practical experience in Vienna with a master builder, Helmuth was the perfect candidate. Bob Roguegnat was impressed with Helmuth's recommendation from his superiors in Elliot Lake, which described him as "very capable, honest, and loyal" with "an alert and aggressive mind," and hired him on the spot for the impressive annual salary of $3,770. In his last letter from Elliot Lake, Helmuth wrote, "Soon, in not quite 116 hours, we will see each other and not need to be writing any letters anymore nor saying goodbye . . . I have been packing diligently and will bring my bed linen along . . . Here in Canada everyone calls their lover 'honey'. But we will probably remain 'Schatz', okay sweetheart?"

On June 10, 1961, 250 wedding guests packed the Mennonite Brethren Church in Kitchener to witness a wedding of surprising grandeur and religious beauty. The engaged couple, who both believed that young people should be financially responsible, refused to accept any money from their parents. Instead, Hanna and Helmuth had saved and planned for months (Hanna brought $13,000 into the marriage) and paid for their own wedding.

It was a genuine family affair. Hanna's brother, Henry, was Helmuth's best man, and Helmuth's sister Hilde was the bride's maid of honour. The service, half in German, half in English, was long and exhausting. At the reception that followed, musicians performed religious music and Hanna and Helmuth received gifts and good wishes from their friends. Luise Buxbaum composed a wedding poem, which included the stanza: "May the Bible be everything to you, tell you only what is true and be your guiding star. May God protect you from misfortune and danger."

That evening, the newlyweds checked into a motel, looking distinctly nervous. It had not helped matters that a relative from the wedding party had chased them to their destination, causing Helmuth to be pulled over for speeding in an attempt to lose him. The groom was all but inexperienced and the bride was a virgin who firmly believed that sex was for the sole purpose of procreation. Before retiring on their wedding night, they knelt by their bedside and prayed. Helmuth later said, "This was the first love-making that we ever had. It was very brief. Hanna was shy. She had never taken her clothes off in front of a man before."

The next morning, the staunchly religious couple felt like a pair of guilty children. Embarrassed by their sexual contact, they drove back to Kitchener where they attended church with Hanna's mother.

A neighbour who knew that the Buxbaums didn't have the money for a proper honeymoon gave Hanna and Helmuth the use of his cottage for a week. The new couple's concern about money led Hanna to purchase four-dozen eggs from a farmer on the drive to Honey Harbour. The frugal lovers proceeded to eat boiled, fried, poached, and scrambled eggs three times a day for the duration of their week-long getaway.

Seven days later, Mr. and Mrs. Buxbaum returned to Kitchener to start working towards a set of financial and intellectual goals that were truly staggering. Their inspiration was Hanna's simple prayer that they would prove to be a blessing for each other. But the young immigrants also knew that the Lord helped those who helped themselves. As Hanna later put it, "We were ready to face the world and work hard."

3

EDEN AND THE SERPENT

"Hanna was a worthwhile, honest, pure person and many times I felt unworthy of having her."
— *Helmuth Buxbaum*

After their week-long honeymoon, Helmuth and Hanna returned to Kitchener and threw themselves into the renovations that would convert the house they had bought on Southdale Avenue into a three-apartment complex. They occupied the main floor, and recouped enough money to cover their mortgage payments by renting out the top flat and the basement apartment. They used the income this freed up to acquire a second house on the same street, working on the theory that each new property could be used as collateral for future real estate purchases.

By paying as little as possible down and using their houses as collateral in borrowing the money to acquire more property, the Buxbaums were able to put together $16,000 to purchase a twenty-eight-acre farm in the sleepy rural community of Komoka, just outside London. (This feat was impressive enough on their modest incomes, but even more so considering that 10 per cent of their earnings was paid as a tithe to the Mennonite Church.) Originally bought as a retirement haven, the farm would soon figure in their more immediate business plans.

Helmuth intensified his efforts to Canadianize his education by taking high-school courses. His parents, who had returned to Austria shortly after his wedding to work for the Mennonite Brethren Radio Ministry, were alarmed by Hanna's accounts of her husband's determination to study his way to financial success. Writing from Melk, Otto Sr. cautioned moderation: "You should not overdo it with the studies. We are satisfied with your success and therefore with you too."

Helmuth refused to slacken his furious pace. By September 1963, he had obtained his Canadian high-school diploma through correspondence courses and enrolled at the University of Western Ontario. The young immigrant had always wanted to be a doctor, perhaps a medical missionary, depending on how his financial plans worked out. Just twenty-four hours before he attended his opening class, Hanna gave birth to their first son, Paul. Helmuth had reluctantly allowed Hanna to work in the first two years of the marriage, but he was now adamant that she stay home with their baby. Accustomed to shouldering heavy loads, he prepared to become sole breadwinner and student, as well as husband and new father.

For the first time in his life, he found he needed more than sheer determination to achieve his goals. His job at Kitchener Water prevented him from studying during the day; at night, the new baby cried constantly. Then Helmuth developed ethical reservations about his pre-med studies at Western. A religious fundamentalist, he found it impossible to deal with lectures and assignments premised on the theory of evolution. By Christmas, he had dropped out of pre-meds and set his academic sights on another goal.

After moving his family to a new house in Waterloo, Helmuth enrolled in a part-time Bachelor of Science program at Waterloo Lutheran University (now Wilfrid Laurier University), hoping to become a high-school science teacher. Now every morning between six and eight, he studied before setting out for the office. At the necessary points during his work day, Helmuth drove to the university for classes, making up the lost time at Kitchener Water with night work. Arriving home after dark, he had his dinner and then settled down in front of his books to log a few more hours of study. There was no such thing as a free weekend, but Helmuth's energy was boundless. He seemed to have been made for the sole purpose of doggedly improving his lot in life, which to both Hanna and Helmuth came down to a single mission – building a sense of security that would finally obliterate the memories of their chaotic childhoods.

In April 1966, the Buxbaums had their second child, Mark, and Helmuth stretched his already tight schedule even further by taking on a part-time job to earn extra money, this time teaching Grade 11 and 12 biology, chemistry, and mathematics at the Adult Education Centre in Kitchener. In accordance with his religious beliefs, he was doing his very best in every respect, and the results were beginning to show. In 1967, Helmuth graduated with a Bachelor of Science degree. He had stayed the academic course while financially supporting his growing family. Another major hurdle on the road to the good life had been cleared.

The best was yet to come.

Just after Helmuth hung his university degree on the wall of his small study in 1967, his brother Otto approached him with a business proposition that had been suggested to him by a London nursing-home operator, Jack Wahl. The Ontario government was offering special grants to any qualified individual willing to operate a nursing home for long-term psychiatric patients. Otto, who had participated in various religious missions to help the sick and destitute, suggested that they build a home on the Komoka farm Helmuth and Hanna had purchased in 1966.

Helmuth had put the farm up for sale, but he was interested enough in his brother's idea to take it off the market. The prospect of starting a family business intrigued him. He and Otto eventually borrowed $33,000 from the Industrial Development Bank to get the project going. But cost overruns forced Helmuth to raise an additional $30,000 by selling his rental properties in Kitchener. Hanna had mixed feelings about investing all they had in what she saw as a make or break proposition. But the woman who had once written that she wanted to be a wife who obeyed her husband proved as good as her word. Despite her misgivings, she agreed to move the family to the Westmount district of London and began to work as tirelessly as Helmuth to make the business succeed. The hardest part for her was leaving behind her mother, Ottilie, in Kitchener.

Excited by the entrepreneurial opportunity he sensed, Helmuth began piecing together the various elements of the enterprise. Knowing that his parents were unhappy in Austria, he offered to accommodate them in the rambling Komoka farmhouse if they would work as custodians at the nursing home. Although this meant dealing with patients who in some cases had been in psychiatric institutions for fifty years, the elderly couple readily agreed. Helmuth and Otto Jr. did much of the construction on the thirty-two-bed facility to cut costs even further. By Grey Cup weekend 1967, the first of what would become an impressive chain of nursing homes was ready to open its doors. Still, the Buxbaums weren't prepared for what they saw when the first batch of patients arrived in ambulances: "They were the worst patients possible from the London psychiatric hospital. My brother asked the ambulance driver if he had also brought the coffins for them," Helmuth said later.

Two weeks after it opened, Komoka was fully occupied. Helmuth took on the responsibilities of administrator, while Otto, who had a way with people, managed the day-to-day operations and oversaw the medical staff. With Otto's wife, Elfrieda, in charge of the kitchen (Hanna helped out occasionally), and the elder Buxbaums patrolling the corridors, it was a family business in every sense of the word.

In 1967, Hanna became pregnant again. After frequent bouts of morning sickness, her doctor prescribed a new medication to ease her discomfort. After taking the first pill, she flushed the rest of the prescription down the toilet. "I believe that it was divine prompting that made Hanna discard that medication. Hanna obeyed without question and saved the life of her third baby," Helmuth said later. The drug was Thalidomide. Later that year, their third son, Phillip, was born whole and healthy.

As soon as they could afford to, the Buxbaums expanded the nursing home to a 90-bed facility under the name Komoka Nursing Homes Ltd. Helmuth owned 51 per cent of the operation and his brother Otto 49 per cent. His appetite for business whetted, Helmuth began identifying lucrative opportunities in other towns. When he found a promising proposition, he was quick to pounce. In 1969, the year his daughter Esther was born, he partnered with Fred Kirkpatrick and established the Canadianna Nursing Home in Chatham, Ontario, a 152-bed facility housed in the former head offices of the Canada Dominion Sugar Company.

In 1970, Helmuth went into partnership with two other couples, including his sister Hilde and her husband, Harry Gottschling. They jointly raised the funds to convert an abandoned public school in Amherstberg, Ontario, into the Richmond Nursing Home, a facility that would eventually boast 103 beds. The following year, Helmuth teamed up with Ken Raphael to purchase the Mountain Nursing Home in Hamilton, Ontario. In partnership with David Bowen, a former Buxbaum boarder, he bought out the Watford Nursing Home, expanding the facility from 20 to 60 beds. In 1973, he built a 120-bed home in Leamington, Ontario, in partnership with David Whitfield, a missionary who had just returned from Africa. Through the frantic days of corporate expansion, Hanna was an invaluable adviser to Helmuth, particularly after the couple bought out Otto's shares in Komoka for $325,000. "She was very supportive of my business activities," Helmuth remembers, "but at times she expressed a concern that maybe we were biting off more than we could chew."

Friends said that Helmuth was the business brains behind the nursing home successes and Hanna was the "conscience" of the operation, a tireless advocate of the view that her husband and his managers had to care for the spiritual as well as the physical needs of their special residents. Hanna, whose fifth and last natural child, Danny, was born in 1972, also insisted that her husband remember his obligations to his own children. In her eyes, the needs of their growing business would always be eclipsed by the needs of her God and her family.

Helmuth didn't need much prodding to assume his paternal role with the children he prized. He showed an avid interest in their educations and a marked aversion to disciplining them, a task that fell by default to Hanna. Remembering, perhaps, his father's obsession with musical training, he bought a piano and insisted that the children take lessons. Sitting in his favourite chair on a Saturday afternoon listening to them play, it was as if a little bit of Melk had come to his rural Ontario Camelot.

As contented as she must have been during such tranquil moments, Hanna never forgot her roots. She was a regular sight at the local post office with her parcels destined for the Soviet Union. To the casual observer, Hanna the millionaire looked much the same as Hanna the meat packer – although after five children she had grown heavier. When friends advised her to pay a little more attention to her person, Hanna listened politely and then ignored them. Lipstick and a lithe body counted for little in her world: the only image that mattered was reflected in a person's immortal soul.

By the early 1970s, the Buxbaums had moved from the Mennonite to the Baptist faith, a short doctrinal trek that put Helmuth in touch with other Baptist businessmen in the London area. Over the coming years, many of Helmuth's friends and business contacts would be drawn from West Park Baptist Church, where he and Hanna sang in the choir and became friends with Pastor Doug Dakin. Even when it came to personal projects, the Buxbaums preferred to deal with fellow Baptists.

In 1970, when they made plans to build their dream home on the grounds of Helmuth's first business success, they chose an architect who was a devout member of West Park. The Komoka residence was built in phases; first the construction of a comfortable bungalow and later the addition of a huge recreation room, a garage, an indoor swimming pool, and a fallout shelter. Hanna eagerly served as Helmuth's prime consultant on the project. The once homeless refugees designed a house big enough to accommodate a large family and several guests. Helmuth hired himself as contractor and completed much of the construction work himself.

By December 1971, Papa Otto was dying of pancreatic cancer. As always, religion was uppermost in his thoughts, which he expressed to his family in a circular letter: "On Sunday afternoon we will have a prayer hour in my sick room. We sing a couple of German songs then we pray, each in his own way, like a child to a father, like a friend to a friend. The very best friend we have is the one in Heaven."

The spectacle of the dying patriarch preparing to meet his Maker prompted one of his sons, Friedrich (Fritz) to confess certain transgressions out of the distant past. Otto was touched, and he wrote, "It is very kind of you to confess to your parents the pranks of your youth and ask them for forgiveness . . . When I turned to God, I wrote to my parents from Siberia to ask for their forgiveness . . . Confessing would be an advantage for other sons, as well, for their spiritual development."

When, on December 15, 1971, Papa Otto died, it was without hearing any confession from Helmuth.

For several years, the Buxbaums ploughed their profits back into the business. But financial success eventually brought grand and giddy changes in their lifestyle. Helmuth and Hanna began taking regular vacations in Florida (their first, in 1970, was to Bible Town Camp in Boca Raton) and in time purchased the Howard Johnson Motel in Ocala, and the East Gate Motor Inn in Kissimmee. Helmuth then used his personal company, Christ is the Answer (CITA), to purchase a comfortable home in Boca Raton.

By the mid-1970s, the family could afford to split its time between Ontario and Florida. Every Christmas, the Buxbaum children transferred from the Christian Academy of Western Ontario to the Christian School in Boca Raton, where they wintered with their mother. Helmuth commuted between their Florida retreat and the family businesses in Canada.

Thankful for God's blessings, the Buxbaums were anxious to share their comfortable, Christian lives with more children. The couple believed they could easily afford to support eight children and there was more than enough room to accommodate a larger family in Komoka. In 1976, Helmuth and Hanna flew to Costa Rica, hoping to adopt a child at a church-run orphanage in San José. Days later, they met Ruth, a beautiful six-year-old who was classified as an "idiot" but blessed with a lovely spirit. It took two more trips to Costa Rica and years of legal wrangling with Costa Rican authorities before the Buxbaums were finally permitted to adopt Ruth Luise in 1978. Confronted with a new round of frustration when they tried to adopt a Canadian child, they eventually helped a Baptist couple start a home for unwed mothers in Watford, Ontario, hoping that one of the women would someday allow them to adopt her baby.

Helmuth's reputation as a deeply religious businessman was rock-solid. Every morning during the work week, he set aside the hectic job of managing his business empire to conduct a devotional service with his office staff, and every weekend, he shuttled between church socials, fundraisers, and religious services. His generosity was legendary. While preparing to move to Komoka, he sold the family house in Westmount at below market value to Real Life Incorporated, a non-profit organization established to help emotionally disturbed children. By the mid-1970s, Helmuth was providing the main support for the Christian Academy of Western Ontario, where he had ensconced his friend Phil Conley as its principal. The Buxbaums also gave $15,000 to each of Helmuth's brothers and sisters. The gift was to make up for the fact that he had been the only child to receive money from his parents for an education, the reason, according to his brothers and sisters, Otto Sr. hadn't been able to leave them an inheritance.

In 1978, Helmuth invited Hanna on a trip to the Soviet Union to offer Christian help to Georgi Wiens, the secretary of the underground Baptist Church and a relative of Helmuth. Wiens had been arrested for his religious activities and sent to a labour camp. Anxious to rescue his persecuted relative, Helmuth had joined the United Evangelists to the Communist World, a lobby group trying to use political pressure to win Wiens' release.

Although sympathetic to Wiens' plight, Hanna had deep misgivings about returning to the Soviet Union; she and her mother had experienced great misery at Russian hands, and it was in the Soviet Union that her father had, as she put it, "left his body." She was reluctant to go to a country where the freedom the Buxbaums had flourished under in Canada was still an unattainable dream. Ottilie Schmidt was terrified at the prospect of her beloved Hanna voluntarily returning to the place they had fled nearly thirty years before. But how, Hanna thought, could she turn down the chance to help a family who hadn't enjoyed their good luck? Sitting on the tarmac at London Airport waiting for their flight to depart, Hanna tried to quiet the butterflies in her stomach with a line modified from the Gospel according to St. Mark: "I will send an Angel before you to prepare your way."

The couple's first moments back in the Soviet Union realized her worst fears. The uniformed customs officers opened and carefully searched each one of their eight suitcases. Hanna turned pale as they lingered over clothes she had brought along for the Wiens family. Noticing her birthplace on her passport, one of them asked Hanna if she spoke Polish. Feeling herself beginning to tremble, she reverted to a habit learned in the prison camps: she gave a one-word answer and fell silent.

Outside the airport, her depression deepened when she saw a crew of elderly woman shovelling snow. She thought of her father and wondered where he might be buried. Try as she might, she couldn't pull free of terrible memories of days long gone. "All my remembrances came like a big wave, like an ocean wave crashing against the shore with a bang . . . I thought I was back in my old life again, in my old country."

Despite her gloom, the trip was a success. The Buxbaums located the Wiens family through the American embassy, and after a daring game of cat and mouse with Soviet authorities, Helmuth managed to deliver the sweaters, stockings, and warm boots Hanna had brought from Canada. Years later, Hanna fondly remembered Helmuth's fortitude during the trip she had been so afraid to take: "My dear husband, my courageous husband. He was just amazing."

As his fortune grew, Helmuth's personal financial philosophy moved to the outer rings of the far right. He was first introduced to the neo-conservative ideas of the economic survivalists in 1979 after reading Howard Ruff's book *How to Prosper During the Coming Bad Years*. Ruff campaigned vigorously for the Republicans, raising more than $1.5 million to put Ronald Reagan in the White House. It wasn't by accident that the foreword to his book, the biggest financial best-seller in American history, was written by Utah's arch conservative senator, Orrin Hatch.

But for America's nervous rich – and the Buxbaums – it wasn't Ruff's politics, but his apocalyptic economic vision that had them flocking by the thousands to hear him talk about a monetary system on the brink of collapse and a social order headed for anarchy. It was a world view whose first principle was the protection of individual assets. Ruff encouraged his followers to invest in gold coins, bullion, and diamonds and to mask all financial transactions from the prying eyes of government. He suggested multiple bank withdrawals in amounts under $5,000 to avoid routine bank reporting to the Internal Revenue Service. Once the money was taken out, he recommended depositing it in a Swiss bank account where American dollars were automatically turned into gold, thereby avoiding the unwanted attentions of Uncle Sam.

But the business of exchanging intrinsically worthless paper money into hard assets, and then hiding one's worldly wealth from authorities who might decide to confiscate it, was only part of the survivalist catechism. Each person also had to provide for his physical well-being in the coming "age of envy." The fallout shelter was to his personal security what the Swiss bank account was to his financial peace of mind. It not only provided protection from the coming nuclear holocaust, but also served as a warehouse for barter goods – tobacco, alcohol, and junk silver and copper – that would be traded for the necessities of life after the nuclear holocaust.

One item eclipsed all others in importance – weapons. Guns and ammunition would command a high exchange value when government finally outlawed their sale in the final breakdown of society. They could also be used to deal with the human predators that survivalists predicted would soon be roaming the bleak American landscape in search of other people's goods. As one of Helmuth's favourite economic survivalists, Gary North, wrote, "When you're dealing with a person in a life and death situation, you had better be the fellow with the gun."

Having been part of Europe's dispossessed during the Second World War, the survivalist message struck a deep and responsive chord with the now prosperous Buxbaums. While many North Americans laughed at what they took to be the paranoid delusions of the right-wing fringe, the Buxbaums had lived through the unthinkable. They religiously followed the financial and personal advice of Ruff and the ten other hard-currency survivalists whose works filled Helmuth's personal library.

The couple began in 1981 by opening two Swiss bank accounts and diverting cash to them – a little at a time – from several different Canadian accounts. By 1982, both Helmuth and Hanna were using their bank cards to withdraw as much as $800 a day from automatic tellers. The money was pooled into amounts between $30,000 and $60,000 and then personally carried to Switzerland for deposit. According to one of Helmuth's Canadian bank managers, Deane Winskill, Helmuth was also a fanatical adherent of Ruff's advice to buy gold as a hedge against inflation:

"I spoke with Helmuth quite a bit about gold bullion . . . I had a bunch of 10-ounce gold wafers and when Helmuth saw them he wanted then and readily paid me double the amount I'd paid. The guy was crazy . . . When I left the bank he had gold bullion in the safety deposit box there. The bullion was bought through a broker legally – from A. E. Ames in Toronto – and delivered prepaid to our bank by Brinks Security trucks . . . Later, we just put it in Helmuth's car. There was so much of it. It came in canvas bags."

In 1981, Helmuth also bought into the last-stand mentality of the survivalists, investing in an elaborate fallout shelter under his two-car garage at Komoka. Before construction began, Helmuth invited a leading American expert on survival homes, Joel Skousen, to review his plans. Skousen also approved the fallout shelter when it was built, even convincing the Buxbaums to install electronic metal shutters in their Komoka home to reduce radioactive contamination in the event of a nuclear war or accident.

The $250,000 fallout shelter had living accommodations, cooking facilities, and doomsday supplies of dehydrated food, water, and items for barter like cigarettes and alcohol. It was also equipped with exactly the kind of weapons recommended by survivalist writer Gary North – two 30-0-6 rifles with scopes, a pump-action shotgun, and a .45-calibre Colt Commander semi-automatic pistol. In 1983, Helmuth took the entire family to Oregon to attend a survivalist camp. Among other things, fifteen-year-old Phillip Buxbaum learned how to fire a machine gun, early training for any unfriendly encounters at the fallout shelter door.

The community benefactor and generous relative could also be a tough businessman. By the early 1980s, Helmuth began to exercise buy-out clauses in nursing home after nursing home, a strategy designed to consolidate his complex and far-flung holdings, to maximize deductible items, and to reduce net taxes. The losers were his former partners, who grumbled about what they saw as Helmuth's ruthless takeovers. All of the profits of the various nursing homes he had managed to buy out now flowed into a new corporate entity – Treugott Management. Helmuth owned 58 per cent of the holding company and Hanna 42 per cent.

Twenty-four years after he had logged his first gut-wrenching day in a uranium mine, Helmuth Buxbaum presided over a nursing-home empire worth more than $25 million. It was as if the Scripture he had once quoted to Hanna in a letter from Elliot Lake had come to pass: "A good man out of the good treasure of his heart bringeth forth that which is good; and an evil man out of the evil treasure of his heart bringeth forth that which is evil."

The good was there for all to see in Helmuth's staggering financial success and selfless Christianity; but there were those who had already seen the dark side.

The shadow that fell across the Buxbaum household crept out from the private corners of their fourteen-year marriage. Over the years, minor complaints had hardened into peevish resentments on both sides. Gone were the days when Hanna was content to play the submissive wife, doing for Helmuth what his mother had once done for Papa Otto. In reality, Hanna had never been quite as slavish as she might have appeared. From the very beginning of the marriage, she had chafed at the regular weekend visits of Helmuth's relatives, which she considered an unwanted invasion of their privacy and which created even more work for her.

Later, she was irritated by Helmuth's long hours at the office and his exaggerated hospitality, which regularly brought five guests to their sprawling house – and even less time alone together. For Helmuth it hardly mattered; he and Hanna now met in the busy intersection of business and domestic banalities, headed in opposite directions. While Hanna regretted the estrangement, Helmuth did not; he had come to regard strictly private moments with his wife as "wasted time."

Although Hanna normally bottled up her frustrations, they occasionally boiled over into shouting matches and painful scenes. Helmuth would back off when faced with his wife's sudden tirades, but not without noting that Hanna's defiance was an affront to his biblical role as head of the household. Helmuth had privately believed from the earliest days of their marriage that Hanna and her mother, Ottilie, had subtly "ruled" him. He had once pointed out to Hanna in a letter quoting from Genesis that the Bible was clear on the subject of marital authority: the husband was meant to be in charge.

Guilt-ridden over her rare emotional outbursts against her husband, Hanna struggled for deeper insights into herself and her role in the marriage. Her reading, once restricted to religious subjects, now included *The Total Woman*, a book that urged her to express her frustrations instead of suppressing them until they exploded under the pressure of Helmuth's insensitivities. Hanna the biblical and matrimonial serf was gradually giving way to Hanna the individual.

Helmuth grappled with the transformation, half approving, half disapproving. On the one hand, he was anxious for his wife to "open up" and blossom, all the more possible now because of their growing affluence. On the other, he never wanted her to forget who was in charge. When

Hanna and some female friends took a trip to Detroit to visit relatives without first seeking his permission, Helmuth lost his temper. Personal development was acceptable, and under certain circumstances even desirable; but patriarchal authority was paramount.

Hanna's growing independence was now only one of Helmuth's many complaints about his wife. He wanted her to buy more stylish clothes and pay more attention to her person; she preferred to shop at discount stores and remained comfortable with the 170-pound woman who looked back at her from the mirror. He provided Hanna with two full-time servants to lighten her domestic burdens; she continued to perform many of the household tasks herself, ignoring her husband's well-intentioned encouragement to become a better supervisor.

A spiritual democrat, Hanna also tended to graft "the help" onto the family. Her Jamaican cook, Donald Campbell, became a personal friend, and her housekeeper, Gizella Toth, a travelling companion. With her six children and legions of church friends, Hanna was often too busy to provide her husband with the constant reassurance he needed, or so it seemed to Helmuth. Her unconscious neglect even began to make him wonder about her true feelings towards him. She may have told others that she had "married the best husband in the world," but did she really mean it?

By the time the couple sought counselling in 1975, the relationship was headed towards total eclipse, and the longest shadow fell across the marriage bed. Ottilie had taught Hanna that sex was solely for procreation and to "watch out for men." Lacking sexual encounters prior to marriage, she had no personal experience with which to temper her mother's rigid views. Although she would permit Helmuth to "tickle" her breasts while they were courting, intercourse had been out of the question. The first night of their honeymoon had been extremely discomfiting. Even the act of undressing in front of her husband had required an act of will. Initially, she had found intercourse painful, and she remained uncomfortable with Helmuth's preference for extended foreplay.

Hanna had also feared getting pregnant, and with good reason. Although their first two children had been planned, the next three had not. Hanna had simply not had time to get her diaphragm in before Helmuth overwhelmed her. After the birth of their fifth child in eight years, she had had her tubes tied.

For Helmuth, sex had always been a fascinating contradiction –

forbidden outside the sacrament of marriage but irresistibly tempting. Unlike Hanna, whose sexual curiosity had been smothered by religious orthodoxy, Helmuth had been an eager sexual explorer from an early age. He was nine when he first masturbated, spurred on by fantasies of a bra-clad model in a magazine advertisement. The awakening adolescent in him was thrilled, the religious zealot mortified: "A Christian should not have fantasies" he later told his doctor. Then, and for a long time to come, lust and guilt were the quarrelling handmaidens of Helmuth Buxbaum's sex life; but lust held the whip hand.

Helmuth was enthralled with the idea of sex, but worried about his ability to perform, and brought a decided awkwardness to his early physical relationship with his wife. "I made a number of mistakes," he candidly admitted to his therapist, not the least of which was pressuring his new bride for favours she did not want to give.

Despite Helmuth's shortcomings as a lover, and his wife's aversion to sexual pleasure, the Buxbaums had a fairly normal relationship in the early years of their marriage. The couple had sex two to three times a week. With one partner propelled by animal instinct and the other tacitly fulfilling her biblical role as wife, their sexual horizons slowly expanded. Hanna didn't enjoy the view. Although she eventually experienced a satisfying orgasm and would occasionally permit Helmuth to perform cunnilingus, she drew the line between conjugal duty and moral impropriety at fellatio. Respectful of Hanna's beliefs, Helmuth didn't force the issue. But his battles with the flesh didn't stop.

At both the physical and spiritual level, Helmuth's choices were clear: sexual fulfilment versus frustration, faithfulness versus fornication. He chose sex, and six years after they were married, Helmuth started to seek out other women, rationalizing that this was actually a way of honouring Hanna. If he could find satisfaction in other beds, she would be spared his unwanted attentions. Although his preference had been for "one wife," it had been Hanna's decision to deny him what he wanted – despite what the Bible had to say on the subject of a woman's duty to her husband.

With his womanizing justified, he considered the issue of sin. Christianity provided a tidy answer. Provided he sought and received God's forgiveness for his sexual transgressions, there was no reason he couldn't have it both ways. After all, wasn't the repentant sinner the apple of the Lord's eye? And if God forgave him, what choice did that leave Hanna?

✦ ✦ ✦

Helmuth's first extra-marital sexual experience took place in the Silver Dollar Motel in London on Grey Cup weekend 1967. It was the same weekend that the Buxbaums officially opened the Komoka Nursing Home with a gala party. It was a dismal flop. Londoners were more interested in watching the Hamilton Tiger Cats thrash the Saskatchewan Roughriders on national television than they were in toasting the Buxbaums' enterprise. After the party, Helmuth and a relative made an uncharacteristic tour of the London bar scene to carry on the celebrations. For fifty dollars, both men had sex with a prostitute they picked up. Helmuth, who felt that he had been led astray, was consumed with guilt.

The next day, he confessed to infidelity. Hanna was badly shaken. Days away from giving birth to their third son, Phillip, she forgave her wayward husband, accepting his vow that this fleshly stumble would be his last. Helmuth later recorded his gratitude for his wife's grace: "Hanna was a worthwhile, honest, pure person and many times I felt unworthy of having her."

He must have felt particularly unworthy on a November morning in 1969 when he received a telephone call from the London District Office of the Department of Social Services. A curt voice on the other end of the line summoned the thirty-year-old father of three to the office to discuss a pressing personal matter. Unbeknownst to his family, Helmuth had recently seduced Donna Hayes, a seventeen-year-old kitchen helper at his Komoka Nursing Home, in the backseat of his car. Social Services had called to tell him, to his horror, that the girl was now pregnant. Helmuth admitted without argument that he was the father and agreed to support payments of sixty dollars a month until the teenager married.

With the easy part out of the way, it was time to face Hanna, who was pregnant with their fourth child, Esther. Hanna was crushed. Through her tears, she agreed that the Buxbaums had a moral obligation to support the mother of what would be his illegitimate daughter. (Helmuth later approached Social Services to adopt the infant, but was turned down.) Once more, Helmuth begged for forgiveness, promising never to stray again; once more, Hanna took him back.

The practical implications of her husband's philandering were inconsequential to Hanna compared to her heartbroken realization that a terrible crack had developed in their relationship. For the second time, Helmuth had demonstrated that there was a part of him that she couldn't trust and didn't understand. Whatever that secret side was, she thought with a shudder, it appeared to have a stronger influence on him than either God or family.

Despite his renewed pledge of fidelity, Helmuth quickly returned to his womanizing, focussing his attention on the female staff at his nursing homes. When his awkward passes and untoward propositions were reported to company managers, it was decided that nothing could be done about the owner's "private life." Instead, women who complained about Helmuth's unwanted attentions were invited to resign. One of them, Ruthann Colwell, had become a favourite of Helmuth's mother, Luise, who was now in the nursing home as a resident. "When I told her I was leaving, she cried and wanted to know why. I didn't tell her," Nurse Colwell recalled.

The goings-on at Komoka and Chatham eventually reached the ears of Fred Kirkpatrick, Helmuth's partner in the Canadianna Nursing Home since 1969. Kirkpatrick knew Helmuth as a good businessman, husband, and father, and a very generous supporter of the church. He also knew that his otherwise likable partner had an eye for the ladies. "He told me it was a problem for him, and we discussed it and I warned him re: the staff. It stopped," Kirkpatrick remembered later.

A change in Ontario's capital gains laws led Fred Kirkpatrick to sell his interest in the business to Helmuth before he could find out how wrong his assessment had been. In the early 1970s, when the family began wintering in Florida, Helmuth had spent a lot of time in Boca Raton. But as the sexual rift between he and Hanna widened, his winter trips back to Canada grew more frequent. The pursuit of his female employees increased until word of Helmuth's misconduct finally got back to the church. The pastor of West Park Baptist Church, Rev. Paul Fawcett, was asked by the parents of one of the girls to speak to the wayward married man.

It was a sensitive task. Pastor Fawcett and his wife were personal friends of the Buxbaums, having travelled with them on church excursions to Haiti and Israel. Helmuth also served on several church committees and generously supported many of its missions and the Christian Academy. Fawcett confronted Helmuth with the incident, but since it didn't involve actual "touching" he treated it as inappropriate rather than immoral behaviour. The affair blew over.

Faced with further evidence of her husband's infidelity and their own disintegrating relationship, Hanna finally convinced Helmuth to see Avinoam and Beryl Chernick, a husband and wife gynaecological team who shared a sex-therapy and marriage-counselling practice in London. The final straw for Hanna had been Helmuth's extended affair with a hitchhiker he had picked up while driving the children home from school. As a result of her husband's year-and-a-half fling, Hanna ended up in a doctor's office with non-specific urethritis – in all likelihood, her considerate family doctor's medical euphemism for venereal disease.

From the very beginning of the marriage counselling, Helmuth made a poor impression on the Chernicks. The doctors' notes refer to him as "rigid and Kraut-like" – a stance they believed was the primary problem behind their "rather frustrating attempt" to work with the Buxbaums.

"Helmuth was most verbose and overbearing during this interview, trying to convince everyone of his views and that whatever he was doing was right, while at the same time protesting that somehow, things were not working." Dr. Beryl Chernick wrote.

Despite his self-righteousness, Helmuth did admit to having had five affairs since his marriage, including one with his London secretary and another with Hanna's personal assistant in Florida. But he wouldn't take all the blame for the condition of the marriage, complaining about Hanna's refusal to try fellatio. (Although the doctors recorded that Hanna was as set in her ways as Helmuth, she, at least, was willing to bow to his desire if it would restore the marriage to health. After one session with Beryl Chernick, she acceded to his wishes with unsatisfactory results.) The Chernicks recommended four joint sessions in which they planned to teach the Buxbaums how to communicate with each other "at a feeling level" to improve "the quality of their life." But for now, the prognosis wasn't encouraging: "Helmuth frustrated, Hanna irritated . . . two wheels going in the same direction but at different speeds. Friction in the axle."

A year later, the couple had still not shown up for their first joint session, but not because their problems were over. For the second time, Rev. Fawcett found himself listening to disturbing allegations against the wealthy pillar of his congregation, this time involving a young teenager. Hanna dismissed the complaints as the exaggerations of a kid. Helmuth's pastor adopted a different assessment according to Doris Sinusac, the woman who brought the complaint forward: "Fawcett and his wife both felt that the incident was due to the girl's flirtation and they refused to believe that Helmuth would do something like that."

Protected by both his wife and his pastor, Helmuth was once again spared the consequences of his philandering.

Despite her gallant if misguided attempts to cover up her husband's inexplicable moral collapse, Hanna Buxbaum knew by 1979 that she had to take action. By that time, there was no doubt that Helmuth had infected her with a sexually transmitted disease. Helmuth not only contracted and re-contracted urethritis a total of fourteen times, he also picked up a virus that caused a growth to form on the tip of his penis. Dr. Gary Nancekievill, the Buxbaums' family physician since 1977, arranged to have the growth removed, surmising that the virus hadn't been picked up from Hanna. But Helmuth didn't confide in Nancekievill, and the doctor asked no questions. "I heard lots of rumours," he said, "but I [didn't] put any stock in them."

Hanna's miseries were aggravated by her own deteriorating physical condition. Suffering from a fallen uterus, she told her gynaecologist that when she was tired, she felt like "her insides were falling out." She complained of spilling urine when she coughed and noted that Helmuth now told her that he felt like he was "on air" when he entered her vagina. Helmuth had all but lost interest in his wife and usually pleaded fatigue or migraines when she initiated sex. When they did make love, he had difficulty maintaining an erection, a change Hanna attributed to the condition of her stretched vagina.

In a desperate attempt to compete with the young women she knew Helmuth was sleeping with, Hanna decided to have a hysterectomy, followed by anterior and posterior "repairs" she hoped would heighten her husband's sexual pleasure. While Hanna looked forward to "[trying] out her new posterior repair for its positive effect on her husband's penis," Helmuth oddly complained to Dr. Chernick that the operation would deprive him of sexual relations with Hanna for eight weeks. The doctor who would perform the operation, Avinoam Chernick, made clear to Dr. Nancekievill that he didn't share Hanna's optimism that surgery was the way to recover her husband's lost attentions: "Knowing his working habits, he may be too tired to enter a virgin-like, reconstructed vagina."

If anything, Hanna's surgery took even more wind out of the couple's sex life; Helmuth later complained that for several months after the operation his wife's sexual desires were "substantially decreased." Helmuth's were not. In the same year that Hanna tried to carry out a medical rescue of their faltering marriage, Helmuth travelled to Fort Lauderdale with

"Catherine," a ski instructor at London's Circle 'R' Ranch. Shortly after being introduced to the young woman in 1977, he invited her to Treugott Management for a job interview. Helmuth began seeing her every two or three weeks and often gave her souvenirs from his travels. The relationship quickly blossomed into an on-again, off-again affair that lasted for three years.

"He arranged to have lunch with me a couple of times, and on the third time we ended up going to one of the motels on Wellington Road," the attractive brunette later recalled. "Helmuth would usually buy a bottle of wine. I had intercourse with Helmuth at the motel. He paid me either fifty or one hundred dollars."

Helmuth made no attempt to hide the fact that he was married. After he made it clear that he loved his wife and children, Helmuth told his latest sex interest that Hanna was "restricting" him from doing the things he wanted to do. "He would describe it as, 'It's too bad I have to go back to Hanna and my responsibilities and my job,'" she said later.

During their three-day stay in a small Florida motel, Helmuth attempted to introduce a new wrinkle into the relationship: "While in Fort Lauderdale, Helmuth wanted me to become involved in group sex. Helmuth wanted me to have sex with him and another woman, but I was not interested."

Despite Catherine's refusal, Helmuth pressed the young woman for a "more permanent relationship." She declined. Their affair began to cool off, and Helmuth decided to organize his search for young women on a more systematic basis. He advertised in several southern Ontario newspapers for "travelling companions" and joined the Phone Club, a dating service on Yonge Street in Toronto that offered its members a list of telephone numbers of willing partners. Although this greatly increased the number of his sexual contacts, what he really wanted was a partner he could keep as a kind of sexual pet.

Monica Taylor, a black nurse who had first met Helmuth during a three-year stint in the Buxbaum's Leamington nursing home, became his mistress during a week-long trip to a Club Med village in Mexico. By early 1980, Helmuth had moved her into a beautiful country house in Lambeth that he and Hanna had recently purchased. As he sipped apricot brandy and made love to Monica, he had no idea that for the first time in his adulterous career, his double life was about to blow up in his face.

Upset by his mother's obvious unhappiness and his father's frequent absences from home, sixteen-year-old Paul Buxbaum decided to get to the bottom of the incessant rumours about Helmuth's infidelities. His inquiries led him to the house at Lambeth, where he found Taylor. Outraged at his father's staggering hypocrisy (at Helmuth's invitation, Taylor had attended West Park Baptist Church and even visited Komoka to meet Hanna and go swimming with the Buxbaum children), Paul decided to leave home. Before he packed his bags, he told Hanna and Paul Fawcett what Helmuth had been up to behind everyone's back. In light of all she had done to make him happy, a wailing Hanna demanded an accounting. Helmuth put up no defence. Instead, he confirmed his son's allegations and begged for forgiveness. "I told her that it [was] true what Paul had told her and that I *had* had an affair with Monica, but that it was all over and finished. I told her that I was sorry it happened."

Anxious as always to demonstrate his remorse, Helmuth quickly removed his mistress from the Lambeth house and installed the principal of the Christian Academy, Phil Conley, and his family in her place. Conley agreed to look after the property and to take in Paul Buxbaum until his anger subsided. (A few months later, Ruthie Buxbaum, unable to get along with her brothers and sisters at Komoka, joined her eldest brother in the Conley household.)

The problem with the church was not as easily smoothed over. Considering the past complaints about his wealthy patron, Rev. Paul Fawcett had no choice but to take firm action regarding Helmuth's self-admitted adultery. He and the board of elders of West Park Baptist Church decided that Helmuth's membership in the congregation would have to be temporarily suspended. Although he was still free to worship there, Helmuth would be readmitted to the fold only if he rejected his "reprobate" lifestyle.

Unknown to his would-be moral arbiters, Helmuth's affair with Monica was only the tip of the iceberg. Unwilling to give up his double life, he continued to visit prostitutes he met through the Phone Club and even set about recruiting an unemployed model as a new mistress. His walk on the wild side grew bolder; by late 1981, he was dabbling in cocaine and group sex. One of the woman he had designs on was the girlfriend of his cook at Komoka, a desire that became painfully clear during a February 1982 jaunt to Las Vegas.

"While in Las Vegas," Donald Campbell recalled, "Helmuth tried to get in bed with Susan and [me], but I told him it wouldn't work and I never had any further problems with him. Helmuth had a couple of hookers while we were in Las Vegas. Helmuth complained about his sex life at home."

But the unhappy multimillionaire would soon have more to worry about than Hanna's imagined shortcomings in bed. One night in April 1982, eternity opened its gaping jaws and Helmuth Buxbaum very nearly disappeared inside.

4

GOD AND THE SATYR

"God had given me a warning. It was a last warning to
smarten up. I resolved not to have any more affairs."
– Helmuth Buxbaum, April 1982

On the morning of April 17, 1982, Helmuth Buxbaum woke from a fitful sleep hoping that the agony was finally over. Ever since the days he
had carried his cross up the hill to the Krems cemetery as a thirteen-
year-old boy, the monthly migraines had struck like hammer blows,
sometimes incapacitating him for days. This one had begun the day
before, and now, as he blinked drowsily at his bedroom, the pain behind
his eyes surged back stronger than ever. On occasions like this, not even
Fiorinal, the powerful painkiller prescribed by Dr. Nancekievill since
1977, could bring relief. Anxious to ease her husband's suffering, Hanna
made an appointment with their London osteopath, whose therapy had
often helped before.

At 4 P.M., Helmuth sat hopefully in a treatment room as the osteopath
performed a series of neck and back manipulations designed to ease the
tension that aggravates migraines. In the course of his therapy, Dr. Douglas Lauder braced himself with his knee against Helmuth's spine and
pulled back on his patient's shoulders, twisting him from side to side. The
doctor then put both hands on Helmuth's head and began rotating his
neck. Suddenly there was an audible crack and Helmuth felt a stab of pain.
After a few uncomfortable moments, it gradually subsided, and he left the
doctor's office feeling a little better.

When Helmuth got back to Komoka, the telephone was ringing. It
was his sons, Phillip and Mark, looking for a ride home from a friend's.

He set out in the family station wagon without noticing that the needle on the fuel gauge was teetering on empty. Just before 6 P.M., as he approached the house where the boys were waiting for him, the car coughed to a stop, out of gas. A neighbour drove Helmuth to a nearby service station and they returned a few moments later with a can of gasoline. The two boys strolled out to help their father. With Phillip holding a makeshift funnel made of rolled up newspaper, Helmuth began refilling the station wagon's tank. Suddenly, he teetered backwards, spilling gas on his pants. Phillip caught his woozy father and assisted him to the ground, while Mark raced back to the house for help.

Fifteen minutes later, an ambulance raced into the emergency entrance of London's University Hospital with a fully alert Helmuth Buxbaum in the back strapped to a stretcher and one of his sons sitting anxiously at his side. He attributed the partial blindness in his left eye and the strange loss of feeling down the left side of his body to having been overcome by gas fumes. But the emergency medical team that attended to him suspected that his sudden blackout had a far deadlier cause.

Helmuth's speech was slurred and his left eyelid drooped noticeably. Through his partially open mouth they could see that his tongue was askew, apparently beyond his control. Nor could he maintain eye contact with a moving object, a tell-tale sign that he had lost muscle control on one side of his face. In fact, the left side of Helmuth's body varied from a state of hemiparesis to hemiplegia – weakness to paralysis. When doctors stuck pins in the sole of his left foot, there was no sensation. As the emergency team searched frantically for the embolism they suspected had interrupted the blood supply to Helmuth's brain, the patient was overcome by waves of drowsiness and began to slip in and out of consciousness. He was rushed to an intensive care room just outside the emergency ward. When Helmuth awakened, Hanna was at his bedside.

"I asked her what happened," Helmuth said later. "She explained to me that I had had a stroke. She was very worried. The doctors told her that I would be in a wheelchair for the rest of my life."

Looking blankly into the eyes of his wife, the paralysed multimillionaire made another unnerving discovery: he couldn't remember long stretches of their twenty-one years together. With his future apparently snatched away, and much of his past eradicated, he found himself sequestered in a terrifying present in which nothing quite made sense.

Four days after his collapse, Helmuth's condition worsened. While making her 6 A.M. rounds at University Hospital, a nurse found him sitting bolt upright in bed, making garbled noises in his throat. "Vital signs stable," she noted on his chart. "Patient incontinent of large amount of urine – could recall no motor events or participating events, other than some tingling in left arm."

Like ten per cent of all stroke victims, Helmuth had suffered an epileptic seizure. An hour later, he was rocked with a second attack. His nurse reported, "patient moaning and grunting as before. This time, left arm extended and twitching. Right arm flexed and jerking. Eyes deviated upwards."

Medical staff at the hospital worked around the clock to determine the nature and extent of Helmuth's affliction. After reviewing the results of CAT-scans (computer x-rays of the brain), carotid angiograms (x-rays of blood vessels), and other tests, physicians at University Hospital confirmed their original suspicion: Helmuth Buxbaum had indeed suffered a massive stroke. His right internal carotid artery, one of two major arteries in the neck that carry the blood supply to the brain, had been "dissected" shortly before his stroke on April 17. The doctors theorized that the tear, which had allowed blood to track under the lining of the artery and harden into a thrombosis, or clot, could have been caused by a sharp twist of Helmuth's neck, possibly during his osteopath's manipulations to relieve his migraine. A number of fragments had then broken away from the main blood clot and proceeded up the artery, eventually lodging in its narrower branches and interrupting the blood flow to several regions of Helmuth's brain. The result was a series of infarcts – masses of brain cells in several areas of his right frontal and parietal lobes that had actually died from lack of blood. The resulting lesions on Helmuth's brain left him suffering from left-side paralysis, partial amnesia, and some perceptual impairment.

In the days immediately following his stroke, Helmuth was subjected to a number of neuropsychological tests aimed at measuring his intellectual impairment, if any, from the events of April 17. The tests revealed some subtle, but nevertheless disturbing abnormalities. Although Helmuth's verbal IQ was measured at 118, a ranking that placed him in the top 25 per cent of the population, doctors discovered that his performance IQ was "disproportionately" lower at a mere 93. Since verbal skills are controlled by the left side of the brain, that clearly indicated damage to the right side.

When the doctors administered the Wexler Adult Intelligence Skill Test, Helmuth registered a "poor performance" in pictorial and visual tests. He had apparently lost a significant portion of his ability to think creatively, abstractly, or logically – yet another indication of damage to the right frontal and parietal lobes. Although he still knew the words "quarter" and "dime," he could no longer put his hand in his pocket and distinguish them by touch alone. But of far greater significance, the damage that had been done to his brain *could* cause dramatic personality change.

Helmuth Buxbaum, a man who had reason to be proud of his intellect, found the endless testing at University Hospital unnecessary and humiliating. "Every day, the psychologist took me for tests. Every day, the doctors came and asked me what my name was, where I was, what day of the week it was, how old I was, where I was born. I felt like an imbecile."

One of his first visitors was his friend and colleague in the nursing-home business, Dr. Cal Stiller, who assured Helmuth that his doctors' treatment was completely appropriate given the seriousness of his stroke.

"Dr. Stiller came to my hospital room to tell me 'confidentially' that, although he was not my physician, he had looked at my CAT-scan pictures and that things looked pretty serious. I had had a massive stroke on my right hemisphere, and as far as he was concerned, I should not go back to work for at least a year since 'destroyed brain cells are dead and you will never have your full capacity again.' I was devastated . . . I felt cheated. Here I was, forty-two years old, in a wheelchair – with the real possibility of spending the rest of my life in a wheelchair . . . All my plans, hopes and aspirations were finished and I felt old, fat, and ugly . . . After my stroke in April 1982, I went through a terrible self-evaluation and as I perceived it, my life was over," Helmuth later wrote.

Through the dark days immediately following the stroke, Hanna Buxbaum was a guardian angel at her husband's bedside. Every day for six hours, she did her best to put back what the stroke had taken away, patiently replacing Helmuth's lost memories with stories from their past, of trips with the children and their astonishing climb to business success. She assured him that there were dozens of ways the family could learn to cope with his affliction if it proved permanent. On the other hand, she did not accept the doctors' prognosis on her husband as final and prayed for God's intervention. As for Helmuth, he believed that the Lord had already made a divine intervention: "God had given me a warning." he concluded. "It was a *last* warning to smarten up. I resolved not to have any further affairs."

Shortly after his sickbed resolution, Helmuth Buxbaum experienced what he justifiably saw as a miracle. "One day while I was still in hospital, Hanna was sitting beside my bed. I suddenly could move two fingers of my left hand. My motor control returned."

Just ten days after the stroke that was supposed to put him in a wheel-chair for life, Helmuth Buxbaum walked out of University Hospital with an anticoagulant to prevent his blood from clotting, a prescription of Dilantin to control his seizures, and a simple cane. Hanna Buxbaum was so happy she could almost forget the strange spectacle just days earlier of walking into her husband's room and finding him masturbating in his hospital bed with all the obliviousness of a man reading a newspaper.

The first sign that Helmuth Buxbaum's recovery wasn't as complete as he believed it to be appeared on May 4, 1982, less than three weeks after his stroke. He was driving with Hanna when, without apparently noticing, he strayed into the left-hand lane of the highway. When Helmuth showed up at Dr. Nancekievill's office the next day for blood tests, he looked "confused" but insisted that he was competent to drive.

Paul Buxbaum made a futile attempt to persuade his father to give up driving until he had properly convalesced. Helmuth was uncharacteristi-cally unreasonable, refusing to discuss the matter. His father's inability to drive safely became so terrifying that Paul went to the Ontario Provincial Police and tried unsuccessfully to have the sick man's licence revoked.

Dr. Nancekievill also noted another peculiarity about his patient that caused him concern. During the year prior to his stroke, Helmuth had twice talked to his family doctor about his fear of nuclear war – a not unreasonable concern in the early 1980s. But in the single month after his release from hospital, he raised the subject with his doctor five times, relating his terror of radioactive contamination and describing the elabo-rate fallout shelter he had built to survive the coming holocaust or a nuclear accident. Struck by his obsessive behaviour, Dr. Nancekievill made note of the fact that his patient appeared to be "over-reacting to the nuclear war threat."

By the time Helmuth walked into Dr. Thomas Feasby's office at Uni-versity Hospital for a follow-up examination on June 17, 1982, he was personally convinced that he'd made "a 100 per cent recovery." Failing to mention his erratic driving, he insisted that his only lingering problem was some mild stiffness in the fingers on his left hand that made it hard for him to button his own shirt.

Dr. Feasby was impressed with Helmuth's remarkable recovery, but he knew it was far from complete. Following an examination on June 17, the doctor noted that Helmuth had not even made a complete physical recovery from his stroke. He was still suffering from a lack of muscle control on the left side of his face and a lack of sensation in the fingers and toes of his left hand and foot. But the most troubling repercussion of Helmuth's stroke was psychological. "Mr. Buxbaum," Dr. Feasby wrote, "has not shown a good ability to appreciate his own condition subsequent to his stroke."

Just days after his discharge from hospital, Helmuth made an appearance in the offices of Treugott Management. He seemed to be trying desperately to convince himself that there was nothing wrong with him, a delusion that got harder and harder to sustain as the symptoms of his disturbing condition mounted in the weeks and months after his release from hospital.

Two days after returning home from the hospital, Helmuth tried to make love to Hanna and made a devastating discovery: he was impotent. Dr. Feasby assured him that sexual dysfunction was common in stroke patients and usually corrected itself in a very short time. But weeks passed and Helmuth still couldn't get an erection with Hanna. He approached Dr. Nancekievill for aphrodisiacs and was given vitamins B and E. When the vitamin treatment failed, Dr. Nancekievill finally prescribed testosterone. "I took the pills," Helmuth recalled. "They helped a little. Hanna and I had sex, but it wasn't the same."

Beneath his shambling, apathetic exterior, Helmuth was in turmoil. Hanna was initially too happy with his new dependency on her to notice that he found her attentions cloying. The truth was he resented being "babied" by everyone around him and worried about the erosion of his authority over his family. Nor did his wife know how preoccupied Helmuth had become with his "fragile penis," although she very nearly found out a few days after his stroke when she and the children had showed up at the hospital for a surprise visit. When she walked into his room, Hanna was shocked to find a pretty young woman sitting on Helmuth's bed. He blandly introduced Roseanne Willoughby, one of the call girls he had begun seeing before his stroke, as an acquaintance from a nursing-home convention.

Soon after his discharge from hospital, Helmuth arranged for Willoughby to take the train from Toronto to London, where she met him in a motel. The first few times he was still too ill to have sex, but after his testosterone treatment, he was finally able to break his sickbed promise to the Lord in a room at the Holiday Inn.

By summer, he was feeling sexually potent enough to offer $300 to Donald Campbell, his former cook, to let him sleep with his girlfriend. Rejected, Helmuth began travelling to Toronto where he resumed his trysts with Willoughby in the Constellation Hotel.

The routine was always the same: drinks, dinner, a porno movie in their hotel room, sex, then a $100 payment and cab fare from Helmuth. At first, he rationalized his dalliances as part of a self-help approach to his impotence. After learning that sex therapists sometimes provide their patients with surrogates to help them overcome their sexual problems, he reasoned that prostitutes were a means to the same end. Later, his justification for his infidelities was less therapeutic. "I wondered if I could still have sex with women other than Hanna. It was easy to satisfy Hanna. I guess I wanted to convince myself that I could still satisfy other women."

On a warm August night in 1982, Helmuth made his usual call from the Constellation to Roseanne's apartment only to find out that she couldn't see him anymore; her steady boyfriend, it seemed, disapproved of her "hooking." But, she wondered, would he like to have dinner with her sister, Corinne? Helmuth eagerly agreed. After wine and a room-service dinner, the businessman and the teenager had sex. Helmuth gave Corinne $200 for her services, double what he paid her sister. Youth always commanded a premium with the wealthy businessman. Helmuth arranged to meet his newest companion again; they were soon seeing each other once a week.

By September 1982, a new element had been added to their relationship. Corinne introduced Helmuth to her friend Lisa Finn, and the two girls now began meeting him in either London or Toronto. Helmuth asked them for a lesbian performance but they refused; he then had sex with both girls and paid each of them $200.

The new experience whetted his appetite. In early October, Helmuth and Hanna attended a conference in New Orleans with three other couples, including Treugott's comptroller, Nick Potocska, and his wife, Pamela. When the conference ended, Hanna flew to Detroit with the others, while Helmuth unabashedly jetted off to Toronto for a tryst with the two young prostitutes, unconcerned about the impression he was making on his wife and colleagues. After spending three days at the airport strip hotel with Willoughby and Finn, the ménage flew at Helmuth's expense to a resort in the Bahamas.

Longing for the close relationship she had had with her husband during his convalescence, Hanna Buxbaum sadly acknowledged that Helmuth had slipped back into his old ways. On the drive back from Detroit to London, she took the Potocskas into her confidence. "Hanna told Pam and I that she was aware of Helmuth's affairs. Her way of dealing with the situation was to be submissive and wait for him to repent," Potocska recalled.

From behind his desk at Treugott Management Inc., Potocska had gathered ample proof that the April 17 stroke had brought about profound changes in his employer's character. He watched his onetime business and religious hero turn into an unpredictable and nearly invisible player in his nursing home empire. The man who had once routinely logged sixteen hours a day running Treugott now spent less than sixteen hours a month in the office.

His new routine was disruptive and caused "anxiety and depression" amongst the staff, according to Potocska. Helmuth walked through Treugott's offices between 7:30 A.M. and 8:30 A.M. and then vanished until after 4 P.M. Since he refused to wear a beeper or to say where he was going, frequently no one, including Hanna, could locate the chief executive officer of the $25-million corporation during business hours.

And then came the dark suspicions. In a business office where every work day began with a prayer meeting led by Helmuth, his mysterious absences created embarrassing problems. The secretaries and receptionists who normally vetted their boss's telephone calls now had to deal with a stream of insistent young women like Corinne Willoughby and Lisa Finn, who regularly called Helmuth from the London train station. Despite his staff's initial reluctance to leap to conclusions, the purpose of the calls soon became distressingly obvious.

Treugott employees also had to deal with frustrated members of the Buxbaum family, who were trying desperately to keep tabs on the changed Helmuth. "During the frequent business or personal trips Helmuth T. Buxbaum made, Hanna often called the office looking for him. There was stress between office staff and Hanna because of her requests for Helmuth T. Buxbaum's address book, whereabouts, or telephone number to reach him at, versus Helmuth T. Buxbaum's direct orders to withhold these things from Hanna," Nick Potocska said later.

Potocska tried to ease the situation by designating one person, Treugott's payroll supervisor, Yvonne Miller, to vet all of Helmuth's calls. But the stress of dealing with a telephone line that was being overwhelmed by prostitutes was too much. Sickened by Helmuth's apparent hypocrisy, Miller resigned on October 14, 1982.

By December 1982, Nick Potocska decided that, as a business colleague and a "Christian brother," he should confront the wayward multimillionaire. During a face-to-face meeting in Helmuth's office, Potocska explained that Helmuth's new life style was seriously disrupting the nursing home business. Stung by the confrontation, Helmuth insisted that Potocska's allegations were based on nothing more than "circumstantial evidence." Besides, Helmuth declared, if his lifestyle had indeed created the business problems Potocska alleged, why hadn't the injured parties in the office approached him directly? Potocska was dumfounded: "His response was . . . to make no comment about the circumstantial evidence and just to stare emotionlessly at me," Potocska recalled.

After his standoff with Helmuth, Potocska confided his concerns in Howard Johnson, another Treugott executive, who had already dropped the occasional remark about Helmuth's "spiritual problems." After telling Johnson about the calls he suspected were coming from prostitutes, Potocska was shocked to learn about the Monica Taylor affair, and even more surprised to find out that Johnson and his wife, Margaret, had actually seen Helmuth around London in the company of another woman. But when Potocska begged Johnson to join him in confronting Helmuth again, the senior manager declined.

Feeling totally frustrated, Potocska decided to make a direct appeal to Helmuth's spiritual confidante, Rev. Paul Fawcett. But even though Fawcett knew about Helmuth's previous sexual escapades, he refused to intervene. "As I remember it, he indicated that he could not act on only circumstantial evidence, so, lacking an eyewitness, that was the end of it," Potocska said later.

A few months later, Howard Johnson had a change of heart and decided to confront Helmuth over his troubling behaviour. With Nick Potocska at his side, Johnson told Helmuth that he had seen him with another woman and "challenged" him as a fellow Christian to overcome his "spiritual" difficulties. Helmuth sat stonily behind his desk staring silently at his accusers. Getting no response, they turned once more to Pastor Fawcett. With an eyewitness standing in his study, the reluctant clergyman had no choice but to confront the congregation's wealthy and powerful patron. His intervention only made Helmuth angrier.

"Within two or three days of their talk, Helmuth T. Buxbaum called both Howard Johnson and I into his office and chastised us for 'meddling' in his personal affairs," Potocska said later. "He told us that our responsibility was to be loyal to him, and not to discuss these or any similar circumstances with anyone but him. This was to include his wife."

Although Nick Potocska sympathized with Hanna's plight, he was too worried about the Buxbaums' business fortunes to give all of his attention to their marital problems. In August 1983, he had received a call from the Royal Bank after the company had exceeded its $1.1 million credit line by $200,000. The bank was concerned about the extent of Helmuth's personal expenditures and wanted him to cut back before they became a problem for the corporation.

Potocska's main worry was a potential cash-flow crisis. The same month the bank called, Helmuth went through another $60,000, and Potocska finally told his boss that if he kept spending at that rate, he would be drawing $720,000 a year out of the company. Helmuth was furious. "It is none of your business. You are the controller of my company, you are not the controller of me," he bristled. What the Buxbaums did with profits made in previous years was, to Helmuth's mind, their business and their business alone. In fact, he was investing the monies in gold bullion, silver, and other hard assets according to the theories of economic survivalism, which had become the centrepiece of the Buxbaums' personal financial credo.

During a later business junket to Florida, Potocska and Howard Johnson both asked Helmuth to redeposit the money in order to avert a liquidity problem. At a second meeting which included both Buxbaums, Hanna's wide-eyed curiosity about the large withdrawals had made it clear to Potocska, at least, that she didn't realize what was going on.

Unhappy that Helmuth had ignored its request for greater prudence in his spending habits, the Royal Bank reduced Treugott's line of credit by $200,000 – exactly the amount Helmuth was overdrawn – and increased its loan rate. Potocska, meanwhile, was busy negotiating a deal with the Toronto-Dominion Bank to take over the Buxbaum account.

Under the new arrangement, the Buxbaums would no longer be permitted to write personal cheques on the corporate line of credit of $1.6 million, but were each given a personal line of credit of $500,000. The potential cash flow problem was averted when Helmuth sold some of the gold and silver he'd been amassing and reinvested it in Treugott, along with $550,000 from the sale of the Manitoulin Island Nursing Home.

Phone calls from Helmuth's women continued to pour in to Treugott, and Sharon Morenz, Yvonne Miller's replacement, soon quit for the same reason as her predecessor. Helmuth's furtive trips to Toronto – and more exotic destinations – kept the Travel Bug travel agency in nearby Byron hopping.

The black sheep was easily outdistancing the shepherd's crook.

Since the earliest days of their marriage, Helmuth and Hanna Buxbaum had admired the Scripture that read: "If we confess our sins, he is faithful and just to forgive us our sins and to cleanse us from all unrighteousness." To Helmuth, the words from 1 John 1:9 were clear: "This means that if I confess to the person and to the Lord, forgiveness would have to come. Hanna believed that as well."

The verse inspired a private ritual: before the sun went down each evening, they would settle any differences between them, confessing their shortcomings and seeking forgiveness from each other. It was a practice that permitted the Christian couple to finish each day with a clear conscience. Although Helmuth had often broken the rule, he had, at least, always acknowledged it. But by the first anniversary of his stroke, Hanna finally accepted the fact that her partner of twenty-two years was now living beyond the pale, a virtual stranger to his wife and family.

The multimillionaire who had once filled his schedule with business meetings, religious commitments, family events – and a busy extramarital sex life – now spent inordinate amounts of time watching television and overeating. During his convalescence, his oldest sons had commented that their father had grown distant, apathetic, and depressed. Then the idiosyncrasies had begun to kick in. Before the stroke, Helmuth had been a stickler for personal hygiene and an impeccable dresser, donning a fresh suit every day. But when Hanna stopped bathing and dressing him a few weeks after his return from hospital, he would forget to shave and wore the same suit for days on end, even when he had spilled food on himself. Phillip Buxbaum found this behaviour "almost funny" and would take Helmuth to his room and make him change his dirty clothes. An old friend, Bill Sergeant, was astonished to see the once fastidious Helmuth walking around with his shirt unbuttoned and "his belly hanging out." They talked one day at the London Bible College, and a disconsolate Helmuth sighed, "They've taken everything away from me."

Helmuth's memory began playing tricks. In the year following the stroke, he forgot Phillip's birthday. When he promised to pick the children up from school, he would often be late or not arrive at all, uncharacteristic behaviour from a man famous for showing up early for his appointments. On several occasions, he asked friends to dinner and then went to bed before his guests arrived, forgetting that he had extended the invitation.

According to staff and friends, he often got confused in the middle of the simplest conversation or completely forgot what he had been saying. He gave specific orders to his groundskeeper, Ken Surette, and then an hour later, when Surette was carrying them out, asked him what he was doing. (This happened so frequently that Hanna began quietly rescinding Helmuth's instructions to their personal staff.) The man who had always displayed a love of animals before his stroke, now mingled acts of extreme cruelty with his former kindness.

"My father instructed me to trap and kill a cat that had attacked our chickens," Phillip later said. "On another occasion, we were out with the chickens and the rooster pecked a bit at our legs. My father grabbed it, chopped its head [off] and staked the rooster to the barn door. He decided to give me an anatomy lesson and cut the rooster open and showed me the different parts of the body."

Helmuth's odd behaviour was impossible to ignore. While wearing a business suit, he gave manure-shovelling pointers to his staff and watered some newly planted trees without seeming to notice that it was raining. One of his less appreciated new habits was discharging his .22-calibre rifle near the nursing home, firing at neighbourhood cats or the blackbirds that were harvesting his fruit trees. Strangest of all, someone had taken to showing up at the nursing home late at night and wandering the halls wrapped in a sheet. Although no one could prove it, the nursing staff suspected it was Helmuth.

He began to lose interest in many of the things that had once sustained him. The man who had personally guided the fortunes of Treugott handed over day-to-day authority to his management team; spending money, not making it, became his new contribution to the business. Once passionately interested in his children's school careers, he now ignored them. Not even Mark, whose German studies had previously fascinated Helmuth, could get his father's attention.

Yet there were odd exceptions to his torpor. Helmuth had usually been lenient with his older sons, but now he seemed anxious to exert his authority over them. When Phillip challenged his father after being ordered to get his hair cut, Helmuth struck him on the head with his open hand. It was the first time he had ever hit one of the children.

As if a secret ego were emerging, Helmuth began to live for the moment in a self-absorbed and peevish way. In sharp contrast to his earlier behaviour, he enjoyed flaunting his wealth. "My father started saying things like, 'I can get that because I'm a millionaire,'" Phillip later explained. One afternoon, Helmuth rolled up the driveway in a $60,000 Mercedes-Benz, breaking the longstanding practice of consulting his wife on *all* purchases. Aghast at what she saw as her husband's profligacy, Hanna forced him to return the car. Later, Hanna confided in her therapist, Dr. Chernick, that her husband had developed "a terrible, sneaky" disposition.

By 1984, the new Helmuth on display at Komoka was no longer just the absentminded autocrat with soup stains on his tie. His attendance at church, once the organizing principle of his private life, dropped off dramatically. (One of the reasons may have been Nick Potocska's picayune vigilance; if he noticed that Helmuth didn't take communion, he would report it to Rev. Paul Fawcett as a sign of a bad conscience.) He began to curse, drink, and smoke in blatant defiance of the very rules he himself had for years so piously imposed on the Buxbaum household. And then came the stunning lewdness. One night Helmuth awakened his eldest son and shouted, "Your mother won't even kiss me on the penis. What's wrong with her? I'm not asking for a blow-job, just a little kiss on the penis."

Phillip Buxbaum got his own jolting introduction to the magnitude of the change that had come over his father. "When I was sixteen years old, my father showed me pictures of girls, saying, 'They want to fuck you.' He told me he loved young prostitutes and, to me, it was as if he did not realize he was an adult anymore. I recall that when I had just turned sixteen and had a driver's licence, I told my father that I was going out cruising on Saturday night with some friends. He asked, 'Can I come?' . . . I was confused because I felt my father no longer appreciated that he was not the same as me. Before, he had always been a real father figure; in control, rational, offering advice and guidance. After the stroke, he seemed to *identify* more with me."

A psychiatrist might have recognized the dark hand of frontal lobe disorder in Helmuth's clearly altered personality, and connected his selfish and often inappropriate outbursts to the condition's pseudo-psychopathic stage, but the Buxbaum children could only watch and wonder at their father's disintegration.

Hanna Buxbaum bore the brunt of the family's agony. Reduced to the status of a single parent, Hanna encouraged the children, helped them with their problems, and tried to fill the vacuum in their lives left by Helmuth's virtual withdrawal from family life.

"It had become regular for my dad not to show up at night. We all got used to it. Sometimes he would phone with some silly excuse – like that his car had broken down. Other times he wouldn't call at all. Most of the time we didn't know where he was," his daughter Esther, fifteen at the time, later recalled.

Hanna may not have known Helmuth's whereabouts during his nocturnal absences, but others clearly did. Members of the West Park congregation were openly whispering about his rampant womanizing. At a home and school meeting, where Helmuth spoke about the moral shortcomings of a proposed policy, one parent turned to Pastor Doug Dakin and said, "How can he say that when he is running around with so many women?" Even Helmuth realized that his wife probably knew what he was up to: "Hanna obviously had suspicions about the other women. I think that she talked to Rev. Paul Fawcett about it. Hanna was reluctant to confront me about it."

In November 1982, Helmuth and Hanna were involved in a serious car accident after he drove through a red light that he insisted was green. While Helmuth explained the incident away by claiming that his mind "went blank," Hanna had a different theory: it was a beckoning hand from heaven, "God telling Helmuth to take me and him."

If Helmuth missed the divine communication that cost him $2,500 in body work to his car, it may have been because his mind was on more earthly matters. Helmuth had been flipping through the pages of the *London Free Press* one day when he came across a classified ad from the Taurus Escort Service that caught his attention. He was intrigued. His sex life at home was as unsatisfying as ever and his recent trip to the Bahamas with Corinne Willoughby and Lisa Finn had left his sexual expectations unfulfilled. It was time to find more willing partners who better understood the rules of the game. On December 14, 1982, he knocked on the door of a dumpy house on Edgerton Street in London ready to pay the twenty-five-dollar registration fee. Noting that Taurus billed itself as a discriminating service catering to single men only, Helmuth listed his marital status as "single/separated" and signed a declaration to certify that all statements on his application were true. Even though he was not asked for identification, he used his real name and Treugott's telephone number – a strangely reckless course for a wealthy businessman who had a lot to lose if his illicit sex life were ever exposed. (The girls themselves showed considerably more concern about Helmuth's anonymity, quaintly shielding him as "Hal" Buxbaum when they noted his appointments on their client cards.) Scrawled across the bottom of his application were the words, "Be discreat [*sic*]."

Helmuth thumbed through a photo album of the Taurus escorts looking for the girls with the largest breasts. As revealing as it was, the album didn't tell the full story. The girls represented a full inventory of social distress: high-school dropouts, welfare recipients, table dancers, drug addicts, and single mothers trying to make ends meet. The real commodity Taurus had for sale was desperation.

The day after Helmuth filled out his application, he received a call at Treugott confirming his membership in the escort service. There were no more high-minded excuses for his untrammelled pleaure-seeking. As one of the many doctors who would later interview Helmuth said, "He told me that he had developed a certain freedom in his thinking after his stroke and said to himself, 'Any day it could be all finished. Why don't you have a little fun!' "

Helmuth's first encounter was on December 15, 1982. Pacing around and apparently drunk, he made the young prostitute nervous. The next day, he tried another. During the course of the next few months, he engaged as many as fifty prostitutes, sampling them like candies from Taurus's well-stocked loot bag.

A pattern was quickly established. On weekdays, Helmuth left Treugott Management early, skipping lunch, in favour of an hour with a bottle of wine and a Taurus escort in a room at the Lamplighter Inn. The first encounters were less than memorable – awkward sessions of haggling over the price (usually $100), followed by speedy and impersonal sex.

"Most hookers I met for the first time just wanted to come to an agreement on the price and were then anxious to hop into bed and get out again for another customer," Helmuth recalled later. "Because I wanted to get service for the money, I told them that my wife did not enjoy sex (untrue), and that she hated oral sex (true); that [way] they would feel like they were good at their profession . . . It made them feel like they were better than my wife."

They were certainly less inhibited. Weeks after joining the escort service, Helmuth began to indulge in "doubles," hiring two girls for his long afternoons at the Lamplighter. Now that he was using full-time prostitutes, he was finally able to get what Corinne Willoughby and others had refused him. It was to become the central feature of his hypersexual double life. "He would ask us to do a lesbian act while he watched or participated. Helmuth liked young girls as well because he would ask me if I knew any girls around the age of fifteen or sixteen years," Faith Fothergill, one Taurus escort, said later.

Helmuth had a soft spot for the chubby call girl with the perpetual smile. Faith had three children, each with a different father. Fothergill's last common-law husband, Gary, was in prison for manslaughter when Helmuth made her acquaintance. He began visiting the twenty-six-year-old outside the auspices of the agency in a rundown house on Salisbury Avenue, an arrangement that saved him Taurus's twenty-five-dollar fee. "She was likable," Helmuth recalled, "She didn't make you feel dirty and unwanted. She made you feel like she enjoyed having sex with you."

Generous with the girls he liked, Helmuth's interest in Fothergill extended beyond the bedroom. He often took her to expensive restaurants around London for candlelight dinners, either not knowing or not caring that the city was filled with curious eyes and wagging tongues. In addition to sex and congenial companionship, Fothergill also provided new contacts. Twenty-five-year-old Valerie Nesbitt met Helmuth at her friend's apartment and was soon helping to satisfy his penchant for voyeurism and troilism, first with Fothergill, and later with an array of others: "It was never singular [sic] meetings with him, it was always two girls and he'd watch, then participate," Nesbitt recalled. She gave Helmuth her address and he asked her to arrange to have a younger girl join them.

Nineteen-year-old Tanya Kosmal now formed part of the sexual threesome that met at Nesbitt's apartment several times over the following months. For Helmuth, the sex ranged from ecstatic to dismal, depending on the still intermittent effects of his stroke. "He usually had a hard time getting it up," Kosmal said later.

One afternoon they were drinking Helmuth's trademark Black Tower wine when Nesbitt added a new twist. After injecting some cocaine in the bathroom, she offered some to her guests. Helmuth partook, although he later claimed that he had snorted, not injected, the drug. "I think the coke made me feel sick," he said.

Helmuth was now beginning to feel more comfortable with his

afternoon companions, more in command. Prominently displaying his wedding band, he began talking more freely about his marital situation. The teenage prostitutes soon learned how unhappy he was at home. "He claimed his wife said it was okay to screw around because she couldn't satisfy him," Kosmal said later. Nesbitt remembered, "He would talk about his wife. She wouldn't give head."

Although the girls appreciated Helmuth's generosity, they were distinctly unimpressed with some of his proclivities. (In fact, some of them told Taurus's receptionist and bookkeeper, Kittie Thomson, that "they didn't want to see Helmuth anymore, that he gave them the creeps.") Like he had with several other escorts, Helmuth asked Nesbitt and Kosmal to recruit twelve- and thirteen-year-old girls into their sexual routine. "He . . . wanted me to bribe young girls at pinball parlours but I wouldn't do it and told him to fuck off," Tanya Kosmal said later.

For Helmuth the afternoon sessions provided a pleasant respite from the pressure and disapproval he was getting from Hanna, the senior management at Treugott, his doctors, and the congregation at West Park. He was London's undisputed king of the rented room and the rented woman, sovereign of a private realm where his wishes were other people's commands and the only judgement that mattered was his satisfaction. But as exhilarating as he found it, he had his moments of guilt: "Sometimes I felt dirty about seeing them. I got used to it. I felt bad for spending so much money on the girls. I could have given the money to a missionary or to the Church. I justified it by thinking the escorts had children of their own to support."

It was a rationalization that he didn't need with Nafisha Somani, a graceful escort he saw fifteen times. From the first time he met the tall, African beauty, he felt that she was several cuts above the others "who were the kind of girls who would steal towels out of motels." Perhaps it was her regular job at a dress shop or her cultured mien. He certainly appreciated her sympathy when he explained that his stroke had made it difficult for him to get an erection. Whatever it was, Helmuth was hooked.

For weeks, he would pick Somani up at a bus-stop near her home and take her to the Lamplighter Motel, occasionally alone, but most often in the company of a second escort. When they were by themselves, Helmuth talked a little about his home life. His unhappiness over the marriage was as obvious to Somani as the liquor on Helmuth's breath: "He didn't like his wife. She was old-fashioned and didn't like sex. She was fat," she remembered being told. "He liked to try new things but she wouldn't go along."

In that respect, at least, the classy prostitute and Hanna had something in common. Somani wouldn't perform lesbian acts for Helmuth, balked at recruiting younger girls for his pleasure, and flatly refused to have his child, despite his offer of $15,000.

While he was still seeing Somani, Helmuth was smitten with another Taurus escort, Debbie Schaeffer. Their first meeting was as bizarre as their torrid six-month affair. When a European relative came for a visit without his wife, Helmuth offered to set him up with a girl. He neglected to tell the man that his partner would be coming from an escort service. As things turned out, the guest got Schaeffer and Helmuth was left with a woman who didn't appeal to him. Helmuth engineered a swap, and quickly fell under the spell of Schaeffer's beauty and youth.

After his first meeting with the twenty-year-old part-time dental assistant, he tried to convince her to leave the escort service and become his full-time mistress. If she would have his baby, Helmuth promised to set her up in a house in California and pay her $20,000. When later asked how he would have explained the child to his wife, Helmuth replied, "Hanna always wanted another daughter. Hanna was a very caring person. She loved babies."

Helmuth did his very best to win the exclusive attentions of the prize escort who was so "good in bed." In addition to the $1,600 a month he paid her for her favours, he gave her $800 for a white rabbit–fur coat. He also chauffeured her to her weekly allergy shots. Then came two international trips. During a European banking junket to buy gold and silver in September 1983, Helmuth took Schaeffer to Switzerland "to impress her." Despite the expensive meals and the designer clothes he bought her, Schaeffer didn't live up to Helmuth's sexual expectations. "Debbie wasn't as interested in sex while she was in Europe," he said later. "She was more interested in sightseeing. I was a bit upset with her because I brought her along to have sex with me."

Undaunted, Helmuth invited Schaeffer to accompany him to Puerto Vallarta, Mexico, just before Christmas 1983 with the clear understanding that "she wouldn't fool around with younger guys at Club Med." Two weeks before they were to depart, he told Schaeffer that two other girls would be coming along. Having already turned Helmuth down on his request for lesbian sex, Schaeffer was understandably wary. But Helmuth was convinced that his special preparations had guaranteed him a good time. "We were going to meet Corinne [Willoughby] and Joanne [Bottaro] in Toronto and then all fly to Club Med. I thought that, with three girls, I would get laid every day."

It was not to be. At the last minute, his other two travelling companions cancelled and Helmuth boarded the plane with Schaeffer, who was already regretting her decision to accompany him to Mexico. Things worsened after their arrival. Schaeffer felt smothered by Helmuth's possessiveness, didn't like the way he downed his wine in uncouth gulps, and was furious that he had smuggled two grams of cocaine into Mexico without telling her. Most of all, she "couldn't handle" Helmuth's incessant demands for sex. During the week they spent at Club Med's Playa Blanca resort, she slept with him only twice. One night after she failed to return to their room, Helmuth threw out all her belongings. Schaeffer grew colder, busying herself with diving lessons and the new companions she met on the beach and at the disco. Helmuth consoled himself with horseback riding and cocaine, privately fuming at the behaviour of his inconstant companion. "I got more and more pissed off with her. She was really stepping on my pride . . . I felt insecure about younger Club Med types. I was really disappointed when she turned around and saw younger guys at Club Med."

When the unhappy duo got back to London, Helmuth refused to pay Schaeffer for the miserable week they had spent in Mexico. She, in turn, informed Helmuth that their relationship was over. In his insatiable quest for more young women, Helmuth asked if she had any girlfriends who might be interested in taking her place. Schaeffer refused to answer, leaving Helmuth to face the fact that he would now have to look elsewhere for his pleasures.

The best and worst of hunting grounds lay just ahead: Kelly's Bar.

5

FEASTING WITH PANTHERS

"It had been a very exciting experience – doing something
illegal and immoral . . . Cocaine made me feel young
and strong again."
– Helmuth Buxbaum to his lawyers, August 1984

In the beginning, Helmuth Buxbaum was regarded with suspicion by the regulars at Kelly's Bar. In the late fall of 1983, he began showing up at Kelly's – and a string of other seedy watering holes around London – to satisfy his growing fondness for beer and to watch the strippers go through their languid routines for the handful of afternoon drinkers who peered at them through clouds of smoke. Eighteen months earlier, Helmuth wouldn't have been caught dead amongst the collection of losers, boozers, prostitutes, and petty hoodlums who called places like Kelly's if not their home, then certainly their office. But his stroke had worked fateful changes. As Helmuth later put it, "That little thing inside you that makes you feel guilty was gone."

One of the dancers he met on his bar crawls, a girl who performed under the stage name Carmen, particularly interested him, and not only because her act featured the novel manipulation of beer bottles between her large breasts. Her real name was Maria Caully, and she was the step-daughter of Helmuth's sister Lydia. No one in the family had known that she was a stripper until the November afternoon in 1983 when Helmuth walked into the Fairside Tavern and caught her act.

Caully was relieved that her uncle didn't seem to disapprove of what she was doing; in fact, he bought her a drink. The former leader of the Baptist Youth Group had come a long way since his pious days in Elliot Lake, when coarse language and dancing had been enough to raise his

Christian ire. But Helmuth wasn't spending much time in church these days. He gave Carmen $100 and told her to call him if she came across any young dancers who would be willing to have sex with him.

Early in 1984, Caully had a chance to return her uncle's kindness when they met again at Kelly's Bar. After paying his stepniece and another stripper for a "table dance," Helmuth asked her if she knew where he could get some cocaine. Like a lot of other affluent North Americans, Helmuth was beginning to dabble in the wonder drug of the 1980s, the rich man's fix that didn't ravish the body like heroin and enjoyed a status in the popular press closer to a health food than a dangerous substance.

Caully knew that Collette Vandenberg, a denizen of Kelly's, was a cocaine addict with excellent drug connections. But when she approached the woman on Helmuth's behalf, Vandenberg was suspicious. The bar stools at Kelly's didn't feature many middle-aged customers in three-piece suits. "I asked her who for," Vandenberg said later, "and she pointed to a man dressed in a suit and said for her uncle. I thought at first he was a narc, but she assured me that he wasn't."

Vandenberg was selling for Robert Barrett, the young man who cleaned the bar after last call and lugged beer from the delivery trucks that pulled up every few days in front of the King Street dive. For Barrett, who in turn worked for drug dealer Cecil Meaney, selling cocaine was a way of keeping himself in drugs, not money. In support of his own cocaine habit, Barrett committed more than a thousand crimes in 1983 alone, most of them illicit drug deals consummated in Kelly's Bar. Initially as wary as Vandenberg, Barrett took Helmuth's $250, handed over two grams of cocaine, and waited. No badge, no bust.

After two or three more brokered deals, the man known on the streets of London as "Squirrel" decided that his strange customer wasn't a policeman. His curiosity was piqued. Judging from the amount of cash the man was spending on drugs – $750 for a quarter-ounce of cocaine every few days – this was a customer who warranted his personal attention. Greedy for the commissions he had been paying Vandenberg to act as his go-between, Barrett broke one of the cardinal rules of the drug culture. "I asked her to introduce me to Buxbaum," Barrett later admitted. "Normally, I wouldn't've asked Collette to introduce me to someone [to] whom she sold drugs. This was the first time that it happened. I saw a dollar sign. I'll do pretty much anything for a dollar."

Born in Welland, Ontario, on New Year's Eve 1959, Barrett, his sister, and two brothers were raised by alcoholic parents. The neglected child began smoking marijuana before he reached puberty. Two years later, he was regularly dropping acid and had become a ward in the care of the Children's Aid Society. By age fifteen, Barrett was hooked on bennies (benzedrine) and had started trafficking to support his habit. Five trips to juvenile court landed him short sentences in the Adelaide Street Group Home and London's juvenile detention centre before he was finally assigned to a court-appointed foster home. At age sixteen, he accidentally overdosed on Tuinal and Valium, the first of five near-fatal drug accidents: "I woke up three days later at University Hospital," he later chuckled.

The grade nine dropout worked briefly at assorted foundries in southern Ontario, and later in Alberta, where he was married in 1980. But the pay was low and the pink slips kept coming. The only other places that would hire him, bars like the Peek 'n' Slide in Grand Bend and Kelly's in London, paid starvation wages – especially for a person with a $700-a-day addiction to cocaine. Even his wife, Kelly Barrett, eventually couldn't take Squirrel's drug abuse, and left her husband and London for a new start in Sarnia, Ontario. Barrett could understand her frustrations: "There were occasions when I would be injecting cocaine up to thirty times a day for five or six days straight," he said.

To pay for his habit, Barrett became an accomplished break-and-enter artist. He approached his work with studious discrimination, regularly visiting the public library to select his victims. There, he and an accomplice would study their favourite book, the *London City Directory*, which listed the occupation of every city resident of a private dwelling. After picking their well-heeled victims, usually doctors, lawyers, or businessmen, they went in for the kill. Barrett broke into thirty or forty houses in 1983 without getting caught. "I made a lot of money from break and enters, like seventy or eighty-thousand dollars," he claimed. Cheating on drug deals, fencing stolen goods, and even, as it turned out, pimping – whatever it took to keep the syringes filled, Robert Barrett was ready to do. His credo was simple: *Money talks.*

Barrett told his wealthy new client that he could keep him well supplied with cocaine. They discussed price, but Helmuth seemed more concerned about the quality of Barrett's product. The experienced dealer had a practical way to settle that concern. Promising that cocaine would also help Helmuth with his weight problem, he led him upstairs to the strippers' quarters and waved him into the washroom. Two girls who were getting undressed ignored Barrett as he took out a syringe.

"I thought we were going to snort the cocaine," Helmuth later wrote. "Then Barrett pulled out a needle. I was surprised . . . I just got caught up in things. I rolled up my sleeve. Barrett stuck the needle in my arm."

Helmuth had dabbled in cocaine before, and may even have experimented with mainlining, but he was unprepared when Barrett injected him with a much stronger dose of the drug than he had ever had before. Fifteen seconds after the needle was pulled from his arm, he showed signs of a first-time user's reaction to cocaine: he couldn't breathe, his stomach cramped, and the top of his head felt like it was going to explode. Barrett led him to a cot, and one of the strippers pressed a cold cloth to his forehead. Half an hour later, after being chewed out by the manager for being in the dancers' dressing-room, Barrett led Helmuth back downstairs. It would take a few more sessions with the needle before the drug's hallmark euphoria would have Helmuth hooked.

Barrett kept the rest of the cocaine Helmuth purchased that day, promising to hold it for him until he was feeling better. Helmuth walked outside, woozy but feeling invigorated. It was as if the sun had risen within him, suffusing his body with a brilliant light that chased away his every care. There was no Hanna, no Nick Potocska, no Pastor Fawcett, no bank manager, no doubts about his virility, no guilt. As Helmuth later put it, "No problems. No anxieties. No worries."

The exhilaration of cocaine masked the fact that this single afternoon in Kelly's marked a radical escalation in the disintegration of his personality that medical experts would later say had begun twenty months before. The stroke victim who had risen from his sickbed with impaired social judgment and an unrestrained craving for sex was now hooked on a drug that further broke down his already flimsy inhibitions and conferred soothing delusions of power, happiness, and swaggering competence. For a man fretting over his sexual potency as much as Helmuth was, cocaine the aphrodisiac seemed like the answer to his dreams. It certainly beat Dr. Nancekievill's bottles of vitamin B. "It was a very exciting experience," Helmuth said, "doing something illegal and immoral . . . Cocaine made me feel young and strong again."

Initially frightened by the power of the dose Barrett gave him, Helmuth vowed never to "shoot up" again. His resolve proved as fleeting as his sickbed vow to curb his adulterous ways. A few days later, he was back at Kelly's looking for the cocaine Barrett had promised to keep for him. Preferring not to shoot up in the strippers' washroom, Helmuth crossed King Street and rented a suite of rooms at the Park Lane Hotel.

A few hours later, a gale-force drug party was blowing through Helmuth's suite with Robert Barrett preparing the cocaine for the strangers who showed up to partake of Helmuth's generosity. Barrett was still carefully studying his new customer and had already made some interesting observations. "Buxbaum never appeared to think in terms of consequences," Barrett later said. "He did not seem to realize that he stuck out in social settings. In many ways, he was like a child."

And then there were the inexplicable mood swings that Barrett observed: "Buxbaum was a person whose personality seemed to change with the snap of a finger. For example, there were occasions when after a night of being with prostitutes and shooting cocaine, he would drive me back towards the nursing home, and as we would pull into the nursing home, he would undergo almost an eerie change. It was as though he became an instant family man who would begin pushing the church at me and also the fact that I should quit cocaine. He really became a man I did not know and would act as though he wanted to be my saviour."

The prominent businessman didn't appear to be worried that he had been seen in the company of London's criminal element, or that his name was on the hotel register beside a room that had been used for a raucous drug party that could easily have come to the attention of the police. (In fact, Barrett would soon be arrested for possession of cocaine on his way out of the Park Lane.) Whether he no longer had the social skills to appreciate the danger to his business and reputation, or merely that his undetected womanizing in motels around London had made him bold, Helmuth blithely entered a new and dangerous phase of his moral disintegration. The day after the Park Lane party, he retreated to his fallout shelter at Komoka and mainlined a gram of cocaine by himself. The experience tightened the drug's grip on the thrill-seeking neophyte. "It was very exciting to do it myself," he said later. "The thrill of the needle was half the enjoyment of coke. I came to look forward to putting the needle in my body even though it hurt."

Realizing that the track marks on his arms could be a problem, Helmuth came up with a plan to hide them. Knowing that he had to have regular blood tests in the wake of his stroke, he went to Dr. Nancekievill's office for more tests. The doctor took blood from the arm that Helmuth had successfully injected and covered the needle mark with a bandage. Helmuth then put a second bandage over the arm that Vandenberg had bruised at the Park Lane. The ruse worked. When Hanna asked about the bandages, Helmuth casually explained that he had just been to the doctor's for some blood tests.

His secret was safe – for now.

For as long as he could remember, Helmuth Buxbaum had been fighting a losing battle with loneliness. A few months after he was born in 1939, he had been deprived of a male role model, the war having swept up his father and older brothers for the first five years of his life. The infant refugee who was weaned on fear had grown into a fretful child who was often picked on by his heartier companions. Virtually friendless throughout his school career in Krems, and a work-obsessed loner during his early years in Canada, he had developed an unhealthy approach to relationships. "Time after time, I made attempts at getting friends by buying them. I did not succeed."

Nowhere was that more obvious than in the friends he cultivated at Kelly's Bar. A week after his first meeting with Barrett, Helmuth threw another drug party at the Park Lane Hotel which was attended by the same collection of strippers, addicts, petty thieves, and pushers as its predecessor. One of them, Pat Allen, was a handy man to have around. An amphetamine dealer who went under the nickname Speedo, Allen was famous for giving the best needle in London.

The supply of cocaine ran out early. Helmuth and Collette Vandenberg set out with Andy Anderson, a well-known London drug dealer, to replenish their supply. With Helmuth behind the wheel of his own car, they pulled onto Clarence Street and stopped at a red light. There was a police car parked on the corner and Helmuth recklessly swerved around it when he made his right turn onto York Street. The lights of the cruiser flashed on and the threesome was pulled over. "The officer asked for my driver's licence. He looked into the car. Anderson just smiled at the cop. The cop seemed to know who Anderson was. The cop warned me that I shouldn't turn right on a red light when other cars are parked at the corner. The officer let me go."

The prominent Baptist and multimillionaire had not only feasted with the panthers of London's underworld, he had now been identified in their company by the police. When he returned to the hotel without drugs, Helmuth's new friends quickly disappeared, including Robert Barrett, who quietly slipped back to Kelly's Bar. Before leaving, someone helped themselves to Helmuth's wallet.

Undeterred, Helmuth kept trying to buy friends and good times. He and Barrett presided over drug-orgies at the Park Lane and other London hotels five times during the month of January and the first weeks of February 1984. Helmuth didn't seem to appreciate his complicity in criminal acts and the risk he was running in exposing himself to blackmail. He seemed equally unconcerned that the denizens of Kelly's were tearing into him like sharks at every opportunity. As Collette Vandenberg later said, "About every second day, Helmuth would come in to Kelly's and everyone would swarm around him to party and do cocaine . . . Helmuth showed everyone that he had lots of money, three to four thousand. Everyone started to rip him off . . . but he was so careless about it."

For a man who had more money than he knew what to do with, it was a small price to pay to be king of the court in Kelly's Bar.

Although Helmuth was thoroughly enjoying his new relationship with Robert Barrett, there was just one problem; he wasn't getting enough sex for the expensive hospitality he was lavishing on Barrett's rapacious friends. A deal was struck in which Barrett became a kind of one-stop shopping centre for his client's vices, providing Helmuth with drugs and women.

Given Barrett's sweetheart drug deal with Helmuth, he hardly needed the extra money. He regularly charged Helmuth $750 for a quarter ounce of cocaine (Helmuth was spending $2,000 a week on drugs soon after his initiation to mainlining), but delivered only half that amount, keeping the other half for himself. He even charged him for the needles he used, two dollars a syringe. Helmuth's wealth and naivety were all the rationale Barrett needed: "I never ripped off anyone or cut my dope with anything. I never overcharged anybody up until the time I met Buxbaum. Until then, I was very honest in my business."

Barrett fattened his purse obscenely for his pimping services. In addition to his $100 "finder's fee," Helmuth gave Barrett $50 expense money to travel around London scouting out new prospects. Every time Helmuth felt the urge, Squirrel scored $500 in cash and drugs. It was a connection well worth protecting. Barrett later said, "I told other people to stay away from him because he was my mark . . . I admit that this was like money from heaven for me. I was still out doing other things as well. I was tapering off those other things because I was making big money from Buxbaum. I didn't want the money from Buxbaum to stop. I had found a lottery ticket."

By supplying drugs and women to Helmuth, Barrett had an insider's view of what he took to be his prize customer's eccentricities. Sometimes Helmuth was easily amused and laughed in "exaggerated and inappropriate" ways. But he could also behave like a petulant child obsessed with instant gratification. Once he had decided on his pleasure, his perseverance bordered on the irrational.

"If the prostitute did not arrive [as scheduled], I would say to him that it looked as though she was not going to meet us and that perhaps we should look for someone else," Barrett said later. "Buxbaum's response was to the effect 'But I want *her*,' to which I would again remind him that there was no one there, and we would look for somebody else and he would reiterate over and over again, 'But I want her *now*' . . . His impatience . . . went to the extent that I wondered whether he had any reasoning ability. He would just keep reiterating his need."

In the early days of 1984, Robert Barrett accelerated Helmuth Buxbaum's reckless descent into crime. In addition to drugs, the young pusher sold him a fur coat he had stolen. He also offered Helmuth two diamond rings that he claimed were worth $200. (Collette Vandenberg had stolen the rings from her mother.) Helmuth agreed to pay half of the real value of the rings, but insisted they be properly appraised first. Once again, he was publicly involving himself in a criminal act with a known cocaine dealer – peculiar behaviour for a man who could have bought the entire stock of the shop in which he found himself haggling over a prostitutes's stolen baubles. Without telling anyone where they had come from, Helmuth made a gift of the rings to his daughters, Esther and Ruth.

A few days later, Helmuth was approached by one of Barrett's friends to buy some loose diamonds. The multimillionaire met with a man named Abercrombie in the parking lot of a local restaurant. He was offered six or seven diamonds for $2,500. Abercrombie explained that he needed the money to complete a cocaine deal with "a guy who would sell him coke cheap."

Again, Helmuth was willing to deal with a criminal, but only after he had the stones appraised; it was as if the businessman inside of him was alive and well, but the moral agent had gone south. The seller insisted he didn't have time to go to a jeweller but Helmuth stuck to his guns. A compromise was struck; Helmuth could take the stones for an appraisal and, in return, Abercrombie would get a $1,000 deposit. The two men agreed to meet later that day to complete the transaction if Helmuth was still interested. Ten minutes later, Mrs. Bucharev at Alexander's Jewellers gave Helmuth the bad news: the stones were worthless.

A week after committing his fraud, Abercrombie called Treugott and demanded the rest of his money. Shocked by the man's brazenness, Helmuth indignantly replied that he wanted the $1,000 back he had paid for the fake diamonds. Helmuth then set up a meeting to settle their dispute in, of all places, the parking lot at Treugott. Fearing "gunplay," Helmuth involved his office manager, Nick Potocska, as a "bodyshield," apparently not caring what his accountant might think of his shady dealings and his even shadier associates.

When Abercrombie arrived, he wanted Helmuth to get into his car, insisting that they had to go elsewhere to recover the money. Helmuth refused. Instead, the three men set out in Helmuth's car with Potocska behind the wheel. Abercrombie claimed that he hadn't known that the first batch of diamonds was fake, but said that he now had a real gem if Helmuth were still interested. Astonishingly, Helmuth agreed to go to a jeweller to have the large stone appraised in the company of a man who had cheated him only a week before.

This time Mrs. Bucharev confirmed that the diamond was genuine and worth about $3,000. After further haggling, Helmuth gave the man an additional $300 and kept the stone, later putting it in his safety deposit box, a glittering addition to his growing inventory of hard assets.

Already alarmed at what he had seen, Nick Potocska heard a snippet of conversation as they concluded their deal that left him deeply troubled. "During the diamond exchange, Helmuth questioned the seller about a man, wanting to know if he had returned from the United States. The seller replied by asking, why, did Helmuth want some coke? Helmuth seemed concerned about my overhearing that, and denied any interest in coke." The worried employee would soon find out otherwise.

Maria Caully did more for her broad-minded uncle than supply him with a cocaine connection. Acting on Helmuth's request that she help him find a "stable" mistress, she was instrumental in steering yet another beautiful young woman into a bed already being kept busy by Robert Barrett.

Twenty-six-year-old Susan Ambrose and her common-law husband, Ron, were employed by George and Lucille Lachapelle as domestics, or at least they were until their car broke down during a winter storm just before Christmas 1983. Lachapelle, a retired doctor with a large estate, had the vehicle towed to a local garage and gave his cook and grounds-keeper three days off to get it fixed.

But the young couple's bank account was as bare as their cupboard. After failing to get a loan from their parents, Ron spent his time off in the apartment, praying that they would somehow find the necessary funds. Ambrose came up with a more practical solution. She promised her depressed companion that she would get the money they needed by waiting tables or, if necessary, dancing on them. The former foster child who had made her living as a waitress in a succession of Toronto restaurants knew how to survive when the chips were down. "I didn't get the waitress job, so I phoned the Abbey Hotel from the Yellow Pages. I phoned the gentleman and asked if I could come down and be looked over."

The attractive young woman with blonde hair and striking blue eyes passed the inspection with flying colours. On January 4, 1984, she was hired as a stripper for forty dollars a day. The club intended to get its money's worth. "Susie," as she called herself, was expected to perform fifteen sets a day, each set consisting of three songs. She also had to table dance for individual customers who were willing to pay five dollars for a closer look. The charge for the private dancing, as well as gratuities, went to her. With her pin-up figure, Ambrose knew she was bound to attract a lot of attention – and tips. As she shed her clothes that first day in the Abbey's tawdry bar, she hoped it wouldn't be long before she earned the money that would put Ron's Volvo back on the road.

Thanks to Helmuth's stepniece, Ambrose's first day on the job was her last. After watching "Susie" perform her first set, Caully called Helmuth at his office to tell him that she had found someone he might be interested in. Her uncle soon arrived at the Abbey Hotel and paid Ambrose and his stepniece ten dollars for a table dance. After conferring with Helmuth, Caully informed Ambrose that her rich uncle was willing to pay $100 to sleep with her. Ambrose agreed, but at double the price. If she were going to use her body to make money, she decided, a private motel room was a better place to conduct business than a seedy bar. The domestic who had arrived at the Abbey as a neophyte stripper left a few hours later as a novice prostitute.

Helmuth took Ambrose to the honeymoon suite of the Motorcourt Hotel, "a screwing place" that Caully had recommended. Forty-five minutes after she had left the bar, Ambrose was back at the Abbey to quit her job, believing, apparently, that Helmuth might be able to help her with more than her car problems. As she explained to Caully, she had "someone to look after her now."

A few days after their first date, Helmuth phoned Ambrose at the apartment she shared with her common-law husband to set up another meeting. Without telling Ron Ambrose what she was doing, she arranged to see Helmuth again, this time at the Golden Pheasant Motel on Highway 22. After the usual wine and sex, the couple engaged in small talk about their lives. Helmuth learned that "Susie" was something of a contradiction – a vegetarian who smoked cigarettes; Ambrose found out how much Buxbaum loved his children and how proud he was of his successful business. She also discovered how unhappy his wife was making him when Helmuth complained that he was trapped in "an arranged marriage" with an "old-fashioned" wife. When Ambrose suggested divorce, Helmuth said that Hanna would never agree, and that even if she did, he would "lose too much of the family estate."

The relationship blossomed. As he had with Debbie Schaeffer, Helmuth attempted to make Ambrose his mistress, offering to set her up in her own house (one of the seedy wartime houses he owned in London) and provide her with a mink coat. He even said he would "get rid" of her troublesome boyfriend so they could devote themselves to one another. But there was still the problem of Hanna.

After a few more motel room meetings, Helmuth suddenly advanced a stunning solution to his marital problems: "He said that he wanted out of his marriage to Mrs. Buxbaum. He proposed to get out of his marriage by murder. He said he wanted her out of his life," Ambrose said. "He didn't have any plans at that time, but he was thinking of plans and making plans."

A lot of people in Susan Ambrose's position would have left the motel room as quickly as they could gather their clothes. Instead, she became a jocular consultant. "I half-heartedly brought up the topic of poisonous herbs," the young prostitute later told police. Since the age of seventeen, Ambrose had made an informal study of herbs to teach herself the medicinal and nutritional value of plants. Although she would later claim that she hadn't been serious about her suggestion about poisoning Hanna, it was clear that Helmuth was: "I knew he took it seriously because he persisted in bringing up the subject at our subsequent meetings."

During a tryst at the Golden Pheasant Motel on January 23, 1983, Ambrose listened as Helmuth embroidered upon what she had "jokingly" suggested. He wanted her to buy poisonous herbs from a farmer and then slip them into Hanna's food. Helmuth later said that Ambrose then launched into a rundown on the various plants that could do the job. He specifically remembered her telling him about a mushroom called the Angel of Death. "She then said, 'But what a way to go. If you eat the mushroom, it causes cramps and paralysis.'"

To execute the plan, Helmuth wanted Ambrose to take a job as the Buxbaums' personal cook or a nursing assistant at the Komoka Nursing Home. In either capacity, she would have access to the house, and she or Helmuth could then administer the poison to Hanna's food. When Helmuth handed Ambrose a job application, she took it without quite believing that he had taken her deadly suggestion seriously.

She wasn't the only one. Joyce Black and Elizabeth Davis were working the 9 A.M. to 3 P.M. shift as chambermaids at the Golden Pheasant when they received a call from their boss. She wanted them to listen at the door of Room 137 "to see if there was more than one person in the room." The proprietor apparently suspected that although a lone man (Helmuth) had signed for the room, it was, in fact, being used by two people. The two women quietly pushed their cleaning carts to a position outside Room 137 where they began to listen. They were soon holding their breath.

"We could hear the conversation between a man and a woman quite clearly," Joyce Black later recalled. "The woman was doing most of the talking in a very clear, carrying voice. She said that she had checked out two or three drugs and she named them but the names didn't mean anything to me . . . Then she said that this certain drug would be the best, but she said you would have to give it to her in her food. Then she said 'But oh my god, what a way to go.' The man would just say yes or mumble as if he were agreeing with her . . . I told my sister [the manager] exactly what I had heard because it sounded to me as if they were planning to murder someone. Betty [Case] more or less laughed at us and told us that *that* man owned several nursing homes. She told us to get on with our work and don't repeat it to anyone."

The chambermaids had wanted Betty Case to call the police, but she refused. The next day, however, she related the incident to an OPP officer who had come to investigate a guest who had skipped out without paying his bill. Case told the constable that while her cleaners may have believed they had overheard a murder plot, the man involved owned nursing homes and was "probably renting rooms to interview staff." She also surmised that he had just been "discussing a patient's medication."

Case apparently didn't stop to wonder why Buxbaum would be discussing a patient's medication with a job applicant – particularly when the "medication" under discussion was poison. The police officer apparently took the incident as seriously as Case: "The officer told me that if I ever hear anyone by that name being murdered that I had better give him a call."

The circle of people who knew about the conversation in the Golden Pheasant soon widened to six. Ambrose looked up Maria Caully to get her impressions of her uncle's sinister intentions: "I . . . told Carmen that Helmuth repeatedly . . . stated he wants his wife killed. Carmen suggested I was lying. Then I made it a little more dramatic and she then suggested that Helmuth was crazy and that he was doing a lot of cocaine, losing a lot of money in cocaine, and that he was not being himself if indeed he was talking like this to me."

Not satisfied with Caully's reaction, Ambrose turned to an old friend for advice. Armando "Army" Gentile, who had known her for five years, and who worked the graveyard shift at a Toronto supermarket stocking shelves, listened patiently as Ambrose told her strange tale.

"I told him that a man whom I knew had been asking me to murder his wife and I didn't know what to do. I told him that I was getting more and more confused. It had never crossed my mind that I would actually do the poisoning."

Army wisely told Ambrose that she was playing with fire and advised her to end the relationship immediately. She agreed, but there was just one problem. "At this time however, the car was not repaired. I hung in with Buxbaum until the car was repaired."

Their last meeting took place on January 28. After placing a call to Treugott, Ambrose met Helmuth for breakfast at the Best Western Hotel. As she ate her eggs and pancakes and Helmuth sipped coffee, the conversation once again turned to murder.

"He asked me to go out and find some poisonous herbs again. This time he had brought the subject up at breakfast when we weren't drinking or in a party atmosphere. I was cold sober. Buxbaum was cold sober. I realized that Buxbaum was serious. He frightened me."

After Helmuth paid the bill, the couple drove to the Lamplighter Motel through a light fall of snow. Once there, Ambrose begged off having sex, using the excuse that she wanted to finish filling out her application for the job at Komoka that he had offered her. When he offered her cocaine, she readily accepted, sensing that he might not have the drug on his person. She was right. Five minutes after he left to get the drugs, she took a taxi home. It was time to tell Ron the truth, but not the whole truth.

Without mentioning prostitution, she said that she had been having an affair that had gone sour and that now both she and Ron were in danger from her former lover. Her half truth must have been convincing. By 4 P.M., the couple had packed up all their belongings and were headed down Highway 401 to Toronto in the Volvo Helmuth Buxbaum's money had put back on the road.

Although she and her wealthy lover had met for the last time, Ambrose never forgot their deadly conversations.

One of the first women Robert Barrett introduced to Helmuth was a pretty black prostitute who had an even bigger cocaine problem than they did. Dawn Watson had become an exotic dancer, petty criminal, and drug addict by the age of sixteen. A year later she was working the street. Then her talent for singing won her a two-year respite from life on the wild side. From 1981 until 1983, Watson toured clubs in Northern Ontario and Quebec with John White Productions, a talent agency that had plans for the street-wise young woman with the exciting voice.

But her music career was brought to a premature end by an uncontrollable appetite for cocaine. Towards the end of 1982, Watson disappeared into a vortex of drugs, using LSD, heroin, cocaine, marijuana, hashish, speed, mushrooms, biodine, uppers, and downers. "I think I've tried it all," she later said.

By the fall of 1983, she had added criminal convictions for theft and assault to her juvenile record for shoplifting. It was a path that by mid-1983 led her to the door of Taurus Escorts. Like Robert Barrett, whom she had known since childhood, Watson wasn't breaking the law to improve her bank balance; the money she earned in bed was quickly exchanged for the loving buzz of cocaine.

After their first meeting at the Park Lane, Helmuth and Watson had sex while Barrett mainlined coke in the bathroom. Helmuth was well pleased with the "raunchy" hooker who called him pet names and gave him her address and telephone number.

Days after their first encounter, Helmuth visited Watson in her Waverly Street apartment. Before they went to bed, Helmuth sipped German wine while Watson played the guitar and sang a few tunes she'd composed. After a few more meetings, a friendship sprung up. Helmuth sensed that Watson knew how oddly vulnerable he was amongst the drug set at Kelly's. She seemed genuinely affectionate towards him and, for reasons of her own, very protective. She also knew how to please the man who quickly became her only sexual customer and whose trust she wanted to gain to the exclusion of all others. Like Robert Barrett, she knew a good thing when she saw it.

Soon after the relationship began, Helmuth began requesting the usual favours. "On various occasions, Buxbaum asked if I could get some younger girls, under sixteen years," Watson said. "Buxbaum wanted to see me with younger girls. I arranged to have Terry Gallagher meet Buxbaum at my house."

Watson and Gallagher became "entangled in a lesbian affair," while Helmuth sat in a black chair, watching them: "Terry laid down on the floor. Dawn started making love to her . . . They turned the lights off. Only a candle was burning. I could hardly see what was going on. I began to masturbate. What else could I do? They already had each other."

In April 1984, Helmuth attended a nursing home convention in Toronto and decided to bring Watson along. She was already stoned before he picked her up at her apartment, and Helmuth soon joined her when the couple stopped along the way to inject cocaine and have sex in a service station washroom off Highway 401. But nothing could have fortified the twenty-year-old prostitute for the conversation she later claimed to have had with Helmuth as they sped towards Toronto. "During the ride, Buxbaum told me he wanted to get rid of his wife. He said he was going to pay someone to do it. He asked me if I knew anybody who could do it. I said, 'I don't know anybody, Helmuth.'"

Since their first meeting in February, Helmuth had made clear to Watson that all was not well at home. He had complained about Hanna smelling his clothes for cigarette smoke, sniffing his breath for alcohol, and checking up on his every move. But the young woman thought that hardly justified Helmuth's talk of having Hanna drowned, shot, or poisoned. Thunderstruck by what she'd been told, Dawn, like Susan Ambrose before her, asked Helmuth why he didn't just get a divorce. "He said he wouldn't divorce her because the children would hate him. She would still have custody of the children. She owns half the assets."

During the trip, Dawn introduced Helmuth to the ultimate high – free-basing crack cocaine. When Helmuth awakened at the hotel from his drug-induced sleep, he found a pantiless Dawn sitting on the couch between two black men she had picked up at a Spadina tavern. They were free-basing his cocaine. Unperturbed, Helmuth introduced himself to Dawn's companions, telling one of them that he "looked like Michael Jackson." He then returned to bed, leaving the others to do cocaine until the pearl grey of a new morning showed through the windows of their suite.

All the way back to London, Dawn was filled with remorse. She told Helmuth that she felt guilty for encouraging him in his cocaine habit and made him promise that he would give up the drug. Was it the cocaine, she wondered, that had prompted Helmuth's chilling question about murdering Hanna? As she would later put it, "Cocaine, when you do it, it makes you feel very euphoric and you talk about anything, everything under the sun." Helmuth agreed that there would be "no more needles" and, as a sign of good faith, handed over the free-base kit and the scales he had purchased in Toronto.

With Helmuth's promise that he would give up mainlining, Dawn was sure that his deadly musings would vanish like those puffs of smoke she had been riding for most of her life between heaven and hell.

6

THE OFFER

"The first time Buxbaum gave me any money for this
purpose would be in mid-May 1984 . . . I believe that part of
the reason that Buxbaum wanted his wife killed was because
she wanted him to go to the United States to get help for his
cocaine problem."
— *Robert Barrett to police, November 1984*

On February 1, 1984, Helmuth and Hanna Buxbaum stepped off a War-
dair flight in Tampa, Florida, ready to enjoy one of the few passions they
still shared together – the annual conference on economic survivalism led
by their financial guru, Howard Ruff. Seven days later, after absorbing
Ruff's advice on how to deal with the coming Deluge, the Buxbaums
were ready to mix a little business and pleasure with some old friends.
Acting on the advice of their auditor, Duncan Findlay, they headed for
Boca Raton to visit Eugene High, an insurance salesman for Christian
Mutual Life, "serving the Saviour and the Saved."

In reviewing the Buxbaums' portfolio, Findlay had noticed that the
couple had no insurance policy for estate-planning purposes, an oversight
that could cost their heirs as much as $2.5 million in capital gains if left
unaddressed. On January 17, 1984, Findlay advised the Buxbaums that the
only way to protect themselves from the huge tax bite was for both of
them to get appropriate amounts of life insurance, something the couple
hadn't done in ten years.

Helmuth and Hanna visited Eugene in his Boca Raton home, and
Helmuth told him that he wanted to take out $300,000 term life insur-
ance policies on both himself and Hanna. Satisfying himself that they
were born again in Jesus, a prerequisite of doing business with Christian
Mutual, High arranged for a retired doctor and a mobile x-ray unit to
conduct their physical examinations in their hotel room. Helmuth paid

High for Hanna's policy, but because of his medical history, decided to wait until his insurance application was approved before paying for his own. High called him back the same day with word that for just $2,500 more he could upgrade Hanna's coverage to $1,000,000.

When the administrative dust had settled, Helmuth decided against a policy for himself because he considered the $13,000 annual premium, based largely on his recent medical history, to be too high. But he did proceed with Hanna's upgraded coverage of $1,000,000 U.S., even though the corporate advantages Duncan Findlay had advised them of would only apply if both of the Buxbaums took out insurance policies and both died.

As it was, Hanna's sole beneficiary was Helmuth.

During their two weeks in Florida, Hanna was almost able to forget about the cloud that had been hanging over the Buxbaum household for nearly a year. But all that changed on the February morning soon after their return to Komoka when she happened to see her husband getting out of the shower after a night of shooting cocaine at the Park Lane Hotel.

"She saw a large bruise on my arm. I wasn't trying to hide it. Hanna asked me what had caused the bruise. I told her that I had been using needles . . . I told her that I was taking shots of cocaine because I was trying to lose weight."

Although Hanna didn't know much about cocaine, she felt a stab of panic on realizing that Helmuth was now engaging in illegal as well as immoral acts. It was no longer a private part of their marital relationship that was in jeopardy, but the entire life they had built together – the children, the business, and their position in the church and the community. The family that appeared to have it all was suddenly one arrest away from disaster.

But the dark cloud of Helmuth's drug use had a silver lining. During the frustrating months after her husband's stroke, Hanna had stoically put up with Helmuth's gross infidelities. Not certain about what lay behind them, there had been nothing for her to do but wait for Helmuth to come to his Christian senses and repent. But now that his altered behaviour could be traced to cocaine, Hanna had an enemy she could finally confront.

She declared a personal war on two fronts against the threat to the world she and her husband had worked so hard to build. A few days after she saw the track marks on Helmuth's arms, she found three-quarters of an ounce of cocaine in his trouser pockets. In the subsequent confrontation, she got her first detailed account of her husband's secret vice. He admitted that he was shooting cocaine in the privacy of the fallout shelter, but neglected to add that he was also regularly taking drugs in London with a variety of pushers and prostitutes. Hanna demanded the name of his supplier. Apparently not realizing that revealing one's drug supply usually meant seeing that source dry up, Helmuth identified Robert Barrett. Hanna then stood by sternly as Helmuth meekly followed her command to flush the drug – all $2,200 worth – down the toilet.

Despite Helmuth's promise, he did not stop using drugs. In April, Hanna was preparing Helmuth's trousers for the drycleaners when she found a hotel key and more cocaine inside a folded magazine page. Just as she made the discovery, Helmuth walked into the room. He snatched the cocaine back, sparking a terrible quarrel in front of Esther. "My dad was desperate and embarrassed about my mom finding the drugs," Esther Buxbaum said later. "He brought his suitcase to show my mother. He said, 'I'm going to leave. Maybe it would be better if we stayed away from each other for awhile.'"

Mark Buxbaum ran into the bedroom to find out what all the yelling was about only to find his father standing beside his packed bags. "I took him for a drive and calmed him down. My mom had found some white powder in a piece of folded-up paper and had showed it to him, and he said it was just flour. I couldn't figure out why it would be wrapped in paper. My dad told me during the drive that my mom was bugging him and yelling at him . . . that he couldn't take it."

Esther, meanwhile, had a good cry with her mother and tried to comfort her as best she could. The brokenhearted woman confided that she and Helmuth "hadn't had sex for a very long time . . . months and months and months." Hanna gradually pulled herself together and determined to cut off the source of Helmuth's drug supply. "She approached me and said . . . 'This is what has been going on around here and I am going to put a stop to it,'" Phillip Buxbaum said later.

When Helmuth and Mark returned, Hanna demanded to know who had sold him the cocaine. Not wanting to finger Barrett a second time, Helmuth lied and told her that it had been Phillip's karate teacher, Chris Browne. The Buxbaums had known Browne and his wife, Angela, since 1975 when they had joined West Park Baptist Church. Later, the Buxbaums had allowed the personable young Jamaican to hold his Saturday morning martial arts classes in their house. Hanna promptly marched Helmuth and Phillip to the family station wagon and drove to the apartment building in London where Browne lived.

It was a painful scene between the former friends. Hanna told the nonplussed young man that her husband's arms were "blue" from injecting drugs she believed he had purchased from Browne. After a stern warning that she would call the police if he sold Helmuth any more cocaine, Hanna swept out of his apartment, deaf to Browne's protestations of innocence. (In fact, Browne, along with Robert Barrett, Dawn Watson, and Rick Balfour was one of four people supplying Helmuth with cocaine by April 1984.) Back at Komoka, Browne's name joined Barrett's on a list of people forbidden to have any contact with her husband, a list Hanna gave to senior managers at Treugott with instructions not to put their calls through to Helmuth.

The second front of Hanna Buxbaum's private war was the medical rescue of the man she had once described as "the best husband in the world." Two days after she gave him a valentine's card festooned with hearts she made another appointment for them with Dr. Avinoam Chernick.

Hanna had high hopes for the session, but Helmuth didn't show up. Hanna explained to the doctor that she was worried about her husband's behaviour and that he, in turn, resented her constant "checking up on him." After talking with Dr. Chernick for several hours, Hanna left the doctor's office, furious that her husband hadn't kept his promise to be there. Later that night, she received a telephone call from Helmuth, a portion of which was overheard by Barbara Musto, an American friend from Illinois who stayed with the Buxbaums for five days in February 1984. "'Oh Helmuth, but you promised,'" Musto heard Hanna say. "She sounded exasperated."

The next morning, a chastened Helmuth appeared for a private appointment with Dr. Chernick. The man who was now using at least seven grams of cocaine a week (thirty-five injections), didn't put up much opposition. "I knew I needed help. I was hopeless on my own."

But once inside Dr. Chernick's office, Helmuth treated the session as if it were an extension of the marriage counselling he had discontinued in 1975, rather than a first step towards kicking his drug habit. In fact, he downplayed his cocaine use to such an extent, describing it, in effect, as a diet drug, that they never really discussed the issue of addiction. What

Helmuth did want to talk about was his unhappy marriage; nine years after the Buxbaums had first sought counselling from the Chernicks, their marriage was still in trouble and, Helmuth thought, for the same reason.

Helmuth had come to believe that he was the real victim of the Buxbaums' marital problems. Had he been free to pick his own wife, instead of acquiescing to a union virtually "arranged" by his mother, he would have chosen someone more compatible. But his lack of experience, and the desire to please his parents, had left him stranded in a frustrating mismatch.

Helmuth explained to the doctor that he and Hanna had drifted apart over the years because of their sexual incompatibility. And while he still had a "psychological craving for sex," he could no longer get or maintain an erection with Hanna who "didn't turn him on." Since Helmuth apparently had no trouble performing sexually with other women, Dr. Chernick concluded that he was suffering from a sexual dysfunction, *not* impotence. Helmuth said that it had been "easy and natural for him to drift off [to] the cocaine crowd," although he recognized that his friendship with the denizens of Kelly's Bar was based on "silliness and loneliness." He also told the doctor that he found himself indulging in things "he intellectually [didn't] think he should." Tired of his current situation, Helmuth told Chernick that "he would enjoy starting his life over again."

The twenty-minute session ended with Dr. Chernick reviewing Helmuth's options: "I saw that he had two – one, to continue with the status quo; two, to move towards change resulting [in] either getting closer or splitting with his wife."

Helmuth himself didn't hold out much hope for a reconciliation; he had grown since their wedding day, Hanna had not. "She got stuck at age four," he complained to Dr. Chernick. The abyss that had separated the Buxbaums since 1975 had become all but unbridgeable. Dr. Chernick offered to start individual therapy with Helmuth or to work out joint treatment with Hanna. But when Helmuth left the office that day, his mind was less concerned about his medical options than the fear that Dr. Chernick might tell the police about his cocaine use.

He needn't have worried. When Dr. Chernick discussed his patient's problems with Gary Nancekievill, the Buxbaums' family doctor, he didn't mention cocaine. In a letter outlining his thoughts on Helmuth and Hanna's troubled marriage, Dr. Chernick wrote: "I saw Mrs. Buxbaum in a very agitated state in mid-February. She was obviously very disturbed about her husband's behaviour . . . He expresses a sincere desire to rehabilitate himself, provided life with Hanna can be somewhat more exciting . . . I recall that Beryl and I had started some therapy with these people several years ago, but that after one or two sessions he dropped out and we got nowhere. Perhaps with a stronger commitment this time, we can help this couple."

For the second time, Helmuth Buxbaum never returned for counselling.

In late April 1984, Helmuth set out in his Ford Bronco to attend a real estate convention, Robert Allen's "Nothing Down" seminar, at the Hillcrest Banquet and Convention Centre in Detroit. His son Phillip had already gone ahead to Grand Rapids to drop off some friends at a musical festival and planned to meet his father that same night, Friday, April 27. Riding with Helmuth in the Bronco were Nick Potocska and Robert Barrett's older brother, John.

Since his release from Warkworth penitentiary, where he had served five years for the 1977 armed robbery of a submarine sandwich outlet, the elder Barrett had found only scattered employment. He was currently working as a caller in a London bingo hall. But after meeting Helmuth in early 1984 through his brother, John had worked for the wealthy businessman as a collector of bad debts and, eventually, a private investigator searching for Helmuth's illegitimate daughter from the 1969 affair with his Komoka kitchen helper. This time, though, John had merely asked to tag along on the trip to Detroit so he could visit relatives in Redford, Michigan.

The first night in Detroit, Helmuth and John planned to shoot cocaine but couldn't find any drugs. The following day their luck changed for the better. Helmuth left the convention shortly after lunch and accompanied John to the home of his American cousin. They made a contact and bought a quarter of an ounce of coke for $700 U.S. Passing himself off as a diabetic, Barrett then bought syringes at a nearby drugstore and the pair headed back to the hotel.

Helmuth began filling the syringes. He enjoyed "hitting" the prostitutes Robert Barrett brought to him and now he revelled in injecting his male companion, first in the arm and then in the ankle. At one point in the night, Phillip knocked on the door, but Helmuth, who was tied off and injecting cocaine, told him he would see him at breakfast. Meanwhile, Barrett had lost control of his body and felt like his head was "coming off." Helmuth prepared a new mixture to make him feel better.

"Bux puts a cold cloth on my head, says, 'It will be okay baby,'" John said later. "Helmuth undid my pants, put a damp cloth on my groin. Helmuth gets out Fiorinal [Helmuth's drug for migraine] and injects it into me to bring me down. Bux injected himself in his penis, and me in my arm, with coke. Then [he] injects me in my penis. Then Bux lies down next to me, says everything will be okay and that he liked me. I watched Bux masturbate."

The next night, Helmuth and John again failed to pick up any prostitutes and returned to their motel room to shoot cocaine. Helmuth began talking to his younger companion about his personal life. He praised Hanna as a good mother and a fine person, but said that he found her sexually unappealing, a poor alternative to the lithe young prostitutes he was seeing in record numbers. Barrett remembered Helmuth saying he liked his women "naive," a quality that explained his preference for girls between the ages of fifteen and eighteen. After his all-night debauchery, Helmuth rose early the next morning and attended church with some of Hanna's relatives.

On the drive home from Detroit, John lay down in the back of the Bronco while Helmuth and Nick discussed real estate deals and other business matters. Barrett would later recall overhearing Helmuth instruct Nick Potocska to look into the possibility of getting kidnap insurance on Hanna. That seemed strange, but what was about to happen as they stopped for lunch left John Barret speechless.

During their meal of Chinese food, Helmuth and John excused themselves and went to the washroom. Before leaving the table, Helmuth slipped a small container of plum sauce into his hand and carried it into the washroom.

"Helmuth injected himself with cocaine, then stood in front of the mirror and dipped his penis in the plum sauce. I went out and sat beside Helmuth's friend [Nick Potocska]. His friend had . . . ordered sweet-and-sour chicken and Helmuth handed him the plum sauce he had taken into the washroom and the man ate it with his chicken. Helmuth didn't eat the plum sauce and I didn't eat," John recalled.

On the way home, John asked for a job as an orderly in one of his patron's nursing homes and Helmuth told him to fill out an application. With each passing day, the netherworld of Kelly's Bar crept closer and closer to Komoka.

✦　✦　✦

It was a doctor, friend, and fellow-Christian who finally convinced Helmuth to seek treatment for his problems. Psychologist Ken Nichols had first met the Buxbaums in 1979 when they sought marriage counselling at the ALIVE (Always Living In View of Eternity) Counselling Centre in Fort Wayne, Indiana. To Nichols, the friction between the couple seemed to be restricted to Helmuth's concern about "the frequency and responsiveness of his sexual contact with Hanna." Although Helmuth wanted a Christian therapist who would respect his privacy, the psychologist at first advised them to find a local counsellor in London to help them with a problem that "did not appear to be anything extraordinary."

The professional relationship soon gave way to friendship. Helmuth would occasionally call Dr. Nichols, expressing his "frustration" with what he called Hanna's "sexual conservatism." On one occasion, the Buxbaums visited Indiana and attended a basketball game with Nichols. Afterwards, they spoke privately about their continuing marital difficulties. Hanna was surprisingly open about her sexual relationship with Helmuth and seemed receptive to advice on how to improve their situation. Dr. Nichols, who was impressed with the Buxbaums and their family, concluded that she was not a prude at all, but merely naive. With a little mutual co-operation, he said with a wink, they could easily work out their problems.

After Nichols left the counselling centre in Indiana and moved to Richland, Washington, he continued to receive occasional phone calls from the Buxbaums. But in the spring of 1983, Hanna's calls took on an ominous tone. She had tried to improve her husband's sex life in the intervening four years, but nothing had worked. By May 1984, Hanna was complaining bitterly to Nichols about Helmuth's drinking, womanizing, and frequent and unexplained absences, which to Hanna, wildly violated her husband's long-held Christian principles. "With each call from Hanna," Dr. Nichols later wrote, "the report became more alarming."

At first, Hanna told the doctor that she thought Helmuth's 1982 stroke was behind his disturbing new life style. But as his mood swings became greater and his emotional instability increased, the world's leading expert on Helmuth Buxbaum didn't know what to do about her husband's escalating problems. Dr. Nichols now heard panic in the desperate woman's voice. "Helmuth's behaviour was far from normal in Hanna's estimation . . . I was alarmed . . . Hanna knew that her husband was in trouble."

Ashamed, perhaps, to admit it, or anxious to protect her husband's reputation with the doctor who was also their friend, Hanna didn't tell him about Helmuth's cocaine use. From her description of Helmuth's actions, Dr. Nichols suspected that he was suffering from a "cyclothymic condition," a personality disorder, as distinct from a mental illness. Still, the exaggerated mood swings between elation and depression that Hanna described were not to be taken lightly, since they could indicate the onset of a more serious mental disorder. In that case, Helmuth might require in-patient care. The only way of being sure was to have him undergo a full medical evaluation.

Nichols knew a place where the work could be done competently and with complete discretion. Located just south of Grand Rapids, Michigan, the Pine Rest Christian Hospital was a first-rate private institution that catered to people who could "no longer cope with life's problems." At the Mulder Therapy Centre, nestled in a quiet wooded corner of Pine Rest's campus, patients received care in a "distinctively Christian healing community." Hanna agreed that it would be better to seek treatment away from London, and insisted that Helmuth admit himself to Pine Rest. Reluctant to give up the drug he found so exhilarating, the patient waffled. When Hanna forced the issue, Helmuth tried to postpone his trip to Grand Rapids by insisting that he had to meet with their family physician, Dr. Nancekievill, to get some advice on how to obtain financial assistance from the Ontario Hospital Insurance Plan. "It was just to stall," Helmuth later admitted. "I really didn't want to go to Pine Rest . . . I still liked doing coke . . . I just didn't want to be addicted to it."

After finally getting her husband's approval, Hanna instructed Dr. Nichols to make arrangements for Helmuth's intake-assessment at Pine Rest on May 17, 1984.

Neither of the Buxbaums understood that Helmuth was on his way to a psychiatric institution.

At the same time as his family was fighting to save him from drugs, Helmuth put his pusher on the payroll. To Robert Barrett, the job at the Buxbaums' Komoka home wasn't so much a favour as a case of honour amongst drug addicts. On January 31, 1984, Barrett had been stopped by police on his way into one of Helmuth's parties at the Park Lane Hotel. As he bent down to get into the cruiser, his jacket had fallen open, revealing the syringe of cocaine he was carrying. The police searched him and found another half a gram of the drug. Barrett was arrested and subsequently fined $500. He immediately acquainted Helmuth with the etiquette of the street in such matters. "Barrett blamed me for the fine because he got busted carrying my coke," Helmuth said later. "I was responsible for it. I wasn't just going to give him money, I thought he should work for it."

Helmuth picked Barrett up at a London doughnut shop the day he was to begin work at Komoka. From then on, it would be the job of the Buxbaums' groundskeeper, Ken Surette, to act as the new employee's chauffeur. Helmuth told Surette to "keep an eye" on Barrett, explaining that if he didn't perform well, they would "let him go." As for Hanna, who knew about Barrett's past role in her husband's drug habit, Helmuth told her that he was trying to turn his life around. He painted the picture of a good kid who had gone wrong, a young husband who wanted to patch things up with his estranged wife and child. Insignificant as it was to the Buxbaums, the temporary eight-dollar-an-hour landscaping job at Komoka was a step in that direction. Helmuth invited his wife to meet Barrett when he came into the Buxbaum house with Ken Surette on their coffee break. Terrified of what Barrett represented, Hanna didn't bother to wait.

"Just after Barrett started, my mom and I went outside to meet him," Mark Buxbaum later recalled. "We introduced ourselves. I thought that he was a weasel . . . I could tell my mom didn't like him. I don't think she came out and said this, but I could tell that she was uneasy having him around the house."

Mark Buxbaum was right. Hanna took Ken Surette aside and told him to keep Barrett away from the Buxbaum children when he came into the kitchen for meals. From then on, whenever Barrett had lunch in the presence of family members, Surette made sure that he was surrounded by other employees.

Despite her wariness of their newest employee, Hanna couldn't resist her Christian desire to help return a lost sheep to God's fold. She asked Barrett and his wife to dinner, and then asked if they would like to attend church with the Buxbaums. Barrett never took Hanna up on either offer but spoke glowingly of her to his brother John. "Rob told me what a wonderful person Hanna Buxbaum was on many occasions," John Barrett later said. "He used to talk about the Buxbaum family and how the family got along."

Barrett's observations couldn't have been further from the facts. Long before Hanna discovered the needle marks on Helmuth's arms, volcanic pressures had been building in the wealthy family. For seventeen of their twenty-three years of marriage, Helmuth had been adulterous, exhibiting truly lecherous behaviour in the two years since his stroke. Paul Buxbaum had left the house at age sixteen as a result of his father's hypocrisy, and only Hanna's superhuman powers of forgiveness – and Phillip Buxbaum's vow that, if a break came, he would choose to live with his father – had headed off a divorce. But now that cocaine had been added to the unhappy mix, other family members were no longer willing to take it sitting down.

One evening, Helmuth came to the table wearing a short-sleeved shirt that exposed the fresh needle marks on his arm. After dinner, eighteen-year-old Mark Buxbaum followed his father to his bedroom and demanded an accounting. "Why are you ruining your life?" he asked. "You have so much to live for. You have five children and you have money galore." Helmuth buried his face in his pillow and refused to answer.

Paul, who returned to Komoka that spring after finishing college in Warsaw, Indiana, was also shocked at his father's casual attitude about his bizarre behaviour. "He wouldn't make efforts to hide his affairs with women or the booze and pornographic films he kept in the bomb shelter," Paul said. "He would not even wash the blood off his leg after shooting coke, and would sit down with us to watch TV, letting us see this."

Phillip was just as alarmed by his father's strange deterioration, and decided to make an appeal to local MP Jim Jepson, whose political campaigns Helmuth had generously supported, and whose daughter, Jane, Phillip was dating. Phillip resented the way that London's establishment men appeared to use his father without ever admitting him into their social circle. It seemed to the young man that Helmuth was good enough to contribute to their causes and run their finance committees, but not good enough to go on their fishing trips. Still, he could think of nowhere else to turn. In the privacy of Jepson's study, Phillip disclosed his father's vices and begged for help. "I told him, 'We are desperate. Our father is into coke and ladies and we need your help.' Jepson assured me he would take care of it. Our phone never rang."

By the spring of 1984, fifteen-year-old Esther Buxbaum had seen enough unhappiness in her family to make a direct appeal to her seemingly lost father. "He was in bed watching TV, she said later. "I asked to see his arm. He said no. I made him pull up his sleeve . . . I saw the marks on his arm. They looked like needle marks. I said, 'Dad, you're hurting yourself.' He agreed. He seemed to be out of it. His mind must have been shot. It was like the drugs were making him senile . . . I made him look me in the eyes. I told him that what he was doing wasn't the right thing for a Christian to do." Helmuth promised to give up cocaine and Esther was encouraged when the marks on his arms began to fade. Then she began noticing the needle's tell-tale work on his feet and stomach.

Helmuth's family beseeched him to do something about his drug addiction. Helmuth felt oppressed. "We had a number of family meetings in our bedroom," he later said. "The whole family stood in the bedroom. They all gave me shit about using cocaine. I told them I would stop . . . I told them I wouldn't do it anymore . . . I told these things to my family because I wanted to get them off my back."

The battle raging inside the Buxbaum family wasn't the only thing that Robert Barrett didn't understand. Unaware that the family knew so much about Helmuth's drug use, including the fact that it was Barrett who had hooked him on cocaine, he lounged around Komoka as if he were welcome there. In fact, he felt so secure in his new position that there were several days when he didn't even show up for work. But it was his drug habits, not his work habits, that finally brought Hanna to the boiling point.

Suspicious that Barrett was still supplying Helmuth with cocaine, Hanna asked him to stay behind one morning after his coffee break. As soon as Ken Surette had closed the door, she lit into Barrett with a vengeance. In a fury, she declared that Helmuth's drug days were finished. She explained that she knew all about his past drug dealings with Helmuth and warned Barrett to stay away from her husband or she would call the police. When Barrett emerged from the house ninety minutes later, he told Ken Surette that no one had *ever* talked to him that way in his entire life.

When Helmuth was told about the meeting, he transferred Barrett to the Grace Villa Home. "I didn't want to lose my friend and I also didn't want Hanna to be upset with me for not firing Barrett."

Behind his role as peacemaker, a cold fact remained: his mutually antagonistic worlds were now on a collision course and the day was fast approaching when Helmuth Buxbaum would have to choose between them.

On the morning of May 16, 1984, the Buxbaum children must have felt relieved as they watched their parents head down Komoka's driveway in the family station wagon, seated side by side. After months of delay, the day had nearly come for Helmuth to present himself at Pine Rest Christian Hospital to begin treatment for his drug abuse. The family's planned trip to Europe was a little over a month away, and everyone was hoping that Helmuth would be well enough to make the journey.

The Buxbaums drove to Grand Rapids, where they spent the night in a motel. Early the next morning, they arrived in front of the gates of the Christian treatment centre to a very unwelcome surprise. "When we got there, it said 'Psychiatric Hospital' on the entrance, and we were both shocked to see that because we did not think that it was a psychiatric hospital that we were being sent to," Helmuth recalled.

The startled couple nevertheless proceeded to their meeting with the institute's director of adult services. Dr. William Van Eerden held private interviews with each of the Buxbaums before speaking briefly with them as a couple. Hanna told him about Helmuth's broad mood swings – from periods of high energy when he turned to other women and alcohol, to a depressed state when he would show remorse, promise to give up his vices and become "somewhat hyper-religious." Just as she had with Dr. Ken Nichols, Hanna couldn't bring herself to tell Pine Rest's staff psychiatrist about her husband's cocaine abuse.

Helmuth gave Van Eerden a different story. Although he admitted to using cocaine (once again, he downplayed the amount) and having extra-marital affairs, he presented these activities as the symptoms of his unhappiness, not its cause. To Helmuth, the root problem was his unhappy relationship with Hanna. Just as he'd done with Dr. Chernick, Helmuth successfully turned what was supposed to have been the first step of his drug rehabilitation into yet another marriage counselling session in which he appeared to have all the answers except one – what to do about his unhappy situation.

"He identifies marriage problems in that his marriage was motivated by his parents' desire to have him marry this *particular* woman; that, although she is a very good mother, he feels unfulfilled particularly in their sexual relationship . . . Some forms of sexual expressions she feels are sinful and unchristian . . . He does not," Dr. Van Eerden later wrote.

After listening to Helmuth analyse his own situation, including his opinion that divorce would be too upsetting for the children, Dr. Van Eerden told his patient that he wanted to admit him to Pine Rest immediately. Although Van Eerden's preliminary feeling was that Helmuth was not psychotic, he suspected that he might be entering the early phase of a manic-depressive disorder. "Dr. Van Eerden wanted me to stay for treatment at Pine Rest for four to six weeks. He wanted Hanna there for the last three weeks. I didn't want to stay," Helmuth later said.

When Helmuth offered to check into the hospital for five days, Dr. Van Eerden pointed out that no useful treatment could be offered during such a short period. Helmuth stubbornly refused to check in for a longer stay, possibly because the admission application to Pine Rest made clear that the director of the hospital could hold him against his will if he saw fit. Hanna acquiesced in her husband's decision, taking small comfort in his promise to check into the institution for a month that September.

"Just after the initial visit to Pine Rest, Hanna called me," Ken Nichols later reported. "She was very concerned. The attending physician at Pine Rest had agreed that it would be very important for Helmuth to stay on for immediate treatment. He viewed Helmuth as an emergency case."

Back at Komoka, the children were devastated by Helmuth's refusal to begin treatment. Under unrelenting family pressure, the reluctant patient wavered and then appeared to change his mind. "Helmuth called back to Pine Rest and said that he needed immediate help. Helmuth then contacted me," Dr. Nichols said later. "I telephoned Pine Rest and they agreed to minimize the red tape involved in Helmuth's admission. An appointment was set for Helmuth. Helmuth did not make the appointment. He offered no explanation for having broken the appointment."

The next time Dr. Nichols spoke to his wealthy friend, Hanna Buxbaum would be dead.

Robert Barrett picked the wrong moment to try and contact the man who had been his meal ticket for almost five months. Several days after the kitchen confrontation with Hanna, he called the Buxbaum house after midnight looking for Helmuth. Hanna and Paul were beside themselves wondering where Helmuth could be and were just about to go out looking for him when Barrett called. Hanna was horrified at Barrett's brazenness in trying to reach Helmuth so late at night after she had expressly warned him to keep away from her husband. Weeping uncontrollably, she threatened that if he tried to call again, she would turn him over to the police. (Faced with Helmuth's renewed cocaine use after their return from Pine Rest, she and Paul had considered going to the authorities, even if it meant that Helmuth might have to spend a short time in jail.) Then, as John Barrett vividly recalled, it was Paul Buxbaum's turn to deliver the same warning.

"I remember Rob speaking to Hanna on the phone once at my apartment," John Barrett said. "It wasn't a friendly conversation. She had told Rob to stay away from Buxbaum, and she was crying (Rob told me afterwards). Then one of the sons got on the phone and told Rob to stay away from his father. Rob told him to fuck off."

The next morning, on May 23, without consulting Helmuth, who was once again away, Hanna and Paul decided to fire Barrett on their own. After collecting a pile of messages Barrett had left for Helmuth at Treugott, proof that the drug pusher had disregarded Hanna's warning, Paul was ready to act. He burst into the shed where Barrett was working at the Grace Villa Home and threw the messages in his face. He then slapped a final cheque for $192 in Barrett's hand. Staring straight into the eyes of their tormentor, Paul delivered an ultimatum on behalf of the family: if Barrett didn't get out of their lives, they would turn him in to the police.

"I was upset. He was in the tool shed. He had a piece of wood in his hand and I took it from him and flung it across to the other side of the shop. I told him that I knew he was the one who started my dad on drugs. That's what my mother told me. And that he should leave my dad alone and that if he saw my dad on the street coming towards him, he should turn around. If my dad called him, he should not talk to him."

A red-faced Robert Barrett left the property wearing a smile. But as Ken Surette observed, it was very difficult to know just when Barrett was angry because he was *always* smiling. But John Barrett soon got a clearer insight into his brother's true state of mind. "Rob told me that he had been fired by Buxbaum's son who had cornered him in some sort of shed one day. I remember Rob being pretty mad about it. He was wondering who this punk was who fired him . . . He was depressed about losing the job at the Buxbaums. To Rob, money was God."

When Hanna told Helmuth about the firing, he was angry at Paul for "overstepping his authority." Paul ignored his father's reaction, reasoning that if he could get Barrett out of their lives, he might be able to curb Helmuth's runaway drug habit. No one in the family knew that Helmuth had in fact visited Barrett at Grace Villa on at least two occasions before he was fired, and that the pair had gone into London looking for drugs. On one of those occasions, they ended up at the Lamplighter Motel injecting cocaine. Nor did the family understand the nature of the relationship between a user and his pusher, or Helmuth's odd personal feelings towards Barrett. "I felt bad that Barrett was fired without notice. He was my friend . . . I liked Barrett. I know it sounds absurd, but I liked him. He gave me the impression that he was like a shy teenager. He had the key to the things I wanted: women and coke."

On the evening of the day Barrett was fired, Helmuth paid his friend a visit at Kelly's Bar. Barrett was busy unloading cases of beer and told Helmuth he would see him after closing. Despite the heavy pressure he was under from his family to change his ways, Helmuth waited around until 1 A.M., accompanying Barrett to the Buxbaum van where they sipped beer and talked.

The next day, May 24, Helmuth did some banking. At 2:38 P.M., he withdrew $1,200 Canadian and $1,000 U.S. from the Oakridge branch of Canada Trust. At 5:08 P.M. he collected another $1,000 U.S. from his Canada Trust account in Byron. Moments later, another teller at the same bank handed him $3,000 Canadian in large bills. At 5:18 P.M., he completed his last transaction of the day, withdrawing $400 from a "Johnny Cash" machine.

His banking complete, he drove to the parking lot behind Kelly's Bar where Robert Barrett was waiting for him and handed Barrett $5,000. Helmuth would later say that Barrett was to have used the money to establish a reliable cocaine connection in the United States. Although Robert Barrett would admit to receiving the money, he remembered Helmuth giving him something else that day; a picture of Hanna Buxbaum reclining in her bed, and another of the family station wagon. The money was not for cocaine, but to arrange a contract killing. The hitman would need the pictures to identify his victim when the time came to take her life.

7

THE DANGEROUS GAME

"I told Buxbaum that I was going to go out of the country
when the murder happened. This is why I went to Florida. I
told him somebody was just going to come to his house and
knock on the door and take Hanna from the house . . . I led
Buxbaum to believe that I was going to get the murder done,
but I was really just going to take advantage of him."
— *Robert Barrett to authorities, December 1984*

For months before he accepted Helmuth Buxbaum's $ 5,000, Robert Bar-
rett had been playing a dangerous game; pretending to arrange a murder
he had no intention of bringing about. It had started in January at a
cocaine party at the Park Lane Motel. After mainlining all evening, Helmuth told Barrett that his wife was a "pain in the ass" and that he wished
"she wasn't around." From that moment on, Barrett had siphoned money
from his favourite mark for supposedly advancing their undeclared murder plot. With Helmuth, all roads led to the bank, and Barrett proudly
told his friend Debbie Barber that he was offered the murder contract in
January 1984 – the same month that two motel cleaners overheard Helmuth and Susan Ambrose talking about how to poison Hanna. After that
first conversation in the Park Lane, Barrett never missed an opportunity of
raising the subject of Hanna's murder with Helmuth – not to actually set it
up, but to obtain more money for his bottomless drug habit.

"Several times prior to receiving the $ 5,000 for my trip to Florida in
May 1984, I asked Buxbaum for money. I usually did this in the context of
saying I was making arrangements or needed money in relation to Hanna.
I do not recall Buxbaum ever raising this matter, but I can recall myself
raising it when I needed money for cocaine."

Without discussing any details about their fuzzy murder plot, Helmuth continued to provide Barrett with inconsequential amounts of cash
– a few hundred dollars here and there that was supposed to magically

resolve the frustrated husband's problem. Meanwhile, Barrett's preferred method of helping Helmuth cope with his unhappy marital situation continued to come in a needle, not a gun. As one of four dealers supplying the wealthy businessman with cocaine, Barrett alone was selling him between fourteen and thirty grams of the drug a week. But as Helmuth's cocaine habit deepened (he was now getting two injections per gram of cocaine as opposed to five when he began mainlining in January), his formerly oblique attempts to have Hanna removed became chillingly direct.

"Sometime in April, I had a brief conversation with Helmuth Buxbaum where he simply asked if I knew anyone who killed for money and his wife was mentioned," Barrett said. "As soon as Mr. Buxbaum made this comment, I saw an opening to obtain more money and more cocaine. I indicated to him that I would look, but I would need money."

Although he later denied that he was serious about arranging Hanna's death at this time, Barrett approached a few of the denizens of Kelly's Bar to see if they would be interested in the job. One of them, Andy Anderson, a London drug dealer, gave his closely guarded telephone number to Barrett scribbled on the back of someone else's business card, promising to look into it. But Barrett wasn't taken in by what he took to be the drug dealer's dark bravado: "I knew Anderson well enough to know that he was just playing the big shot. Anderson never agreed to do it."

With the exception of that half-hearted inquiry, everything about the fantasy murder remained shadowy and unresolved until Barrett was fired by Paul Buxbaum. Then, just a day later, a comprehensive deal was struck. For $25,000 plus expenses, a job in Helmuth's nursing home in Prince Edward Island, and a $10,000 bonus if the victim's body wasn't discovered for at least a year, Barrett agreed to set up a contract killing. His only condition was that he wanted to be in Florida when the murder took place. "Buxbaum was under the impression that I went to Florida because the killing was going to happen while I was away. When he gave me the $5,000 I told him I was going to be leaving the country and that part of the money was for a downpayment for the killing."

After leaving $1,500 of the murder money locked in the safe at Kelly's Bar, and buying three grams of cocaine, Barrett decided to head south to enjoy the Florida sunshine and Helmuth Buxbaum's money. All he needed was a little company for the road.

John Barrett was faintly uneasy when his younger brother showed up at his London apartment in late May with a healthy bankroll and an invitation to take a holiday. Although Robert claimed that the money was to buy two ounces of cocaine for Helmuth, John was suspicious. Thanks to his brother's none too discreet inquiries on his employer's behalf, the Hanna Buxbaum murder contract was already common knowledge in Kelly's Bar. In early April, John Barrett himself was confronted with the deadly proposition when he stopped in for a beer.

"Have you heard anything about Helmuth asking Rob to knock his wife off?" an acquaintance asked him.

"No, and I don't want to," John replied.

"Rob was probably just going to burn him for some money," the man laughed.

Three weeks later, just before Robert Barrett began his job at Komoka, John had confronted him about the rumour. "Rob admitted to me that it was true, Helmuth *had* asked him to find someone to kill his wife. I tried to talk Rob out of seeing Helmuth and . . . [to] seek some help for his cocaine use."

Now as Robert Barrett stood in front of his older brother, all smiles and alluring propositions, his boyish charms belied the deadly dealings he had been party to over the last twenty-four hours. Over his wife's objections, John decided to take a week off work and accompany his well-heeled brother on a brief and unscheduled vacation.

On May 25, 1984, two days after Robert was fired from his job at Komoka, the Barrett brothers boarded a train for Windsor, Ontario. From Windsor, they took a cab across the river to Detroit where they visited with relatives and hit the clubs. Robert got drunk at a break-dancing contest in Cagney's Bar. John grew more and more concerned at the rate he was spending Helmuth's money on everything but cocaine. Later that night, he asked his brother what the money was really for, even though deep down, he already knew. "Rob told me it was money that Helmuth Buxbaum gave him to have his wife murdered. But Rob said he had no intention of arranging the murder. He was just scamming Buxbaum."

After partying in Detroit, Robert Barrett bought two tickets on a south-bound Greyhound bus. Thirty-eight hours later, on May 28, they stepped out into the brilliant sunshine of Orlando, Florida, and made their way to a motel that had been recommended to them by their mother, Sadie Barrett. Robert paid for a safety deposit box into which he stuffed what remained of his bankroll, a little over $3,100. From the privacy of room 114 of the Gateway Inn, he called his estranged wife, Kelly, who had left him a year and a half earlier, and invited her to join him in Florida. He then called his mother and instructed her to pick up his stash from Kelly's Bar, explaining that Kelly would be by to collect it before joining him in Orlando in a few days time.

For the next week, Robert and John sipped beer by the pool, mellowed out with marijuana and cocaine, and visited Disneyworld, the Epcot Centre, Sea World, and Daytona Beach. Both brothers acquired tans water-skiing and racing around in rented hydrofoils. The only cloud over their vacation was when Robert badly cut his hands and feet scrambling up a palm tree, necessitating a trip to the hospital. The same day that Kelly Barrett arrived, Robert gave his brother $350 for airfare back to Canada and continued his idyllic vacation at Helmuth Buxbaum's expense. Helmuth had always said he wanted to get the Barretts back together again and now he finally had.

But Robert Barrett's ever-smiling face disguised a worry that gnawed a little more deeply at him every time he watched the sub-tropical sun go down, reminding him that another day had passed. The murder money was running out and he still had no plan.

The day after the Barretts arrived in Orlando, and just twelve days after he had given his word to enter Pine Rest Christian Hospital for drug treatment, Helmuth Buxbaum boarded a transatlantic flight with Dawn Watson to do some private banking in Zurich. But the businessman and his favourite prostitute were headed for the rocks. Helmuth was put off by Dawn's loud-mouthed obscenities, sour disposition, and lack of co-operation in bed; Dawn was humiliated by his child-like bluntness in seeking out the pleasures she had grown tired of providing. "It seemed to me that his entire trip was to see how much sex and how much drugs he could use," Dawn later said. "In Amsterdam, Helmuth was acting really stupid and strange by walking up to complete strangers and asking for drugs or a couple of lesbians."

The break came at Zurich Airport when Helmuth demanded that Dawn return 1,500 guilders that she had taken from his wallet while he was asleep. With curious onlookers taking in the shouting match, Dawn demanded that Helmuth buy her a return ticket to Toronto. He calmly refused, insisting that she give back the money. Dawn snatched up her suitcase and stormed away. As her high heels clicked across the terrazzo floor, she offered a parting shot: "You are going to be sorry for this."

Relieved to be rid of his shrewish companion, Helmuth completed his banking errands, making deposits of cash and traveller's cheques in Lloyd's Bank and the Ueberseebank on Zurich's Limmatquai, where he and Hanna had joint accounts. It was a far cry from his boyhood trip to Switzerland with his mother; the city she had once visited seeking donations for the Lutheran church had now become the secret vault for the overflow of Helmuth's growing fortune.

Helmuth passed one afternoon with his twenty-five-year-old nephew, Andrew Aerne, the middle son of his sister, Esther. Aerne had been a favourite of his uncle's ever since a 1981 visit to Florida, when he had impressed Helmuth with his ability to memorize Bible verses. Helmuth had lunch with the young man and his father, Paul Aerne, and they agreed to help their wealthy relative find a suitable house – preferably large with a self-contained apartment – in Switzerland.

After Andrew's father had gone, it became clearer to the young man why his rich uncle was interested in Swiss real estate. Helmuth began to complain that Hanna was "narrow-minded" and didn't "appreciate" sex, and that his son Paul was a "bigot" who, along with his mother, kept poking into Helmuth's affairs. Aerne concluded that Helmuth wanted to make major changes in his life after taking care of his wife and children financially.

"Helmuth told me he was taking money to Switzerland where he could go away. He said he just wanted to go away. He wanted to disappear forever . . . It was like his life with Hanna was like being in prison. Helmuth said that he couldn't live with Paul and Hanna looking into his life. He wanted his own life."

Helmuth invited his nephew on an all-expenses paid two-week holiday to Canada and told him that they could fly back to Europe together and look for women in Holland and Denmark. He repeated his request that Aerne keep his eye out for an appropriate Swiss residence for reasons the young man had already guessed. "Helmuth told me that he wanted the house for himself and a young wife. He still hadn't found the woman. He wanted me to help him find a nice woman in Europe. He [didn't] like the mentality of North American women."

Before they parted, Helmuth took Aerne to a travel agency and bought him an airline ticket to Buffalo, New York. While they were at a bar for a farewell drink, Helmuth took out a small, blue appointment book. Beside the date of Aerne's planned arrival in North America, he drew a picture of an eye from which four tears were falling. Beside the drawing he wrote the words, "*Mon ami.*" Long afterwards, Andrew Aerne explained the reference: "Helmuth said, 'You are my only friend.'"

Over the next two days, Helmuth played tourist, taking in some English movies and dining in fine restaurants. Before leaving for London, he called a few of his relatives, including his brother Fritz, who reminded him that Isbrandt was having financial difficulties with his taxi business in Langley, British Columbia. Helmuth promised to meet both brothers there in mid-June to see what could be done.

On his way home, Helmuth's luggage went astray in Buffalo. People's Express traced it to Newark and promised to send it out on the next flight. While he was waiting, he met Lucy Addis, a young woman whose luggage had also failed to arrive from Newark. They shared a drink and Addis told him that she had just come out from Ireland and was on her way to Canada. Helmuth offered her a ride across the border and she gratefully accepted. But there wasn't much time to socialize when they reached her brother's Toronto apartment. Helmuth gave Addis his business card and told her to call him if she had trouble finding a job.

Back in his car, Helmuth headed down Highway 401 towards London, thinking briefly about Dawn Watson and the pleasant young woman he had just met. But he had weightier matters to consider than a jilted prostitute's menacing goodbye or the possibilities in a pretty, new face. With the industrial wasteland of southern Ontario passing by in a blur, Helmuth stepped heavily on the accelerator and turned his thoughts to what might be waiting for him when he pulled in through Komoka's stone gates inscribed with the Scripture *God is love.*

Paul Buxbaum couldn't wait for his father to get back from Switzerland. Ever since he had taken Robert Allen's "Nothing Down" real estate seminar in Tampa, Florida – the same seminar Helmuth, Phillip Buxbaum, and Nick Potocska had taken in Detroit – he had been fascinated with the idea of making his fortune by buying and selling properties with what the course promised was little or no financial risk.

Helmuth himself was mildly interested in the concept of "nothing down" real estate, possibly because he and Hanna had followed a similar approach in accumulating properties when they were just beginning their climb to financial success. During March break in 1984, Helmuth and Paul had travelled to Florida to investigate potential property investments. Helmuth was also considering involving his nephew, Reinhold Buxbaum, who lived in Sebring, Florida. Although the young man was a teacher by profession, he had experience in hotel and apartment-building construction and Helmuth wanted his nephew to help the Buxbaums develop property. To Helmuth, the key was to find the appropriate vacant land at distress prices.

Paul Buxbaum had grander ideas. A few months after the March trip with his father, he had returned to Florida on his own to scout out real estate opportunities. Browsing through the *Tampa Tribune*, he came across the name of David Howard, a developer who specialized in taking over and finishing distressed projects. Paul set up a few breakfasts with Howard and became convinced that, with virtually no risk, there was money to be made in "flipping" fully leveraged properties. But in order to get involved, Paul would first have to win his father's approval – and more importantly, his financial support.

So when an exhausted Helmuth arrived at Komoka on June 3 to find a very much alive Hanna waiting for him, Paul asked him to take a trip to Florida. Over the next two days, he kept up the pressure, convinced that if his father acted decisively, there was a fortune to be made. Although Helmuth was reluctant to go, largely because he had promised to meet Fritz and Isbrandt in British Columbia to grapple with the problem of their troubled taxi business, he finally gave in to Paul's youthful enthusiasm.

The young man had no way of knowing that his father had another reason for agreeing to accompany him to Florida. One of the first things Helmuth had done when he had gotten back to London was to visit John Barrett to find out the exact whereabouts of Robert Barrett. "I said, 'Why, don't you know where he is?'" John recalled. "Helmuth said, 'Yes, Florida, isn't he?' I said, 'Yes, he is at the Gateway Inn in Orlando.'"

When Helmuth checked in at Treugott, he found a June 4 telephone message from Robert Barrett. He called the Gateway Inn and spoke to Barrett, who told Helmuth that "something had screwed up" and that he would need more money to stay in Florida a little longer, until the murder contract could be carried out. Helmuth said he was coming to Tampa in a day or two himself and would stop off in Orlando to see Barrett.

On June 6, Helmuth and Paul drove to Buffalo and took a People's Express shuttle to Newark, where they caught a flight to West Palm Beach, Florida. Helmuth quietly snorted some cocaine in the washroom at the Buffalo Airport, using up the remainder of his supply on the flight to Newark. When they reached West Palm Beach, he rented a Cadillac limousine and they started out for Orlando, two hundred miles to the north. Helmuth had already made reservations at the Gateway Inn where

Barrett was waiting for him, but fatigued by their journey, the travellers decided to stop at a motel part way to their destination.

The next morning, June 7, they continued to Orlando, where Helmuth insisted on stopping at the Gateway Inn, even though Paul was worried about missing their 11 A.M. business meeting in Tampa. "I told Paul that I would only be a minute. I had to give him some excuse to go to the Gateway, so I used the excuse that I wanted to cancel the reservation," Helmuth remembered. He was apparently unconcerned that Paul might wonder why his father would be cancelling a reservation they had already missed the previous night.

With Paul waiting in the Cadillac, Helmuth went to Barrett's room, where the two men held a ten-minute meeting. Kelly Barrett, who was there when Helmuth arrived, excused herself to get a coffee. Helmuth explained to Barrett that Paul was waiting in the car and that he didn't have much time. Barrett later recounted what took place: "While we were in the room, Buxbaum gave me $2,000. This was for me to stay longer because the murder was going to happen while I was in Florida."

When Helmuth hadn't returned after five minutes, his impatient son went into the Gateway Inn looking for him, unaware that his father was just finishing a meeting with the same drug dealer Paul had fired and driven off the Buxbaum property just two weeks before. When Helmuth suddenly appeared in the lobby, there wasn't time for Paul to find out where he'd been; anxious to make their appointment, he hustled his father back to their waiting limousine and headed off to Tampa.

If Paul Buxbaum had high hopes of getting Helmuth involved in a Florida real estate venture, they were soon dashed. The two men met David Howard and Reinhold Buxbaum in a Tampa restaurant and then inspected a few properties. Having already lost money in the motel business in Florida, Helmuth was wary, particularly when he found out that other Canadian investors were trying to get their money out of the project that had attracted Paul. Helmuth felt that Paul, for all his enthusiasm, was "just a kid" who didn't understand the responsibilities of doing business. Helmuth said he would need more information before making a decision on the deal. He gave his nephew, Reinhold, three post-dated cheques for $2,000 as a sign of good faith that they indeed wanted him to be available for a construction project should the right piece of property be found.

On June 8, the Buxbaums flew out of Tampa with Paul upset at his father's refusal to launch him on his real estate career, and Helmuth wondering if Robert Barrett would prove as good as his word. He had just twelve days to fulfil their contract before the Buxbaums jetted off on their long-planned vacation to Europe.

By the time father and son drove into the labyrinthine parking tower at Toronto's Pearson International Airport, they had only a few hours before their flight was scheduled to depart for Vancouver. Helmuth was not looking forward to dealing with the mess Isbrandt had made of the taxi business he jointly owned with Fritz Buxbaum. He had already given his brothers $60,000 and wasn't anxious to pour more money into their poorly managed enterprise. The family connection made it all the more difficult, particularly since Helmuth was so fond of Isbrandt's fourteen-year-old son, Roy. But he had already decided that family or no family, this time he would assess the situation as a business problem, not a fraternal obligation.

While they were waiting for their flight to Vancouver, Helmuth broke away from Paul, explaining that he needed "some space" after living at close quarters with him during their two days in Florida. In fact, he met with a prostitute he had called from Buffalo airport.

When their Air Canada flight landed in Vancouver, there was still a discernible chill between Helmuth and Paul. They were picked up by one of Isbrandt's taxis and taken to his apartment for a brief and awkward reunion. Since Fritz had not yet arrived from Austria, their business discussions were put on hold, and Helmuth and Paul decided to check out some foreclosure sales of real estate in Vancouver. On the spur of the moment, Helmuth decided to fly up the British Columbia coast to Bella Bella for a few days' fishing. On the first day, Paul hooked a seventy-five-pound halibut, a trophy their guide convinced Helmuth he should get mounted. The wilderness outing was a pleasant respite from the outside world and all that was unfolding there. "Paul and I were quite close during the fishing trip. We talked mostly about our future business plans. We talked about Paul coming into the nursing home business. We also talked about the potential Florida development."

But every day during their week-long visit to British Columbia, Helmuth called the Gateway Motel, believing by now that the plot to murder Hanna was well underway. Despite the money he had already given to Robert Barrett, and the young man's cocky assurances, delay seemed to follow on delay.

When they got back from Bella Bella, Helmuth finally had to deal with his brothers' business crisis. Fritz had by now arrived from Austria and was openly concerned that the $30,000 Helmuth had given him, and which he had invested in the taxi business with Isbrandt, might be lost. In no position to buy his brother out, Isbrandt wanted more venture capital to make a go of their troubled company. Helmuth had ostensibly been called in as a peacemaker, but it quickly became clear that Isbrandt merely wanted more money from his wealthy younger brother.

Instead, Helmuth told Fritz that Isbrandt was a "poor manager" whose cabdrivers made more money than he did. Confirming Fritz's fear that his money was at risk, he offered him some tough advice: either take over management of the company or pull out his investment. Helmuth also rebuffed Isbrandt's offer of non-voting shares in the troubled company in return for an infusion of cash. Other family members were furious that Helmuth, though prepared to shower the Church with generous gifts, had abandoned his own relatives. Fritz's daughter, Ilse Webb, later recalled her father's version of the encounter: "Isbrandt is supposed to have said that he could cut Helmuth's guts out."

Before leaving British Columbia on June 15, Helmuth made a small peace offering. He had always liked Isbrandt's son, Roy, and when he found out that the fourteen-year-old hadn't been able to find a summer job, he invited him to Komoka to work as a landscaper. The boy happily accepted and it was agreed that he would bring Paul's prize fish when he came east. Helmuth bought him a plane ticket to Toronto, and told his nephew that arrangements would be made to pick him up at Pearson International Airport at 4 P.M. on July 5.

As the Buxbaums winged their way back home, Hanna and the others were busily packing for their long-planned European vacation. Meanwhile, Robert Barrett had finally accepted the fact that he was caught in the trap of his own greed. He had gone through nearly $7,000 of Helmuth's money without lifting a finger to advance the murder contract he had been paid to arrange. Having gone from crumbs to the whole cake, he knew there could be no more make-believe murder plans. Something would *have* to be done and sooner rather than later.

Robert Barrett had no intention of replacing Hanna Buxbaum in Helmuth's deadly disfavour.

8

PLAYING FOR KEEPS

"I realized that I had taken quite a bit of money from
Buxbaum and figured that if he was willing to have his wife
killed, he wouldn't think bad about killing me . . . My being
afraid of Buxbaum was only part of the reason I hired John
and Brigitte to kill Hanna. The other part was that Buxbaum
answered the majority of the dreams I'd had, a nice house,
getting away from London, money and a good job."
— *Robert Barrett to authorities, December 1984*

When the desk clerk at the Gateway Inn registered the young couple
from Quebec, Canada, he had no way of appreciating the small joke that
Paul Ringuette played on him. Next to the alias Ringuette used, Gilles
Hébert Bouchard, he gave his address as 8000 Arthur Sante, Laval, Quebec. Unlike the false name, the address was real. It was not Ringuette's
home, however, but the French Canadian headquarters of the Hell's
Angels.

Ringuette and his companion, nineteen-year-old Brigitte McCurdy,
had been on the run since March 17, the day he walked out of Cowansville Institution on an eight-hour pass and never went back. Ringuette
had been serving a five-year sentence for armed robbery when he perma-
nently settled a jailhouse difference of opinion with a crowbar. He was
convicted of involuntary manslaughter and sentenced to twelve more
years. Given his violent history and close connections with the notorious
motorcycle gang, his recapture was given high priority by both correctional authorities and the police. But Ringuette got by with a little help
from his friends, including his beautiful blonde companion.

McCurdy was seventeen when she met Ringuette through her
brother-in-law, who was serving time in the same prison. By April 1983,
she had become his girlfriend. When he escaped a little less than a year
later, they hid out in a Laval apartment with the help of Laurent Vion, the
president of the Hell's Angels. After McCurdy overdosed on cocaine in

Montreal, Ringuette decided to take her on a recuperative holiday to Florida.

From the moment he spotted the forbidding tattoos on Paul Ringuette's arms, Robert Barrett had a feeling that his lackadaisical search for a hit man might be over. He and Kelly struck up a pool-side conversation with McCurdy and an introduction to Ringuette soon followed. With McCurdy translating his colloquial French, Ringuette told Barrett that he was "a good friend of the Hell's Angels" and that he was on the run from Canadian authorities. Barrett's interest sharpened when Ringuette said that he had escaped from prison while serving time for murder. Making sure that the other man saw his own tattoos, unspoken proof that they belonged to the same outcast tribe, Barrett invited Ringuette to his room to do lines of cocaine. They became instant friends.

Over the next few days, the two couples visited the local sights and regularly took meals together. Kelly Barrett took several pictures of the group, including one of Robert, McCurdy, and Ringuette at the Epcot Centre. When Barrett decided that the right degree of camaraderie had been achieved, he got down to business. With McCurdy translating, he made his deadly proposal. Ringuette listened in silence, his dark head bowed. In any language, Barrett's intentions were chillingly clear. "He wanted me to kill a woman, Hanna Buxbaum. She was in London, Ontario. He told me that her husband had paid him to find someone to kill the woman," Ringuette said later. "He drew a map of the house and gave me two Polaroid pictures, one of the woman and one of the house with the car in front . . . He told me to kill her, but said it would be better not to do it in the house. He said it was preferable to kidnap her, then take her on the road and arrange that her body would not be found. To prove that I had killed her, I was supposed to bring her ring and watch back to show the husband that they came from the wife."

Ringuette agreed and a rough plan was worked out. The escaped convict would pick up a gun in Laval and travel to London, Ontario, where he would kidnap and kill Hanna Buxbaum. Barrett wanted McCurdy to remain behind to make sure that her boyfriend carried out the contract, but she refused. Instead, the couple agreed to leave one of their suitcases with the Barretts to show good faith. Only one detail remained – the price.

Ringuette wanted $5,000 up front, a request that Barrett discussed with Helmuth shortly after his return from Vancouver. Though Helmuth later admitted that Barrett had asked for the money, he claimed that it was for cocaine, not murder. According to Ringuette and McCurdy, who were in the motel room when the telephone conversation had taken place, Barrett discussed the contract killing with Helmuth, and made it clear that he needed additional funds. When the haggling was over, Buxbaum had agreed to wire Barrett $1,500 the following morning.

The funds, as promised, arrived on the morning of June 16. The two couples took a cab to the closest Western Union office, and while the women waited in the cab, Barrett and Ringuette picked up the money. Barrett insisted on a photocopy of the money order with both his and Helmuth's names on it, even though the clerk handed him $1,500 in cash. He then snapped several pictures inside and outside Western Union, later claiming he had wanted irrefutable proof that he had been elsewhere when the murder took place. But since he already had his hotel receipts for that purpose, and the Western Union receipt would only show that he had been there on a day the murder couldn't possibly take place, the more likely explanation is that he was now toying with the lucrative possibilities of blackmail.

With yet another stack of Helmuth's money in his hands, Barrett worked out the final terms of the contract. Imputing his own high standards to Ringuette, he suspected a rip-off and offered only a small cash downpayment with a further $10,000 *after* Hanna was dead and another $60,000 once things had cooled down. Ringuette agreed, and Barrett counted out $500 U.S. The convicted murderer knew exactly what was expected of him. "Barrett told me to go the fastest way to London, make the woman disappear, then take a plane back from Detroit to Orlando."

That night, Ringuette and McCurdy flew to New York courtesy of Helmuth Buxbaum. They arrived with the Polaroid pictures of Hanna and the station wagon given to them by Barrett, and one less suitcase than they'd taken to Florida. When they reached Albany, they called the Gateway Inn and told Barrett that everything was going according to plan – just before they headed to Vancouver and what they hoped would be a new life. While still in Florida, they had decided not to follow through on the murder plot. Ringuette and McCurdy had simply scammed the scammer in order to get back to Canada.

Between June 16, when Ringuette and McCurdy left Orlando, and June 19, the day the Buxbaums left for Europe, there were nine telephone calls between Helmuth and Barrett, seven of them placed by Buxbaum. The last one was made from the quiet offices of the Komoka Nursing

Helmuth Buxbaum's parents, Otto and Luise, on their wedding day in Russia, July 1920.

Two-year-old Helmuth practising on a stringless violin. Later, his misery at learning the instrument at the knee of a martinet made him think of suicide.

The Buxbaum family *circa* 1941, with Helmuth on his mother's knee. L.-r., back: Isbrandt, Gottlieb, Otto Jr., Friedrich, Maria, Elizabeth; front: Luise and Helmuth, Lydia, Esther, Otto, Hildegunde.

Otto Buxbaum, home from the Russian Front, holding his youngest child, Helmuth.

Helmuth between sisters Hildegunde and Lydia just before the family fled Labiau, East Prussia, during the Second World War.

Unhappy in his rocking chair, Helmuth cries for his teddy bear. In Labiau, *circa* 1940.

The Buxbaum family reunited after the war, *circa* 1946.

Hanna Schmidt with her mother, Ottilie, and brother, Henry, just before leaving West Germany for Canada in 1949.

Hanna as a young teenager shortly after her arrival in Canada, *circa* 1950.

Helmuth as a teenager in Melk, Austria, *circa* 1957, shortly before his emigration to Canada.

Hanna in the Schmidt family garden in Kitchener at the time she met Helmuth.

Helmuth and Hanna
leaving the Mennonite
Brethren Church in
Kitchener after their
surprisingly elaborate
wedding in 1961.

The newlyweds on
the eve of their
honeymoon.

Hanna in her wedding dress, June 1961.

Hanna with the Buxbaums' first child, Paul, Christmas 1963, in London, Ontario.

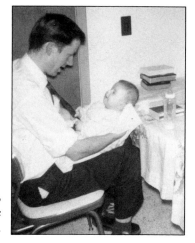

University student, sole breadwinner, and new father: Helmuth takes time out to play with Paul.

The good life: Helmuth, Hanna, and Paul vacationing in Florida, *circa* 1970.

The growing family: Helmuth and Hanna with their four children, Paul, Mark, Phillip, and Esther seated on her now bearded father's knee, *circa* 1970.

The complete family: Esther, Mark, Hanna, Helmuth, Phillip, Paul, Ruth, and Danny at Komoka, *circa* 1978.

Home shortly after midnight on June 19, long after the rest of the family had gone to bed. Both men had waited and waited for Ringuette to make his move, but nothing had happened. As he had half-suspected, Robert Barrett had met his match. Accepting the fact that he had been double-crossed by Ringuette, a disconsolate Barrett checked out of the Gateway Inn on June 20, spending a final night in Florida at the home of the motel's bartender, who had befriended the Barretts. When their Grey-hound bus pulled into London a few days later, Barrett tried to contact Helmuth at Treugott, but he was already out of the country.

Barrett had now spent $8,500 of Helmuth Buxbaum's money with nothing to show for it but a Florida tan and some souvenirs from Disneyworld. Realizing that he would have to arrange the contract by the time the Buxbaums returned from Europe, Barrett turned to the only people he knew might be interested in making some money: his friends at Kelly's Bar.

The vacation may have been over for Robert Barrett, but it was just beginning for the Buxbaums. Helmuth's brother and sister-in-law came up from Florida to look after Komoka while the family was in Europe. Early on the morning of June 19, 1984, Douglas [Gottlieb] Buxbaum and his wife, Rosita, waved goodbye as everyone but Ruth piled into Hel-muth's red and white van and headed for Buffalo to catch a People's Express flight to Newark. From there, the Buxbaums took a bus to Ken-nedy Airport in New York, where they met up with a group setting out on a religious pilgrimage through central Europe sponsored by Bryan College, a Baptist school in Dayton, Tennessee.

The Bryan College tour was organized around a seven-hour play celebrating the Passion of Christ performed in the Bavarian village of Oberammergau. The Passion Play had begun there in 1634, the year after God had answered the prayers of the desperate inhabitants by sparing them from the Black Plague that had threatened to wipe out their village. Every ten years since, the villagers had kept their word to stage the epic performance that began with Christ entering Jerusalem and ended in his resurrection and transfiguration. The 1984 performance marked the 350th anniversary of what had become both a major German cultural event and a lucrative tourist attraction.

Although the Buxbaums were anxious to see the play, they had care-fully checked the brochure sent to them six months earlier before paying $15,000 to join the excursion. They wanted to make sure that the tour

schedule would allow them time to visit relatives in Austria and Switzerland, members of the Buxbaum family that Hanna and the children
had never met and whom Helmuth himself hadn't seen in thirty years.
With Lucerne and Vienna on the tour's itinerary, it was a perfect fit with
their plans.

Weighed down by the misery of the last year, Hanna Buxbaum was
visibly apprehensive about the trip as they cleared French customs at Orly
airport and headed for the Nikko de Paris hotel. Although she was
encouraged that Helmuth had agreed to cut short their European vacation in order to check in to Pine Rest Christian Hospital in August, she
didn't know if he would follow through on his promise. He had, after all,
already delayed his treatment at Pine Rest once and broken Hanna's heart
many times with false promises to give up cocaine. But the ever-optimis-
tic woman was praying that a family trip to witness the passion of their
Lord would somehow bring her prodigal husband back to the fold.

Their first two days in Paris were promising. Drug-free, Helmuth
seemed to enjoy the company of his children. The first night, he took his
youngest son, Danny, to the top of the Eiffel Tower, where they spent an
hour looking at the City of Light through the world's busiest pay-tele-
scopes. As he would on every night of the trip but one, Helmuth slept
with Hanna, a dramatic departure from their life at home, where he had
taken to staying out all night. The next morning, Paul knocked on their
door to go down to breakfast, and for the first time in months, found
himself intruding on a happy moment between his parents. "My mother
and father were both sitting on the bed laughing . . . They couldn't
stop laughing . . . I didn't know about the joke or anything, but I had to
sit down and laugh myself . . . They were in a very good mood that
morning."

Hanna took heart from the reappearance of the old Helmuth. The
couple talked as they hadn't in years. There was so much to discuss: college plans for Mark and Phillip, preparations for their silver anniversary
(Helmuth had missed their twenty-third anniversary during his most
recent trip to Vancouver with Paul), and their own eventual retirement.
Fellow Baptists on the tour couldn't get over how much Helmuth and
Hanna looked like sweethearts, holding hands and whispering together in
a string of European cafés and restaurants. But it was the Buxbaum children who most appreciated the difference in their parents. "They had
drifted apart in the last few months. I guess most of this was due to my
dad's use of drugs," Mark Buxbaum said. "The fact that he wasn't using

drugs on the trip gave my Mom some reassurance. I think it brought them a lot closer together."

Then came Lucerne. After taking in the Swiss town's mediaeval walls, covered bridge, and famous Lion Monument, Helmuth returned to his room at the Europaischer Hof and called his nephew, Andrew Aerne. Aerne met the Buxbaums in Lucerne, and Helmuth explained to the family that he had to inspect a chalet the young man had found for them in Lausanne that he might be interested in buying. Hanna, who had never quite approved of Andrew after he showed his aunt and uncle his paintings of nude women on one of their banking trips to Zurich, was upset at Helmuth's departure. Her apprehension increased at word that he would be away overnight.

As Aerne drove through the Swiss Alps towards Lake Geneva, his uncle began to tell him about his unhappy relationship with Hanna, just as he had on his earlier trip to Switzerland at the beginning of June. Aerne was left with the impression that Helmuth wanted out of his marriage, but couldn't find a way: "Helmuth said that he had asked Hanna a number of times over the last two years for a divorce. Hanna wouldn't do it. 'What would the neighbours think?' was her reaction."

Along the way, Helmuth asked his nephew to take him to a club "where there were people with whom he could have fun." After checking Helmuth into a hotel, Aerne gave his uncle's words the broadest possible interpretation. They arrived at a nightclub where they were soon joined by a bevy of attractive women. Helmuth began buying drinks and looking forward to the pleasures ahead. Regrettably, the women turned out to be men. "We drank with the transvestites. Helmuth thought [one] transvestite was a woman. He put his hand on her crotch. The transvestite got an erection."

Shocked by his discovery, Helmuth made another strategic mistake; he tried to get rid of his camouflaged companions by buying them drinks. Approximately 3,400 Swiss francs later ($2,000 Canadian), Helmuth saw the error of his ways.

"The transvestites kept on drinking. They were really putting away the booze . . . They started to get obnoxious. One started feeling my leg," Helmuth indignantly recalled. "One of the transvestites called one of the strippers over. Her name was Cindy. Before I knew it, the transvestite had arranged for Cindy to come with me after the show was over."

At 4 A.M., his accommodating nephew delivered the stripper to Helmuth's room; for 400 Swiss francs, she did her best to make him forget the employees of Taurus Escorts. Later, she told him she wanted to come to Canada, and Helmuth gave her his address at Treugott. An hour after Cindy left, Aerne reappeared at his hotel for the two-and-a-half-hour drive back to Lucerne and Hanna.

Luckily for Helmuth, his nephew's parents, Esther and Paul Aerne, were already at the hotel with fresh strawberries and ambitious plans for the rest of the day. Hanna covered her anger at her obviously debauched husband by showering attention on her guests. The two families toured the city, circling Mount Pilatus by aerial cable car and cogwheel railway. The pleasant day gradually smoothed Hanna's ruffled feathers, and she and Helmuth dutifully smiled for the photographs that were *de rigueur* at each new sight. Later, the couple made love for the first time in months, and once more Hanna had reason to believe that her husband might finally be on the mend.

Two days later, the party arrived at Oberammergau in the Bavarian Alps. The next morning, at 8:15, the pageantry of the world's most celebrated religious folk play began, performed by a cast made up exclusively of Oberammergau's villagers. It was a Christian pilgrim's delight, an enactment of the Bible's four gospel texts in fourteen acts with all the haunting formality of a Greek tragedy. One player introduced the scenes in a prologue written in classical metre, and later a chorus musically linked each *tableau vivant* to the next act of the Passion. One of the most poignant moments in the performance came with the biblical prefiguration of Christ's agony on the Mount of Olives, when the chorus sang:

> *Cursed be the man who betrays,*
> *Who pretends love with dissembling face,*
> *Who approaches with the Judas kiss of innocence,*
> *But means betrayal in his heart.*

After the Passion Play, the rest of the tour headed for Cortina d'Ampezzo in the Italian Dolomites, while the Buxbaums travelled to Munich where they caught the Orient Express for Vienna and a family reunion. The first night in Vienna, Helmuth and Hanna had an excellent view of the Danube from their palatial quarters, a suite in the Biedermeier hotel that had often been used by the former Shah of Iran. "I was flabbergasted," Helmuth later said. "It cost me a bundle."

The next day, the family roamed through Vienna, marvelling at St. Stephen's Cathedral and the splendour of Maria Theresa's summer palace of Schonbrunn with its 1,441 rooms. After a midday stop at one of Vienna's irresistible *Konditorei* (pastry shops), they continued their sightseeing in the city's entertainment district, before making their way to a downtown beer garden where twenty-five relatives were eagerly awaiting them. Revelling in the company of her temporarily reunited family, Hanna was exhilarated. There was food and drink, much talk and even more picture-taking, until late that night the tired but happy Buxbaums made their way back to their hotel.

After the family reunion, the Buxbaums rejoined the tour for a journey down the Danube Valley to Salzburg. While the others took in the cathedral with its world-famous Glockenspiel and visited the birthplace of Mozart, Helmuth descended into the city's salt mines. As the only tourist fluent in both English and German, Helmuth ended up translating for the unilingual tour guide. After passing through Munich and the mediaeval town of Rothenburg, the tour came to an end in front of the glass doors of Frankfurt international airport. On July 3, the family boarded a Pan Am flight bound for New York.

When they reached Buffalo airport just before midnight on July 3, the wealthy family pooled their remaining U.S. currency, barely scraping together the $103 parking fee owing on their van. Everyone was anxious to get going, though for Helmuth, returning to Komoka raised the unpleasant prospect of having to enter Pine Rest Christian Hospital.

With Hanna behind the wheel, the weary travellers set out on the last leg of the long journey home.

When the Barretts had returned from Florida in late June, they had picked up their daughter, Robin, from Sadie Barrett and begun the search for a place to stay. Broke as usual, Barrett turned to the one person in London he could always depend on for help: Debbie Barber.

The single mother of two had a soft spot for the boyish drug dealer and petty thief. They had first met in 1982 when Barber started dating the man who fenced the stolen merchandise from Barrett's break-and-enters. The Barretts had been boarding with Barber when Squirrel got nine months in jail in May 1983 for break-and-enter. Barrett's family continued living at Barber's apartment, but after he got out of jail, the couple "fought all the time" and Kelly and Robin finally moved out. Barrett wore out his welcome shortly afterwards.

In early 1984, Barrett asked Barber if he could return to her apartment, this time as a paying boarder. During this second stay, Barrett was constantly after his landlady to join in the string of cocaine parties that were being paid for by his wealthy drug client. But the more she heard him talk about Helmuth Buxbaum, the farther away Barber decided to stay. Barrett's stories of the man's insatiable appetite for cocaine and young women were only part of her revulsion: "During this time, Rob was always talking about a hit on this guy's wife, and in February 1984, he was asking everyone down at Kelly's to do the hit, or if they knew of anyone that could do it for him."

Although Barber liked Barrett, there were limits to her tolerance. She disapproved of his increasing cocaine use and constant run-ins with the police and was horrified by his talk of a contract killing. Then, in early February 1984, she finally threw him out after he was arrested for possession of cocaine.

For the next few months she heard nothing, until a postcard arrived from Florida from the Barretts. Barber was pleasantly surprised to learn that Robert and Kelly were back together again. Then, in late June, they unexpectedly showed up on her doorstep "dressed in Florida clothes" with nowhere to go. In the interests of helping the couple work out their reconciliation, Barber once more extended her hospitality, but only to Kelly and Robin. Although he was free to visit, Robert was to make his own living arrangements.

For the first few days at the apartment, the Barretts lived out of their suitcases, depending on Barber for food and cigarettes while Robert looked for more permanent accommodation. During their stay, Kelly Barrett told their hostess all about the trip to Florida. It became obvious that they had spent a lot of money, and Barber finally asked Barrett where it had come from. "Rob told me that Helmuth Buxbaum flew to Florida at one point and met Rob there to give him some more money . . . He also told me that the hit on Helmuth's wife was supposed to happen when he was in Florida and Helmuth was in Europe [the Dawn Watson trip]."

With a temporary base secured, Barrett returned to the only real job he had: finding someone to kill Hanna Buxbaum. Allen Pickrem remembered being approached by Barrett at Kelly's Bar while playing cards with four other people. Pickrem, who had already heard that Squirrel "wanted to get someone dusted," was told that the contract was worth $75,000. "I was told that it didn't matter if it only cost me $1,000 for the murder, I could keep the balance of the $75,000."

Barrett later had trouble remembering that encounter, but not his

meeting with Terry Kline, a booking agent for exotic dancers and a sometime underworld bailiff. To settle a drug debt, Kline had once collected a
pet boa constrictor which its owner had then reported missing. After police broadcast an appeal for information about the dangerous reptile, Kline
turned it over to the police, his face hidden behind a black T-shirt with
eyeholes cut into it. He had asked the *London Free Press* to be present
when he turned the snake over to ensure that the police would live up to
their bargain not to charge him. Thanks to his press escort, Kline's picture
had made the newspaper, greatly impressing Robert Barrett. Would a
man capable of snake-napping, he wondered, ever consider murder?

"I was in Kelly's one night and I met Terry Kline, 'Sunshine.' I told
Sunshine that I knew a guy who wanted to have his wife killed and that he
had $25,000 to have it done. Sunshine just looked at me like I was crazy."

Taking a breather from his contract problems, Barrett was swimming
with his wife and daughter in London's Thames Park when his predicament suddenly got much worse. Unbeknownst to Barrett, his two
cocaine suppliers, Cecil Meany and Burt Merrow, had been arrested for
drug trafficking and were now in custody. According to the rules of the
street, Merrow's girlfriend was given a list of outstanding drug debts to
collect, the money to be used to post their bail. The woman in turn
hired a local thug known as "Big Jim" to encourage London's delin-
quent cocaine buyers, including Robert Barrett, to clear up their
accounts. Together with the 225-pound Pat Allen, Big Jim showed up at
Debbie Barber's apartment looking for Squirrel. Barber directed them
to the park.

"I met Allen in the park with Big Jim on June 29 or June 30," Barrett
said. "They wanted to speak with me. This Jim guy said that I owed
$1,000 for cocaine. He said if I didn't pay it to him in a week, he was
going to break my legs."

It was the holiday weekend, and Barrett decided to take Kelly to Har-
vey's Hotel in Grand Bend, hitching a ride with Debbie Barber. Barrett
wasn't particularly worried about the drug debt; although he did, in fact,
owe the $1,000 to Burt Merrow, Cecil Meany was indebted to Barrett for
the same amount in stolen goods. Since Merrow and Meany were partners, Barrett decided that made everything square, an interpretation he
hoped Big Jim would share when he checked into the matter.

Sitting on the Lake Huron beach trying to figure out his next move,
Squirrel had an idea. If Big Jim was prepared to break legs for money,

maybe *he* would be interested in the Buxbaum contract. In London a few days later, Barrett was at Kelly's Bar when he ran into Pat Allen, who had some drug debts of his own to worry about. By this time Allen himself was curious about the murder contract, having heard about it from Terry Kline. Barrett got a surprise when he asked his old friend about Big Jim. "I asked him if this Big Jim guy would be interested in doing the murder. Allen said, 'Forget about Big Jim, *I'm* interested.'"

Allen wanted $5,000 up front, but Barrett refused, explaining that he had already been ripped off in Florida. Instead, he struck the same deal with Allen as he had with Ringuette and McCurdy; a small downpayment to cover the expenses of the murder, and a main payment of $10,000 after Hanna Buxbaum was dead. At last, Squirrel had good news for Helmuth when he returned from his religious pilgrimage.

The Buxbaum van pulled into the moonlit grounds of Komoka at 12:15 A.M. on the morning of July 4. Tired as they were, the family briefly stopped to admire the haunting beauty of their gardens, now in high bloom. After everyone else had retired, Helmuth slipped down to the fall-out shelter, where he quickly broke out his hidden stash of cocaine. It had been almost a month since his last fix and he made up for lost time by mainlining all night.

Sleepless and still high on cocaine, Helmuth emerged from the shelter at 8:30 A.M. Esther and Danny were still sleeping, and Hanna and Rosita Buxbaum were fixing breakfast for the rest of the family. Helmuth, who rarely ate breakfast, had a quick cup of coffee, scooped up his briefcase, and headed out the door before Hanna could confront him over his nocturnal activities.

He may have been feeling guilty about his speedy return to cocaine, but he was hardly repentant. As soon as he arrived at Treugott, he tried to contact Rick Balfour, a drug dealer who had gradually supplanted Robert Barrett as his main supplier of cocaine. He liked Balfour's more discreet approach to his illegal trade, even if he was somewhat unnerved by the man's habit of giving his dog beer caps to chew on.

Getting no answer when he telephoned Balfour's Adelaide Street apartment, Helmuth showed up at his door. The dishevelled drug dealer, his dog snarling at his side, told his anxious customer that he was still sleeping and to come back later. Desperate, Helmuth then tried to score from Chris Browne, who lived just a few blocks away. Again, he failed.

Around noon, Helmuth headed back to Treugott to tackle the pile of mail that had accumulated on his desk during the family's European vacation. Helmuth was on the telephone when he heard Hanna's voice in the outer office. She had been talking to Treugott accountant Robert Bell while waiting for Helmuth to finish his call so that they could go to lunch. Their conversation was interrupted by another telephone call, which Bell answered. He soon found himself in an awkward position. It was one of the people Hanna had strictly forbidden Treugott's staff to put through to her husband: Robert Barrett.

Momentarily befuddled, Bell put the call on hold. Since Helmuth was the only other person in the office on the telephone, Hanna knew that the call was for him. She asked Bell for the name of the person behind the telltale, blinking light. When she found out who it was, Hanna was rocked by a wave of betrayal and fear, emotions she had hoped were forever behind her after Helmuth's apparent moral rejuvenation in Europe. She walked into his office to personally deliver the telephone message – and to register her searing disapproval. "Hanna told me that Barrett was on the phone," Helmuth remembered. "She just shook her head."

Her resolve to get her husband into Pine Rest Christian Hospital now touched with a sense of urgency, Hanna left, closing the door behind her. For the first documented time since shortly after midnight on June 19, the customer and the contractor finally got a chance to speak.

Barrett explained that he was back from Florida and had now made all the necessary arrangements they had discussed, but needed more money to take care of expenses. Ten minutes later, Helmuth left the office for a meeting with Barrett at Debbie Barber's apartment. Kelly Barrett, who had last seen Helmuth in a motel room at the Gateway Inn in Orlando, briefly encountered him again as she stood over the kitchen sink doing the dishes. Fresh from her shower, a towel-clad Debbie Barber had a short conversation with Helmuth about a red ceramic D (for Debbie) hanging on the wall that had caught his eye. Before the two men left, Barrett told his wife he was going to Toronto and asked her to pack him a bag that he would pick up later.

During the ride to Kelly's Bar, Barrett explained that Pat Allen had accepted the contract. As soon as he received expense money and a co-ordinated plan could be worked out, he was ready to act. Barrett also told Helmuth that he would need more pictures of Hanna and the station wagon, since he had given the previous set to Ringuette and McCurdy before they had absconded with Helmuth's money.

After dropping Barrett off at Kelly's Bar around 1:30 P.M., Helmuth withdrew a total of $5,146.41 from three different London banks. He then contacted Barrett and set up their second meeting of the day, this time in the parking lot behind the bar.

"Buxbaum telephoned me at Kelly's . . . He met me there . . . He gave me another $5,000 and two more pictures. Buxbaum told me that he was going to go to Toronto to pick up his nephew the next day. He said his nephew was flying in from B.C. Buxbaum said that we would get together later on July 4 . . . He called me later at Kelly's and asked me to meet him at McDonald's at Oxford and Wonderland Road," Barrett later said.

With his alley bag bulging with yet more of Helmuth Buxbaum's money, Barrett once again had the means to put the murder plot into action. Shortly after his parking lot rendezvous with Helmuth, he met Pat Allen to invite the triggerman to the meeting with Buxbaum at 4:30 that afternoon. There was only one item on the agenda: selecting the location of Hanna Buxbaum's execution. In a coded conversation designed to keep his female companion, Anita Pitcher, in the dark about the murder, Barrett told Allen that the event would take place the next day, while the Buxbaums were on their way to Toronto to pick up their nephew.

"Rob produced between $190 and $200 and a picture of Hanna Buxbaum," Allen later said. "At this point, Anita Pitcher was with him . . . Anita saw the $190 or $200 and the picture of Hanna Buxbaum."

Leaving Allen to take care of his end of the deal, Barrett then went to work on building his alibi, a high-profile drug party in Toronto that would place him far away from London when Hanna Buxbaum was murdered. Drifting from bar to bar, Barrett bought drinks for various friends and acquaintances, inviting a select few to accompany him to Toronto. As the afternoon wore on, Rick Diorio, Anita Pitcher, and Janet Hicks agreed to come. Allen claimed that he wanted his sometime girlfriend, Janet, to represent his interests in a drug deal in Toronto, promising her $1,000 for her trouble.

At 4:30 P.M., Helmuth drove across the parking lot at McDonald's in the station wagon that he and Hanna would be taking to Pearson International Airport in less than twenty-four hours to pick up Roy Buxbaum. He parked on the back of the K-Mart portion of the lot at the edge of a ravine. Barrett and company showed up late for the meeting driving a blue Chevy Nova that Pat Allen and Anita Pitcher had rented earlier in the day with the money Barrett had given them in the bar.

After dropping Pitcher off at the K-Mart with twenty dollars and instructions to go shopping, Barrett and Allen followed Helmuth through the early evening rush hour to Komoka. While Barrett and Allen waited on a nearby country lane, Helmuth entered his grounds through the back entrance, operating the electronic gates with a remote control device in his car. Opening the garage door the same way, he retrieved a brown mink coat from behind a mirror in a clothes closet where he had hidden it six months earlier. He then drove back to where Barrett and Allen were waiting for him and motioned for them to follow him.

A hundred yards west of the main corner in Komoka, by a gas station, Helmuth pulled over onto the right shoulder of County Road 14 and waited for Barrett to join him. He made clear that he wanted the murder to take place on that spot when he and Hanna were on their way to the airport the next day. Barrett got out of the car and relayed the information to Allen, who protested that there were too many houses in the vicinity. "Follow me," he told Barrett, "I'll find a better place." Barrett returned to the station wagon. Allen pulled out around the other car and headed towards Highway 402, with Buxbaum and Barrett following at a comfortable distance.

"During the ride from the first spot to the second spot on Highway 402 with Buxbaum, Buxbaum mentioned about making the killing look like a kidnapping," Barrett remembered. "Whoever killed Hanna was supposed to take her jewellery and deliver it to me . . . I agreed that I would mail Buxbaum Hanna's jewellery and a ransom note from the United States . . . It would look like a kidnapping. That would take all suspicion away from him."

After learning from Helmuth that the Buxbaums would be on the highway at approximately 8:30 the next morning, Barrett told him that the Nova would be on the side of the road with the hood up. Helmuth was to pull over to offer assistance, and Pat Allen would take care of the rest.

Less than ten minutes after they left Komoka, Allen parked on the shoulder of the eastbound lanes of Highway 402, adjacent to a spot with bulrushes, wild wheat, and a deep ditch. Scrambling down the embankment, he discovered a large drain with a heavy metal cover. Lifting off the cover, he decided that it was the perfect spot. When he dragged Hanna out of the car, she would fall directly into the gully, where she could be shot out of sight of the traffic. It would then be an easy matter to stuff her into the drain and conceal the body by replacing the metal cover.

A moment later, the station wagon pulled to a stop six or seven car lengths behind him. Barrett ran over to the Nova and threw a mink coat into the back seat. He had sold it to Helmuth six months earlier, and he didn't want the police connecting it to him when the Hanna Buxbaum murder investigation got underway. Barrett leaned against the car with both hands and lowered his head to the driver's side window where Pat Allen was looking up at him. Allen's words came in a hoarse rush: "This is where I want it to happen."

Helmuth never got out of his car, leaving it to Barrett to shuttle back and forth between the two vehicles until everyone agreed on the plan. When the conference was over, Helmuth was the first to leave, anxious to keep his promise to Hanna to be home for supper. Then Barrett and Allen headed eastward down the 402 until they reached the first cutoff that would take them back to London and Janet Hicks' apartment. After checking out the sub-machine gun, they returned to K-Mart to pick up Anita Pitcher. They let her try on the mink coat but wouldn't tell her where it had come from. The next stop was Kelly's Bar where Allen parted company with Barrett and his female companion.

By 7:30 P.M., Robert Barrett was on his way out of London in a rented limousine with Rick Diorio, Anita Pitcher, Janet Hicks, and the cocaine he had purchased for the epic drug party that would rage at Toronto's Westbury Hotel for the next few days.

Pat Allen, meanwhile, picked up another gun, a Harrington & Richardson .32-calibre revolver, and then went looking for some help. By chance, he ran into Gary Foshay and Terry Armes, who joined the murder plot after injecting speed with their new boss. Afterwards, the three men paid a brief visit to the murder scene where Allen explained what would happen.

"Buxbaum will be driving a brown station wagon. He will pull up behind our car, at which time we are to open the passenger's front door of his car and pull her out," he croaked. "At that point, if you pulled her out, she would fall right into the gully."

Returning to London, the killers spent the rest of the night drinking, shooting speed, and sleeplessly awaiting their morning rendezvous with their paymaster.

True to his word, Helmuth made it back to Komoka in time for supper. To his surprise, he discovered that Douglas Buxbaum had decided to go to Windsor to meet their brother Otto, who had come up from Florida to visit his daughter. But there were still plenty of people in the house. John

Fangrad, a friend of Mark Buxbaum had come over to visit and was invited to spend the night. Hanna had prepared goulash and she, Helmuth, Rosita, and a few of the children and their friends enjoyed a quiet dinner together.

After supper, Helmuth retreated to the den to watch the news channel. Later, he and Hanna took a quick dip in the Jacuzzi. Just as they were getting ready for bed, the telephone rang. It was Isbrandt calling to remind them that Roy would be arriving from Vancouver the following day at 4 P.M. to begin his summer job at Komoka.

The Buxbaums finally climbed into bed just before midnight. After making love to Hanna, Helmuth waited until she had drifted off to sleep before slipping out of their room. The lights were out on the tennis court, the trout pond was still, and no one was seeking relief from the humid summer night in the Buxbaum's indoor swimming pool. Helmuth made his way to the fallout shelter he had built beneath his twenty-eight-room mansion.

Bolting the door to what had become his personal sanctuary, he unlocked the tool box where he kept his collection of pornographic videotapes, slipping one of his favourites into the VCR. After expertly loading a syringe with cocaine, he gave himself his first injection of the day. Euphoria came quickly as the drug hit his bloodstream and made the fifteen-second trip to his brain. High, he watched the naked bodies gyrating impersonally on the screen in front of him. Fascinated with the sexual pleasures he took for the North American norm, and which he had so diligently tried to duplicate with a string of paid companions, Helmuth Buxbaum repeatedly injected himself until his five-gram supply of cocaine was exhausted.

Like the revellers at the Westbury, and the occupants of the blue Nova, Helmuth remained stoned and awake all night.

9

THE LAST BREAKFAST

"He just stood there looking at me, and as Hanna Buxbaum
was trying to pull away from Gary Foshay . . . she is looking
up at Helmuth and said, 'No, honey, please not this way' . . .
And he didn't even blink an eye, he just stood there."
— *Terry Armes, on the July 5, 1984, slaying of Hanna Buxbaum*

July 5, 1984, was the kind of day that made you glad to be alive. The air smelled of freshly cut grass, and Komoka's gardens blazed in the early morning sunlight. Listening to the birds as he filled his lungs with the sweet summer air, Helmuth Buxbaum was grateful to be outside, and not only because of the weather. At 7:30 A.M., he had just stepped out of the shower when Hanna noticed the fresh needle marks on his arm. She bluntly asked if he had been injecting cocaine the previous night; Helmuth ruefully admitted that he had. Her silent and sorrowful reproach was more than he could bear. Using the excuse that he wanted to see if the groundskeeper had remembered to water the potted flowers while the family was away in Europe, he hurried outside where he could be alone.

Helmuth was standing in the garden when their housekeeper, Gizella Toth, arrived for work a little before 8 A.M. After exchanging pleasantries, Helmuth told her that he and Hanna were stopping in Kitchener that morning to visit Hanna's mother at the Millwood Manor Rest Home on their way to pick up Roy Buxbaum at Pearson International Airport. Trying to make amends with his wife, Helmuth asked Toth to prepare "a big breakfast" for the Buxbaums and their guests.

During the eight years she had worked for the family, Gizella Toth had been responsible for cooking, cleaning, and looking after the children when Helmuth and Hanna were travelling. At first, it had seemed like the perfect household. Both of the Buxbaums were generous and considerate to the widowed mother of five, treating her more like a member of the family than an employee. But as loyal as she was to both of them, it had soon become impossible to ignore the trouble in the Buxbaum marriage.

It had started with disturbing rumours about Helmuth's affairs. Then one night when Hanna was away, Helmuth had brought a strange woman into the house. They went for a swim together and then disappeared upstairs. To Toth, it was as if Helmuth had become another person after his stroke, a man who "had lost his sense of responsibility towards his family."

Although Hanna kept her private life to herself, there was an unspoken intimacy between the two women that ran deep. Toth always knew when something was bothering Hanna because she would fall silent and work even harder around the house. For the last few years, she had been working very hard indeed. One day, Toth had found a packet of white powder when she was dusting Helmuth's dresser. Only then had Hanna reluctantly admitted to her that her husband was addicted to drugs.

Toth had half expected Hanna to talk about her marital problems during a three-week trip to Hungary the two women had taken in March 1984, a trip to Gizella Toth's homeland paid for by the Buxbaums as a reward for her faithful service to the family. But telling tales out of marriage was not Hanna's style. Other than wondering out loud how her husband and children were doing without her, she had said nothing about her problems. But back home again, the signs of her private misery were unmistakable. There were many days now when Hanna would simply sit quietly by herself knitting, as she fretted over the bizarre forces that were destroying everything she and Helmuth had built.

By 8:30 A.M., Toth had finished cooking and the family sat down to breakfast. Esther, Danny, and Phillip were still sleeping, but Paul and Mark joined hands with their parents and aunt to pray, a family ritual whenever they shared a meal together. Rosita Buxbaum said grace in German, reciting a prayer she had learned as a girl from her father, a Lutheran minister. It was one of Hanna's favourites. "As I said grace, I began to cry," Rosita later remembered. "I had a strange feeling. I couldn't explain it."

The sobbing woman got up from the table and retreated into the living room. Hanna followed. After a few minutes, the women returned to the breakfast table. As if to make up for her inexplicable show of emotion,

Rosita did a hilarious impersonation of a local Baptist minister, whose shallow sermon she had recently attended. The only thing he managed to get out properly, she told her laughing audience, was the Lord's Prayer.

Breakfast proceeded at a leisurely pace until it was finally time for the Buxbaums to set off. Helmuth had filled up the Oldsmobile station wagon at the Buxbaums' private pump. He was the picture of casual elegance in his grey slacks and sports jacket with a white shirt open at the neck. But Hanna knew better. Fully aware that her husband had been injecting cocaine all night, and had probably not slept, she wanted to drive. Despite his fatigue, Helmuth insisted on getting behind the wheel, promising Hanna that if he became too tired, she could take over.

The couple looked happy enough, but when they started down the driveway on their way to visit Ottilie Schmidt, the same mysterious emotion that had overwhelmed Rosita Buxbaum at breakfast overcame her again. "I began crying as they left. It seemed odd. It seemed like the last time I would see them . . . This is what I honestly felt."

About the only thing that had gone smoothly for Pat Allen on the morning of July 5 was the piss he had taken on the ramp leading from Middlesex County Road 14 to Highway 402 at 7:45 A.M. Since then, he and Terry Armes had been waiting in vain behind their jacked-up Chevy Nova, while Gary Foshay hid in the ditch clutching the KK9. They were exactly two kilometres along the eastbound lanes of the highway at the spot Buxbaum had agreed would be the site of his wife's execution. By 8:30 A.M., Allen was getting nervous.

"If he's not here in twenty minutes, we are leaving," he said.

"Why?" Terry Armes asked.

"At five to nine the OPP will go by," Allen answered.

"How do you know?"

"I just know," Allen told Armes. The previous night, Allen had, in fact, called "Porky," a former police officer who occasionally acted as a consultant to London's criminal element. Porky told him that an OPP cruiser would pass their location on Highway 402 at 8:55 A.M. After Allen's twenty-minute deadline passed, he walked to the rear of the Nova, took the car off the jack and was just putting the spare tire and tire iron into the trunk when a shout from Terry Armes stopped him in his tracks. "Here he comes."

Gary Foshay was just climbing out of the gully, when Helmuth Buxbaum's brown station wagon sent him scurrying for cover. Helmuth stopped three feet behind the Nova, directly adjacent to the spot in the ditch where Foshay now waited beside the open culvert that was to be Hanna's grave. Allen, who recognized their victim from the picture Robert Barrett had given him, walked back to the passenger door of the station wagon and tapped on the window. Although Hanna was unnerved by Allen's unkempt appearance, she rolled down the window.

"You wouldn't have an extra pair of panty hose?" he asked in a deep voice. "My fan-belt is broken."

"No," the nervous woman answered.

"Is there something I can do?" Helmuth asked. It was an odd question from a man who knew nothing about cars.

"Come and have a look," Allen suggested.

The two men walked towards the Nova. Allen called out to Armes to pull the hood release. As Helmuth and Allen made their way to the front of the car, Helmuth saw the other man lying across the front seat with a baseball cap pulled down over his ears. Armes shouted that he couldn't find the release. Allen then poked around above the grill until he located it himself, popping the hood with a metallic thud. Protected now from Hanna's vigilant gaze, the two men had a brief conversation about what was really going on.

"How come you are late?" Allen hissed.

"I got up late," Helmuth replied.

Just then, the horn honked in the station wagon. Helmuth went back to see what his wife wanted.

"Take these," she said. "They have holes in them anyway." Helmuth returned to the Nova and handed his wife's panty hose to Allen.

"It is kind of late, there is a lot of cars out now," Allen said, remembering what Porky had told him. Helmuth looked down the highway but couldn't see any traffic.

"Hurry up and get her out of the car and get it over with," he demanded.

Luckily for Pat Allen, he decided to follow his instincts.

Const. Philip Medlyn of the OPP's Strathroy Detachment was travelling eastbound on Highway 402 enroute to London District Headquarters when he noticed two vehicles pulled off on the south shoulder of the road just west of Middlesex County Road 14. Had the vehicles been east of the road, they would have been in the jurisdiction of the OPP's London Detachment. But as it was, they were in his territory, and he was duty-bound to stop and offer assistance.

As Constable Medlyn's cruiser slowed down and began to pull over, Terry Armes shouted "NG" (no good) to Allen, and Allen in turn barked out "Six," the street warning for trouble. Aware now that something had gone wrong, Gary Foshay remained in the bushes, cradling the fully loaded KK9 in his lap. Terry Armes, who was flattened across the front seat of the Nova, heard Pat Allen telling Helmuth that their mission was officially aborted.

"It's off," he said sharply, adding that Helmuth could reach Barrett at the Westbury Hotel.

"It's all right. I will get back to you later," Helmuth answered.

As he stopped his black and white cruiser, Constable Medlyn saw Helmuth and Allen standing by the right front fender of the Nova. By the time the policeman straightened his hat and got out of his car, the older man was walking back towards the passenger door of the brown station wagon. Stopping at the back of the police car, Medlyn asked if the men needed help.

"No," Pat Allen answered, slamming down the hood and deciding to shoot the policeman if he came any closer. "I just fixed it."

As Medlyn pulled away, unaware of how close he had come to dying, he stuck his head out the window of the cruiser to check approaching traffic; Helmuth was standing beside the station wagon now, the sun glinting off his balding head. Hanna watched uneasily as the last angel the Lord would send her disappeared down the highway.

If she was having trouble making sense of what was going on, her confusion was understandable. Although the stocky man with the black beard had wanted help from her admittedly non-mechanical husband, he had waved away the police. Her puzzlement must have increased when Allen returned to the station wagon with her panty hose, the problem apparently fixed.

"I don't need them, thank you," Allen said, lowering his dark face to look into the eyes of the woman he had come within minutes of helping execute.

Hanna was unable to keep the irritation out of her voice when she and Helmuth were alone again.

"I took them off expressly for him," she complained. But she was more relieved than angry as Helmuth eased the station wagon back onto the highway and the couple resumed their strangely interrupted journey.

"That guy gives me the creeps," Hanna said.

"Me too," Helmuth replied.

Accelerating smoothly down the 402 towards Kitchener, Helmuth watched the blue car shrink to insignificance in the rear-view mirror before his mind turned to other matters.

Coming down off their speed run, and foiled in their early morning attempt to pick up some easy money, the unhappy band of killers drove back to Janet Hicks' apartment to work out their next move. Foshay and Armes were of the opinion that Buxbaum still ought to pay them because it had been Helmuth who had "fucked up" the plan by arriving late. At 9:58 A.M. Allen called Robert Barrett at the Westbury Hotel and told him what had happened. During their six-minute conversation, Allen made clear that the threesome still expected to be paid for their trouble. Barrett said that he was waiting for a phone call from Helmuth, and would talk with the killers again between noon and 1 P.M.

Allen dropped Foshay and Armes at the Wellington Tavern in downtown London before returning to his apartment to check on his pregnant girlfriend, Lisa Mattalo. The expectant mother was still asleep. At noon, he picked up his accomplices and went back to Hicks' apartment to call Robert Barrett. Barrett, who had by then spoken to Helmuth, told Allen that there would be no payment for the botched morning attempt.

But there was still a way to get the money. Helmuth now wanted the killing to take place at the same location, but on the opposite side of the highway, when the Buxbaums returned from picking up their nephew at the airport that night. Spooked by the roadside encounter with the OPP, Pat Allen bailed out. "I don't want anything more to do with it," he said. "It screwed up once and it wasn't meant to be done."

Gary Foshay, who had been listening in on the conversation, signalled to Allen to give him the phone. Until then, Barrett had been under the impression that Allen alone would be killing Hanna Buxbaum. Foshay told Barrett that *he* was willing to carry out the murder, and that Barrett should stay in Toronto until he and Armes picked up the contract money at the Westbury the next day. Without even knowing who he was talking to, Barrett agreed. "He said that he knew me and it didn't matter if I knew him." Assuming that Allen had already given Foshay the other details about the hit (he hadn't), Barrett explained to the new gunman where the murder was to take place. "Buxbaum had told me . . . that he'd be going there at about 7:00 or 7:30 P.M. Buxbaum had also told me that his nephew wasn't to be hurt because the nephew would be in the car at the time. I told Foshay this."

Before hanging up, Barrett asked to speak to Pat Allen again. He instructed Allen to give Foshay the keys to the Nova and the .32-calibre revolver. Before they left Janet Hicks' apartment, Allen locked the KK9 in a suitcase and returned it to its hiding place. Foshay then dropped Allen off at his mother's house, where he spent part of the afternoon fixing her refrigerator. Foshay and Armes headed back to the Wellington Tavern, where Molson's was throwing a free beer bash.

After a rocky start, the day wasn't turning out too badly after all.

The last person Heinz Wagner expected to find when he laid down his paint scraper and turned around to see who had said hello was Helmuth Buxbaum.

Since the early 1970s, when the two men had been in competition in the nursing home business, they had only two things in common; their hearty dislike of one another, and the fact that their wives were sisters. During a confrontation at their mother-in-law's, Helmuth had once told Wagner that he would put him out of business after finding out that Heinz and his brother Kurt were planning to build Sunhaven Nursing Home only a few miles from Komoka. Seeing his once-menacing business competitor in the guise of casual visitor was a shock for Wagner. "I couldn't believe my eyes . . . Before we [had] even started building the nursing home, Helmuth told me to my face that he was going to ruin me no matter how much it cost him."

According to Wagner, Helmuth tried to make good on his threat by reporting his brother-in-law to government authorities over alleged problems at Sunhaven. Wagner was questioned by officials from the health department, and later confronted Buxbaum about the false reports he had made: "I told him he had told lies to the government against me. I asked him why he did it. He said he did it because he promised to ruin me and that was what he was doing. He said he told the lies, but if I was a Christian, I had to forgive him."

But there were some things that even the spirit of 1 John 1:9 couldn't fix. Although the antipathy between the two men had tapered off a little after the Wagners sold their nursing home in 1972, there was never any love lost between them. Hanna tried to establish family gatherings at Christmas, but whenever she cajoled Helmuth into going to the Wagner home, he would sleep in the van until it was time to leave.

Helmuth thought of Heinz as a domineering ignoramus who enjoyed playing the role of patriarch of the extended clan, a title Helmuth wasn't about to cede to his imperious brother-in-law. When their mother-in-law, Ottilie, tried to patch things up by telling the feuding men that they were both headed for the same eternity, Helmuth replied that he didn't want to go anywhere with Wagner, including heaven.

But at 10:30 on the morning of July 5, he entered the Wagner house and sat drinking grape juice and chatting amicably with his old enemy. Helmuth explained that Hanna was giving her mother a bath at Millwood Manor Rest Home two blocks away and would be joining them after she had finished her visit. Martha Wagner invited the Buxbaums for lunch, but Helmuth said they had already made plans to stop in nearby Preston on their way to pick up Roy Buxbaum at the airport.

Knowing that Helmuth had planned to take the family on an extended visit to Europe that summer, Wagner asked why they had come home so early. Helmuth cited the Protestant work ethic and the need to be frugal. "He replied that the boys should learn how to work, that they had too much of everything and that it was a lot of money in Europe," Wagner recalled.

As they made small talk about the family's trip to Europe, Wagner was struck by how nervous Helmuth seemed to be. He gulped three glasses of grape juice, even though he complained that it was artificial and "tasted like tin." Unable to sit still, he wandered in and out of the Wagner's living room, repeatedly checking his watch. He had banking to do, he explained, and then there was the task of picking up Roy. Finally, Helmuth asked his host if they could go outside and see his fruit trees. "I said, 'Sure we got fruit trees,' and we went to the backyard. I set out a lawn chair for Helmuth to sit on and he fell off it. He continued being very nervous," Wagner remembered.

At noon, Hanna arrived. Martha Wagner again extended a luncheon invitation but Hanna, following Helmuth's lead, declined: "When my honey invites me, I always go for lunch with my honey," Hanna cooed.

As the Buxbaums were saying their goodbyes, Hanna realized that she had forgotten her purse at the nursing home. Helmuth accompanied her back to her mother's room. Before leaving Millwood, Hanna took a Polaroid picture and the three of them prayed together. Back in the car, Hanna noticed the presents she had picked up in Austria for her sister and nieces – five candlesticks. After another brief stop to drop off the gifts, they were on their way again. As Hanna got into the car, Martha noticed something strange for her very proper sister. Hanna wasn't wearing any panty hose.

With Helmuth behind the wheel, the Buxbaums drove to the Knotty Pine Restaurant in Preston, where they began a relaxed lunch at around 1 P.M., knowing that the airport was only an hour's drive away. After lunch, Hanna took over the driving and the Buxbaums passed the time on the way to the airport talking about the relatives they had met on their European vacation. Helmuth mentioned that he was planning another banking run to Zurich. They arrived at the airport at approximately 3:30 P.M. and parked across from Terminal 1.

Leaving Hanna to nap in the station wagon, Helmuth went into the airport to pick up Roy. While he waited, he bought himself a glass of orange juice and drew $400 out of a banking machine. He then went into the washroom and snorted some cocaine. Canadian Pacific flight 060 arrived at 4 P.M. and Helmuth was there to greet his nephew when he walked into the terminal. While waiting for Roy's luggage, which included a box containing fifty pounds of frozen fish from Paul Buxbaum's prize halibut, Helmuth told his nephew that he had to make a private business call. According to Robert Barrett, the business was murder. "I believe altogether Buxbaum called me three times," Barrett said. "He called me once from the airport, which was the last time. He said that he was on his way back to London."

After getting Roy's luggage, Helmuth and his nephew walked back to the parking tower where Hanna was just waking up. Roy greeted his aunt and then made some room in the back seat where he could stretch out after his long flight. With his aunt driving, and his uncle sitting beside her in the passenger seat, the fourteen-year-old drowsily fielded Hanna's questions about himself and his parents, happy that his Komoka summer was finally beginning. After a few kilometres, Roy no longer answered her affectionate inquiries, and she nudged Helmuth to look at the sleeping boy in the back seat, his face burrowed into Hanna's sweater.

Fresh from her own nap, Hanna navigated through the heavy airport traffic to the westbound lanes of Highway 401. Roy didn't wake up until they pulled into McDonald's restaurant in Milton, a traditional stop for the Buxbaums whenever they were returning home from Toronto. After drinks and a snack, they got back into the car for the last leg of the trip home. Roy kicked off his shoes and curled up in the back seat. Everything was as it had been when they left the airport except that a light rain had begun to fall.

There was one other difference; Helmuth was now driving.

✦ ✦ ✦

After a long day of drinking at the Wellington Tavern, Gary Foshay set out in the blue Nova for the second rendezvous on Highway 402 with Helmuth Buxbaum. Sitting beside him was Terry Armes, twitching from the prodigious quantities of speed and beer he had consumed over the past twenty-four hours. Foshay attempted to pull over just before the turn-off to Komoka, where it had been agreed he would wait for their victim, but Armes objected. Drunk as he was, the same instinct that had once inspired him to save a girl from being raped, now halfheartedly kicked in to prevent a woman from being murdered. He insisted that Foshay park well beyond the Komoka turn-off by a railway overpass west of the County Road 14 exit. His hope was that when he didn't see their car, Helmuth would simply take his exit home and it would all be over. "I know he [Foshay] was going back to kill that fucking broad. So I got him to pass the turn off . . . I didn't want nothing to do with it," Armes later claimed.

When they reached the location Armes had selected, Foshay got out of the car and opened the trunk. Taking out a piece of green felt, he covered the licence plate and quickly pulled on a stocking mask and a black and gold United Auto Workers baseball cap he had borrowed from Janet Hicks. With Armes leaning against the car, his head in the passenger's window to avoid identification by Roy Buxbaum, Foshay took up his position behind the cement pillar of the railway overpass and waited. At 7:25 P.M., Armes saw the brown station wagon, its headlights on, approaching down the westbound lane of Highway 402. Just as he had hoped, Helmuth slowed down and started up the exit towards Komoka. "I saw him turning up, okay," Armes said later, "and I felt good, you know, I did the right thing. I was just going to say to Gary, 'Fuck man, let's go,' when I saw the car coming back."

Helmuth had just begun to take the Komoka exit, when he noticed the Nova parked several hundred feet ahead of him down the highway under a railway overpass. He made a U-turn at the top of the exit ramp and headed down the westbound entrance to the 402. As he swerved sharply back onto the main highway, his dozing wife was jostled awake. "You missed the turn-off," she said sleepily. "Aren't we going home?"

Helmuth told her about the broken-down car ahead and said that it looked like their neighbours, the Richardsons. Anxious to get home, Hanna asked him not to stop. Roy Buxbaum shook away the cobwebs of his own nap in time to overhear his aunt agree that the distressed vehicle might indeed belong to the Richardsons. Ahead of them, Roy could see a car by the side of the road with its trunk open and a lone man leaning into the passenger-side window. When the station wagon came to a halt, Helmuth turned off the ignition, even though he, and Hanna, could now see that this was definitely not the Richardsons' full-size Chrysler.

Without warning, the rear passenger door flew open and a masked man pointed a gun at Roy's right eye, ordering him to "get down and keep down." The fourteen-year-old buried his face in the sweater he had been using as a pillow. The man jabbed him in the kidneys with the barrel of the gun before turning his attention to Hanna. Opening the front passenger door, he grabbed her by the hair with his left hand and put the gun to her right temple.

"Give me your fucking money, give me your fucking jewellery," he shouted. As deep and menacing as it was, his voice seemed oddly nervous, as if he were as frightened by what was going on as his victims. Terrified, Hanna turned and looked at Helmuth. "Just do what he says," he told her.

Hanna struggled in vain to get one of her rings off and then began sliding down in her seat to reach her purse, which was on the floor between her feet. Foshay again demanded her money and jewellery, grabbing Hanna by her right arm. While his wife was being assaulted, Helmuth slipped out of the car and stood by the door. Terrified, Hanna tried to claw her way across the front seat to the driver's side of the car, screaming through the glass at her impassive husband. Then the iron hand was at her throat, pulling her back.

"Okay, okay. Please, you're hurting me."

"Get the fuck out of the car."

Turning back to her assailant, Hanna pleaded for mercy. "Don't hurt me, I have five children at home."

Terry Armes, who had covered his head with his hands, looked up to see his partner pulling the frantic woman towards the guardrail. As much as he wanted to distance himself from what was happening, Armes was riveted to the spot. Helmuth continued standing outside his car by the driver's door, looking over the top of the Oldsmobile at Foshay, who was now shoving Hanna across the metal cable of the guardrail. Trying to turn and look at her husband, her beige slip now showing beneath her dishevelled navy dress, the struggling woman begged Helmuth for her life: "No honey, please, not this way."

There was a momentary silence, then Foshay pointed his gun at Helmuth. "It should be you, you son of a bitch," he roared, his eyes blazing through the holes in his home-made mask.

Turning abruptly to Hanna, he fired point-blank into her left temple just above the ear, sending her crashing to the ground face-first in the mud. As her body went into convulsions, Foshay tried to fire again, but the gun jammed. Armes noticed Roy Buxbaum getting up in the back seat. Rushing over to the car, he pushed his face back down into Hanna's sweater. "Keep your fucking head down," he screamed, trying to prevent the youngster from seeing what was happening. Helmuth, still standing by the car, added, "You do what you're told."

A second shot rang out, creasing Hanna's left bicep. Helmuth got up on his tiptoes and watched as Foshay fired a third round at his fallen wife. Clutching Hanna's purse, Foshay hurdled the guardrail, dodging between the two cars on his way to the driver's door of the Nova. Turning around his baseball cap with the brim to the back, Foshay yelled, "I've got the purse. Let's go, let's go." Armes rushed from the passenger side of the station wagon and jumped into the front seat of the Nova.

As the killer's car started to pull away from the shoulder, Helmuth got back into the station wagon and slammed the vehicle into reverse. Still cowering in the back seat as he felt the Oldsmobile backing up, Roy suddenly heard his uncle shout, "Put your head up and look." But when Roy tried to get the licence number of the car, which was now ten feet further away from them thanks to Helmuth's manoeuvre, he saw that it was covered. Strangely, when the men who had shot Hanna left the scene, they didn't appear to be in any rush. "They just drove off," the boy later recalled. "They didn't throw dirt or spin the tires."

Only then did Helmuth and Roy get out of the station wagon and run over to the guardrail. "Oh, my God, they shot her," Helmuth cried. His nephew jumped over the metal cable in his stocking feet and ran over to his aunt, who was lying face-down in the mud, her white sandals lying in a puddle. "She had a bullet hole in her left temple area," he said later. "There was no blood coming from the bullet hole. It was a reddish colour hole. She didn't say anything. She was jerking."

Helmuth never approached his wife's body. Roy quickly rejoined his uncle and they scrambled onto the highway to flag down help. The first westbound vehicle, a stake-body truck that had just come onto the highway from County Road 14, nearly ran Helmuth down as it thundered by. But help was on the way.

Colin Lawrence, a professional trucker with thirty years experience on the roads of southern Ontario, was travelling westbound on Highway 402 when he noticed two people standing beside a brown station wagon on the north shoulder of the road. He watched as a young boy went over the guardrail and down around a cement pillar before rejoining his companion. The second person, a middle-aged man, walked towards the rear of the station wagon and then began waving at oncoming traffic. Lawrence braked his tractor-trailer to a stop four feet behind the station wagon. The older man tried unsuccessfully to open the passenger door and then ran around to the driver's side of cab.

"Do you have a CB?" the man asked.

"No, what's your problem?" Lawrence inquired.

"My wife's been shot," the man said.

"What!" the astonished trucker replied.

"Yeah, two guys shot my wife."

"Where is she?" Lawrence asked.

"Over there," Helmuth answered, pointing towards the trestle.

As Lawrence vaulted over the guardrail, Helmuth told him that she had been shot in the head. The trucker rushed over to the fallen women, halting for a stomach-tightening moment when he saw her twisted body lying on the ground. Blood was now coming out of her mouth and nose, as well as from the hole in her temple. Lawrence could see that she was still breathing, and found a faint pulse in her neck.

Afraid that she would choke on her own blood, he tilted Hanna's head to the right with the wound up. Helmuth wanted to load Hanna into the station wagon and take her to the hospital, but the experienced trucker insisted that the injured woman not be moved. Knowing how badly she needed help, Lawrence raced back onto the highway to flag down another vehicle. There wasn't any westbound traffic, but he noticed an eastbound tractor-trailer and started waving frantically at its driver.

"How long ago did this happen?" he asked Helmuth, as the other truck began to gear down.

"A little while ago, a light blue car," Helmuth answered, explaining that he hadn't been able to see the licence plate number because it had been covered.

By now, the eastbound tractor-trailer, an Imperial Oil tanker, was pulling to a stop on the south shoulder of the highway. When he opened the door of his cab, Alec Johns was greeted by a desperate request:

"Have you got a radio, this man's wife has been shot. We need an ambulance and the OPP. She has been shot in the head," Lawrence said.

"You're kidding," the incredulous trucker replied.

"Two men in a blue car just shot my wife. They just shot my wife," Helmuth said, telling the others that they had been after her money and jewellery.

Johns noticed that the boy seemed to be in shock, repeating over and over again, "I don't believe it." Johns first tried to raise the OPP on channel 9. In desperation, he switched to channel 19, the trucker's emergency frequency, hoping to contact a CB base station, finally reaching a pair of CBers known as "Tiny Bubbles" and "Lucky Lynn." The women promised to alert the authorities and to bring help to the scene of the shooting.

Just then, Johns noticed a car backing up on the south shoulder of the 402. A man got out and ran over to ask what had happened. When the others explained, Mark Halden, a trained medic, rushed back to his car to get a first-aid kit. With Lawrence leading the way, the two men ran across the 402 towards Hanna. Helmuth and Roy momentarily remained behind talking to Alec Johns, who managed to flag down a tow-truck. Its driver, Daniel Kerslake, crossed the highway to see for himself what had happened, and then ran back to his truck to get blankets and a pillow. His face was chalk white.

Mark Halden found Hanna Buxbaum lying face down in the mud with her legs partially drawn up and blood pouring from the wounds in her head and upper arm. He placed a pad under her head and cleared her air passages to ease her laboured breathing. Halden noticed Helmuth standing on the other side of the guardrail with Roy, looking "cool, detached, plastic." Unaware that Helmuth was the husband of the injured woman, he told him to "drive like hell" to Strathroy to get a doctor and ambulance. "Stratford?" Helmuth inquired. "No," an exasperated Colin Lawrence replied, "*Strathroy.*"

As Lawrence watched Helmuth and Roy drive off, he couldn't help shaking his head. The veteran trucker had seen a lot of different reactions from people whose relatives had been seriously injured or killed on the highway, but never anything like this. There had been many times when he had had to pry relatives away from an accident victim, but Helmuth Buxbaum had not once crossed the guardrail to check on his wife's condition or offer her comfort. Nor, in Lawrence's opinion, had he helped very much in getting her medical assistance. Now he was leaving her in the care of total strangers, with no assurance that she would be alive the next time he saw her. But what troubled him most was Helmuth's coolness, hardly the reaction one would have expected from a man who had just witnessed robbers shoot his wife.

Brushing aside his misgivings, Lawrence hurried over to assist the group of people who were now attending to Hanna Buxbaum. Mark Halden wrapped Hanna's head in a bandage and placed a pillow under her abdomen to keep her on her side. Daniel Kerslake folded one blanket over her legs and another across her shoulders. Everyone felt sick in the pit of their stomach at the sight of the widening pool of blood around Hanna's head. A few moments later, an ambulance arrived, and the truckers helped the attendants load the mortally wounded woman into the back. Mark Halden packed up his first-aid kit and climbed in beside her for the trip to Victoria Hospital in London.

As the ambulance pulled away, with its lights flashing and siren blaring, Helmuth Buxbaum was nowhere in sight.

Const. Roger Aisladie got news of the shooting on his police scanner at 7:36 P.M. He immediately parked his cruiser on the median of Highway 402 at the intersection of County Road 39, hoping to spot the blue car that early reports said had fled the crime scene heading west. Less than a minute after he parked, a brown station wagon screeched to a halt in front of him. He got out of his cruiser and ran across the highway, where he met Helmuth and Roy. Helmuth told the officer that his wife had been shot, and Aisladie assured him that help was already on its way. After Helmuth gave him more details about the suspects' car, Aisladie radioed the information to his dispatcher. He then pressed Helmuth for a better description of the two men in the car, and a brief account of what had happened after the Buxbaums had pulled over to offer assistance. "I can tell you, that will be the last time I stop and try to help anyone," Helmuth said.

Like Colin Lawrence, Constable Aisladie was struck by Helmuth's demeanour. He seemed cool and collected, never once asking the policeman to check on his wife's condition. There was no self-recrimination, no tears, just a "very patient" man answering the policeman's questions, one after another. "He did not seem as upset as I would have imagined a husband to be who [had] seen his wife shot," Aisladie noted.

When he radioed in the information Helmuth had given him about the two suspects, Aisladie was told to stay with the victim's husband until other officers picked him up for questioning. Moments later, constables

Chris Lewis and Mike Rutigliano arrived from the scene of the shooting and Helmuth was introduced to the cold realities of professional police work. Acting on the orders of Const. Greg Calcott, who had taken charge of the investigation at the scene, they impounded Helmuth's station wagon and called a tow-truck to transport the vehicle to OPP headquarters for expert examination. They explained to Helmuth that he and Roy would have to come to the police station for questioning. In keeping with an OPP policy of searching anyone who rides in its cruisers for weapons, the Buxbaums were quickly frisked and then put in the back seat of the police car. Helmuth, who was sweating heavily, asked the officers to open the passenger windows. At 8:20 P.M., Milliken's Towing arrived and hooked up the station wagon. Lewis gingerly opened the door and turned off the lights, careful not to disturb potential evidence. The police then escorted the tow-truck back to the London Detachment.

During the ride, Constable Lewis asked Helmuth to describe what had happened. After relating a patchwork account of the roadside shooting, Helmuth said that he didn't want Roy going home and telling the family about Hanna before he, Helmuth, had a chance to speak to his children. Lewis told him that he could call any relatives he wished from the police station. On reflection, Helmuth said he would rather talk to his pastor to get advice on how to handle the dreadful task ahead of him.

The three vehicles arrived at London Detachment at 8:42 P.M. Constable Rutigliano took charge of the Buxbaum station wagon, guarding it until just after midnight, when he and another constable sealed it in an OPP garage to await the attention of experts from the Identification Unit. Lewis escorted the Buxbaums into the police station, where Roy was questioned while Helmuth called Pastor Paul Fawcett. Although he normally called his spiritual mentor several times a week, under the pressure of the moment he forgot his telephone number and had to look it up. Call after call, he was greeted with a busy signal.

Ten minutes after arriving at the police station, Helmuth and Constable Lewis headed for London's Victoria Hospital to check on the condition of Hanna Buxbaum. There was no need for them to rush. From the moment the ambulance carrying her inert body had arrived at the hospital just after 8 P.M., the head of the emergency unit, Dr. Robert Anthony, knew that there was little hope. The unconscious woman had no vital signs or blood pressure, but Dr. Anthony and four other surgeons tried desperately to bring her back to life. Fifty minutes later, the emergency team stopped administering drugs, and Dr. Anthony ordered an end to the heart massage. Hanna Buxbaum was pronounced medically dead at 8:52 P.M.

Helmuth was in the waiting room with two OPP officers, Chris Lewis and Richard Pellarin, when Dr. Anthony introduced himself and broke the news. The widower's first reaction seemed one of disbelief. Then Helmuth asked why Hanna hadn't been taken to University Hospital where all the specialists were. "I mentioned something about Reagan's press secretary [James Brady] who had been shot in the head and lived. I thought it could be the same for Hanna."

Dr. Anthony once again expressed his regrets, assuring the bereaved man that every possible procedure had been tried to save his wife's life. Helmuth finally broke down, but Constable Lewis, who was watching him closely, noted that there were no tears. When he stopped sobbing, Helmuth looked at the doctor and said, "We have six children."

The grieving husband was left alone with the doctor and a nurse to compose himself before police began taking his formal statement. Helmuth repeatedly asked the doctor for a sedative. In the five minutes they spent together, Dr. Anthony's "sixth sense" told him there was something wrong with the whole situation. Like Colin Lawrence and Constable Aisladie, the doctor couldn't help noticing Helmuth's remarkably unemotional reaction. He had seen stoicism in the face of tragedy before, and was even familiar with Teutonic reserve, but this was different.

At 9:15 P.M., Dr. Anthony and his nurse emerged from the small room where they had been comforting Helmuth and told the waiting police officers that he wanted to see his wife's body. Everyone proceeded to the emergency room, where Hanna's corpse lay on a stretcher under a sheet. At a nod from Dr. Anthony, the nurse slowly drew back the cover to reveal the murdered woman's face, a gruesome death mask spattered with blood and dirt, the mouth agape. "I don't want to remember her like that," Helmuth shouted. "Cover her up!"

He ran out of the room and again demanded a sedative. After asking Constable Lewis to call Pastor Fawcett on his behalf, Helmuth returned to the quiet room with Constable Pellarin to begin his formal statement.

Before the questioning began, Pellarin asked Helmuth if he needed more time to pull himself together. Helmuth assured him that he was all right and, at 9:20 P.M., for the fifth time that night, he began to describe what had happened. But he was curiously short on details, or so it seemed to the experienced investigator. "Throughout the statement, I had to continually ask questions in order to get a better description of the day's activities and details of the incident. Buxbaum seemed very vague when it came to detail," the police officer noted.

Fifteen minutes after it began, the session was interrupted by the arrival of Pastor Fawcett, his wife, Violet, their daughter, and her boyfriend. Fawcett had assumed that the whole Buxbaum family would be at the hospital, and had brought his own family along to comfort them. As he was embraced by his pastor, Helmuth began to sob; Constable Lewis again observed that there were no tears. Helmuth wanted Fawcett to tell the Buxbaum children what had happened before Roy Buxbaum did. Convinced that this was Helmuth's duty, the clergyman gently insisted that they go to Komoka together once the police were finished with their routine questions.

Pastor Fawcett sat quietly in the room, listening to Helmuth tell Constable Pellarin how Hanna had died. At first, the grim tale of robbery and murder made his blood run cold. He could almost picture her attacker terrorizing the poor woman for her purse and jewellery before dragging her out of the car and shooting her in cold blood. But the more detail Helmuth went into, the more questions began occurring to Fawcett. Why hadn't Helmuth challenged his wife's assailant? Why hadn't he sped away when the robber had closed the back door and started for the front of the car? No matter how you looked at it, one thing was puzzlingly clear: throughout the entire calamity, Helmuth had done nothing to protect his wife from a man he said he thought was wielding a toy gun.

For as long as he could remember, Ron Piers had always wanted to be a policeman or a professional athlete. An avid baseball and basketball player, he had ultimately chosen to join the police. Most days he was happy about his decision, but lately he was beginning to wonder. Ever since his recent promotion to the London Unit of the OPP's Criminal Investigation Branch, Piers' daughter and son had been upset about their imminent move from Georgetown to London, and there had been more than a few tears shed around the Piers household as the day drew nearer.

A career policeman, the forty-one-year-old native of Pugwash, Nova Scotia, had moved many times since the day in 1964 when he joined the RCMP. During his two years with the national police force, he served in Nova Scotia, Newfoundland, and Quebec, before leaving for a job in Chatham, Ontario, with the OPP. That same year, he married Judy

McKay, his high-school sweetheart from Tatamagouche, Nova Scotia. Over the years, Piers had worked his way steadily up the promotional ladder, exhibiting a ferocious work ethic learned from his earliest days at home.

By 1979, Piers had shown sufficient flare for criminal investigations that he was transferred to the OPP's Anti-Rackets Branch as an acting Detective Sergeant. He enjoyed the methodical process of building a case and had unusually well developed "people skills," the result, perhaps, of growing up in a household with eight brothers and sisters.

All of his talents as a policeman were tested to the limit in his first big assignment, the $100-million Astra Trust bankruptcy. After a long and painstaking investigation into the Niagara Falls company, Piers was part of the investigative team that charged financier and real estate mogul Carlo Montemurro with fraud. Montemurro's preliminary hearing alone lasted a full year. He was eventually convicted and sentenced to ten years in prison. Piers worked on the case from the spring of 1979 to the early summer of 1984, a marathon assignment that convinced him that when it came to fraud investigation, with its long hours and months without apparent results, there was no substitute for hard work. "You learn to take one little piece of information, keep going with all kinds of other pieces of information, and eventually, down the road, watch as they develop into the full picture."

It was a fitting *modus operandi* for the assignment of his life. On the evening of July 5, 1984, Detective Inspector Piers was getting ready for bed when the phone rang in his Georgetown kitchen. It was Tom O'Grady, the director of the Criminal Investigation Branch, the man who had been instrumental in bringing Piers into the CIB as an inspector. O'Grady explained that there had been a serious shooting and robbery in London, and asked Piers to head up the investigation.

"Do you think you can handle it?" O'Grady rasped.

"Well you brought me into the branch, so *you* must think I can handle it. Yes, I can handle it," Piers replied.

After packing clothes for what he thought would be two days away from home, Piers slid in behind the wheel of his unmarked cruiser and started out on the two-hour drive to the London Detachment. Despite his answer to O'Grady, he was nervous about assuming control of his first criminal investigation as case manager. "I'm wondering in my own mind, 'Are the other officers going to have confidence in my being able

to handle this case? Am I going to portray that confidence to them?'
Because that's what you have to do."

The butterflies in his stomach got busier just after midnight when Piers
arrived at London Detachment to learn that the victim of the apparent
shooting-robbery had died; he was now in charge of a murder investigation.

It would be forty hours before he slept.

At 10:10 P.M. Helmuth finished giving his statement, and Constable Pellarin spoke to the coroner for twenty minutes before asking Paul Fawcett
to confirm the identity of the victim. With Helmuth waiting outside the
door of the emergency room, Fawcett and Pellarin examined the body a
final time before it was moved to the hospital morgue, where it would be
guarded all night by Constable Lewis. It was imperative that nothing be
disturbed until Hanna's remains made the journey to the OPP's headquarters in Toronto for examination by forensic experts. The attending nurse
gave Fawcett Hanna's necklace, watch, and engagement ring after he
made the identification.

As Helmuth got ready to leave with Fawcett and Roy, Pellarin
informed him that he would have to come back to the OPP's London
Detachment to give a more detailed statement. The policeman was still
not satisfied with Helmuth's sketchy account, and didn't want to release
him until he had gathered all the information he could. For the third time,
Helmuth asked Dr. Anthony for a sedative and was finally given a package
containing two tablets of Serax. Even though Pellarin didn't want him to
take any medication before he completed his next statement, Helmuth
swallowed one of the pills before leaving the hospital at 10:40 P.M.

On the way back to the OPP detachment with Constable Pellarin (Pastor Fawcett followed on his own), Helmuth asked if he could retrieve his
briefcase and the fifty pounds of halibut that were still in his car. Pellarin
explained that the station wagon was off limits until the police identification experts had combed it for evidence. They arrived back at detachment at 10:55 P.M. Pellarin left Helmuth with Fawcett while he spoke to
the officers who had taken Roy Buxbaum's statement. It was an hour
before Pellarin returned to lead Helmuth into the OPP's Crime Office for
what would be his sixth and final statement of the evening.

Throughout most of the next hour, Helmuth was anxious to leave,
protesting that he didn't want to keep Pastor Fawcett waiting any longer

than necessary and wanted to be with his family. He appeared tired to Constable Pellarin and generally indifferent about what had happened. Just after midnight, two other officers arrived to apply the standard "hand wash" test the police administer to everyone involved in a shooting incident to see if they have been recently exposed to gunpowder.

Pellarin then made Helmuth go through the whole story, starting from the time he drove to Toronto that morning at 9 A.M., until he met Const. Roger Aisladie on the median of Highway 402 at 7:37 P.M. When he signed his statement at 1:15 A.M., it contained the number of the parking level the Buxbaums had used at Pearson International Airport, Roy's flight number from Vancouver, and even what Helmuth had had to drink when the Buxbaums stopped at McDonald's on the way home from the airport. What it did not contain was any reference to the morning stop behind a blue Nova on the eastbound lanes of the 402.

After he signed his statement, Helmuth joined Pastor Fawcett, who was sitting with Roy Buxbaum in the lobby of the OPP building. Genuinely touched by the tragedy, Pellarin expressed his deepest condolences to Helmuth. Helmuth was just about to leave when Pellarin stopped him one last time. Standing beside the uniformed OPP officer was a slight man in civilian clothes with thinning, slicked-back hair and a neatly trimmed moustache. Pellarin introduced Helmuth to Det. Insp. Ron Piers. Helmuth looked just about as Piers would have expected – haggard, rumpled, "a person who had just gone through the mill." When the detective spoke, his words came softly.

"I just wanted to tell you how sorry I am, and that I'll do everything in my power to find the people who did this."

"I appreciate that," Helmuth replied.

The two men looked into each other's eyes as they shook hands and then headed off for the dread tasks ahead of them; for Buxbaum, the journey home to tell his children that they no longer had a mother; for Piers, a 2 A.M. visit to Highway 402 to make sure that the murder scene was properly secured and all short-lived evidence had been gathered.

It would be a sleepless night for both of them.

The killers would not be caught this night. With the puffs of white smoke from Foshay's .32 revolver still floating above the murder scene, the pair had driven off down Highway 402 with their victim's purse on the seat between them. They exited at Highway 81 and drove north to Hickory

Corner, and then east towards London. Armes was furious at Foshay's choice of an escape route when he looked out the window and saw that they were passing the tiny OPP Detachment at Strathroy.

Two kilometres past the police station, Foshay jammed on the brakes and jumped out of the car. Running to the rear of the Nova, he ripped off the green felt pad covering the licence plate and threw it in the ditch. Back behind the wheel, Foshay knew exactly what he had to do next: ditch the car, get rid of Hanna's purse, and most important of all, dispose of the murder weapon.

Shortly after 7:30 P.M., Gary Foshay pulled into the driveway of the London home of his estranged wife, Robin. The couple had married in 1977 and separated five years later, largely because of Gary's violent temper. Robin, whose nose Gary had once broken, now lived on mother's allowance with their two daughters, Melissa and Aimee. In the past two and a half years, Gary had regularly visited his children, but had given Robin only $300 towards their support. Still, fatherhood conferred its privileges, and Gary Foshay now exercised a big one.

Both men looked edgy to Robin Foshay when they came into the house through the back door. Foshay immediately asked for cleaning supplies and headed back out to the car, where Armes began wiping down the inside of the Nova. Moving into the garage, Foshay called to his wife to bring him a garbage bag, then asked her to hold open an ivory-coloured woman's purse while he riffled through its contents. He removed everything of value, including a pair of gold sleeper earrings with floating hearts that belonged to Esther Buxbaum, and a large quantity of coins. Without a word, Foshay scooped up the coins and poured them into a glass jar. Robin noticed a driver's licence inside the bag bearing the name Hanna Buxbaum of Komoka, Ontario. She looked quizzically at her husband, ready for anything but what happened next: the street-hardened tough guy suddenly began to cry. "He said he'd really done it this time," Robin Foshay said later. "He told me not to say anything to anybody, or he'd have to do me too."

After checking with Armes on how the cleaning of the car was going, Foshay hid Hanna's purse above the garage door. Armes buried the jar of coins in Robin's backyard. Finally, they dragged an orange tarpaulin out of the garage and pulled it over the Nova. Tossing the keys into the mouth of a porcelain frog sitting on the window sill, Foshay told his wife not to drive the car, explaining that someone would be by the next day to pick it up as he would be going to Toronto in the morning to collect some money. Before leaving, he went back to the house and gave the earrings he had taken from Hanna's purse to his daughter Melissa.

Their work complete, the killers headed for the apartment of Kathy Laine, one of Foshay's many girlfriends. Armes took a shower and Foshay hung up the leather jacket he had worn at the murder scene, telling Laine's father that its owner would be stopping by to get it in a day or two. It was now time to hit the Wellington Tavern for a badly needed drink.

Around 9 P.M., Foshay called Pat Allen from the bar and asked if he and Armes could drop by for a visit. Half an hour later, they showed up at his door with a case of beer. When Allen opened the door, Armes winked and held his hand in the shape of a gun, nodding his head. Foshay called the Westbury Hotel to tell Robert Barrett that the hit had gone down, and that the boys would be coming to Toronto in the morning to collect their money.

After a few beers, Foshay asked Allen if he wanted to party, but the former ringleader of the murder plot declined. Foshay and Armes left to go drinking. As they walked over the Rideout Street bridge, Foshay reached under his shirt and pulled out the .32 revolver that was still stuck in his belt. Checking to see if anyone was watching, he tossed the gun into the Thames River. With the car and the murder weapon taken care of, and Hanna's purse hidden for the time being in his wife's garage, it was time for a little fun. After closing down the bar, Foshay and Armes went to a house party with people they had never met before. When the beer ran out, Armes headed over to Kim Drennan's, his ex-wife's cousin, where he spent the night. Although he was living at his brother's house, Foshay returned to Pat Allen's.

Trent Foshay's wife didn't like it when Gary came in after midnight. This way, the killer thought, he wouldn't get into trouble for waking up the kids.

The first inkling that there might be substance to the dark premonition Rosita Buxbaum had felt on the morning of July 5 came early that same night. All day she had felt strangely uneasy, and when the Buxbaums hadn't shown up or called by 9 P.M., she began to worry. When the phone finally rang at Komoka at 9:30 P.M., she felt relieved. But when it turned out to be Pastor Paul Fawcett instead of Hanna or Helmuth, her sense of foreboding flooded back. Without telling her why, the clergyman said that he and his family would be coming over that night for a visit. He then spoke briefly with Paul Buxbaum before hanging up.

While Rosita prepared tea and cookies for the mysterious visit, Paul walked into the den where Phillip and Esther were watching television and abruptly switched off the set, just as Pastor Fawcett had instructed. He then checked the entire house to make sure that no radios were playing. Whatever he did, Pastor Fawcett had told him, he was to keep the children from seeing or hearing any newscasts.

His task complete, Paul explained to his brothers and sisters that Pastor Fawcett was coming to Komoka for an important visit. After an hour passed and Fawcett still hadn't appeared, Paul sent Esther to bed. Gradually, the three eldest sons concluded that Roy's flight must have been delayed and that Pastor Fawcett had been distracted by church business. After sipping tea and nibbling at the cookies Aunt Rosita had prepared they went to bed.

At 1 A.M., just before Helmuth and Roy got into Pastor Fawcett's car for the short drive from London to Komoka, the clergyman called Phil and Chris Conley and asked them to meet him on the road in front of the Buxbaums' Komoka estate. During the ride home, Helmuth kept falling asleep. By 1:20 A.M. both cars had arrived at the house, where a few lights were still burning. Helmuth was awakened, and the group proceeded slowly up the driveway to tell the children.

After sending Roy to bed, and with his suitcase still in his hand, Helmuth opened his sister-in-law's bedroom door and poked his head inside.

"We were worried," Rosita said. "Where's Hanna?"

"She's not coming," Helmuth replied, motioning to her to follow him.

In the dining room, Pastor Fawcett and the Conleys were barely visible in the light of a small lamp hanging above the piano. One by one, the older Buxbaum children filed in, still woozy from their interrupted sleep. It had been decided that the younger children should not be told until morning. Mark knew something terrible had happened when he saw his father sitting on one of the dining-room chairs, sobbing. "I had never seen my father cry before," Mark said later. "I didn't see my mother or Roy in the room. I got apprehensive."

When they were all there, Paul Fawcett leaned forward from his seat on the piano bench and finally ended the suspense. He told them about the roadside robbery that had ended in Hanna's death, giving the details of the attack just as Helmuth had related the story to him a few hours earlier.

"Your mother has gone home to the Lord," the clergyman told them. "She is already in heaven."

Shock momentarily paralysed everyone in the room. Mark glanced helplessly from face to face, first at his brother Phillip, who was crying, and then at his Aunt Rosita, who began swaying silently back and forth in her chair.

"My dad said, 'It's fortunate that I'm home. Roy's okay . . . There could have been three caskets. It was by the grace of God that we are still alive,'" Mark later remembered.

Helmuth, who appeared to Rosita Buxbaum to be deeply confused, began talking disjointedly about the plans he and Hanna had been making for their silver wedding anniversary. After a few sentences, he began nodding off, feeling the effects of two nights of cocaine-induced wakefulness and the Serax tablet he had taken at the hospital. Rosita, Phillip, and Mark went to bed after Pastor Fawcett left, and Helmuth now said good-night to the Conleys, who remained behind talking to Paul. But his empty marriage bed provided no rest this night. "I drifted in and out of sleep," Helmuth said later. "I was very depressed . . . I just wanted to die. I remembered that my shotgun was in the sitting room adjoining the bedroom. A thought had crossed my mind that I could just blow my brains out and I wouldn't have to face this mess."

Slipping his trousers on over his pyjamas, he started down to the fallout shelter at 3 A.M., only to be surprised by Paul who was still in the TV room talking to the Conleys. Afraid that his father might harm himself (either with the guns that were stored in the shelter, or by an overdose of cocaine), Paul demanded that Helmuth turn over his key to the shelter. Helmuth handed him the key ring he was carrying, minus the key in question, and defiantly continued on his way.

Unable to sleep, he tried to get into the shelter's large supply of alcohol, but Hanna stopped him. Aware of Helmuth's alcohol abuse, she had secured the liquor in a cabinet with a special chain lock to preserve it for its intended purpose – trading for other necessities of life in the event of a nuclear war. Frustrated, Helmuth turned to the gun cases that held the small arsenal recommended by his survivalist tutors, once more considering suicide.

In the end, he reached for a syringe rather than a rifle. Opening a small desk where he kept his cocaine, Helmuth expertly prepared a shot of forgetfulness. Equipped with a large elastic band to tie off his leg, and a jar of vitamin E cream that would help erase the needle marks, he pulled up a chair in front of the television and made himself comfortable. For the next three hours he injected himself with cocaine every twenty minutes, staring mindlessly at the television screen.

He was watching the news channel, but all he saw was Hanna's face.

10

THE BILL

"It was either me or Rob that gave out the envelopes. Gary
got the $5,000, Terry . . . got $3,500, and I had my $1,000."
— *Pat Allen, on the distribution of the murder money, July 6, 1984*

The morning after her murder, Hanna and the men who had killed her set out for Toronto within twenty minutes of each other, their final destinations separated by only a few city blocks.

The hearse from McNiece's Funeral Home arrived more than an hour before the CN train carrying Foshay, Armes, and Allen. It pulled into the cavernous garage under the OPP's general headquarters at 90 Harbour Street at 1:45 P.M. Dr. Archie Grace, London's coroner, had decided that, in the circumstances, it was better to conduct the post-mortem examination of Hanna's remains at the Centre of Forensic Science (CFS) in Toronto. Ron Piers, who had been working on the murder case all night, agreed.

The body was immediately taken upstairs to be photographed and checked for fingerprints. Still fully clothed, Hanna was removed from her white plastic shroud and placed on the examination table on a sheet of brown paper. Under the watchful eye of Det. Insp. William McGregor, a Toronto-based investigator, Hanna's body was carefully undressed. Every article of clothing, from her muddied white sandals to her bra, was placed in a separate plastic bag by Corp. H. E. McNally of the Identification Unit. As McNally collected the exhibits, Const. Chris Lewis made up a numbered tag and placed it directly into the bag with the evidence. McNally also took photographs of the body. Every time his shutter clicked, constables Calcott and Lewis recorded the particulars of the shot in their notebooks.

Fifteen minutes after the examination began, Finn Nielson, a CFS firearms expert, arrived. He watched patiently as the officers from the Identification Unit completed their work, conducting a hand-wash test and collecting loose hairs from the body, including a single grey strand found beside the bullet wound on Hanna's left arm. They also took control samples of Hanna's hair for later comparison with the loose hairs found on the body or in the suspect vehicle, should it ever be recovered. Before turning the remains over to OPP technicians for detailed fingerprint examination, Corporal McNally took a tape lift from the left side of the victim's face that would pick up any gunshot residues, as well as fingernail scrapings from both hands in the event Hanna had been able to scratch her assailant.

After the exhibits were packaged and boxed, Donald Huwka conducted a laser examination, training a brilliant beam of light over every square centimetre of the body in the hope of turning up foreign objects. The grim business of gathering all possible evidence now complete, Hanna's body was taken back to the OPP garage and loaded into the hearse for the short trip to the CFS's pathology building on nearby Granville Street, where the autopsy would take place.

Just after 6 P.M., Dr. Richard Hutson, a pathologist from Toronto's East General Hospital, began the post-mortem examination of Hanna Buxbaum. After a series of photographs and x-rays were taken, Dr. Hutson placed a probe through the centre of the wound on her left temple to show the angle of travel the bullet had taken through her brain. Having established the cause of death as a gunshot wound to the head, he also removed a piece of bone containing lead fragments, possibly embedded there when the bullet ricocheted off the right side of Hanna's skull.

An hour into the autopsy, Dr. Hutson removed a .32-calibre slug from the deceased, the piece of evidence that Finn Nielson had been waiting for so that he could conduct some critical tests of his own. After gathering samples of various body fluids, removing the liver, and taking Hanna's fingerprints, Dr. Hutson finished his work.

Having yielded up all that it could to help police investigators capture her killers, Hanna's body was again loaded into the McNiece's hearse for the journey back to London, where she would be buried three days later.

The afternoon of July 6 began with a wake-up call Robert Barrett would never forget.

As soon as their train had squeaked to a stop at Union Station, Foshay, Allen, and Armes hurried to Front Street, where they hailed a cab to the Westbury Hotel. Without announcing their presence, they took the elevator straight to the fourteenth-floor suites Barrett had rented. Even though he had been alerted by earlier telephone calls that the killers were coming to present their bill, the master-mind of the Hanna Buxbaum murder was sound asleep when they arrived. Shaking him out of his drug-induced stupor, his angry accomplices demanded their money for the hit.

"Hold on, I just woke up," he protested. He was surprised to see Terry Armes in the room, and more than a little discomfited. Just a year before, Armes had held a knife to Barrett's throat and strip-searched him, looking for money he suspected Squirrel had stolen from a friend.

"Where's Jan?" Allen demanded.

"Where's the rings?" Barrett countered, hoping that the killers had remembered to keep Hanna's jewellery, which he believed was worth as much as $20,000. Exasperated with Barrett's evasiveness, Allen went looking for Janet Hicks. After he left, Gary Foshay and Terry Armes took a harder line with the man who had apparently contracted a murder that he didn't have the funds to pay for. They dragged him out of bed, expressing their displeasure as forcefully as they could without actually killing him. Hearing Barrett's screams, Pat Allen rushed back to see what was going on. "I came in the room and watched them hang him over the balcony . . . I knew they were mad."

Dangling by his ankles fourteen stories above the sidewalk, Robert Barrett got the message. After Allen and Rick Diorio persuaded Foshay and Armes to pull their captive back on to the balcony, Barrett quickly promised to get in touch with Helmuth Buxbaum to get their money. As usual, he tried to get someone else to take on the risky job of making the contact. This time, the lucky candidate was his wife, Kelly.

In London, Debbie Barber and Kelly Barrett had been buying eggs and milk at a corner store, when Barber happened to pick up a newspaper with a banner headline about Hanna Buxbaum's murder. She immediately connected Rob and Helmuth from their meeting at her apartment and angrily threw the paper at her companion. "What's going down here?" she demanded to know. Kelly read the article and, remembering the encounter with Ringuette and McCurdy in Florida, blanched.

At Debbie's apartment, the collect calls soon began arriving from the

Westbury Hotel. After Kelly got off the telephone, she told Barber that Barrett wanted her to get in touch with "Andy," the code name he used for Helmuth to fool Treugott's snoopy office staff and Helmuth's family. She was to tell him to get Rob more money, "because he is sitting in a room with three guns pointed at his head." Kelly refused to call Helmuth, and Barber herself hung up on Barrett when he called collect a second and third time. Squirrel now had just two choices: the telephone or the balcony.

It was not the best timed telephone call Robert Barrett had ever placed. Helmuth was standing beside the casket he had chosen for his wife (the simplest oak coffin the undertaker had) when Pastor Paul Fawcett walked into the basement of Needham's Funeral Home and told him he was wanted on the phone. Picking up the receiver in the reception area, the grieving widower was expecting another heartfelt condolence and was dumbfounded when he recognized Barrett's voice on the other end of the line. It was all Helmuth could do to control his temper while Barrett talked. Blurting out his desperate situation, Barrett begged Helmuth to bring $20,000 to the London airport at 7:30 P.M. that night.

After Barrett got off the phone, another argument broke out amongst the conspirators. Foshay and Allen didn't trust Barrett to collect the money on his own, but they themselves didn't want to risk a meeting with Helmuth less than twenty-four hours after murdering Hanna. Pat Allen, who was taking a surprisingly active role for someone who had bailed out of the murder plot, worked out a compromise. He would send Janet Hicks with Barrett to meet Buxbaum and *she* would make sure that Squirrel turned right around and flew back to Toronto as soon as the payoff was made. The killers reluctantly agreed.

At 5:19 P.M., Barrett quietly placed another call, this time to Lenny Peltier, a truck driver who dabbled in drugs, asking him to meet him at London airport with half an ounce of cocaine. Running behind schedule thanks to a last-minute shopping expedition by Janet Hicks, "Mr. and Mrs. Barrett" took a cab to Pearson International Airport to catch a flight and keep their appointment with Helmuth Buxbaum.

Knowing that the youngest of the Buxbaum children still didn't know about the murder of their mother, Pastor Paul Fawcett arrived at Komoka early on the morning of July 6, frowning as he saw the throng of reporters assembled on the front lawn. Helmuth was still sleeping, but the Conleys had spent the night at the house and were still comforting family members when the pastor walked into the recreation room. Esther had been awakened by Phillip Buxbaum at 6 A.M. and told about her mother. At first, she had thought it was just another of her older brother's sick jokes, but reality had quickly set in. "I was so shocked. I cried. I used a whole box of Kleenex," the then Grade 9 student remembered.

At word of his mother's death, twelve-year-old Danny Buxbaum had fallen deathly silent, huddling alone on the couch with a blanket pulled over his head.

When he finally climbed out of the fallout shelter at 11 A.M. on July 6 high on cocaine for the third straight day, Helmuth made his way upstairs, where he found that Pastor Fawcett, Phil Conley, Gizella Toth, Rosita Buxbaum, and the children were already grappling with the aftermath of the tragedy. Helmuth directed that the relatives be informed and that funeral arrangements be worked out. (His brother Otto had learned about Hanna's death when he called from Detroit on his way from Florida, and was now en route to Komoka with Douglas Buxbaum.)

Although Helmuth wanted Hanna's service conducted by the same funeral director in Mount Brydges who had buried his mother in 1980, Pastor Fawcett recommended the Needham Funeral Home in London, pointing out that it would be closer for most of the mourners. Helmuth agreed, and after satisfying himself that the children knew the appropriate relatives to call, set out for the funeral home with Pastor Fawcett.

They stopped briefly at Treugott, where Helmuth waited in the office with Fawcett until the pharmacy across the street called to say the prescription of Serax given to him by Dr. Anthony the previous night was ready to be picked up. Afterwards, they drove to Needham's, where the resident mortician assured Helmuth that Hanna's body could be made sufficiently presentable to have an open-casket service. It was after Helmuth had gone downstairs to order a concrete burial vault that Robert Barrett had tracked him down. As curtly as possible, Helmuth agreed to bring the money to the London airport that night and promptly hung up.

After finishing their business at Needham's, Pastor Fawcett drove Helmuth home, stopping along the way to look at the Buxbaum's family plot in Campbell Cemetery. When the pastor left, Helmuth got into his van and drove into Byron, where he picked up a refund cheque for $798 from the Travel Bug travel agency. He then drove to London to collect the rest of the money Barrett had requested.

Unshaven and still dressed in the grey suit he had worn on the day of the murder, his first stop was at a branch of the TD Bank, where he cashed a $3,000 personal cheque. The teller, Jennifer Flatman, didn't have enough $100 bills to complete the transaction. While she was away gathering the money, Pamela Sharpe, the supervisor, offered her condolences to Helmuth. "I can't talk about it now, Pam," the unkempt widower brusquely replied. When Flatman returned, Helmuth stuffed the cash into an envelope and got another $400 on his VISA card after he discovered that the branch's banking machine was out of order.

When Helmuth walked into the Byron branch of Canada Trust an hour later, the teller he talked to, Casy Clarke, thought the businessman looked uncharacteristically nervous. He withdrew $3,400 from one account and then presented Clarke with a cheque for $8,496.41. It was Hanna's monthly income-equalizing annuity from Victoria and Grey Trust. The cheque was dated July 1, 1984, and had been endorsed by Hanna on July 4. Knowing that Mrs. Buxbaum had been murdered, Clarke took the cheque to her supervisor to discuss whether or not it should be honoured. After checking the signature, and taking into account who the customer was, it was decided to give Helmuth the money. Quietly patient throughout his twenty-minute wait at the counter, Helmuth asked Clarke to put $2,500 in an envelope and deposit the balance into his account. Eighteen hours after her death, Hanna Buxbaum was about to make a payment on her own murder.

The manager of Chris Brooker Coins was as surprised as Pamela Sharpe had been when Helmuth walked through the front door of his shop just after 4 P.M. Brooker couldn't imagine what Helmuth could be doing in the coin shop when he obviously had so many more important things to worry about. He was even more taken aback when Helmuth produced a five-ounce gold bar that he wished to sell.

Just over a month earlier, Helmuth had tried to cash in the same gold bar, but decided against the transaction because Brooker's price, $2,440, had been too low. Brooker now called Toronto for a new quote and didn't expect to be making any deals when it came in even lower than the earlier price at $2,260. To his amazement, Helmuth accepted his offer of $2,100, and walked out of the store with $700 in cash and an IOU for the remaining $1,400.

Helmuth completed his banking expedition by cashing his refund cheque from the travel agency and hitting a few more instant teller machines. By the time he headed back to Komoka to check on the funeral arrangements with other family members, he had amassed $13,000 for Hanna's impatient killers – $7,000 less than Barrett had requested. Satisfied that everything was in hand on the home front, he swallowed a Serax tablet and set out in his van for the airport. Despite his overnight fame, he didn't seem in the slightest concerned about what others might make of his dishevelled appearance, or his bizarre airport meeting with a known drug dealer so soon after his wife's murder.

Diane Tachauer was checking boarding passes for Air Ontario at Pearson International Airport's gate 74A when a young couple rushed up to her station out of breath and out of luck. They held tickets for the 6:50 P.M. flight to London, but moments earlier, their plane had taxied away from the terminal and joined the line of aircraft awaiting clearance for takeoff.

It was not the first time Tachauer had dealt with the frustrations of travellers who had missed their flight. But she was startled when Robert Barrett asked if he could charter a plane or a helicopter for the thirty-minute trip to London. She recommended that he wait for the next scheduled flight to London, which was departing in only forty minutes. The still impatient customer then asked for the latest departure time from London to Toronto that same night. Tachauer checked her computer and told him that Air Ontario's last flight back to Pearson Airport left London at 9:15 P.M., a mere fifty minutes after the couple would now arrive in London.

"That doesn't give you much time," she said, "It's not worthwhile."

"Oh it's worthwhile," Barrett said with a smile.

"It's well worth it," Hicks chimed in, winking at her companion.

Barrett asked to use the telephone to call a party waiting at the London airport. Explaining that she couldn't give him a free long-distance call, Tachauer took the party's name, Helmuth Buxbaum, and promised to have him paged by Air Canada personnel in London. When she asked what message she should leave, Barrett gave his new flight number and arrival time, as well as a phone number to call for more information. Squirrel's inexperience in the murder business was beginning to show.

Their revised travel plans completed, Barrett and Hicks left the gate area and Janet called the number they had just given, her own, and spoke to her sister, Karen. Barrett got on the line and told Karen to expect a call from Helmuth. He told her to explain that Squirrel had missed his flight and would be arriving an hour late. Barrett then phoned Lenny Peltier a second time to let his cocaine connection know he would now be meeting him at the London airport shortly after 8:30 P.M.

Meanwhile, back at gate 74A, Diane Tachauer was troubled. What sort of business or personal affair, she wondered, would prompt a scruffy man in Levis to want to charter a plane to another city when there was a commercial flight to the same destination leaving in less than an hour? And what could be so important that he needed just fifty minutes at that destination before turning around and flying back to Toronto?

Shortly after 7 P.M., she called airport security and asked to speak to the RCMP. Five minutes later, Const. Rex Jenkins appeared and the Air Canada employee explained her misgivings. Jenkins took up a position near the gate and jotted down a description of the Barretts in his notebook when they appeared at 7:25 P.M. to board their flight.

They would not be hard to spot. With a ring on every finger, four earrings in each ear, and heavy eye make-up, Janet Hicks looked to him like a "table dancer," an impression that was reinforced by her low-cut blouse, skin-tight jeans, and three-inch spiked high heels. At five foot ten, she towered over her younger companion, a scrawny man in jeans with dirty blond hair and a gold stud in his ear.

Jenkins called RCMP security at the London airport and spoke to Const. John Mark. Mark told his Toronto counterpart that Barrett was a well-known figure in London's petty crime scene. Police in both airports sniffed a possible drug deal in the air.

Even before Air Ontario flight 817 took off from Toronto, the police surveillance that would document the meeting between Robert Barrett and Helmuth Buxbaum the day after Hanna Buxbaum's murder was already in place.

With three envelopes containing $13,000 in cash stuffed into his jacket, Helmuth arrived at the airport well before the time Barrett had set for their meeting. Inside the terminal, he learned that all flights from Toronto were late because of a severe thunderstorm. Armed with several copies of the *London Free Press*, which he wanted to save because of their coverage of Hanna's murder, he settled down in the coffee shop to wait for Robert Barrett's flight.

Half an hour later, Helmuth wandered back to the waiting room, where he scanned the papers for reports of Hanna's murder before nodding off to sleep. His fitful dozing was suddenly interrupted by someone jostling his shoulder. It was his old friend, Dr. Cal Stiller, who was just returning from a business trip to Cleveland. Dr. Stiller had read the news of Hanna's murder on the plane and was stunned to see Helmuth sitting by himself at the airport so soon after the tragedy.

"What are you doing here, Helmuth?" he asked.

"Waiting for my nephew," Helmuth replied. Dr. Stiller thought he looked alarmed and confused.

"I was so sorry to hear about your wife's death," Stiller said.

"Yes, she deserved a better death than that," Helmuth sadly answered.

After Helmuth assured the doctor that he was all right, Stiller continued on his way to the washroom and then left the airport. Moments later, an announcement came over the public address system for Helmuth Buxbaum to proceed to the Air Canada counter for a message. After going to two or three locations, he was handed a written message to call Karen at the number indicated. Helmuth went to a pay phone and dialled the local number. A young girl answered.

"This is Helmuth Buxbaum," he said.

"Squirrel phoned and said he missed the plane," the voice said. "He will be in on the next one. He wants you to wait for him. He will be in at 8:30 P.M."

Without even knowing who he was talking to, Helmuth complained that he couldn't stay because his children were bound to worry about him. But after a sentence or two, his voice trailed off. He realized it was an appointment he couldn't afford to miss.

Many miles away, as the Stillers cruised towards Tillsonburg, Ontario, to visit a cousin, Mrs. Stiller expressed her concern about what she and her husband had just witnessed at the airport. "Surely this doesn't make sense," she told her husband. "He is alone waiting in a room, when his wife was destroyed and the children are at home."

Cal Stiller agreed that it seemed very strange. Concerned that his friend might be deranged with grief, he decided to call Pastor Paul Fawcett to let him know where Helmuth was and what he was doing. But the pastor had other Buxbaums to comfort and there was no answer at the rectory.

Const. John Mark was already positioned by the airport gift shop, his normal surveillance location for incoming flights, when Robert Barrett and Janet Hicks walked into the terminal at 8:30 P.M. to meet Helmuth Buxbaum. Recognizing Mark as a police officer, Hicks nudged Robert Barrett.

"There's a friend for you," she joked.

"Stand here and wait for me," Barrett answered.

The RCMP officer kept Barrett under visual surveillance, talking nonchalantly to airport employees and various travellers without realizing that his cover was already blown. Barrett headed straight for a middle-aged man in a grey suit, with a dark moustache and a receding hairline. The pair started into the public washroom, but after looking back toward the police officer, headed outside instead. Mark watched them get into a customized, red and white van before ambling outside himself, where he kibitzed with the drivers on the taxi stand as he took down the licence-plate number of the vehicle.

Inside the van, Helmuth gave Barrett the money he had gathered that afternoon, explaining that it was all he could collect on such short notice. "When Helmuth gave me the $13,000, I made arrangements with him to pick up the other $7,000. I said that I would get it later," Barrett said.

When Barrett got out of the van four minutes later, Mark followed him back inside the terminal building, talking to various people along the way in a continuing effort to disguise his surveillance. Barrett walked up behind Hicks, who was on the telephone with her sister, and slipped the envelope containing the money into her purse. Although Mark missed the transfer of the money, he did observe Barrett dialling a number that had more than seven digits, a call that in all likelihood went to Pat Allen at the Westbury to report that the murder money had been picked up.

Hanging up the phone, Barrett asked Hicks to get him some water. He then sauntered over to the policeman who had been watching him and asked for a light – an act of bravura that greatly amused his female companion. Mark obliged him before disappearing into his office, where he ordered a motor vehicle registration search of the suspect van from the RCMP's Canadian Police Intelligence Computer. Afterwards, he called Constable Jenkins in Toronto to report what he had so far observed.

But Robert Barrett's business at the airport wasn't finished yet. As he stood by the front door, a yellow 1979 Chrysler Cordova cruised to a stop in front of the terminal building. Barrett jumped into the passenger seat and the car squealed away. The driver, Lenny Peltier, pulled over a few hundred yards from the terminal and handed Barrett a package containing half an ounce of cocaine. Barrett passed Peltier an envelope bulging with brand new fifty-dollar bills. All told, there was $1,700 – $1,600 for the drug dealer at the Park Lane Hotel who had provided the cocaine and $100 for the delivery man.

"Where'd you get all the money?" Peltier asked.

"Don't you read the papers?" Barrett replied with a smile, boasting that the lady he was with had $30,000 more in her purse.

Hicks was on the telephone when she noticed Barrett crossing the terminal in her direction. She had already filled up an empty Dristan bottle with the water Squirrel needed to shoot some cocaine. Winking as he took the bottle, he hurried to the public washroom and mainlined until he realized with a start that they still had a plane to catch and killers to pay.

Constable Mark, who by now had returned from the security office, was getting concerned that the couple may have left the airport. Air Ontario flight 826 had already taken up its steps and closed its doors, and Air Canada personnel at the security wall were getting ready to call it a night, when Barrett and Hicks ran up to the ticket counter demanding to get on the plane. They didn't have their boarding passes, but airline attendant Shirley Ludlow stopped the flight, which was empty, and hurriedly checked them through security. She had been watching the suspicious couple during their brief stop at London airport and wondered what the x-ray machine might turn up in their hand luggage. Hicks' purse passed inspection, but Ludlow asked Barrett about the Dristan bottle and the object wrapped in Kleenex in the bottom of his small carry-on bag. He told her it was medicine. "We sent them through and they boarded the plane to Toronto. I didn't feel right about their behaviour so I reported it to the RCMP," Ludlow said later.

After Ludlow reported what the security check had revealed, Const. Mark headed back to his office to update his colleagues at Pearson airport about the movements of their now airborne suspects. He told Jenkins about the suspicious objects in Barrett's hand luggage and also had news about the van in which the young man had held a brief meeting before catching his return flight to Toronto.

It was registered to the Watford Nursing Home in Watford, Ontario, under the name Helmuth T. Buxbaum.

It looked like the night was going to end quietly for the crew of Air Ontario flight 826 as the commuter plane prepared to leave London with no passengers.

After a three-hour break between flights, a boring respite spent in the crew lounge of the London airport, purser Becky Hess and flight attendant Kathy Say made their way to their aircraft. They were buckled into their seats when the pilot rang for Hess to go to the cockpit as the main engines shut down. A few moments later, two passengers, who had obviously run all the way from the terminal building, appeared at the aircraft's hastily reopened doors.

The first thing Robert Barrett asked for was a gin and tonic. Hicks nudged him in the back and asked to sit in the smoking section. The couple was assigned seats in the last row of the empty cabin. Becky Hess had just begun her safety instructions when one of her strange passengers abruptly cut her off.

"Don't bother, we just came in on the last flight from Toronto," Barrett said.

"Don't you like London?" the purser joked, referring to their brief layover.

"Yeah, we're *from* London," Barrett replied.

The plane was barely off the ground when the twitchy, young man asked to use the washroom. Hess explained that he would have to wait a few moments. While she was fixing their drinks, she noticed Barrett enter the washroom with the small yellow bag he'd carried onboard.

Hess served Hicks, unaware that Barrett was shooting cocaine in the washroom. Hicks tried to pay the six-dollar bar bill, but couldn't find anything small enough as she fumbled through a thick wad of fifty-dollar bills in her purse. When Barrett returned from the washroom, he paid for the drinks out of his own bankroll. Hess returned to the front of the cabin and sat down beside Kathy Say. After she'd gone, Barrett tried to get Hicks to take the murder money out and count it; she refused.

Midway through the short flight, Hess went back to check on her passengers' drinks only to find Barrett snorting lines of cocaine from a compact mirror lying on his meal tray. "To shut up" her pestering companion, Hicks had been partaking as well, spilling her rye and ginger in the process. Covering the cocaine with his hand, Barrett looked up sheepishly at the purser.

"Are we in trouble?" he asked.

"No," Hess calmly replied. After conferring with Say, it was agreed that they should go to the cockpit, but just at that moment, the captain announced that they were about to land. Hess and Say sat in the flight attendant seats behind the lone passengers. Suddenly, the young man wheeled around:

"Do you want some dope?" he asked.

"No, I'm not into that kind of stuff," Hess replied.

"How about some hash?"

"No, thank you," she replied.

"How about some coke, I've got lots of that," Barrett continued hopefully.

"No, thank you," Hess said, mustering as much finality as she could politely put into her voice.

As soon as the plane landed, Hess reported the conversation to the captain. Barrett, meanwhile, had begun a frantic search for his cocaine knife. Hicks called him an idiot and told him that he had probably left it back at the hotel, a conversation that was overheard by the flight attendants. On the way out of the plane, Barrett stopped for a final word with Kathy Say.

"You're not going to tell them anything, are you?"

"Tell them what?"

"Do you want some stuff?"

"What stuff?"

"Oh, coke, dope, anything you want," Barrett chirped. Looking into her eyes, a smile spread slowly across his face. "You look like you use pills, I've got lots of pills. Would you like some?"

"No," Say told him, relieved when the couple finally left the plane and headed down the arrival ramp, higher than they had ever been on the flight from London.

At 9:50 P.M., Const. Rex Jenkins and four other RCMP officers were standing by gate 740 when Barrett and Hicks walked into Pearson Airport's Terminal 2. The couple was apprehended and taken to the security office, where Hicks was led off by a female officer and Barrett was questioned by Jenkins. The policeman asked him why he had gone to London for such a short time. Barrett said that he had to pick up some money. The officer asked how much, and Barrett said $50 — a less than convincing reply considering that the return trip for two had cost the couple $325. To back up his claim, Barrett pulled a $50 bill out of his pocket, and also, unfortunately for him, a cocaine sniffer.

When he was informed that he would now have to be strip searched, Barrett took the quarter-ounce of hashish he had purchased at the Westbury Hotel and deftly slipped it under the RCMP officer's desk. But there was a limit to what the quick-thinking drug addict could hide. The police found six grams of cocaine in a plastic bag tucked inside the waistband of his underwear, and a second bag with five more in his left sock.

Barrett was taken to a nearby police station, where he was allowed to make a phone call before questioning continued. He told police he was calling his lawyer, but called the Westbury instead, anxious to let Pat Allen know that his delay in returning to the hotel was beyond his control. Barrett was charged with possession of a narcotic, but after police discovered that there were no empty cells in the jail, he was released on a promise to appear in court.

Remarkably, the RCMP didn't find the $13,000 Hicks was carrying, and didn't charge her with possession, even though they found six "bennies" in the bottom of her purse. The pair was driven back to the airport, where, at Hicks' insistence, their first stop was a pay phone.

It was just after 1 A.M. when the telephone rang in suite 1405 at the Westbury Hotel. Pat Allen had been waiting for nearly three hours to learn the outcome of Barrett's run-in with the RCMP. Relieved that the police hadn't seized the murder money, Allen told Barrett that he expected to see him back at the hotel in half an hour. Ten minutes after Barrett's call, Foshay, Armes, Pitcher, Diorio, two hookers, and a drug dealer named Randy Leslie walked into the room.

"I brought two girls," Diorio beamed, "One for you."

"I'm going home," Allen answered.

"The more the merrier for me," Diorio replied, smiling at his new companions as they drifted into the adjoining suite with the others to shoot speed.

When Barrett and Hicks arrived, the only person left in the room was Pat Allen. Barrett counted out $10,000, placing $5,000 in one sealed envelope and $3,500 in another, before handing both of them to Allen. He then flipped another $1,000 to Allen for the "bullshit" he had put him through, and $500 to Hicks. When the killers came back, Allen gave Foshay the $5,000 envelope, Armes the one containing $3,500, and then "borrowed" the $500 back from Hicks.

Their business finally completed, the killers prepared to leave. Foshay, Allen, and Hicks stopped for a coffee at a doughnut shop and then hailed a cab for the long ride back to London. Over Barrett's objections, Anita Pitcher decided to leave with Armes, checking into the Seaway Towers on Lakeshore Blvd. for the rest of the weekend.

The party at the Westbury was almost over.

At 3:15 A.M. on July 7, Manuel Mendoza was watching the fourteenth floor of the South Tower of the Westbury Hotel through a pair of night vision binoculars when he saw a man climb out of the window and jump to the balcony of the next room. The hotel's director of security snapped to attention, thinking that he might be watching the perpetrator of a rash of thefts in the Westbury over the past few weeks. He alerted the supervisor of Checkmate Security, who was already patrolling the South Tower, and then called security at the front desk, instructing the guards to stop and check any person getting out of the south elevators or stairwells.

The hotel's night manager joined Mendoza in his room and confirmed that the rooms in question were 1404 and 1405, both registered to a Robert Barrett from London, Ontario. Barrett had already been involved in one incident with security since checking in on July 4, when he had tried to force his way into another guest's room, thinking it was his own; it turned out that he was on the wrong floor. Hotel security had put the incident down to an honest mistake, but Mendoza still had a bad feeling about the skinny guest with the peculiar friends and the cocky manner.

After the night manager left, Mendoza watched as the balcony-hopper returned to his original room. When he saw a second man following him, he again contacted the night manager and they decided to confront the occupants of Room 1405.

Robert Barrett had had a busy night. After the killers had left, he and Rick Diorio organized a card game in their room – gin rummy at fifty dollars a card. One of the players was Randy Leslie, Diorio's Toronto drug contact. Although Robert Barrett didn't know it, Diorio had invited Leslie to the game expressly to win some of the bankroll he knew Squirrel was carrying – money that Diorio told Leslie had come from organizing the murder of Hanna Buxbaum. During the game, someone mentioned the front page story in the *Toronto Sun* about the Buxbaum murder. Racing along on speed, it was all the encouragement Robert Barrett needed to tell his story.

"Early Saturday morning, Barrett was bragging to Leslie about the murder. We're sitting playing cards – the kid is bragging . . . He didn't say, 'I killed the woman,' but he said he had something to do with it," Rick Diorio said later.

After losing so much money that he had to get more from his safety deposit box at the front desk, Squirrel decided to give up cards for a little aerial gymnastics, unaware that he was under surveillance. Shortly afterwards, there was a knock on the door of room 1405. Barrett explained to hotel security that he had unwittingly locked his keys in room 1404, and had had no way of getting inside except via the balcony. Mendoza asked Barrett, who now had both sets of keys, to open room 1404. When the security director found Randy Leslie in the other room, he knew that Barrett had been lying. After checking to see if guests in rooms 1403 or

1406 had been robbed, the hotel told Barrett and his friends to clear their accounts and leave the premises.

Security accompanied them to the front desk, where Barrett reclaimed his remaining cash from his safety deposit box. Upset by charges run up by Hicks and Pitcher, he refused to pay his bill. But when the night manager began dialling the police, Barrett paid in full and left the hotel in a huff. It was 4 A.M. The bell captain hailed a cab for Barrett, Diorio, and Leslie, carefully noting down its number, which he gave to Bill McCarthy, the supervisor of Checkmate Security. On a hunch, McCarthy called 52 Division of the Metro Toronto Police to see if there were any outstanding warrants on Barrett. The computer came up empty.

The three men ended up at the apartment of Leslie's girlfriend, Edith Sturge. When Sturge left on an errand, Barrett insisted on tagging along. But after he bought cigarettes, syringes, and orange juice at a local drugstore, he vanished, leaving the puzzled woman to walk home by herself. She told Leslie and Diorio what had happened, and the two men went out looking for Barrett, returning half an hour later without him. Diorio emptied Barrett's duffel bag on the bed and carefully searched its contents for cocaine and money. Finding nothing but his friend's change of clothes, he repacked the bag and left with Leslie.

Their plans for the day were put on hold shortly after they entered the Cantina Restaurant on Parliament Street, where Leslie was arrested on an outstanding warrant by two uniformed officers of the Metro Toronto Police. Leslie was taken to 52 Division for booking. He wasn't very far into his description of the previous twenty-four hours before he told them about the drug party at the Westbury and the card game with Rick Diorio, and another man he called Bob.

The routine interrogation changed dramatically when Leslie told police that Bob had boasted that he had set up the roadside slaying that had been in all the papers. He said the "small, blond guy" claimed that he'd already received two payments for arranging the murder and was expecting a third. Leslie explained that the three men had been kicked out of the Westbury after their party had gotten out of hand, and that Barrett's bag was still at a friend's house down the street. The police got a search warrant and at 11 P.M. that night seized Robert Barrett's duffel bag from Edith Sturge's apartment.

A mere forty-eight hours after he had gunned down Hanna Buxbaum in a roadside ditch, Gary Foshay was treating his co-conspirators and friends to a lavish dinner in London. As they ate lobster and drank champagne and mixed drinks called orgasms, they didn't know that their loosely-knit conspiracy was already beginning to unravel.

After losing Rick Diorio and Randy Leslie, Robert Barrett had gone on a mind-blowing cocaine binge, injecting $900 worth of the drug in less than twenty-four hours. He had a dim recollection of spending part of the night at a girl's apartment, but when he woke up in Toronto's Regent Park, he couldn't remember her name or how he had ended up sleeping outside on a bench. With all his money gone, Barrett went door-to-door looking for Rick Diorio, before heading back downtown alone.

Edith Sturge had spent the afternoon of Sunday, July 8, at the cinema with her children. At 5 P.M. they were waiting for the streetcar in front of the Bend Hotel when she saw the small, blond man who had been at her house the previous morning. Sturge called Barrett over and asked him why he had disappeared the previous day. Ignoring her question, he asked where he could find Randy Leslie. Sturge directed him to the Cantina Restaurant and warned him that the police had already been to her apartment and seized his duffel bag.

"He showed me a newspaper page which had the story of the shooting in London. I told him I'd seen it and he said something like, 'Yeah, they're looking for me' or 'I'm involved,'" Sturge later recalled.

In just four days, Robert Barrett had run through $18,000, including the $8,000 he had personally received to arrange Hanna Buxbaum's murder. Penniless and wanted by the police, the man who had ridden to Toronto in a chauffeur-driven limousine returned to London in the back of a Greyhound bus.

11

PROJECT ANGEL

"In a murder investigation, you always talk to hundreds of
people about the victim. We did that in the Buxbaum case
but there was a big difference. Not a single person had
anything bad to say about Hanna Buxbaum. Everybody loved
the woman. None of us had ever seen that before. That's why
we put her picture on the squad room wall and called the
investigation Project Angel."
— *Const. Mel Getty, September 1993*

Within hours of Hanna Buxbaum's murder, Ron Piers knew that he had a
tiger by the tail. The roadside slaying of the pious mother of six sent shock
waves through conservative London, where violent crime was rare. The
fact that Hanna and Helmuth were two of the city's best-known business
figures made the public revulsion even stronger. The story was immediately picked up by the national media, who were waiting to see what sort
of people could perpetrate such a heartless crime.

As Piers mulled over the organization of his investigative team, he
knew that their daily activities would be scrutinized in every newscast
until the high-profile crime was solved. Wary of reporters, like most police officers, Piers also understood the enormous power of the media and
set out to harness it.

One of his first acts was to appeal through the press for all motorists
who had been in the vicinity of the crime scene between 6:45 P.M. and
7:15 P.M. on the night of July 5 to contact the OPP. He believed that the
recovery of the murder car, which might lead police to the identity of the
killers, would be the key to cracking the brutal slaying.

Long before the first call from the public was logged at the OPP's London Detachment, Piers was mildly uneasy with the facts as the police then
knew them. He had been briefed by Const. Greg Calcott on the night of
the murder and had since reviewed early reports from various officers
who had been at the scene minutes after the shooting. It was impossible to

ignore the sheer number of witnesses who had remarked on Helmuth's unusual demeanour; Piers was particularly struck by reports of the husband's aloofness from his wife's body.

Then there was Helmuth's own account of the shooting, a story that several police officers had found irritatingly vague. Corp. Leo Sweeney had written in his notebook after interviewing Helmuth on the night of July 5: "Statement not the most helpful." After studying the various oral and written statements Helmuth had given, six all told, Piers decided that they raised more questions than they answered.

Why would the suspects take pains to stop Roy Buxbaum from witnessing the crime, but allow Helmuth to roam freely outside the car? If robbery were the real motive behind the attack, why had the killer gone first to the boy in the backseat of the station wagon, but ignored Helmuth and his valuables while he assaulted, and finally murdered, Hanna – without taking her rings or watch? Strangest of all, *if*, as Helmuth told police, he had not witnessed the actual shooting, why hadn't he run to check on his wife's condition after the suspects had fled the scene?

Piers had been a policeman long enough to know that violent crimes often unfold irrationally, and that victims and witnesses sometimes behave out of character in the stress of the moment. Further investigation would be needed to see if any of the officers' crime-scene observations were relevant to the case. For now, Piers' attention focused on something he could check – the exact circumstances under which Helmuth had stopped and offered assistance to Hanna's killers.

On this point, Helmuth had been straightforward. He had just been turning off Highway 402 onto the Komoka exit at County Road 14, when he noticed a man waving frantically from the shoulder of the highway. The distressed motorist had been standing behind a blue car parked under the railway overpass some distance ahead. Thinking it might be a Komoka neighbour, Brian Richardson, he drove back onto the highway and continued along to the apparently disabled vehicle, where the attack had taken place.

One of the first facts gathered in the investigation was simple and, perhaps, inconsequential, but it had done nothing to assuage the Inspector's uneasiness with Helmuth's story. On July 6, Piers dispatched Const. Bart Linker to interview Brian Richardson and check on the make and colour of car he drove. Linker discovered that the Richardsons had been in Florida since June 30, a fact the police noted that Buxbaum should have known. Linker learned that the Richardsons owned "a large family car," a light blue 1979 Chrysler Newport – a vehicle difficult to confuse with a dark blue, mid-size car.

But even if Helmuth had made such a mistake that evening as he looked west from County Road 14 down Highway 402 towards the railway overpass, he would certainly have realized it as he approached the disabled car. So why, as he had told police, had he turned off his ignition when he stopped behind a vehicle he certainly knew by then did not belong to the Richardsons?

Piers also wondered why a man who had been driving all day, and had a guest in the car who had just flown in from the other end of the country, would go out of his way to offer help rather than proceed home? He decided to visit the 402 to determine for himself exactly what could and could not be seen at the railway overpass from County Road 14 – a distance of just over a third of a mile.

Piers returned to the scene of the crime on the morning of July 7. He parked a 1984 dark blue Chevy Malibu under the overpass, and placed a man beside the car with instructions to wave his arms when signalled. Piers then backtracked to County Road 14, and looked long and hard down the westbound lanes of the 402 towards the overpass, just as Helmuth had on the night of the murder. It was a clear, sunny day, and the July heat shimmered in waves above the sparsely travelled highway. Although it was barely possible to see the officer waving his arms under the overpass, just as Helmuth had claimed, another part of his story didn't check out according to the Inspector's admittedly unscientific test. "At that distance," Piers wrote in his notebook, "it was impossible to tell the colour or type of vehicle."

Unless, of course, you were looking for it.

On the morning of July 7, Helmuth got up early and went out for a walk, ending up on the veranda of his next door neighbour, Mrs. Morrow. He spent a restful hour on the widow's porch, talking about the tragedy and reaffirming his still unshakable trust in God, telling her "that there was a purpose in everything we go through."

Even so, he admitted to Mrs. Morrow and her daughter that he didn't know what to do, since the children were still young and needed a mother. Declining their offer of coffee, he returned home to prepare for a trip to the OPP's London Detachment to retrieve his briefcase from his impounded station wagon. Later, he planned to visit the funeral home with his children and close family friends to see if the mortician had been able to make Hanna sufficiently presentable to lie in an open casket.

While Helmuth was on his way to London Detachment, the police got their first big break in what would prove to be a remarkable day. At 12:30 P.M. Inspector Piers received word of a telephone call from Const. Philip Medlyn, who reported that on the *morning* of July 5, just before 9 P.M., he had stopped to offer assistance to two vehicles stopped on the south shoulder of Highway 402, just beyond County Road 14. One of the cars had been a blue Chevy Nova, the other, a late-model, brown station wagon with woodgrain side panels and roof-racks. Medlyn was immediately summoned to London Detachment to see if the Buxbaum vehicle was one of those cars.

When Helmuth and Roy Buxbaum arrived to pick up his briefcase, Calcott and Sweeney were already waiting for him. Acting on Piers' instructions, they asked if they could get some additional details from Helmuth. Just before 1 P.M., Calcott escorted Helmuth to an interview room and inquired about a missing item of Hanna's jewellery, a diamond engagement ring, which subsequently turned up at the Buxbaum residence. They went over other details of his earlier statements before Calcott casually raised Constable Medlyn's new, and potentially explosive, information. "They asked me if anything unusual had happened in the morning of July 5. I had completely forgot about stopping for a car in the morning," Helmuth said later.

He had made no mention of this in his six previous statements to police, two in writing and four verbally. But now, Helmuth proceeded to describe for the first time the strange encounter with another apparently disabled blue car on his way to Kitchener with Hanna on the morning of July 5. He said that the strangers had at first asked for Hanna's stockings to fix their car, but then had slammed down the hood of the Nova when an OPP cruiser arrived on the scene, hastily explaining to the officer that everything was all right. After the cruiser had pulled away, the man had inexplicably returned the panty hose to Hanna, telling her he didn't need them anymore. When asked if the blue car he had tried to help on the morning of July 5 was the same blue car he had stopped behind that evening, Helmuth told police he "couldn't say."

The interview would have continued but Helmuth explained that he was late for the family's planned trip to the funeral home that afternoon. The boys, he solemnly reported, had already been to Westmount Mall to buy new suits for their mother's funeral. At 2:40 P.M., Corporal Sweeney ended the interview and began taking down the new information in statement form. Just under an hour later, an impatient Helmuth signed the statement and got ready to leave.

In the foyer of the cell block area, Helmuth found Inspector Piers talking to another police officer. He interrupted their conversation to ask about his briefcase. The other officer, Constable Medlyn, who had just arrived at London Detachment to inspect the Buxbaum station wagon, immediately recognized Helmuth when he glanced in the policeman's direction. "I recognized him by the receding hairline as the sun reflected off his scalp when he was standing beside the station wagon. I had looked back through the open window as I pulled out onto the roadway."

While Helmuth was signing a receipt for his briefcase, Medlyn told Piers that Buxbaum was definitely the man he had seen behind the blue Nova during his morning stop on Highway 402. Piers' sense of uneasiness stirred once again. He decided that he would offer Helmuth a ride back to Komoka, but not before taking a brief detour to the scene of Hanna Buxbaum's murder. Before the case was done, Piers would return to the scene twenty-five times, trying to visualize what had happened from the evidence his investigators gathered.

Corporal Sweeney, Helmuth, and Inspector Piers drove to Highway 402 in a 1983 maroon Pontiac Grand Prix. Helmuth talked wistfully about the family's recent trip to Europe, and said that after the funeral he planned to "get away from it all." His hideaway of choice, he said, was the family cottage in Huntsville. He also said that he wanted to erect a marker in Hanna's memory at the place where she had been killed, telling the two policemen that it was a common practice in Europe. Conversation flagged until Helmuth volunteered that, after what had happened, he had decided never to travel on Highway 402 again. Piers let the remark pass and the men rode in silence until they reached the spot where the police now knew the Buxbaums had stopped behind a blue car on the morning of July 5.

"I asked him whether the car he had stopped for in the morning was the same blue car he saw in the afternoon [sic] and he said he didn't think so," Sweeney later wrote in his notebook.

When the men reached the scene of the shooting, Sweeney asked Helmuth where he had stopped on the evening of July 5. Taking precise directions from Helmuth, he parked the Grand Prix exactly where the station wagon had been, beside the abutment of the overpass. Helmuth said that the blue car had been parked directly in front of him. Piers asked if Hanna had mentioned anything about the vehicle being the same one they had stopped behind in the morning. Both officers were struck by his oddly insensitive reply: "He said his wife had a grade-three education . . . He doubted her ability to tell one car from another," Sweeney later said.

Inspector Piers asked Helmuth to go over exactly what had happened, prompting a protest from their passenger that he had already done that at least half a dozen times with other police officers. Piers calmly replied that *he* had never heard it before. Sweeney gently reminded Helmuth that it was also the first time he had returned to the scene of his wife's murder since the shooting.

Resigned to the fact that the officers were only trying to do their jobs, Helmuth once again related the terrible events of that July 5 evening — how when he stopped behind the blue car after being flagged down by a man with dirty blond hair, a second man wearing a stocking mask had accosted Roy in the backseat, before pressing what looked like a toy pistol to Hanna's head and demanding her money and jewellery. Helmuth described how he had been inching his way out of the car when the gunman suddenly ordered Hanna to get outside. After the masked man had dragged her onto the shoulder of the highway, Helmuth had run to the middle of the road, waving his arms to attract the attention of westbound traffic. While he was in the centre of the highway, he heard three shots that did not sound like the reports of a real gun. He didn't see what happened to his wife, or what the second man, who had been standing beside the blue car, had been doing during the attack. Clutching Hanna's purse in his hand, the gunman and his accomplice had then jumped into their car and made their escape down Highway 402, headed west.

With Piers and Sweeney listening hard, Helmuth took them through the aftermath of the shooting, describing how he and Roy had managed to flag down a trucker, and then a second trucker, who made a call for help on his CB radio. Other vehicles soon arrived, and several people rushed over to the mortally wounded woman. By his own admission, Helmuth wasn't one of them. He explained that he didn't want Roy "to see that" and left the care of his wife to "a guy with medical training." Piers asked Helmuth if he had gone to his wife's side at *any* point after the attack. Sweeney recorded the reply in his notebook: "I didn't go over. I didn't go over the railing at any time."

After standing silently by the guardrail looking at Hanna's blood, still visible on the ground, Helmuth got back into the police car and had the officers drop him off at Komoka.

Piers was as disquieted as before. It wasn't so much that he didn't believe what Helmuth had told them, as that "there were a lot of troubling aspects" to his story. And then there was his strange demeanour. "Clearly, he wasn't emotional. He wasn't what you would expect a man to be who had just lost his wife," Piers later recalled.

On the drive back to London Detachment through the gently sloping southwestern Ontario farmland, its fields of corn, tobacco, and soya golden in the fading afternoon sun, Piers considered the possible implications of Helmuth's belated recollection of the morning meeting with the blue car on the day that Hanna had been murdered. It could, of course, have been a bizarre coincidence, stopping behind two different cars on the same day that just happened to be the same colour and style. But how likely was it that someone could forget such a meeting, given the strange behaviour of the man whose broken-down vehicle apparently repaired itself when the OPP arrived, especially in light of what had happened later that same day? And if the cars at both stops were one and the same vehicle, was it again mere coincidence that placed it on the exact stretch of highway the couple had travelled in both the morning and the evening? Or had its occupants known in advance the route the Buxbaums would be taking?

As devil's advocate, Piers considered one important difference between the two incidents. In the morning, the men the Buxbaums stopped to help hadn't made any attempt to disguise their identity or that of their car; in the evening, the vehicle's licence plate had been obscured and the gunman had been wearing a stocking mask. Piers pondered the mystery and then reflected on another difference between the two encounters. In the morning, Roy Buxbaum hadn't been sitting in the back of the station wagon.

In the morning, the only person who could have identified his wife's assailants was Helmuth Buxbaum.

By the evening of Saturday, July 7, Const. Greg Calcott and his fellow investigators had already interviewed twenty-three people, many of whom had called the OPP in response to Piers' appeal for information from the public. Bothered by his transaction with Helmuth so close on the heels of Hanna's murder, coin dealer Chris Brooker had reported to the London police the businessman's sale of a gold bar on the afternoon of July 6, adding another oddity to a growing list of unlikely occurrences. Like Brooker, police wondered why a wealthy man like Helmuth would cash in gold bars less than twenty-four hours after his wife's murder – and at such a low price.

The eyewitness accounts from motorists driving by the murder scene raised even more puzzling questions. More than ten people had seen the suspects' vehicle parked by the overpass with its trunk open as they went about their lives on the evening of July 5. Marcel Elderhorst had been on his way home to Bright's Cove when he noticed a shiny, dark blue car parked on the westbound shoulder of Highway 402. He had seen two men, one standing at the rear of the vehicle, and the other running east in the ditch of the westbound lanes towards the overpass. "I do recall thinking I [should] stop to see if they needed help, but I didn't because they were both mean-looking characters," he told Const. Gary Aspden. "They looked like someone who may have been from jail."

Bill Hines, an electrician with Imperial Oil, had been driving home to Sarnia when he, too, had passed a blue car with an open trunk parked under the overpass on Highway 402. Like Elderhorst, he had considered stopping, but decided that the lone man he saw walking towards the rear of the parked car, "just didn't look friendly." But what caught the attention of OPP constables Brady and Edwards as they took the man's statement was another observation, a detail that would be repeated by several other drivers over the next few days. "He didn't appear to need any help. He didn't try to wave me down," Hines said.

Other motorists supplied police with information that backed up Elderhorst and Hines. Gary Foster had noticed two men in conversation beside a dark blue car whose licence plate "was covered over with a thick material" and whose trunk was open. Neither man had tried to flag Foster down. Kenneth Huizinga told Const. Paul Edwards that he had seen a man in a black leather jacket behind the west face of the cement abutment under the overpass, "with his back to the pillar."

But by far the most unsettling evidence came from two drivers who had seen both the Buxbaum's station wagon and the suspects' car in the vicinity of the murder scene on the evening of July 5. One of them, Jeffrey Smith, had been driving west on Highway 402 when he passed a brown station wagon with three passengers. As Smith approached the Komoka-Mount Brydges interchange, he noticed a blue vehicle on the side of the road by the next overpass. There was a man crouched by the back of the car with a jack set up off to his right.

"It struck me odd that the guy was just crouching there looking back. As I slowed down he just stared at me. He wasn't making any effort to fix the tire if he had a flat, he just kept looking back down the road towards the interchange," Smith told Const. Mel Getty.

As he drew up to the older model blue Nova, Smith saw the upper body of another man standing up in the ditch, looking back down the highway in the same direction as his companion with what appeared to be a pair of binoculars. "It struck me really strange because both of them kept looking down the road, like staring. It looked like they were after one particular vehicle."

It was an intriguing speculation, but that was all it was. Which is what made Robert Mitchell's information all the more sensational. Mitchell appeared to have driven his truck by the overpass while the murder was actually being committed. As he barrelled down the entrance ramp to the westbound lanes of Highway 402 from County Road 14, he saw two vehicles parked on the right-hand shoulder. The first was a two-tone, brown and cream, late model station wagon; the second, parked just in front of it, a dark blue, smaller car. But it was not primarily his description of the vehicles that so interested Constable Mel Getty as he took down the trucker's statement, but rather what he saw happening at the scene.

"I saw a man in light coloured clothing, a heavy-set, older man, run-ning from the passenger side of the brown station wagon past the front of the car, between the two vehicles, then down the driver's side towards the driver's door," he said. Just as the man he was watching started towards the driver's door, Mitchell saw two other men jump over the guardrail and run towards the back of the blue car with the open trunk. The trucker was a mere thirty to forty feet from the two cars when he made his observa-tions, which included the fact that both of the men who had come from the direction of the ditch appeared to be wearing baseball caps. He noticed that one of them had something else on his head that came down the left side of his face and under his chin, like an aviator's leather helmet with the chin-strap done up.

When Mitchell was directly adjacent to the scene, he saw a small cloud of smoke hanging three or four feet above the ground on the far side of the guardrail. As he swooped under the overpass at 120 kilometres an hour, he glanced in his left mirror and saw the blue car pulling onto the highway. It quickly gained on him, then shot past at high speed. As the car accelerated away, Mitchell noted that it was an older Chevy Nova, possibly the 1977 model because of its squared-off tail-lights. He noticed that the two white men inside had taken off their caps and that both had dark hair. As the Nova drew farther ahead of him, he also saw that its licence plate was covered over with what looked like a piece of green felt. Mitchell followed the car westbound until it turned off Highway 402 at County Road 39, thinking no more about the strange incident until he had heard about the murder the next day and had called the police.

As tentative as observations made at highway speeds necessarily were, these early drive-by accounts troubled police investigators. If the occupants of the blue Nova had, in fact, waved frantically to the Buxbaums as Helmuth said they did, why hadn't they tried to attract the attention of other motorists who had passed the scene moments earlier? And what had the man in the black leather jacket seen by Kenneth Huizinga been doing behind a cement pillar with his back to the wall? It certainly wasn't consistent with someone repairing a vehicle, but he could have been lying in wait for something. And then there was Mitchell's description of the two men in the Nova. His claim that both men had dark hair did not square with Helmuth's statement to police in which he claimed that the man who had waived the Buxbaum car down was blond. Such questions were made all the more provocative in light of the Buxbaums' morning stop behind another distressed blue car that also, apparently, had had nothing wrong with it.

But the really big question arose from Robert Mitchell's detailed observations. Assuming that the heavy-set man he had seen running from the passenger side of the Oldsmobile station wagon had been Helmuth Buxbaum, what had he been doing beside the guardrail when he told police that he had bolted to the middle of the highway to flag down help as soon as his wife had been pulled from the car? To Piers, it was too early to make much more of the motorists' observations than that they were "the direct opposite" of what Helmuth had told police. But it was another piece of the investigative puzzle that didn't seem to fit.

The police were still chewing over the discrepancies when, at 6 P.M., Const. Greg Calcott got the first of two phone calls that electrified the murder investigation. Const. Courtland Booth of the Metropolitan Toronto Police called to report that the Metro police had arrested an informant, Randy Leslie, who claimed that a man he had been playing cards with at the Westbury Hotel, a Robert Barrett from London, had "set up" the roadside murder on behalf of a man who wanted his wife killed to collect on a life insurance policy. Booth also informed Calcott that the Metro police had already executed a search warrant at a Toronto residence and seized a duffel bag allegedly belonging to Barrett.

Less than three and a half hours later, the name the OPP had been given by the Toronto police took on a grim significance. At 9:26 P.M., the RCMP rocked the murder investigators by informing them that they had evidence of a meeting at the London airport between Helmuth Buxbaum and a man named Robert Barrett. Astonishingly, the meeting had taken place on July 6, only hours after Helmuth had sold a five-ounce gold bar to Chris Brooker and twenty-four hours after his wife's murder.

Inspector Piers and his investigators worked late into Saturday night evaluating the windfall of information that had come their way. "It appears that there's more to this case than meets the eye," Piers told his team. They still had more questions than answers, but there was now, at least, a definite possibility that Hanna Buxbaum's murder was a wider-ranging conspiracy than early evidence had indicated. Piers gave orders for his men to begin building a case for an authorization to intercept the communications of Buxbaum and Barrett. He also ordered physical surveillance of the two men early the next morning. The central target of the covert activity would be Helmuth Buxbaum.

Forty-eight hours after Hanna Buxbaum's murder, her husband had become a key suspect.

Early in the morning of Sunday, July 8, the phone rang in the home of Robert Eaton, the security manager of Bell Telephone's London office. Corp. Leo Sweeney advised him that the OPP needed some telephone data, records of calls made from phone booths, and possibly also line information or wiretaps. Eaton dispatched John Heatherington to the OPP's Criminal Investigation Branch (CIB) offices on Adelaide Street in London, where he sat in on a meeting to plan the operation. Corp. Ken Allen, an intelligence expert and former Bell Telephone employee, was also brought in to prepare the necessary affidavits for the wiretap authorizations and to manage the operation.

Meanwhile, the OPP investigators hit the ground running in an all-out attempt to follow up on the sensational leads of the previous evening. Const. Andy Fotheringham, an intelligence expert, traced the whereabouts of off-duty RCMP officer John Mark, who had witnessed the meeting between Helmuth Buxbaum and Robert Barrett at London Airport on the evening of July 6. Just after 1 P.M. Fotheringham knocked on the door of the Mark family's summer trailer at Spring Lake Recreational Vehicle Park outside London. As the two policemen discussed Robert Barrett's lightning visit to the Airport for a four-minute meeting with a middle-aged man in a rumpled grey suit, Mark noticed a picture of Helmuth Buxbaum resting on the seat of Fotheringham's cruiser. "I immediately knew what I had seen at the airport," Mark recalled.

Fotheringham then drove to the airport, where he interviewed the Air Canada employee who would have received any paging requests on the evening of July 6. He asked Claudia Langford if, on the evening in question, she had logged any messages from a Robert Barrett at Pearson airport in Toronto to a Helmuth Buxbaum. Lady luck smiled on the officer's inquiry. On July 6, severe thunderstorms in Toronto had played such havoc with evening flight schedules that airport staff had switched on the telephone printer to handle the flood of messages streaming in from stranded travellers. Langford was able to hand Fotheringham a typed copy of the message Robert Barrett had sent to Helmuth Buxbaum. Part of that message contained a London phone number that police quickly learned belonged to one Janet Hicks.

The hounds had had their first sniff of blood.

Anita Pitcher's sojourn to Toronto ended on Sunday, July 8, on a platform at Union Station when Terry Armes put her on the train for London with a goodbye kiss and some final instructions. Pitcher, who had been given $800 of Armes' murder money, was to pick up the blue Nova from Robin Foshay's house and return it to Rent-A-Wreck. After the train pulled out, Armes called Robin Foshay to tell her that Pitcher would be coming by later that afternoon to pick up the car. He stressed that she should tell Pitcher to take it through a car wash before returning it to the rental agency.

Back in London, Pitcher took a cab to Robin Foshay's, where she picked up the keys to the blue Nova. After passing along Armes' instructions, Robin helped Pitcher take the tarpaulin off the car, relieved that it was finally going to be taken away. Pitcher drove the Nova through a car wash and then parked it on the lot of Rent-A-Wreck, placing the keys in the ashtray and leaving one door unlocked. Her task completed, she took a bus to Janet Hicks' apartment, where fresh orders awaited her.

Hicks explained that Pat Allen had called to say that he wanted 300 miles put on the car before it was returned to the rental agency. That way, the Nova's odometer would back up Pitcher's previous story to rental agent Maureen Dennison that she was taking the car to Canada's Wonderland, north of Toronto. Like a good soldier, Pitcher did as she was told.

As Anita Pitcher drove aimlessly around London's peaceful Sunday evening streets in the car every policeman in Ontario was looking for, the Buxbaum family was putting in an emotional appearance at West Park Baptist Church. Surrounded by his children and a phalanx of relatives, Helmuth took his usual seat in the pew three rows from the back of the church. As the pastor mourned the loss of one of the congregation's gentlest souls and greatest benefactors, (the Buxbaums had donated more than $100,000 to West Park in the last year alone) Helmuth openly wept.

After the service, the Buxbaums greeted their friends in the lobby of the church, where Pastor Fawcett kept a book with a family picture of every congregation member. Stopping a friend, Helmuth pointed out his own family's portrait, which had been taken just before the Buxbaums' pilgrimage to Oberammergau.

"I started crying again," Helmuth said later. "I thought of how impossible it was for Hanna to be dead. I could see her sitting with all the children and me in the photograph. It all seemed so unreal. Several people came to me and shook my hand and tried to comfort me. I couldn't stop crying."

After lunch at Swiss Chalet, the family returned to Komoka, where Helmuth, a self-admitted "emotional disaster," knelt down in his and Hanna's bedroom and prayed before setting out with the others for Needham's Funeral Home. Cocaine-free for the first time in four days, Helmuth was taking prescription sedatives like candy, but there was no relief from his jangled nerves. When he arrived at Needham's, he was overwhelmed by the crush of well-wishers. Working his way through the throng, he found himself in front of his wife's open casket. As he had done so many times as a child in Melk's cemetery, Helmuth stared into the face of death. "I looked at Hanna. I couldn't see any marks on her forehead. I leaned over to take a closer look. I still couldn't see any marks."

Dazed by the whole affair, Helmuth found himself at the head of an impromptu reception line leading to Hanna's casket. He shook hands with the visitors and awkwardly told them that coffee was being served downstairs. It was a relief when the funeral director interrupted his macabre duties to call him to the telephone. He was stunned to hear the cheerful voice of Robert Barrett asking for more of the murder money. "I told you I would phone you at ten on Tuesday," Helmuth snapped, abruptly hanging up on his indecorous caller.

Phil Conley was speechless. For the past two days, he and his wife Chris had been looking after the Buxbaum children. While talking to Paul Buxbaum late one evening, Conley had been stunned to find out about Helmuth's secret life of cocaine and prostitutes. Intent on making sure that Helmuth didn't touch off a scandal during this period of high public mourning by using drugs, he had followed him like a shadow ever since. Standing by his side at the telephone, Conley simply couldn't imagine that the call had been about legitimate business.

"I asked Helmuth who would be phoning him at the funeral home, for what reason. He said, 'It was a fellow from Toronto named John that needed some money for food and clothes,'" Conley recalled. Having learned about the Barrett brothers from Paul and Phillip Buxbaum, he asked Helmuth point-blank if his caller had been John Barrett. Helmuth, who was anxious to get Conley off his back, brusquely shook his head and hurried downstairs for coffee.

Unwilling to believe that the call had been as innocuous as Helmuth let on, Conley buttonholed Nick Potocska and asked him to write down the snippet of conversation he had just overheard. With Conley dictating, Potocska recorded Helmuth's words on the back of a business card. Conley read the card over to make sure that Potocska had written it down accurately. Convinced that Helmuth was in the clutches of drug dealers, Phil Conley decided that for the next few critical days he wouldn't let Helmuth out of his sight.

That night on the way back to Komoka, Conley confronted Helmuth about his drug problem. He wanted to know more about the people who had been supplying him with cocaine and whether he intended to enter a detoxification centre for treatment, as he had promised Hanna and the children he would once they had returned from Europe. To Helmuth, Conley's questions sounded more like meddling than concern. "I told him, 'You can't believe everything that Paul tells you.' I meant Paul Buxbaum. I said it was a personal matter and that he didn't need to concern himself with it."

But Phil Conley was already concerned; so concerned, in fact, that when they got back to Komoka and Helmuth got ready for bed, Conley decided to sleep in the same room. He wanted to make sure that the sinister forces that clearly had his friend and mentor under their spell couldn't reach him before Hanna Buxbaum was laid to rest the next day.

It was the least he could do for the woman who had been so kind to him from the first time they had met.

On the day that Hanna Buxbaum was buried, the OPP were up early. At 8:15 A.M., Const. Mel Getty called Bill Ashby, the superintendent of the Middlesex County Board of Education, and requested the use of Parkview Public School in Komoka, which was closed for the summer, as the command centre for the police wiretap operation. Ashby readily agreed, and a 9:30 A.M. meeting was set up between a member of the OPP's Technical Support Branch and the school board's supervisor of maintenance, Hugh Zapfe, to work out the details.

At 9:20 A.M. Inspector Piers ordered a grid search of the Komoka-Mount Brydges cloverleaf by a police Tactical and Rescue Unit (TRU), after learning from a drive-by eyewitness that one of the suspects in the blue Nova may have thrown a beer bottle into the ditch — a beer bottle that might still have his fingerprints on it.

The fourth day of the murder investigation generated more tips and leads than there were homicide investigators to check them out. Const. Malcolm Lees of the OPP's Intelligence Unit received a flurry of calls from a well-placed female informant who deeply implicated Robert Barrett in the slaying of Hanna Buxbaum. The informant told Lees that Barrett had called his wife, Kelly, from the Westbury Hotel in Toronto and asked her to go to Needham's Funeral Home to get more money from Helmuth Buxbaum. She claimed that Barrett had told her the previous January that he had been offered $20,000 to arrange Hanna's murder. Although Barrett had set up the contract killing, she said, it was likely that one of his associates, Pat Allen, had actually pulled the trigger. As a final contribution to the investigation, the informant gave police a copy of Robert Barrett's personal telephone book.

Supt. Don Andrews of the London police learned from another caller that Helmuth Buxbaum had a two-ounce-a-week cocaine habit, and that his main drug supplier for the past six months had been one Robert Barrett. Barrett, the caller said, also procured young girls for Buxbaum during drug parties at London's Park Lane Hotel. Later that day, members of the London vice squad confirmed the drug bashes at the Park Lane and learned from the doorman that Helmuth had been barred from the hotel after a particularly rowdy party in his suite on January 27.

One of the strangest, and totally unsubstantiated, tips police received came from one of Helmuth's own brothers. During a 10:35 A.M. meeting in the Hi Fi restaurant with Staff Sgt. James Balmain of the London police, Otto Buxbaum insisted that the murder was a "set-up deal," but said that he wouldn't talk to OPP investigator Paul Edwards until after Hanna's funeral.

The initial flood of information had turned into a torrent. Inspector Piers assigned his six-man team of general investigators to check out the most crucial leads. Const. Greg Calcott was dispatched to Toronto to investigate Robert Barrett's arrest by the RCMP, as well as his three-day stay at the Westbury Hotel. Crucial to Calcott's inquiries were any calls Barrett may have made to London before and after the murder.

One of the first things the detective learned was that Barrett had, in fact, made ten such calls, including three to Debbie Barber, three to Pat Allen, and three to Janet Hicks, whose telephone number police already had from the message Barrett had left for Helmuth at the London airport on the night of July 6. He also learned that Pat Allen had made four calls to the Westbury from his London apartment, the first one two hours after Hanna's murder, and the rest within the next twenty-four hours.

While Calcott prepared to visit 52 Division in Toronto to find out more about police informant Randy Leslie's remarkable story, his colleagues in London were investigating Helmuth's banking transactions in the days immediately before and after his wife's murder. They also looked into allegations that Helmuth hosted drug parties at a local hotel, retrieving registration slips from the Park Lane for January 17, 18, 19, 26, and 27. Remarkably, Helmuth had registered the rooms under his own name. There was more to the wealthy pillar of West Park Baptist Church, it seemed, than charitable contributions and Christian principles.

With the Identification Unit, TRU teams, and general investigators all hard at work (up to seventy officers at any one time would be assigned to the case), Piers was anxious to get the other elements of the homicide investigation in place. The key to his operational plan was physical and electronic surveillance, the most labour-intensive part of any major investigation. The first element of that plan, round-the-clock watches on the residences of Helmuth Buxbaum and Debbie Barber, was already in place. If there was, in fact, another instalment due on the murder contract, as Randy Leslie had told police, Piers wanted his men to be there when it went down. He also dispatched three two-man teams to cover London's airport, train station, and bus terminal to make sure that none of the known suspects fled the city. Finally, he assigned a five-man surveillance team to the funeral and burial of Hanna Buxbaum scheduled for 1:30 P.M. that afternoon. Their base would be a nondescript house directly across the street from the church.

There was no telling who might show up at the funeral, and the Inspector wanted to know exactly how Helmuth would bid farewell to his partner of twenty-three years.

On the morning of his wife's funeral Helmuth woke with a strong craving for cocaine. Forgetting about the six grams hidden behind his desk, he reached instead for his bottle of Serax tablets. "Walking around like a zombie," he began looking for the codicil to their will that he and Hanna had both signed before leaving on their trip to Europe. His brother Douglas had urged Helmuth to name one or two of his brothers and sisters as administrators of the estate in the event that Helmuth and Hanna died simultaneously on the trip. That way, Douglas had pointed out, Ruth's natural parents, who were still alive in Costa Rica, couldn't make a claim against the Buxbaum's multimillion-dollar estate. Now that Hanna had "predeceased" him, Helmuth reasoned, there was no need for the codicil. When he finally found it, he put it away for safekeeping in his briefcase – an odd beginning to the day he was to bury his wife.

Even stranger, Helmuth had engaged a security firm in the days immediately after Hanna's death, based on the seemingly irrational fear that he "might be next." (Helmuth told reporters that his wife's death was a sad comment on the state of Canada's gun laws, and even sent a telegram to Ottawa complaining of the proliferation of weapons in the country.) Although he said he had no idea of who might be after him, when it came time to leave for West Park Baptist Church with his children and the collection of close relatives who were staying at Komoka, the paranoid widower climbed into the car beside Ian MacFadgen, a bodyguard from Burns Security.

As eight hundred mourners filed past him on their way into the auditorium of the church, Helmuth stood in the lobby, missing a private family prayer session he didn't seem to know was taking place in the basement. With the church jammed with mourners, Helmuth walked up the aisle holding the hand of his youngest son, Danny, taking his place in the second pew from the front only a few feet from Hanna's now-closed coffin. Despite the drowsiness induced by the tranquillizers he was taking, Helmuth was overwhelmed by the service.

Pastor Fawcett spoke briefly about Hanna's good works, before Georgi Wiens took his place in the pulpit. The Baptist dissident, who had finally been released from exile in Siberia in 1978 after a diplomatic protest in which the Buxbaums had played a prominent part, told the congregation that Hanna was now with God.

During hymns performed by Hanna's old friend, Barbara Musto, Helmuth openly wept. After Paul Buxbaum read some selections from the Bible, a tape was played in which Hanna herself told the story of how she had become a Christian. Esther Buxbaum delivered her mother's eulogy. The fourteen-year-old schoolgirl began sobbing after reading a few verses from Proverbs 31:

> *"Who can find a virtuous woman? for her price is far above rubies.*
> *The heart of her husband doth safely trust in her, so that he shall have no need of spoil.*
> *She will do him good and not evil all the days of her life . . .*
> *Her children arise up, and call her blessed; her husband also, and he praiseth her."*

"My Dad cried a little at the funeral. He was very sad. He listened to the service. He was too upset to say anything," Esther said later.

After the service, the cortège set out for Campbell Cemetery in Komoka, where the family, including Helmuth, gathered under a tent erected over Hanna's grave. Among the many people who extended their sympathies to Helmuth was Chris Browne. After the Jamaican native had left, Helmuth told Phil Conley that the man was a drug dealer, hardening Conley's resolve to stay by his friend's side. With the surveillance team scanning the crowd and noting down Helmuth's every action, the distraught man broke down again. As Hanna's coffin was lowered into the ground, the mourners surrounding her casket began to sing one of her favourite hymns in German; Helmuth remained silent. "I couldn't sing," he said later. "I was choking in my tears."

Helmuth remained at the cemetery with his children until the mourners had gone and attendants began filling in Hanna's grave. The family then drove back to the church, where they hosted a reception in Hanna's honour. Old friends like Bill and Ruth Sergeant expressed their condolences to Helmuth and the children. When Phillip Buxbaum embraced his grieving father, he felt something hard under his jacket – a .45-calibre Colt Commander hanging barely concealed from his vest pocket. When Phillip asked why he was carrying a gun, Helmuth explained that he had to be ready to protect himself "if anyone came for the family."

After the reception, Phil Conley drove the worried man back to Komoka and put Helmuth to bed at 4 P.M. At the same time, Anita Pitcher was handing the keys of the murder car to Sharon Lawrence at Rent-A-Wreck. Lawrence gave her a refund of $30.97 – and a lecture for returning the Nova three days late.

Ron Piers, meanwhile, had more to think about than the eyewitness observations of the surveillance team at the funeral. Late that afternoon he received a startling report from Constable Davies at London Detachment that a woman named Susan Ambrose had called to say that she had been offered money by Helmuth Buxbaum to poison his wife in January 1984. The caller, who claimed to be Helmuth's former girlfriend, left a telephone number in Toronto where she could be reached. Piers gave the number to Const. Mel Getty, unaware of the remarkable corroboration of Ambrose's story that would very shortly be coming his way.

As the mourners gathered to bury Hanna Buxbaum, the man who had shot her in the head for $5,000 was spending part of that money on new shoes and a haircut to attend a funeral of his own. On Saturday, July 7, Gary Foshay, who had been partying with a vengeance since the murder, called his brother Trent to tell him that their grandfather had died suddenly in Lindsay, Ontario. Gary and a cousin, Rick Langley, had then made plans to attend his funeral.

On Monday, July 9, Foshay was stopped by the Lindsay police for having open liquor in his car. After giving police a false name (his brother's), he was arrested. Hanna Buxbaum's killer was in jail for his grandfather's funeral and wasn't released until the afternoon of July 11. He immediately returned to London, where he spent several days with his girlfriend, Debbie Trollope, squandering nearly every penny of his murder money on cheap motel rooms and expensive drugs.

But the free-spending killer hadn't completely forgotten about his family obligations. Before setting out for Lindsay on the day of Hanna's funeral, he had picked up his wife and two daughters to take them for a drive. While at the house, Foshay retrieved Hanna's purse from above the garage door where he had hidden it on the night of July 5, and loaded it with two bricks. During the drive with his family, he stopped the car by the Thames River across from 1 High Street, took out the purse and tossed it into the same river in which he had already disposed of the murder weapon.

Before leaving for his grandfather's funeral, Foshay gave his wife fifty dollars to buy the girls new shoes.

After waking from his post-funeral nap, Helmuth joined the children and made plans for the family to go to their Huntsville cottage later in the week. Still concerned about a possible attack, he went outside with Phil Conley and talked to his security guards about their plans for patrolling the property that night. Although Helmuth told them to be vigilant, he made clear that they were not to disturb patients from the nursing home who often wandered onto the Buxbaum property during their evening constitutionals.

Back in the house, Helmuth excused himself and disappeared upstairs to use the washroom. It was a welcome relief for Phil Conley, who was so determined not to let his charge out of his sight that he had even defied the call of nature. Conley bolted to the downstairs bathroom; when he returned, Helmuth was gone. Rushing to the window, he saw him sitting behind the wheel of his van with the motor already running. Conley caught up with his charge as he was getting ready to back down the driveway to keep an appointment with Robert Barrett.

Helmuth explained that he wanted to get some cash at the bank and Conley, concerned about the amount of tranquillizers his friend had taken that day, as well as the darker urges Paul Buxbaum had warned him about, offered to act as his chauffeur. Helmuth refused. Exasperated, Conley reached in through the open driver's side window and plucked the keys out of the ignition. Helmuth exploded, accusing Conley of treating him "like a child."

Helmuth eventually calmed down and agreed to go for a walk on the grounds of Komoka. As they strolled by the pond in the summer dusk, the trout making feeding circles on the dark water, Conley began quizzing him on his cocaine use. Although Helmuth resented Conley sniffing around his private affairs, he gave him an honest answer. "I told Phil that coke took the confusion and pressure from my mind."

Conley told Helmuth of his suspicion that the undesirables Helmuth had fallen in with over the last six months were now blackmailing him "for whatever reason." Helmuth finally admitted that, although he was not the victim of an extortion scheme, he did owe a local drug dealer $2,000 and that "it would make this person happy if they were paid."

Certain now that Helmuth's unsavoury associates were pressuring him, Conley advised him not to go to the Park Lane Hotel to make the payment, pointing out that if he did, the man would only demand more money. Instead, Conley said that he would wait at Komoka for the man's call and tell him that Mr. Buxbaum wasn't available. Reluctantly, Helmuth agreed.

Later that evening, the phone rang at the Buxbaum residence. With Helmuth listening in on an extension, Conley answered the call and explained to a person who identified himself as Steve that Helmuth was busy. "Well, just give him the message that we are sorry about his wife," the man said. "We will be in touch with him."

Steve didn't say who the "we" might be, and Conley didn't ask. Helmuth's terse explanation was that the caller had simply been his unpaid drug dealer. Less than convinced that Helmuth wouldn't try to meet his mysterious caller, Phil Conley once more bedded down at Komoka to keep an eye on his restless charge.

As Helmuth was climbing into his bed, County Court Judge R. J. Flynn was climbing out of his to sign the necessary authorizations to intercept the private communications of Helmuth Buxbaum, Robert Barrett, and Debbie Barber sought by Crown attorney Michael Martin and Corp. Ken Allen of the OPP. In Helmuth's case, the authorizations covered wiretaps of his main residence, his Komoka Nursing Home, and his cottage at Mary Lake in Huntsville.

From now on, every facet of Helmuth's private life would be scrutinized by the hidden eyes and ears of the police.

On Tuesday, July 10, the run of perfect summer weather was finally broken by a gentle rain that fell steadily all day. Inside the unmarked surveillance van parked outside Debbie Barber's home, no one was complaining about the weather. It was the first day of electronic surveillance on the principal suspects in the case, and the rain had persuaded one of them, Robert Barrett, to conduct his business on the telephone, which suited Corp. Ken Allen just fine. Before the day was over, the quarterback of Hanna Buxbaum's murder would place fourteen telephone calls, five of them to Helmuth Buxbaum.

Barrett never reached Helmuth, but his conversations with his mother and brother intrigued the investigators. At 11:45 A.M., he called Sadie Barrett to chastise her for a July 6 telephone call she had made to the Buxbaum residence, in which she had expressed her condolences on behalf of Rob and had left her telephone number.

"Why did you call the Buxbaums?" he demanded.

"Well, you wanted *somebody* to do it," Sadie Barrett replied, recalling her son's frenzied phone calls from the Westbury to get Kelly Barrett to collect money from Helmuth to pay Foshay, Armes, and Allen.

"Are you fucking crazy or what?"

"He wasn't even around," she protested.

"But you left your phone number," Barrett snapped, repeating what Helmuth had told him.

"Oh well, you kept bugging Kelly all the time."

"It's got *nothing* to do with you," Barrett said desperately.

"Okay then."

"Okay then, yeah, it's okay then," he mocked. "Want me to go to jail for *twenty-five* years?" The surveillance officers listened hard; there was only one offence that carried that kind of sentence, and it wasn't peddling drugs at Kelly's Bar.

"I didn't mention your name," Sadie replied defensively.

"You didn't have to, you left your phone number. All they gotta do is call up Bell Canada and find out who owns that phone number."

"Yeah, and you gave them Debbie's number, too," Sadie said, reminding her son of an earlier call that Barrett himself had placed to the Buxbaum residence.

"To Andy [Helmuth's code name], yes, *not* to his fucking son."

"Now don't swear at me."

"Swear at you?" Barrett said angrily. "I was gonna come over last night and belt you in the head."

After hanging up on his mother, Barrett called Pat Allen and reluctantly agreed to a 6 P.M. meeting in Thames Park. He then called his brother, John, looking for money.

"It's just until I can pick up mine," Barrett said in a shaky voice.

"When's that?" John asked.

"In the next few days."

"How do you know that?"

"Well, 'cause that's the way it was set up," Barrett replied, obliquely referring to the $7,000 Helmuth still owed him.

"Have you been talking to him lately, like yesterday or today?" John asked.

"Yesterday. He was supposed to meet me last night but he didn't show up, so something must've come up."

"Where'd you get in contact with him?"

"At his house, from a phone booth," Barrett replied, sounding sleepy from the drugs he was using.

"An' when's he supposed to be goin' back to work?" The pauses were beginning to get longer between John Barrett's questions and his brother's answers.

"I don't know," Barrett replied, yawning and trailing off into a cough.

"So he said within the next couple of days?"

"Uh huh. Oh, I'm expecting a couple of airline tickets, too."

"To where?"

"Anywhere I want."

"Sure he ain't gonna fuck you around?"

"You kidding?" Barrett replied, suddenly brimming with confidence.

"Well, why didn't he show up last night then?"

"Well, obviously something came up that he couldn't get away an' he didn't want to take the chance."

"How's he supposed to get in contact with you then?"

"He's got the number here."

Barrett told his brother that he needed a place to stay and was considering renting an apartment for a month, or until he could get out of London. John told him it was a good idea, provided Buxbaum came through with the money.

"Oh yeah, well, I told him, that was the insurance. To make sure that he does pay me. Two's as easy as one," Barrett said.

"What insurance?"

"Well, if he don't pay, he's number two."

The officers in the van looked at each other as Robert Barrett broke into a short, nasty laugh. These words would later explain for the police Helmuth's mania for security guards and personal weapons. John tried to keep the conversation going but Barrett broke it off, telling him that he was expecting a call and didn't want to tie up the line. Unaware of how closely Helmuth's every move was being watched by Phil Conley, Barrett was still hoping that he would keep his promise to call him on Tuesday, July 10. But, by 4:20 P.M. the phone at Debbie Barber's apartment still hadn't rung. Exasperated, Barrett called the Buxbaum residence for the third time, this time reaching the man who had fired him from his landscaping job at Komoka six weeks earlier and whose mother he had had killed.

"Ah, yes, has Mr. Buxbaum come back in yet?" Barrett asked, nervously clearing his throat.

"Could I please have your name?" Paul Buxbaum asked.

"Yeah, it's Andy Ross calling back."

"Ah, let me get a pen here. Could you spell that for me please?"

"R-O-S-S," Barrett replied.

"Okay and, ah, could I have your phone number?"

"Um, I'm at a kind of phone booth," Barrett said, as he paced back and forth in Debbie Barber's kitchen. "I don't have one."

Paul tried to get the number of the pay phone, but Barrett said he would call back later. He made a final attempt to reach Helmuth on July 10 just before 8 P.M., once again Helmuth wasn't available.

Fifteen minutes later, Robert Barrett had more serious problems than Helmuth's maddening silence. A furious Pat Allen called Debbie Barber's apartment to find out why Barrett hadn't kept their appointment in Thames Park – a meeting Squirrel had hoped would somehow just go away.

"Where were you?" Allen asked angrily.

"Where was I?"

"Yeah."

"Where was I suppose to be?" Barrett innocently replied.

"Six o'clock. At the park."

"I forgot all about it, I was sleeping," Barrett said, breaking into the high-pitched, silly laugh that often disarmed his friends, even when they were angry at him.

"Well, do you wanna get your ass over here *right now*," Allen replied sternly.

"I got no money to get there," Barrett protested. Allen sighed before making his frosty reply.

"I'll send a cab for you. Be fuckin' ready, okay."

"Okay."

"Because we got some talkin' to do."

The officers inside the wiretap van immediately contacted the physical surveillance team and told them where the meeting between Barrett and Allen was to take place. When a cab pulled up in front of Pat Allen's home with Barrett riding in the back, five officers were already in position around Thames Park. They observed Allen and Barrett meet briefly on the porch of the house before Barrett left again. Although the officers didn't know it, the topic of conversation was the Hanna Buxbaum murder.

"Gary Foshay and Terry Armes were looking for Rob for more money. Gary Foshay had called me earlier and said . . . Terry and him were short," Pat Allen later said.

It was beginning to dawn on Robert Barrett that arranging a murder wasn't necessarily the answer to all his problems.

By July 10, Helmuth Buxbaum was beginning to feel more like Phil Conley's unruly child than his wealthy benefactor. The younger man chaperoned the widower all morning as he went through the melancholy aftermath of Hanna's funeral. Helmuth opened an envelope sent over from Needham's Funeral Home containing Hanna's jewellery – her own wedding band, her mother-in-law's wedding band, a ruby ring, and a brooch with a floral design.

The two men then opened the stack of condolence notes that had poured in from across the country. Bryan College, which had organized the Buxbaums' trip to Oberammergau, sent a note to say that it would be placing Gideon Memorial Bibles in Hanna's memory in motel rooms across the United States. Mario Bruno, a preacher from British Columbia who found out about Hanna's murder while visiting a church in Mississauga, beseeched Helmuth to keep his faith: "No amount of writing could fill the vacuum in your life you now must feel. I have read that when godly men lose their wives, they seem to go to pieces more so than when godly women lose their husbands. I want you to know that I am praying for you. Keep your testimony strong and true. Continue to live a holy, blameless life in the Lord."

When Helmuth looked up from the stack of condolences, he saw Martha Wagner inscribing the visitors book from her sister's funeral with decorative letters. Just inside the front cover was the frail signature of Ottilie Schmidt. The children kept to themselves and the house was strangely quiet, filled now with the flowers from Needham's Funeral Home. Helmuth felt a mild sense of relief as he set out for Treugott Management to meet with his staff for the first time since Hanna's murder.

After a subdued lunch at the Horse and Hound restaurant around the corner from Treugott, Phil Conley drove Helmuth to his lawyer's office to sign some papers. On the way, Conley once again asked Helmuth if his drug connections were trying to blackmail him. "No, believe me, I'm not being blackmailed," Helmuth insisted. "If I pay these guys for the drugs, they will get off my back."

Phil Conley was still not convinced. Helmuth had told him that he never bought more than four grams of cocaine at a time, which at $125 per gram would mean a debt of only $500. But Helmuth kept insisting that he owed a London pusher four times that amount. So was the debt an outstanding drug bill, or, as Conley feared, hush money to keep Helmuth's cocaine habit from becoming public?

When they came to the intersection of Wharncliffe Road and Stanley Street, Helmuth ordered Conley to pull over, explaining that he needed to pick up some money he was owed. Suspecting a darker purpose, Conley refused. When Conley stopped at some traffic lights, Helmuth jumped out and crossed against the red light, threading his way through the traffic towards Chris Brooker's coin shop. Conley watched in the rear view mirror as his reluctant passenger entered the coin shop. When the light changed, Conley pulled over at the first pay phone and called Pastor Paul Fawcett for advice. They agreed that Conley should pick up Fawcett, who would talk with Helmuth about the things that were clearly clouding his life.

Helmuth, meanwhile, was collecting $1,400 in cash from Chris Brooker – the balance owing on his July 6 sale of a five-ounce gold bar. With Conley nowhere in sight, Helmuth then took a cab to Del McLennan's law office, arriving just after 3:30 P.M. Half an hour later, Conley and Pastor Fawcett showed up. The three men left together and Helmuth immediately began complaining to Fawcett about Conley's custodial behaviour. "Isn't this ridiculous?" Helmuth inveighed. "Phil doesn't want to give me the keys to my own van!"

Pastor Fawcett dropped Conley off where he had parked the van and then took Helmuth to his office. "While I was alone with Fawcett, I complained to him that everyone was trying to control me and I resented being treated like a child," Helmuth said later.

After listening patiently to Helmuth's complaints, Fawcett recommended that he see Dr. Ken Nichols to talk over his problems, knowing that Helmuth had already dealt with the psychologist when he and Hanna had entered marriage counselling in 1979. Helmuth agreed, and Pastor Fawcett arranged for the doctor to fly up from his Washington clinic on Thursday, July 12.

It was certainly a lot better than going to a Michigan psychiatric hospital, even one run on Christian principles.

✦   ✦   ✦

Curiosity finally got the best of Kimberly Louigne.

For the past two days, the sixteen-year-old girl had been moving her belongings into the back apartment at Robin Foshay's place and couldn't help noticing the tarpaulin-covered car parked in the driveway. When she asked Robin, for whom she regularly babysat, who owned the car, the nervous young woman evaded her question.

But on July 10, the day after Anita Pitcher collected the car, Robin invited her babysitter into her kitchen and asked a question of her own. What would Kimberly do if she knew someone who had committed a murder? When the teenager replied that it would depend on who that person was, Robin quickly took the conversation out of the realm of the hypothetical. "Gary pulled Mrs. Buxbaum out of the car and shot her," she whispered.

Robin went on to say that Gary had been hired by the person Helmuth Buxbaum had paid to arrange his wife's murder. The terrified young girl didn't know what to say, and found herself wishing that she hadn't rented the back apartment – particularly when Robin Foshay added a final detail: "Robin warned me that Gary had told her, 'If you or Kim say anything about this,' he wouldn't hesitate to blow both our brains out."

While the twin tape recorders of the electronic surveillance team kept whirring, other elements of the investigation pressed slowly ahead. Const. Andy Fotheringham was detailed to check all telephone numbers that the investigation had so far turned up, running them through the police intelligence computer. He was also instructed to obtain telephone tolls for the various suspects for the previous six months.

The TRU team searching the murder site recovered a number of Player's Light cigarette butts, which were turned over to the Identification Unit for fingerprint examination. After being guided to the spot by Constable Medlyn, they also found a syringe at the site on Highway 402 where the Buxbaums had stopped on the morning of July 5. No usable prints were recovered.

The assistance of other police forces continued to be invaluable. In Toronto, the Metro police gave Corporal McNally of the Identification Unit the duffel bag containing Robert Barrett's clothing that had been seized from Edith Sturge's apartment. Sgt. Dave King of the London police informed the investigators of Helmuth's July 6 gold transaction at Chris Brooker's coin shop. Finally, Sgt. James Balmain of the London force set up a meeting between OPP Const. Paul Edwards and Otto

Buxbaum in a car parked in the lot of the Lamplighter Motel, the place where Helmuth had often entertained his "dates" from the Taurus Escort Service.

"I heard she was shot three times. Why didn't he [Helmuth] chase the car and put it off the road?" Otto mused to Constable Edwards. "I also talked to some family members who said, 'Could it be Helmuth removed Hanna because she knew too much?' It was my wife that said that. To me, this whole thing smells like a contract murder. Why was Helmuth not hurt? Why was Helmuth's money or credit cards not taken?"

Edwards listened patiently, but by the time Otto finished rambling, he knew that the only thing the businessman had to offer was his opinion that Helmuth had been involved in Hanna's murder.

When Piers learned of the meeting, he dismissed Otto's remarks, but noted the oddity of a man coming forward against his own brother. "It's terribly unusual," he thought, "but then this is turning into a very unusual case."

The morning of July 11 began with an 8:30 A.M. conference of the detectives working on Project Angel: constables Bart Linker, Greg Calcott, Andy Fotheringham, Gary Aspden, Paul Edwards, Mel Getty, and Det. Insp. Ron Piers. The meeting took place under the peaceful gaze of Hanna herself, whose enlarged photograph smiled down on them from its place of honour on the squad room wall. In every murder case, a crucial part of the basic police work is a thorough investigation of the victim, a routine that often yields valuable clues about the motive and identity of the killer. But in this case, it had also revealed something else.

"In a murder investigation, you always talk to hundreds of people about the victim. We did that in the Buxbaum case, but there was a big difference. Not a single person had anything bad to say about Hanna Buxbaum. Everybody loved the woman. None of us had ever seen that before. That's why we put her picture on the squad room wall and called the investigation 'Project Angel'," Const. Mel Getty said later.

After the detectives exchanged information on the Toronto and London ends of the case, Inspector Piers assigned Getty to gather the necessary information for an authorization to wiretap Janet Hicks' apartment. Andy Fotheringham was to check with Needham's Funeral Home to see if Helmuth had received any telephone calls while he was on the premises. The other officers were to continue interviewing witnesses and checking out Helmuth's business and personal affairs around London.

The meeting broke up at noon. All afternoon information continued to flow into the homicide team's Adelaide Street command centre, some of it from surprising sources. A prominent London criminal lawyer called to arrange a private meeting with Piers on the parking lot of a local A&P store. During their hour-and-a-half talk in the man's brown truck, he gave the detective general tips about some of the people he thought might be involved in the crime, a few of whom had been clients.

The Joint Forces surveillance team reported that Helmuth was on his way to Chatham in a Ford Bronco with one of his sons and a bodyguard. Later he would be observed checking his boat at the Merritt Marina in Chatham, where it would be noticed that he was carrying a gun. Shortly afterwards, the probate office called to say that Hanna Buxbaum's estate had been evaluated at $4 million.

But the best news of the day was supplied by Const. Randy McNaught of the OPP's Strathroy Detachment. McNaught turned over a pad of green foam rubber that had been found by Earl Pincomb on the northeast corner of County Road 16 and Concession 7. It would turn out to be the material Foshay and Armes had used to cover their licence plate on the night of the murder.

The electronic surveillance team added tantalizing information to the now bulging murder file. The police had listened in as Debbie Barber explained to a female caller that Robert Barrett had set up the contract killing, but that someone else had actually committed the murder.

They had also heard Barber read the riot act to Kelly Barrett. Ever since Barber had returned from her weekend in Grand Bend to find the Barretts snuggled down in her bed, she had been unhappy about their continuing presence in her apartment. But after the events of July 5, tensions between Barber and her guests had been stretched to the breaking point. She now told Kelly Barrett that if they didn't get out of her apartment immediately, she would call the police. Everyone, it seemed, was beginning to feel the heat.

Shortly after 1 P.M., Robert Barrett treated police to another interesting conversation, this time with his Westbury bodyguard, Rick Diorio, and Helmuth's former playmate, Dawn Watson:

"Where're you gonna go?" Diorio asked.

"I don't know yet," Barrett replied.

"Well?"

"Ah, I just bin sitting here waitin' for fuckhead [Buxbaum] to call, but that could take some time so I gotta –"

"Yeah, well, better off not fuckin' talkin' to him anyways," Diorio advised.

"Yeah."

"He's an idiot."

"Hmm, yeah."

"You know what I mean?"

"Yeah, yeah, I was gonna wait till he contacts me," Barrett replied, saying he had to go.

"Hold on, someone wants to talk to you."

"Who does?" Barrett asked.

"Hey, Squirrel!" a female voice squealed.

"Who's this?"

"Guess."

"I don't know."

"Fuckin' Dawn, asshole!" Watson shrieked.

"*Oh*. Howya doin'?"

"Do you believe it?" she asked, a thinly masked reference to the Buxbaum murder.

"No."

"Fuck, eh!"

"No shit."

"Fuck me, I don't fuckin' believe it. What a fuckin' goof!"

Getting uncomfortable, Barrett tried to change the subject.

"So whatya been up to?" he asked.

"Nothin' much," Helmuth's old girlfriend said laughingly. "He's gonna get nailed you know."

"Probably."

"For sure. As long as my fuckin' name don't come into it."

"It's pretty wild."

"It *is*. Everybody's fuckin' talkin' about it."

Whether it was the prospect of Helmuth getting arrested before Barrett collected his final payment or just itchy impatience, Squirrel put in another call to Treugott after finishing his conversation with Diorio and Watson. Once more, he got the same exasperating reply he had been getting for the past three days: Mr. Buxbaum wasn't taking calls.

At 6:30 A.M. on July 12, Helmuth Buxbaum finally broke away from the unwelcome shadow of Phil Conley to take care of some private business. Dressed in a dark blue suit and wearing green sunglasses, he slipped quietly out the back entrance of his Komoka home while the rest of the household slept. His briefcase was somewhat heavier than usual from the more than two pounds of gold in five-ounce bars he had stowed inside. He got into the family van and headed to the airport. Inside the terminal, he bought a ticket and then headed into the restaurant to wait for his flight.

As he settled down to an order of coffee and toast, an RCMP special constable was already on the telephone to the OPP with the news that Helmuth Buxbaum had just bought a ticket on Air Ontario flight 802 to Toronto – a *one-way* ticket. The OPP called the RCMP's Special Squad at Pearson airport and arranged to have the suspect followed.

Const. Barry Stewart of the Intelligence Branch was ready and waiting at Pearson when Helmuth arrived and made his way to a pay phone on the departure level of Terminal 2. If the homicide investigators were afraid that Helmuth was preparing to flee the country, their fears were somewhat allayed when Stewart reported that Helmuth had called a Mrs. Toth in Komoka and told her he would be returning to London at 12:30 P.M. He also left instructions with her to have someone take the Bronco and pick up the speedboat so that it would be ready for the trek to the cottage later that night.

Helmuth then took a limousine to downtown Toronto. Constable Stewart and Corporal Bell of the RCMP's Special Squad followed the car to the Guardian Trust Company at 123 Yonge Street, where Helmuth sold two gold bars. His next stop was the Deak-Perera Foreign Exchange at 10 King Street West, where he sold two more. His final banking stop was at the Deak-Perera office at Square One plaza in Mississauga, where he sold three more five-ounce bars, for a total gold sale of thirty-five ounces. It was a tidy morning's work. In just a few hours, Helmuth had collected nearly $16,000, including several thousand dollars' worth of Swiss, German, and American currency.

Moments after he left the Mississauga foreign exchange, Constable Stewart questioned Deak-Perera tellers Lisa Thomson and Angela Johnson about Helmuth's transactions. Both women reported that, although it was company policy to issue cheques for large gold purchases, Helmuth had insisted on being paid in cash. "He said a cheque was no good to him because he was from out of the country," Johnson told police.

When Piers learned of the gold transactions, he wondered why Helmuth would need so much cash. Was it, as an informant had already told police, because there was another payment due to Hanna Buxbaum's killers? Or did he need the foreign currency because he was planning to leave the country? The answer, he reasoned, would come if Buxbaum tried to contact Robert Barrett, something that the wiretaps showed he hadn't so far attempted. Patience was the order of the day.

By the afternoon of July 12, patience was in short supply at Debbie Barber's apartment.

Barber had put up with a lot from Robert Barrett, but murder was where she drew the line. Ever since she had read the accounts of Hanna Buxbaum's slaying on the morning of July 6, she had refused to believe that Helmuth's and Barrett's meeting at her apartment on the afternoon of July 4 had been mere coincidence. Nor had she been persuaded by Kelly Barrett's story that Barrett had gone to Toronto for a major cocaine deal, particularly after he had called collect the morning after the murder asking Kelly to go to Needham's Funeral Home to get more money from Helmuth Buxbaum. She knew you didn't interrupt a man visiting his wife at a funeral parlour to finance a drug deal. Besides, hadn't Barrett himself boasted to her after his Florida trip that Hanna's murder, which he had been paid by Helmuth Buxbaum to arrange, was supposed to have taken place while he was in Orlando?

For days now, Barber had listened in on the extension as Barrett had used her upstairs telephone to discuss matters that were obviously related to the murder. Barrett had even grudgingly told her some of the details of the crime, including the fact that Pat Allen was supposed to have carried out Hanna's execution but had backed out at the last minute.

Then the calls from Helmuth Buxbaum, using his code name, "Andy," had started to come in. In a call that Barber took before the wiretap had been authorized, Helmuth told her that he didn't know how he was going to get away from Komoka to "do some coke with Squirrel." Barber smiled, having recently listened in on another of Barrett's calls in which he had talked about having Helmuth killed.

"Rob's talkin' on the phone the other day and he's going, 'Well, I don't know how they're gonna do all this because his house is surrounded by security or something.' Rob says, 'Where do you want me to take a poke at him?'" Barber said later.

The sinister atmosphere the Barretts brought into her house was more than Debbie Barber could bear. For two days she had been trying to evict them. They always agreed to leave but never seemed to get around to moving – even after Barber threatened to call the police. The last straw came on July 11 when Barrett phoned the Mounties in front of Barber's children to find out the date of his court appearance on cocaine charges arising out of the July 6 incident at Pearson airport. "I just went nuts, because you don't talk like that in front of little kids . . . I told them to pack their shit and get out."

The tension between Barber and the Barretts was at the breaking point on the afternoon of July 12 when the Barretts returned to pick up the last of their belongings. Barber, who was on her way to a job interview, insisted that the couple come back later, fearing that Squirrel would otherwise help himself to some of her belongings. Barrett ignored her request and began taking Barber's pictures off the wall and throwing them into boxes. Barber finally exploded when he yanked out some speaker wires and carelessly tossed more of her possessions down the stairs to his wife, Kelly. The spirited young woman, whose only criminal conviction had been for assault, ordered the couple out of the house, giving them two minutes to leave before she called the police. Barrett responded by shaking his fist in Barber's face and threatening her life.

The surveillance officers in the van outside the apartment listened in as Debbie Barber picked up the telephone and dialled 911. A police car quickly arrived at the scene, and the Barretts noisily moved their belongings into two cabs. After a few parting words for their former landlady, they made the short drive over to the latest of their temporary living quarters, London's Brunswick Hotel.

Less than fifteen minutes after the Barretts rolled out of her driveway and, she hoped, her life, Barber picked up the telephone and called Sgt. Bob Cann of the London police. Infuriated by Barrett's threats and violence, she set up a meeting with the police officer to talk about the Hanna Buxbaum murder the next morning.

It would be a long conversation. Next to orchestrating the roadside killing, Robert Barrett had just made the biggest mistake of his life.

Police at the Adelaide Street offices of the OPP's Criminal Investigation Branch were frantically busy all through the long, hot day of July 12. Not since the stunning revelations of July 7 had the murder investigation taken so many dramatic turns. Shortly after the Mounties' call saying that Helmuth Buxbaum was on the move to Toronto, Const. Mel Getty had received a collect call from a woman who claimed that Helmuth had asked her to kill his wife in January 1984.

Susan Ambrose had already called police on July 9, but no one had had time to return her call. After reading the press coverage of the murder, she hadn't been able to wait any longer. As she explained to Getty, she was afraid that Helmuth, her former boyfriend, would try to "silence" her. While Getty scribbled the distraught woman's words into his notebook as fast as he could write, Ambrose recounted how she had become Helmuth's lover shortly after New Year's, regularly meeting him in various London motels during their steamy, three-week relationship in January 1984. The nervous woman claimed that, after a few dates, Helmuth had complained about his unhappy home life. Ambrose claimed that he had then asked her point-blank if she would help him kill his wife. It was a measure of how overwhelmed the police were with quality tips that Getty didn't get a chance to take a statement from this crucial informant until August 13 – a month later.

It was a different matter with Betty Case. The proprietor of the Golden Pheasant Motel had been on vacation when Hanna Buxbaum was murdered. But when she learned about the sensational crime after returning to London, chilling memories of January 23 had come flooding back. She remembered that two of her employees, her sister, Joyce Black, and another woman, Elizabeth Davis, had come to her that day to tell her that, while listening outside the door of Room 137, which was registered to a Helmuth Buxbaum, they had overheard a couple planning to poison a woman by lacing her food with deadly herbs. Case and her husband called the police on the morning of July 12, and Const. Gary Aspden drove out to the rural motel to interview Black and Davis.

Aspden was able to confirm Case's story with the two chambermaids, who readily gave signed statements. But it would be several more weeks before police realized a startling coincidence: the young woman who had called Mel Getty earlier in the day, claiming that Helmuth had asked her to murder his wife, was the same person the chambermaids had overheard talking about poisoning someone.

One of the most disquieting developments for Inspector Piers that day was a small detail provided by Colin Lawrence, the truck driver who had been the first person on the scene after the roadside shooting on July 5. In his July 12 statement to Const. Mel Getty, he described how he had tried to assist Hanna Buxbaum from the moment he found out from her husband that she had been shot. Piers was struck by a single sentence in Lawrence's statement: "As I was walking to the place where she was lying, the husband said to me she had been shot in the head."

Piers read the words over and over again. Helmuth had told investigators that he had been in the middle of the highway when the gun was fired and had not witnessed the slaying. He had also told Piers and Corporal Sweeney that at no time had he gone over the guardrail to his fallen wife. The trucker's recollection raised a very large question: if Helmuth's previous statements to police were true, and he hadn't witnessed the shooting, how had he been able to tell Colin Lawrence his wife had been shot in the head? And if they were not true, what had he been trying to hide?

After completing his gold transactions in Toronto, Helmuth decided to drive back to London. Const. Barry Stewart followed his limousine as far as the Milton exit from Highway 401. Helmuth, it seemed, had decided to treat his driver to lunch at McDonald's. The Mountie took up a position in one of two adjacent phone booths with a clear view of both the front entrance of the restaurant and the limousine.

Ten minutes later, Helmuth left the restaurant and entered the phone booth beside Const. Stewart, who heard him place a collect call to Komoka to see if Mark had picked up the boat. The limousine then continued west on Highway 401 to Highway 2, where it pulled into a Co-op gas bar, where Helmuth again used the pay phone. He then continued his journey towards London. Constable Stewart followed at a discreet distance until he reached Highway 74, where an OPP team was waiting to pick up the surveillance. They followed Helmuth to the London airport, where he paid the limousine driver $200, retrieved his van, and set out on the short drive back to Komoka.

Anxiously awaiting him there were Paul Buxbaum, Pastor Paul Fawcett, and Dr. Ken Nichols. Helmuth's unannounced trip to Toronto had taken everyone by surprise. Paul was afraid that his father had forgotten about his appointment with Dr. Nichols, who had flown all the way from Seattle on a very tight schedule to see him. He was also worried that his father was slipping back into the familiar vices.

Nichols was devastated by Hanna's death and depressed by the "very foreboding" atmosphere at Komoka created by the presence of security personnel and guard dogs. Many years ago, Helmuth had told the young psychologist that he was "struggling," but he had never openly admitted to any marital infidelities or a serious drug problem. So Nichols could scarcely believe his ears when Pastor Fawcett and Paul Buxbaum told him about Helmuth's bizarre behaviour during the months leading up to the murder. When Paul expressed the fear that his father might even be involved in his mother's murder in some unknown way, Nichols could only shake his head. Helmuth's son and his pastor told him that it was absolutely essential that Helmuth check into Pine Rest Christian Hospital as quickly as possible.

If Nichols had any doubt about that, it vanished when he met Helmuth again for the first time in five years. He was shocked by the "drastic" change in the once warm and articulate businessman who had contributed $200 a month to help Nichols establish his own clinic in Richland, Washington. Preferring to speak to Helmuth alone, Nichols suggested they walk to Hanna's grave. The doctor expressed his heartfelt regret that he had missed her funeral. Helmuth told his old friend that he didn't know what he would do without his wife. When they reached Hanna's grave, both men got down on their knees to pray. As he had every day since his wife's funeral, Helmuth picked a rose from her grave and put it in his lapel.

Despite Helmuth's show of grief, Nichols sensed that something was terribly wrong. "I met with Helmuth only briefly. He was very distant . . . He refused to make eye contact with me . . . He mumbled and his speech was unclear . . . I confronted him openly about the drugs. There was really no response at all . . . I also confronted him about any possible involvement in Hanna's death. Again, he really gave me no response."

Nichols tried to persuade Helmuth to seek immediate psychiatric help in Grand Rapids. Although he agreed to go, Helmuth pushed his admission date into the future, protesting that his children needed him too much right now. It was a replay of his May visit to Pine Rest with Hanna, when he had promised to check in, but put off his treatment date because of the pending family trip to Europe. A stay in a psychiatric hospital where his personal freedom might be snatched away by a doctor's assessment simply wasn't in Helmuth Buxbaum's plans.

Once Nichols and Fawcett had left for the airport, frustrated in their attempt to help the troubled businessman deal with his personal demons, Helmuth called the OPP and asked Const. Paul Edwards if the police were finished with his station wagon. Edwards said it was ready, and Helmuth arranged to have Ken Surette pick it up the next day, explaining to the detective that he was on his way to Huntsville for a week. He then rounded up the children, including his nephew, Roy, and a family friend, fourteen-year-old John Lauenstein, and got ready to leave for the cottage. He also brought along a security officer and a guard dog for his personal protection and arranged for around-the-clock patrols at the cottage by a four-man team with dogs.

The only holdout was Helmuth's eldest son. Paul Buxbaum refused to accompany the rest of the family north, declaring that if Helmuth wouldn't go to Pine Rest to get help, then he wouldn't go to the cottage and pretend that everything was normal.

Shadowed by the OPP surveillance team, the Buxbaums set out on the long drive to Mary Lake. At Port Severn Landing, Helmuth left his party to use the pay phone. At 8:16 P.M., the officers in the surveillance van outside Debbie Barber's London apartment fell silent, as the call they had been waiting for finally came in:

"Hello?" Barber said.

"Yes, is Rob there?"

"Who?"

"Rob."

"Ah, who's calling please?" Barber replied.

"Ah, Andy," Helmuth answered.

"Ah, yeah, listen Andy, I, uh, asked Rob to leave today."

"Did he?"

"Yes, so I assume that you could find him back at his brother's."

"His brother John?"

"Yeah. Okay?"

"Okay."

"Right, bye-bye."

Thanks to Barber and Barrett's parting of the ways a few short hours before, police lost the opportunity to listen to a conversation between the two key suspects in the Hanna Buxbaum murder. All that remained after the cryptic call was a tantalizing question: why would Helmuth Buxbaum call Robert Barrett on the same day he had quietly amassed $16,000 in cash after a swift and solitary trip to Toronto?

At 10:30 P.M., the physical surveillance team watched as Helmuth disappeared inside the family cottage carrying three bags of groceries. Half an hour later, the lights winked out after the Buxbaums' generator failed. For a few moments, the officers watched the dark silhouettes of the dogs and security guards posted at the gates of the cottage. When all fell silent under the starry northern sky, they headed back to the Hidden Valley Inn for a few hours sleep.

It would be a long week.

✦　✦　✦

While the Buxbaums were basking in the sun at their cottage, Debbie Barber was blowing the Hanna Buxbaum murder case wide open. In a statement to Sgt. Bob Cann of the London force, she gave the police a shadowy but essentially accurate outline of the entire crime, describing how her former friend, Robert Barrett, and his "mark," Helmuth Buxbaum, had spent months talking about killing Hanna Buxbaum.

In the weeks leading up to the roadside slaying, Barrett had been "talking about murder all over the city. Now the people he's asked . . . to do it last month is incredible," she said. Whenever their schemes back-fired, the pair doggedly hatched a new plot. "This guy is like dirt that I walk on," Barber said of Komoka's most respected citizen.

For the first time, police learned of Robert Barrett's trip to Florida. Barber explained how Helmuth had given him the money to take his wife, Kelly, to Orlando. "The whole job was supposed to go down when Squirrel was in Florida," she said. "That's why Squirrel has all these receipts. He keeps telling me that 'I have all these receipts to prove where I was.'"

Although she didn't know the details, Barber explained that the per-son Barrett had hired in Florida to do the job had cheated him, and that Squirrel had returned to London in late June desperate to hire another contract killer. Sometime before July 5, he made a deal with Pat Allen, a well-known petty criminal, whose London apartment had been searched by police in March 1984 in relation to a rash of assaults and robberies in Hamilton. The former militiaman and weapons expert had a "box full of guns" and a clear plan to kidnap and then execute the millionaire's wife. Barber said that Helmuth Buxbaum was so heavily involved in the plan-ning of his wife's execution that on the eve of the murder he had even had to rid himself of a piece of stolen property that could tie him to Robert Barrett.

The article in question was a "brown mink that [Barrett] stole . . . last winter when he was doin' all those B and ES, and he sold it to Helmuth for $900, and Helmuth gave it back to him. He said, 'I don't want this hot coat 'cause if the cops come over . . .' He says, 'You get rid of it again . . . All I want is $200 out of it and you can have the rest.'"

Although Barber was fuzzy on the details of the Toronto trip Barrett had taken on the night of July 4, she told Cann that he and Rick Diorio left London in a rented limousine to do some high-profile partying at the Westbury Hotel. The real purpose of the junket was to establish a firm alibi for Barrett when the murder took place the next morning in

London. But the plot had gone awry. "Pat Allen screwed it up in the morning," Barber said, explaining that Allen had then bailed out of the deadly ambush, forcing Barrett to hire two other men; she didn't know who they were. It was one of those two men, Barber said, who had actually carried out the July 5 execution. "He was only supposed to shoot her once. I guess he ended up shootin' her three times because he missed. So you can tell he was just someone stupid, one of Pat Allen's friends," she said.

Barber then clarified for the police some of Barrett's frenetic movements on July 6. She explained that he had flown back to London that night to pick up money from Helmuth Buxbaum to pay the killers. Buxbaum, she claimed, had gathered part of the money by selling gold bars so there would be no record of the transaction in his books. But the account was still outstanding. Buxbaum hadn't yet delivered on a promise to move Barrett and his family to Prince Edward Island and to give him a job at his nursing home there.

By 2 P.M., Cann had briefed Inspector Piers on the contents of the Barber interview and had arranged to provide the OPP with a taped version of her story later in the day. Fully appreciating the import of the new information, Piers called a meeting of the entire investigating team to listen to the tape. With the names of other possible conspirators to the murder now in his hands, Piers instructed Mel Getty and Ken Allen to prepare the necessary affidavits so that the wiretap effort could be broadened to include Kelly Barrett, Janet Hicks, Pat Allen, and Rick Diorio.

Piers gave one other assignment to OPP wiretap technician G. B. McVicar. He asked him to bug the basement conference room and the detention cells on the main level of the London Detachment. It was now only a matter of time before some of the suspects in the Hanna Buxbaum murder would be confined there. If they talked about their crime, Piers wanted to hear exactly what they had to say.

After his official duties were over, the detective drove up to Campbell Cemetery and "just stood a couple of minutes" in front of Hanna's grave. It was hard to believe that a little over a week ago, she had been as alive as her killers.

It wouldn't be long now.

Inspector Piers wasn't alone in believing that it was only a matter of time before the truth would out. Since the night his mother was murdered,

Paul Buxbaum had been sure that the intensive police investigation would uncover his father's secret life of cocaine and prostitutes. Even if Helmuth had not in some way been involved in Hanna Buxbaum's death, the exposure of his vices would be enough to destroy his nursing-home empire. All of the homes required annual government licences to operate, and one of the opposition leaders in the Ontario legislature, Bob Rae of the New Democratic Party, was already a staunch critic of the province's institutional care of elderly. For Rae, Helmuth Buxbaum, who had grown fabulously wealthy warehousing the elderly, symbolized all that was wrong with the nursing-home system. Paul knew that even if the police didn't actually charge Helmuth for cocaine use, just one leak to Rae about the drug addiction of Treugott's sole owner would be enough to put the wealthy family out of business.

Paul had already discussed the precarious situation with Treugott's senior managers, who in turn had taken the matter up with Helmuth's lawyer, Del McLennan. It was decided that the best way to protect the family business would be for Helmuth to put his shares of Treugott into trust. That way, if the scandal ever broke, it could be argued that he no longer owned any nursing homes. The only job that remained was to get Helmuth to agree to transfer his shares.

By July 14, Paul knew the unpleasant task couldn't wait any longer. At 9:55 A.M., detectives Calcott and Edwards showed up at the Buxbaums' Komoka residence and interviewed him about some of his mother's allegedly missing jewellery, jewellery that Debbie Barber mistakenly believed was now in Pat Allen's hands. In the course of the hour-long interview, the investigators tried to extract more information about Helmuth from Paul, who quickly realized that they already knew about his father's immoral and illegal activities.

As soon as the officers left, Paul called the cottage, getting Phillip on the line. The mood in the surveillance van became electric.

"Hi Phil,"

"How're you doin'?"

"Not too good," Paul replied.

"Why?"

"Well, cops were just here."

"Yeah." Phillip listened as his brother heaved a long sigh.

"They talked to me."

"What happened?"

"Nothing. I didn't give them much," Paul said a little breathlessly.

"Do they know?" Phillip asked, referring to Helmuth's cocaine use.

"Sure, Phillip. They've known for a long time."

"Yeah. What are they saying?"

"Nothing," Paul answered. "They don't tell me much, but it's getting closer. Let me talk to Dad."

The previous day, the wiretap had picked up Paul telling his father that he "disagreed" with what Helmuth had done and advising him to get a lawyer. He now reinforced that message by telling him about the visit from Calcott and Edwards.

"I hate to ruin your day, but the police were just here. They know a lot. I just wanted to let you know."

"And?" Helmuth asked.

"And, ah, they know a lot . . . Just wanted to let you know."

"Yeah. What?"

"I can't talk over the phone. I think the phone's probably bugged."

"Well, why don't you come up here?" Helmuth suggested.

"No, I gotta hold onto things down here," Paul said stubbornly.

"Well, what did they say to you?" Helmuth asked again.

"Nothing. They just, ah, tried to squeeze stuff out of me and they made it known that they know what's going down in your life. If I were you, I would seek legal counsel. Dad, I'm serious, from a financial and a personal point of view."

At 11:30 P.M. the OPP monitor at Komoka listened in as Paul called Phil Conley and told him about the visit from the police. He asked Conley to call Howard Johnson from a pay phone and tell him what had happened. Arrangements were then made for Johnson and Del McLennan to drive to Huntsville early Sunday morning to persuade Helmuth to transfer his shares in Treugott into trust.

"They were eager to set up a trust agreement for the company. I thought it was odd that they came so far to discuss the matter. They also advised me to engage a criminal lawyer. I couldn't understand why they wanted me to do so," Helmuth said later. He listened to the two men but refused to discuss any trust arrangement until he returned to London in five days' time.

After they left, Helmuth went back inside the cottage, turned on the air-conditioning and made a fire in the hearth. The day before, a member of West Park Baptist Church had come by to drop off his daughters for a visit with the Buxbaums and noticed that both the air-conditioner and a fire were going. "He said he had enough wood for the fireplace to last a thousand years, but that he would not likely live that long," Michael Dunn said later.

Back in London, the OPP's general investigation and the expanded wire-tap operation were adding important details to the murder case. Charles Downswell, the limousine driver who had taken Barrett, Diorio, Pitcher, and Hicks to the Westbury on the night of July 4, gave investigators a detailed picture of his passengers, describing how Barrett had paid him with a pair of crisp $ 100 bills. Police also interviewed several employees of the Westbury Hotel, who described the people in the Barrett party and their behaviour during their three-day stay. Finally, Air Ontario purser Becky Hess gave detectives an account of her strange encounter with "Mr. and Mrs. Barrett" – Robert Barrett and Janet Hicks – the night after the murder, telling them about the wad of bills and what appeared to be a bag of cocaine she had seen in Hicks' purse during the flight to Toronto. Meanwhile, surveillance officers listened in as Debbie Barber explained to a female caller that Barrett had to sell all of his belongings "because Helmuth won't be giving him the money for another month or so, or until it dies down."

As the case continued to dominate the media, several of Helmuth's call girls began phoning one another to discuss their experiences with the wealthy businessman, providing police with a clearer picture of his private activities in the months leading up to the murder. Terry Gallagher and Dawn Watson, who had catered to Helmuth's desire to watch lesbian sex, discussed his May trip to Europe with Dawn. Debbie Schaeffer, who had been asked by Helmuth to bear his child, traded stories with Dawn Watson about the days of sex and drugs the women had spent with the murder suspect.

One of the lighter moments in the investigation came when Dawn Watson, not realizing that her phone was wiretapped, called the OPP's London Detachment to leave an anonymous tip. Before the police even answered the telephone, the surveillance team heard Watson shout, "Buxbaum did it, I know he did it," to someone else in the room. When an officer finally picked up the receiver, Dawn said, "Buxbaum did it," and abruptly hung up.

But one new piece of information police wiretaps picked up was no laughing matter. At 3:09 A.M. Janet Hicks placed a call to Pat Allen's apartment, a call that added a critical new name to the growing list of conspirators in the Hanna Buxbaum murder investigation.

"Hello," Allen said irritably, having been awakened just moments before by the first of Hicks' two early morning phone calls.

"Hi, I forgot to tell you that Gary Foshay's gettin' in touch with me tomorrow, okay?" Hicks said. Allen sighed heavily, tired of telling his associates not to use names over the telephone.

"Yes."

"Goodnight."

Thanks to Janet Hicks' growing flair for cloak-and-dagger theatrics, the police had just been handed the name of Hanna Buxbaum's killer.

Sequestered in his well-guarded Huntsville retreat, Helmuth Buxbaum was unaware of the powerful forces that were slowly closing in on him. He and the children fell into a lazy pattern of recreation and worship that Helmuth felt was helping to take the edge off the shock and terror everyone had experienced at Hanna's murder. The Buxbaums and their friends took turns churning up Mary Lake on a Ski-Jet and there were frequent joy rides in the family's twenty-one-foot inboard powerboat.

The phone at the cottage never stopped ringing. Dr. Ken Nichols called to see how Helmuth was doing, advising him to stay away from London until some of the scars of the family's recent tragedy started to heal.

Christine High, whose father-in-law had sold Helmuth the $1-million insurance policy on Hanna's life, called to offer her condolences. When Helmuth got on the line, she asked him if he intended to check into the hospital in Grand Rapids, reminding him that it had been Hanna's wish. He told her that he still intended to seek treatment, but not just yet.

Finally it was the turn of Helmuth's nephew, Andrew Aerne, to telephone from Switzerland to see if his uncle still wanted him to come to Canada on July 24 for the all-expenses-paid vacation he had been promised during Helmuth's last banking junket to Zurich. Thinking he would make a return trip to Europe with his young nephew to look for women in Holland and Denmark, Helmuth told Aerne to call him from Buffalo airport when he arrived on the afternoon of July 25.

There were nearly as many visitors to the cottage as there were phone calls. In addition to Howard Johnson and Del McLennan, Phil and Chris Conley dropped by, as did several members of West Park Baptist Church who were staying at Muskoka Bible Camp. Ab Birch, who was staying in another cottage owned by Helmuth, twice invited the Buxbaums over for dinner. They ate the rest of their meals at McDonald's in Huntsville or at the Bible Camp, a twenty-minute drive away from the cottage.

Not all the calls Helmuth made were picked up by the surveillance team. While waiting for the children one day, just two weeks after Hanna's murder, Helmuth slipped into a phone booth to arrange an appointment with one of his call girls. "I called from Muskoka Bible Camp to E. D. in Toronto. I wanted to see how she was. I wanted to know if I could see her when I got back from Europe. There was no answer when I called. I called her grandmother's number, which E. D. had given me. She wasn't there either."

Women weren't the only thing on his mind. While at the cottage, Helmuth talked to his stockbroker, Garth Bechtal, about taking possession of some gold he had just purchased, explaining that even though it was more expensive to take delivery in five-ounce bars, they were much easier to sell than the ten-ounce variety. "I don't want some oddball refinery," he cautioned, telling Bechtal that he planned to pick up the gold bars at the TD Bank when he returned to London. He also gave instructions to his broker to pick up options on 300 ounces of gold at three different rates, a transaction with a price tag of $14,000.

Police listened with interest as Helmuth next talked to a man named Mark (not his son) about creating a "captive insurance company" in the Bahamas, a tax shelter he was told could be set up by the San Francisco law firm of Parks, Lewis & Silsby. Rounding out his financial transactions, Helmuth visited the TD Bank in Huntsville, where he filled in and deposited into his account two blank cheques that had previously been signed by Hanna, one in the amount of $50,000, the other for $60,000.

"Hanna had given me these cheques some time before. I dated them at a period before her death so that the transaction of the cheques wouldn't be frozen with Hanna's estate," he explained later, saying that he planned to use the money to pay for renovations to the cottage. Although the bank accepted the deposits at the time, both cheques were later returned to Helmuth uncashed, with an explanatory form bearing a check mark beside the words "Drawer Deceased."

Towards the end of his stay at the cottage, Helmuth once again took the children into Huntsville for lunch at McDonald's. Afterwards, he sauntered across the street to a shoemaker's, where he produced his .45-calibre Colt Commander from his briefcase, explaining to the proprietor that he wanted a custom leg holster made with enough room inside to accommodate a spare clip. Although Helmuth told the man that he needed the holster for a September hunting trip, he had a more immediate use in mind.

One night when the Buxbaums had been returning from the Muskoka Bible Camp, two men on motorcycles tried to flag down Mark and Phillip on the gravel road leading to the cottage. The terrified boys drove back down the road to warn their father, who was following in the Bronco with a security guard. By the time the police arrived, the bikers were gone, leaving Helmuth more convinced than ever that self-defence was necessary. "I was still afraid that I may need to protect myself and my children," Helmuth said later. He also told Phil Conley that he thought the men who had murdered Hanna might try to kidnap Esther or Danny.

On the morning of Friday, July 20, some of the Buxbaums returned to London. Esther and Mark left the cottage in one vehicle, and Helmuth and a security guard left a little later in the Bronco for the journey back to London. While still at the cottage, Helmuth had conferred with a security company about retaining his personal bodyguard and twenty-four-hour protection at Komoka. He arranged a Monday morning meeting with Phil Thompson of Burns Security to discuss his needs, emphasizing that all security arrangements were to be made through him and him alone.

Back at Komoka, Helmuth was safe from everything but the telephone. As he unpacked from his trip north, he received a call from the girl who had first sold him cocaine at Kelly's Bar.

"Hi, Helmuth," Colette Vandenberg purred.

"Yes?" Helmuth replied cautiously.

"This is Colette."

"Oh, yes."

"How you doin'?" she asked.

"I'm very busy," he replied curtly.

"Are you?"

"Uh-huh."

"When can I get ahold of you?"

"Oh, sometime tomorrow."

"At your house or at work?"

"At work," Helmuth said, keeping in mind Paul's warning that the Komoka phone was bugged.

"Okay. Can you give me that number? I've lost it."

Exasperated, Helmuth sighed and hung up without replying.

Eight minutes later the phone rang again. If Helmuth thought it was Vandenberg badgering him again for his office telephone number, he was in for a surprise. It was Ron Piers. As the two men talked, Helmuth kept hearing clicks on the line and asked the detective if his telephone was being bugged at either Komoka or Treugott. Trying to protect the integrity of the wiretap, Piers replied that they weren't. He then asked Helmuth if he and Roy could come in to London Detachment to look over a piece of very important new evidence. Helmuth agreed to bring his nephew to the police station at noon on Monday, July 23.

The OPP had finally found the blue car used by Hanna Buxbaum's killers.

The most sought-after piece of evidence in the sensational murder case had been recovered by police just after 5 P.M. on July 19. After two weeks of sifting through licence-plate numbers on police computers and stopping scores of blue sedans in spot checks, Const. Paul Edwards finally hit the jackpot. Acting on a tip from the London police, Edwards visited the Rent-A-Wreck outlet in London to check out a blue Nova registered to the company. Piers was delighted with the break; within forty-eight hours of the murder, he had requested a print-out from Motor Vehicle Registration of all blue Chevy Novas licensed in Ontario for the model years 1975, 1976, and 1977. Had his men failed to come up with the murder car, he would have been forced to check each one – all 80,000 of them.

According to a copy of the rental agreement supplied by Rent-A-Wreck manager Allan Morris, a woman named Anita Pitcher had rented the 1976 Chevy Nova at 4 P.M. on July 4 and returned it on the afternoon of July 9. The dates worked and, best of all, Edwards knew that Pitcher had already been picked up on police wiretaps at Janet Hicks' apartment. Edwards also noted that the licence plate of the rental vehicle began with the letter V, one of the few pieces of detailed evidence Helmuth Buxbaum had given police about the blue car at the scene of his wife's shooting. Although the licence plate had been covered, what looked like a "v" was still visible at the left edge.

Edwards reported his findings to Piers, who also connected Pitcher to Pat Allen and Janet Hicks through two July 13 telephone calls that had been intercepted at the Hicks apartment. It was a big moment. Edwards explained that the blue Nova was currently rented to a John Lennon McLung, and Piers decided to assist in its retrieval. When the two detectives located the car on Southdale Street in London, McLung volunteered to drive the Nova back to London Detachment. When he handed the keys to Const. Ray Gilleno of the Identification Unit, McLung told him that the collection of refuse on the front passenger floor belonged to him. By the time Gilleno finished examining the Nova, he had bagged sixteen exhibits, including several fingerprints from inside and outside the vehicle, and a number of hair samples.

The next morning, a muggy shirt-soaker, Constable Edwards returned to Rent-A-Wreck and interviewed both Maureen Dennison and Sharon Lawrence. Dennison, who had done the original paperwork on the rental, described both Anita Pitcher and a male companion who fit Pat Allen's description. She said that Allen claimed to be a truck driver from Alberta who told her that authorities there "had screwed up on transferring his driver's licence." Lawrence confirmed that Pitcher had returned the car at 4 P.M. on July 9 and put the $30 refund from her $150 deposit into a shoulder bag.

The blue Nova wasn't the only piece of evidence that had Inspector Piers pondering his next move in the investigation that humid July afternoon. A few days before, Sgt. Bob Cann of the London police had run into Robert Barrett, who was in court for his July 6 cocaine charge at Pearson Airport. Barrett, spruced up for the occasion, told Cann that he was going to check himself into the St. Thomas Psychiatric Hospital in the next day or so to get help with his cocaine addiction. He also told the policeman that he had once worked for Helmuth Buxbaum. Cann relayed the information to the OPP, adding, "It would be a good time to sweat him now."

Earlier in the week, Bill Pierce of Canada Trust had provided Piers with a computer print-out of all recent transactions on Helmuth Buxbaum's two bank accounts. Piers now sent investigators to interview Trudy Tomlinson and Casy Clarke, the tellers who had dealt with the wealthy businessman on two dates the Inspector was particularly interested in – May 24 and July 6.

Tomlinson confirmed that just after 5 P.M. on May 24 Helmuth had withdrawn $3,400 Canadian and $1,000 U.S. from his account at the Byron branch of Canada Trust, taking receipt of the cash in large bills, which he placed in his briefcase. She told detectives that earlier that same day he had withdrawn $2,000 Canadian from the bank's Oakridge branch.

Casy Clarke, from the Byron branch of Canada Trust, told detectives that around 2 P.M. on Friday, July 6, a mere seventeen hours after his wife's death, Helmuth had deposited a cheque for $8,496.41 into his personal account made out to, and endorsed by, Hanna Buxbaum. He had asked for $2,500 in cash, which the teller placed in an envelope on Helmuth's request. Clarke told police that she had watched the well-known customer fumble with the money as he tried to put it into his jacket pocket, which already contained two other envelopes.

When his officers reported these findings, Piers saw a clear and troubling pattern. Immediately after Helmuth's withdrawals on May 24, Robert Barrett had left London for a month in Florida, where, according to Debbie Barber, he was to arrange a murder contract on Hanna Buxbaum. After putting together another large sum of money on the afternoon of July 6 from a combination of bank withdrawals and gold sales, Helmuth had met Robert Barrett at the London airport. Barber claimed the purpose of that meeting was to make a further payment on Hanna's murder. And on July 12, following his secretive trip to Toronto, where he raised $16,000 by selling thirty-five ounces of gold without realizing the police were watching, Helmuth had called Debbie Barber's apartment, looking for the same man, Robert Barrett.

Everywhere Ron Piers turned he found Helmuth Buxbaum and Robert Barrett, the multimillionaire and the social disaster. The question was *why*. The policeman hoped that the blue car parked in the basement of London Detachment would soon provide the answer.

Helmuth Buxbaum woke on Saturday, July 21, with guns and grizzly bears on his mind.

After a brief stop at Treugott to thumb through his mail, Helmuth and one of his Burns security guards paid a visit to George Wood Guns, where the businessman explained to the owner's son, Bobby Wood, that he needed a high-powered rifle for a September bear hunt in British Columbia. The young man produced a chart showing the impact rating of various weapons and promised Helmuth he would order him "a particularly effective model." Helmuth also ordered a spare clip for his .45-calibre Colt Commander.

With his guard in tow, Helmuth returned to Komoka where he prepared to spend a quiet weekend in the country. On Saturday night, he received a telephone call from Hank Unrau, an old church friend who had been away when Hanna had been murdered. Unrau apologized to Helmuth for missing her funeral, and offered to visit the Buxbaums to give what belated comfort he and his wife could. The subject then turned to the latest development in the case.

"I saw in the paper this morning that they found the car," Unrau said.

"Yeah, they want us to come down on Monday to identify the car," Helmuth replied.

"Yeah, isn't that incredible?"

"Well, I'll tell you, I think it's safe to say that it's a good idea to have a gun in your house," Helmuth said.

"Oh dear, yeah," Unrau answered.

"I think it's come to that point in time now in Canada where it is not safe to be unarmed."

"Is that right?"

"I feel that way . . . Not just a handgun, I got a shotgun and a rifle, too." Unrau considered Helmuth's answer and then steered the conversation directly back to Hanna's murder.

"What's so unusual is they must've had such *clear* intentions."

"I don't think so," Helmuth quickly replied. "We just happened to be the victims. I think if somebody else would've come along, they would've done the same thing to them."

After agreeing to get together with Unrau for a barbecue when his schedule became more settled, Helmuth hung up and retired for the evening. The next day, he and the children attended church with Hanna's brother and sister. Afterwards, Helmuth treated everyone to lunch at Swiss Chalet. On Sunday afternoon, Phillip brought Roy back from the cottage so that he could keep his appointment at the OPP Detachment with Helmuth the following morning.

That evening after dinner, Helmuth walked through the summer fields to Campbell Cemetery, where he picked a rose from Hanna's grave. Before going to bed, he took a Serax tablet to help him sleep. In the middle of the night, he woke up with a crushing migraine and took another Serax pill and two Fiorinal tablets. But sleep moved off beyond the reach of tranquillizers and painkillers, until dawn showed grey and pink at the window and birds began to sing.

It was July 23.

12

JULY 23

"Suddenly Piers jumped up. He stood in front of me and
lowered his face directly in front of mine. I thought he was
going to hit me. He was very red in the face. He said to me,
'You know and I know who killed your wife.'"
— *Helmuth Buxbaum, on his final interview with Det. Insp.*
Ron Piers, July 23, 1984

At 8:15 A.M. on Monday, July 23, every detective working on the Hanna
Buxbaum murder case gathered in the conference room of the OPP's
London Detachment to get their assignment from Ron Piers. The
policeman had spent a restless weekend in the room at London's
Ramada Inn that had been his home since the investigation began two
and a half long weeks earlier. His problem was to decide his next move,
now that authorities had found what they believed to be the car used by
Hanna Buxbaum's killers and the name of the young woman who had
rented it.

Piers had decided to bring in Anita Pitcher and Janet Hicks for questioning. But first, there was some unfinished business with Helmuth
Buxbaum. From early in the investigation, police had been working
on the theory that Robert Barrett was at the centre of the murder plot,
with Helmuth off to one side and Pat Allen off to the other. But in the
seventeen days since the shooting, the OPP had gathered powerful
circumstantial evidence that Helmuth *might* have been involved in his
wife's death.

Piers had four key concerns: Helmuth's June phone calls to Robert
Barrett at the Gateway Inn in Orlando; his July 6 meeting with Barrett at
the London airport; his July 12 phone call to Debbie Barber's apartment
looking for Barrett; and any phone calls he might have made on the day of
his wife's murder. Piers decided that he would talk to Helmuth about

these and other matters when he came to inspect the blue Nova parked in the OPP's garage. The suspect was not advised of the planned interview.

Piers asked Greg Calcott to help him interview Helmuth and assigned Paul Edwards and Gary Aspden to re-interview Roy Buxbaum at the Criminal Investigation Branch's London office. Bart Linker was to check Helmuth's dealings with the Bank of Montreal in Komoka, and Andy Fotheringham was to collect more telephone tolls from Bell Canada and to see if Helmuth had had any other financial dealings with Guardian Trust or Deak-Perera in Toronto.

Piers had barely finished deploying his men when he received a verbal report from the wiretap team that Helmuth Buxbaum had just finished a call they thought the Inspector should know about.

For a few days now, Helmuth had been toying with the idea of moving his family to Europe, and on the morning of July 23, without telling his children about his plan, he called the Black Forest Christian Academy in Germany to arrange a visit to the school. He spoke to Mrs. Albert Martin, the wife of the institution's business administrator. During their lengthy conversation, Helmuth gave her as many details about his private life as he garnered about the school, including a fact the electronic surveillance team found very interesting: the wealthy businessman was apparently preparing for an imminent move to Germany, where he planned to live for two years.

"What is your profession" Martin asked.

"I'm in the nursing home business. We have homes, they look after the elderly and, ah, the retired people," Helmuth told her.

"Yeah. And you say your wife passed away two weeks ago?"

"Yes."

"Oh, I'm sorry about that."

"Yes, she was murdered," Helmuth added.

"No kidding."

"Unfortunately."

"Oh, my goodness," Martin exclaimed.

"The reason we would, ah, like to spend some time away," Helmuth explained to Martin, "is really basically, ah, [to] allow the children, you know, and myself, to be together and be in a Christian environment . . . And also, you know, having the, ah, German culture around us for two years would be very, I think it would be a very enriching experience for the children."

After arranging to call Dr. Henry Toew, the school's director of enrolment, who happened to be visiting Canada, Helmuth prepared for his noon appointment with Inspector Piers, unaware that the police were alerted to the possibility he may leave the jurisdiction.

Inspector Piers and Constable Calcott met Helmuth and Roy when they arrived in the lobby of London Detachment just before noon. Piers escorted Helmuth to the garage to examine the Chevy Nova, leaving Roy with constables Edwards and Aspden. He had given a lot of thought to the questions he would ask Helmuth this day and began with three crucial ones: "I would like you to look at the vehicle, both sides, the front, and the back and tell me: One, was this the vehicle you stopped to assist on the morning of July 5, 1984? Two, was this the vehicle you stopped to assist on the evening of July 5, 1984, when your wife was killed? Three, was it the same vehicle on both occasions?"

With Calcott poised to take down his responses, Helmuth circled the car, noting that the colour was right, the licence plate started with the letter V, as he had claimed in previous statements, and the general size and shape of the vehicle matched the one he had stopped for on July 5. Helmuth asked the officers to open the garage doors so he could see the car's colour in natural light. He then walked around the Nova again, remembering that he had touched the vehicle during the morning stop when he had looked under the hood with Pat Allen. Had the police, he wondered, found his fingerprints?

After a brief pause, Helmuth turned to Piers and said that he thought that this was the car he had stopped for in both the morning and the evening. Calcott wrote down his response.

Piers now knew that Helmuth had not only neglected to tell police about the morning stop behind a car *similar* to the one driven by his wife's killers; he was asking them to believe that he had forgotten about pulling over behind the *same* car just ten hours before the roadside slaying. Questions the detective had hoped to resolve recurred now with a vengeance: How had the blue car managed to "break down" by the side of the highway on the precise route the Buxbaums had taken in both the morning and the evening? And why had the car's licence plate been exposed in the morning but covered in the evening, along with the killer's face?

Helmuth, who was expecting to leave after his five-minute stop in the garage, didn't protest when he was asked to accompany the two detectives to an interview room to answer a few questions. Piers sat behind a table with Helmuth in a chair to his right and Calcott in another to his left. He had his questions written down, more than twenty of them, and Calcott prepared to make notes of Helmuth's responses.

The note-taking was a necessary charade. The real record of the proceedings would be supplied by the hidden tape recorders whose reels were already revolving. The law on surreptitious taping of a suspect was about to change, but on July 23 it was a perfectly legal interception, requiring only one consenting party. Ron Piers was that person.

Piers began by taking Helmuth through some details of his European trip, clearing up an earlier misunderstanding about when the Buxbaums had returned to Komoka, a confusion that had initially led the detective to mistakenly conclude that the suspect had been lying to him about his banking activities on the afternoon of July 4.

In revisiting the events of that day, Helmuth said that he had done some banking and eaten lunch in town with one of his managers. Piers already knew about the July 4 meeting between Helmuth and Robert Barrett at Debbie Barber's apartment, and was also aware that Barrett had given her $300 after disappearing with Helmuth for a few hours. Piers pressed Helmuth for more details about how he had spent the rest of the afternoon. The weary suspect, perhaps feeling the effects of the tranquillizers he had been taking, couldn't remember. Nor could he recall what he had done on the evening of July 4.

"Listen, you're going to have an empty sheet," Helmuth said, looking at Calcott's notebook, "because you're asking me things that I . . . I wish I could help you."

For what seemed to Helmuth to be the hundredth time, Piers next asked him to recount in detail the events of the July 5 morning stop behind the blue Nova. Helmuth described how he thought it was strange that the driver of the car had asked for panty hose to fix his vehicle. Piers thought it was even stranger that Helmuth accompanied the man to the front of the car to look under the hood, given that he readily admitted that he knew as much about "what is under the hood of a car as what's behind a clock."

Helmuth described how Hanna had removed her panty hose and given them to him to assist the unlucky motorist. When Piers asked him to describe the man police believed was Pat Allen, Helmuth became as vague as he had been in his first statements to police. At first the man's hair was "dark brown, almost black." Then it became "not really dark, not really blond, something in between, brunette." He said the man was "taller than the car" and "didn't have a tie on." Helmuth apologized for

his unhelpful answers, reminding the officers that a 1982 stroke had affected his memory. To their surprise, he even suggested that hypnosis
might help him to recall more about his ordeal.

The last detail Helmuth said he remembered about the morning
encounter was the strangest of all. When the police officer arrived on the
scene of the morning stop, the scruffy motorist had quickly waved him
away, saying that everything was all right. He had then walked back to the
station wagon and returned the panty hose to Hanna, telling her that he
didn't need them after all. Helmuth's own description of what had happened simply didn't clear up several troubling questions: How could he
have forgotten such a peculiar encounter with the same car that Hanna's
killers would use a few hours later? Why would the man return the panty
hose Hanna had given him without making any attempt to use them?
And why had a man who claimed he was having car trouble solicit help
from the admittedly nonmechanical Helmuth and turn it down from an
OPP officer with a radio?

It was now time to go through the events surrounding the murder,
something he sensed Helmuth wasn't anxious to do.

"I just want to go through it all again," Piers said with characteristic
matter-of-factness.

"You're kidding?" Helmuth replied.

"You picked Roy up –" Piers coaxed.

"You don't want to do all this again?" Helmuth complained.

"Well, I just want the sequence of events that will make sure we have it
absolutely correct."

"You've written it down four times now, I think that's plenty," Helmuth bristled.

"I know. We make sure we have every detail."

"You've got all the details I can give you."

"You're now leaving the airport –" Piers said, ignoring Helmuth's plea
and giving him the starting point for the story he was bent on hearing
again.

As Helmuth began to describe the drive from the airport back to
Komoka, the tape that had been recording his answers ran out. By the
time the operator switched to side B, the suspect was talking about how
he had taken over the driving after he, Hanna, and Roy had stopped at
McDonald's for a snack. Helmuth was telling the officers how Hanna and
Roy were both snoozing as they headed west towards London, when
Piers suddenly interjected a question:

"All through the day up to this point did you make any phone calls at any of the places you stopped?"

"What time?" Helmuth asked.

"Oh, any time during the day?"

"Any time during the day," Helmuth repeated as he contemplated his answer. "Yeah, I think I called in Toronto at the airport. I called, ah, a place in Toronto . . . I had met a girl that I dropped off at her brother's place in Toronto and I phoned to see how things were going because she was looking for a job and, ah, she, she said she would call me, and she never called me back, so I called her."

Assuming that Helmuth had been involved in a conspiracy to murder his wife in the morning, as Barrett had told Debbie Barber, the police knew he would have needed to contact his co-conspirators once the first attempt on Hanna's life had failed. Now he was admitting that he had, in fact, made a local call from Toronto a few hours before his wife was shot. Although it would take further investigation to determine if that call had been to Robert Barrett at the Westbury Hotel, Helmuth's own words had raised yet another question: Why, in four detailed statements to the police about the events of July 5, had he neglected to tell them about his Toronto phone call?

Piers asked Helmuth for the name, address, and phone number of the girl he had called on the afternoon of July 5, but Helmuth couldn't oblige him; he'd changed suits, he explained, and had inadvertently left his day book behind. "I can give it to you as soon as I get home," Helmuth said, before broadly hinting that he was ready to go. "I gotta drop Roy off anyway because, ah, he's gotta get back to the cottage . . . He was supposed to leave early this morning, but I postponed the whole thing because of this identification of the car. I didn't expect *this* you know."

"I'm sorry to inconvenience you, but it's one of those things that have to be done," Piers replied.

Once again, Helmuth reluctantly told the story of Hanna's murder, starting with the man at the back of the blue Nova who had waved to the Buxbaums for help, a man Piers knew had *not* tried to flag down at least three other passers-by just before the shooting. Helmuth claimed that after he had pulled over, the man walked, not to the driver's door, but to the front passenger door – a peculiar move for someone who needed help. As the detective's questions became more detailed, Helmuth's frustration flared again:

"Do you *have* to go through this?"

"I'm sorry, Mr. Buxbaum, but we have to get the sequence of events down completely," Piers replied.

"But we did."

"And accurately."

"We, we, we got it four times," Helmuth stammered.

"I know, but as we go along I have some questions, and then I'll tell you some stuff," Piers replied.

The reluctant witness continued, describing how a masked man had then leaned in through the right rear door and pointed what looked like a toy gun at Roy's face. Helmuth said his mask was brown and made of a double-knit material, like "the top of the stockings that ladies wear." Like the panty hose Hanna had given the stranger during the morning stop, panty hose Helmuth claimed the man had returned but that police had never found in the station wagon, Piers thought.

Piers then asked Helmuth to describe the killer's clothing. Again, the businessman was short on details, claiming that the man had worn a light jacket, greyish-brown in colour. Pressed for a better description, Helmuth added that "it wasn't black," a flourish that didn't square with the statement of one of the drive-by witnesses who had seen a man in a black leather jacket hiding behind the cement pillar of the overpass.

Piers turned his attention to the killer's associate, the man who had flagged the Buxbaums down. Apart from describing him as just under six feet tall and wearing a baseball cap, Helmuth couldn't remember what he had been wearing. Remembering Helmuth's claim that the man lying across the front seats of the Nova during the morning encounter wore a baseball cap, Piers asked his most pointed question of the afternoon:

"Could you say that the person who was standing by that car was one of the same people that you saw in the morning in the blue car?"

"It's possible," Helmuth replied. "I wouldn't say it for sure, but it's possible."

It was an astonishing answer, given that Helmuth had never before suggested that any of the men he encountered on the morning of July 5 may have been there in the evening. If he could now say that it was possible one of the men had been with the Nova on both occasions, why hadn't he been able to say that without police prompting much earlier in the investigation?

"Do you know for sure if it's the same car that you saw in the morning?"

"I think I can say that that was the same car, yes, yeah."

The same car and maybe one of the same people on both stops, Piers thought, as he prodded Helmuth into a description of the fatal attack itself. The weary man described how he had slipped out of the car and run to the middle of the highway to flag down help, without ever seeing the gunman pull Hanna from the car and drag her over the guardrail. As he tried to wave over an oncoming truck, Helmuth had heard three rapid shots. He had then seen the masked man running back to the Nova between the two cars holding Hanna's purse in his hands. As the car sped off westbound on Highway 402, its licence plate covered with what Helmuth described as brown material, he kept trying to flag down a truck to get help for his wife.

"Okay, now that the car's speeding off, travelling west, you're out on the highway waving down traffic. What happens next?" Piers asked. Finally, Helmuth told him, he had been able to get a trucker to stop. "I ran up to him and I told him that, ah, somebody shot my wife, 'Have you got a CB?' That's what I first asked him. 'Gotta get help.'"

Helmuth claimed that he and the trucker had then looked over the guardrail at his wife's fallen body. Although he didn't see any wounds on Hanna, Helmuth said that he did see "some blood on the ground." He then flagged down another truck while he tried to convince the first trucker to help him get Hanna to the hospital.

Piers listened carefully to everything Helmuth said, waiting to hear something that would reveal whether Helmuth had been on the passenger side of his vehicle at any time *before* he had flagged down the first truck driver. In four previous statements, Helmuth had denied going to the passenger side of the vehicle until *after* he had flagged down Colin Lawrence. But that wasn't the way trucker Robert Mitchell had remembered it in his July 12 statement to Mel Getty. And that created a problem any way Piers looked at it.

If Mitchell was right when he said he saw Helmuth run from the passenger side of the station wagon around the front of the car towards the driver's door just as two men emerged from the ditch, then Helmuth was lying. And if Helmuth was telling the truth, and had never witnessed the shooting or been on the passenger side of the station wagon by the ditch until *after* he flagged down Colin Lawrence, then how had he been able to tell Lawrence that Hanna had been shot in the head?

"Okay," Piers said, gathering his thoughts on this crucial element of

Helmuth's story. "If I have the sequence of events right, you were never on the passenger's side of your vehicle until after you had stopped help. And then you went over by the guardrails, ah, talking to the trucker that your wife was hurt?"

"Do you mind if I make a telephone call?" Helmuth calmly replied. Piers nodded. When Helmuth returned to the room five minutes later to answer the detective's question, he made a major alteration to his previous story.

"Oh boy, maybe we got the sequence wrong here. I think, uh, after he ran across the car, this gunman, I think I *did* go first and look to see what happened to my wife."

"Did you go over the fence?" Piers asked.

"No, I didn't go over the fence."

"Okay."

"I just looked."

"Where do you mean you looked? Where were you when you looked?"

"On Roy's side of the car."

Helmuth explained how he had then run between the guardrail and the station wagon, looped around the back of the car, and headed out on the highway again to flag down help.

"I'm just trying to get it straight in [my] mind, the sequence of events," Piers said. "You were out on the highway waving down traffic. You hear the shots. You run around the rear of your vehicle to the passenger side of your car. You see your wife's been shot –"

"No, I didn't see that," Helmuth protested.

"Okay."

"I didn't see any gunshot wounds. I heard the shots, but for all I knew, he could've missed."

"Okay, okay."

"Maybe he was just trying to scare us, or whatever, to get the purse," Helmuth speculated.

"So if I understand you correctly," Piers said, straining to make his point perfectly clear, "you never at any time *ever* crossed the guardrails."

"Not that I remember."

Helmuth's revised story added further twists to the big question on Piers' mind. If he hadn't seen any gunshot wounds on his wife, hadn't gone over to her body at any time after the shooting, and was now suggesting that the gunman might even have missed when he fired at Hanna, how could he know to tell Colin Lawrence that his wife had been shot in the head?

Piers found himself in the familiar position of being left with more questions than answers. It was time to confront Helmuth with some of the other matters the police had uncovered, which until now had been among their most closely guarded secrets. This time, Helmuth couldn't complain that he had been through it all before.

"Back some time ago, there was some telephone calls made from Treugott Management to the Gateway Inn in Orlando, Florida," Piers said.

"Oh yeah?" Helmuth replied, sounding surprised.

"There was a call on June 5, 1984, for four minutes. Can you tell me who you were calling down there?"

"Yeah, I think that was, um . . ." Helmuth began haltingly, pausing in mid-sentence as he realized that the police must have talked to Barrett. "Oh what was his name?" he asked aloud, pausing again. "I think it was *Bartlett*, yeah."

"Who?" Piers asked, knowing that Helmuth and Barrett had been well acquainted for the past six months. Helmuth's mood had changed dramatically. No longer businesslike, he began shifting in his seat, becoming "agitated and excited."

"Bartlett, something like that," Helmuth repeated.

"And who is he?"

"Oh, he's a guy that I met some time ago," Helmuth said, suddenly remembering Paul Buxbaum's words that the police knew about his double life.

"Bartlett?" Piers asked again.

"Bartlett, yeah," Helmuth said for the third time.

"B-A-R-T-" Piers said, spelling the name out. Helmuth interrupted him.

"Oh, *Barrett*, pardon me, Barrett, not Bartlett. Barrett."

"Okay. And what would you be talking to him in Florida for?"

"Ho boy," Helmuth said, pausing for a moment. "You, you know him. He's a, he's a cocaine dealer . . . He called me from there. He told me that he was there."

"What was he doing there?" Piers asked, bearing in mind Barber's story to police that Barrett had left the country to set up a murder contract on Hanna Buxbaum.

"I dunno," Helmuth replied.

"Okay. Why were you calling him?"

"'Cause he had left a message that I should call him back."

"Okay. And what was the message when you eventually talked to him? What was the message about?" Piers asked.

"Well, he told me that there was some real good blow down there, some real good coke, and he wanted to, ah, bring some up to Canada," Helmuth replied. Without warning, the firm bottom of the interview had dropped away, and Helmuth suddenly found himself treading water.

"When you talk about blow, does that mean cocaine?" Piers asked.

"It means coke, yeah."

"Okay. So that's what you discuss, is it?"

"Yeah."

Piers then confronted Helmuth with the other phone calls he had made to Barrett in Florida and asked what they had discussed.

"Well, we were talking about coke back and forth and . . . I told him that I didn't – I was straight – that I wasn't gonna get into the stuff anymore," Helmuth said. If true, it was a lot of phone calls to say no.

"What was Barrett?" Piers asked. At last Helmuth saw an opportunity to change the subject; he began talking about how Barrett had desperately wanted to get on Buxbaum's payroll.

"He wanted a job so bad, and he kept badgering me about employing him, and I told him I couldn't *make* a job," Helmuth replied, adding that Barrett used to work at Kelly's Bar in downtown London.

"Okay. What's he doing in Orlando, Florida?" Piers asked.

"I don't know, just looking for coke and –" Helmuth began slowly. Piers interrupted him.

"Did you send him to Florida?"

"No, I didn't send him."

"Okay. Mr. Buxbaum, on the way to your cottage on Thursday, July 12, 1984, you made a phone call from a tourist information booth north of Port Severn –"

It was now Helmuth's turn to interrupt. "From where?"

"From a telephone booth north of Port Severn. You made it at 8:16 P.M. Who did you call?" Piers asked. Helmuth realized that there were only two ways the police could have known about the call: either Debbie Barber had told them, or he had been followed.

"On July 12?" Helmuth asked.

"Yes sir, on your way to Huntsville. That was one week from the day your wife was shot. That's Thursday, July 12."

"Well I'd like to know the number to find out who I called," Helmuth answered.

Piers could have supplied it, but since he already had proof of Helmuth's call to Debbie Barber's apartment looking for Barrett, he asked another question.

"Do you remember making the call?"

"No."

"Okay." Piers now decided to give Helmuth the chilling message that the police knew about his airport meeting with Robert Barrett. "At about 7:30 P.M. on Friday, July 6, you made a telephone call from London airport as a result of a pager message from a person by the name of Barrett . . . What was the reason for that call?"

"I was supposed to meet him and, ah, that he wasn't gonna arrive because the plane wasn't gonna arrive," Helmuth said, beginning to flounder.

"What do you mean? You were supposed to meet him at the airport?" Piers asked sharply.

"Yeah."

"Well, for what reason?"

"I don't know," Helmuth stammered. "I think that he probably had some coke on him or something. I didn't want to buy any more, but he kept badgering me to buy more."

It was not the best of excuses. Helmuth had already told Piers that he had been "straight" during the June phone calls to and from Orlando and wasn't using cocaine anymore. Now he was saying that he didn't want to buy cocaine, yet had nevertheless met with a drug dealer the day after his wife's death.

"Okay. Why did you go to the airport in the beginning on Friday, July 6?"

"You know, I think you're trying to put me into something here that —"

"Mr. Buxbaum, all I'm trying to do is get the answers to some questions," Piers replied.

"Yeah, I know, and I wanna talk to a lawyer before I answer any more questions here," Helmuth said.

"That's fine. Do you want to call a lawyer?" Piers asked.

"Yeah," Helmuth replied.

"Okay . . . What I'm trying to do is get all of the events that transpired immediately before, and all of the events that transpired after your wife was shot," Piers stated for the record.

"Okay," Helmuth answered.

"If you would prefer to have a lawyer here while I'm talking to you that's fine," Piers said, making clear that the interview definitely wasn't over.

"Well I think I should."

Helmuth stepped outside the interview room to call his lawyer, with Inspector Piers and Constable Calcott at his side. Del McLennan said he would be down right away. After hearing the gist of what was going on, McLennan decided to bring along his partner, Timothy Price, a criminal lawyer who had once acted for Helmuth in a nursing-home inquest. After making the call, Helmuth went to the water fountain, where he took another Serax tablet to calm his jangled nerves.

The three men returned to the interview room to await the arrival of the lawyers. After a few uncomfortable moments, Piers broke the silence.

"If there's any questions you want to ask of me, go ahead."

"Yeah? Well, have you talked to Barrett? I'm sure you must have talked to him."

"No sir, we have not," Piers replied.

"Because if you have all this information, obviously, ah, you checked him out."

"You asked me the question whether or not I'd been talking to Mr. Barrett. No, I have not," Piers repeated. Noting the look of puzzlement on Helmuth's face, he continued. "These questions are questions that I have amassed through investigative means. The phone calls from Treugott Management, I obtained those from your company."

Piers and Helmuth had strayed into a discussion about Helmuth's lawyers when side B of the first tape reel ran out. By the time it was replaced with a fresh tape, Piers was once again explaining to Helmuth he was only trying to do a thorough investigation of Hanna's death.

"That's all I'm trying to do," he protested.

"I think you're trying to frame me, that's what you're trying to do. Trying to connect me with a crook, a drug pusher," Helmuth shot back.

"I'm *not* trying to connect you with a drug pusher, Mr. Buxbaum. I asked you certain questions. *You're* the man who gave me information. All I'm trying to do is get the answer to questions in order that I can do the investigation."

"Well naturally when you talk about cocaine," Helmuth replied, "I'm not gonna get myself into the spot where –"

"Mr. Buxbaum –"

"– this information could, you know, not only damage me and my reputation, but also –"

"Mr. Buxbaum, this is a murder investigation," Piers said firmly.

"I know, I know."

"It's not a cocaine investigation *per se*, it's a homicide investigation."

"I understand. I guess you're doing your job."

"That's all I'm trying to do, and I know that you want to help me in every way you can to find the persons responsible for your wife's death."

"Well, sure," Helmuth replied. Piers started out of the room to pick up some refreshments.

"Is there anything else you want besides a coke?" he asked.

"No," Helmuth answered gloomily. "My whole day is shot."

Constable Calcott then asked Helmuth about his family, wondering if Paul would follow in his father's footsteps. Helmuth said that his eldest son was interested in the nursing homes, but that a cocaine scandal could "ruin the business for good."

"Just on a personal level," Calcott asked, "I was just curious as to how a man of your stature would even come into connection with something like this?"

"Well," Helmuth replied, "I don't know either. Only I was just very, very stupid."

Their conversation over, Helmuth asked to use the telephone. At 2:15 P.M. the phone rang at Komoka, and Phillip Buxbaum knew it would be his father calling. Helmuth and Roy had been gone for quite a while, much longer, Phillip decided, than would be necessary to look at a car. Helmuth sounded "spaced out," and Phillip asked him if he had had one too many of his pills. "Well, I've taken four altogether," Helmuth admitted. "That should knock out the biggest horse around." Helmuth told Phillip that he thought the car the police had seized was the same one that was used in Hanna's murder. He then asked his son to have Paul Buxbaum or Phil Conley call the OPP station when they got home. A dull alarm went off inside the apprehensive teenager, and he asked why his father hadn't come home.

"Well, they're questioning me," Helmuth replied.

"Are they questioning you about that thing?" Phillip asked, convinced that the cocaine scandal was finally about to break.

"Uh huh," Helmuth replied guardedly.

"I'm coming down to pick you up right away," Phillip replied, slamming down the receiver. He ran to get his friend, Bill Dakin, and the two boys then sped into London in the Buxbaum family van.

No one could drive fast enough to overtake the events that were unfolding at London Detachment. When Helmuth's two lawyers showed up at the police station, they were directed to the office of the communications corporal, where they met privately with their client. Standing outside the office, Piers and Calcott observed the meeting through a glass partition.

"What is this all about?" Del McLennan asked Helmuth.

"They're asking me questions about cocaine and about phone calls," Helmuth replied. "I don't want to get involved in a cocaine case."

To McLennan's amazement, Helmuth admitted that he had been using cocaine. Putting aside his personal reaction, the corporate lawyer dealt with the issue at hand, advising Helmuth to continue the interview with the homicide detectives. He was afraid that if Helmuth arbitrarily ended the session, it might trigger his arrest. Timothy Price disagreed. He was not in favour of Helmuth answering any more potentially incriminating questions without finding out more about his client's status with the police.

Price then met privately with Inspector Piers and bluntly asked if Helmuth were under arrest. Piers answered that he was not, and Price returned to the office where Helmuth and McLennan were waiting for him. Ten minutes later, Piers knocked on the door to find out what the men had decided. Price replied that his client would not be answering any further questions on the advice of counsel and that he would like to leave.

Piers considered for a moment and decided he couldn't let that happen. Armed with a new statement from Helmuth that was inconsistent with his four previous signed statements, and unsatisfied with his answers in the four specific areas of concern he had had the chance to question him about, Piers looked straight into Helmuth's eyes and, at 2:47 P.M., advised him that he was under arrest, charged with the first degree murder of his wife, Hanna, on July 5, 1984. After giving him the standard police warning, Piers asked Helmuth his final question of the case:

"What, if anything, do you wish to say?"

"Is there any way we can keep this out of the press?" Helmuth asked, looking at his lawyers. They shook their heads, and he turned back to Piers. "Nothing to say."

After his lawyers left, Helmuth was taken to an office in the cell-block area. There, he later said, Piers was sitting behind a desk, going over his notes. He appeared to Helmuth to be upset or annoyed.

"Suddenly Piers jumped up. He stood in front of me and lowered his face directly in front of mine. I thought he was going to hit me. He was very red in the face. He said to me, '*You* know and *I* know who killed your wife.'"

Piers would later deny that the encounter had ever taken place.

A few moments after Helmuth's arrest, two uniformed officers confiscated Helmuth's personal effects, the first step in booking him. With one policeman writing down descriptions of the articles as the other handed them to him, Helmuth began the official transformation from free citizen to accused prisoner. The pile of objects in the middle of the table revealed the world he was leaving: two diamond rings, a gold watch, a gold wedding band, $1,300 in cash and traveller's cheques, and a gold chain with a cartouche bearing the names of Hanna and the children in hieroglyphics.

The moment Phillip Buxbaum arrived at London Detachment, he asked to speak to his father. At the mention of Helmuth's name, the officers looked silently at the anxious teenager and then at each other. They summoned Inspector Piers. Thinking of his own son, the detective broke the news as best he could. "It's painful for me to say this, but your father has just been arrested for the murder of your mother. I'm sorry, there's nothing I can do about it."

Weeping uncontrollably, the devastated teenager was taken to a room where he found Helmuth sitting in a chair dressed in his shirt, trousers, and socks – the contents of his pockets spread out on the table in front of him.

Phillip tried to speak to his father in private, but Piers informed them that they couldn't leave the room. With the detective watching, Phillip asked his father what was going on. Helmuth replied that he had been charged with first degree murder.

"What evidence?" the heartbroken boy asked.

"I don't know. They lured me here and ended up charging me with the murder of Mom."

"How can they charge you with no evidence?"

"I don't know, but they did," Helmuth replied.

Phillip broke down. Helmuth told him to "go home and be a good example" to the rest of the family, instructing him to tell Pastor Fawcett what had happened. The sobbing teenager left, stripped of his father eighteen days after his mother had been snatched away. Bill Dakin, who had been waiting at the desk, took the wheel for the sad trip back to Komoka.

The depersonalizing rituals of incarceration continued the moment Phillip was gone. Stripped of his personal possessions, including the Fiorinal he relied on for his frequent migraines, Helmuth was told to take off his clothes. After a desultory body search, the officers handed him a T-shirt, some jeans, and a pair of running shoes.

Just before 4 P.M., Const. Bart Linker escorted the accused man to the cells, lodging him in the one farthest from the offices. Fifty minutes later, Helmuth called out to Linker, and appearing cool and calm, requested a Bible. "When I gave one to him, he said, 'Thanks, I really appreciate it.'"

A few moments later, the policeman noticed that he had already started reading. He had begun with the first page of Genesis.

After eighteen days of investigation and 104 interviews, the number one suspect in the Hanna Buxbaum murder was finally under arrest. But the day's work was far from finished. Inspector Piers drove over to the office of the Criminal Investigation Branch, where he met with Const. Paul Edwards and informed Roy Buxbaum that his uncle had just been arrested for murder. Edwards was just putting the finishing touches to his interview with Roy. The boy had repeated basically the same story he had given in his previous two statements, with one important exception. He now told police that Helmuth had, in fact, called someone from the airport just hours before his aunt's murder. But if what the boy was saying was true, Helmuth had apparently lied to his nephew about the call. "He was on the telephone for two or three minutes. I think he said it was a business call."

Piers and Edwards escorted Roy back to the OPP garage, where he identified the blue 1976 Chevy Nova as the vehicle his aunt's killers had been driving on the night of July 5. After making arrangements to get Roy back to Komoka, Piers and Edwards returned to London Detachment.

It was time to talk to a man called Squirrel.

For days, Robert Barrett had known that the police were following him, but mistakenly assumed it was in relation to the non-prescription drugstore he was running in Kelly's Bar. To demonstrate his knowledge of their presence, he walked up to the two policemen who had started to follow him on the afternoon of July 23 and asked them for a ride downtown. Constables Wil Cranston and Jim Pinnegar were only too happy to oblige. What Barrett didn't know was that they had been asked by Inspector Piers to pick Barrett up and bring him in for questioning in the Hanna Buxbaum murder case.

After Piers made clear to Barrett that he was not under arrest, he asked him about his lengthy stay at the Gateway Inn in Orlando and his July 4 trip to Toronto in a limousine he had paid for with a couple of $100 bills. Barrett acknowledged both trips and told police that they had been paid for by Helmuth Buxbaum. When asked why Helmuth would finance Barrett's travels, the twenty-four-year-old gave the same one-word reply as Helmuth: cocaine. But when the subject shifted to his July 6 airport meeting with Helmuth, Barrett's memory deserted him as completely as the cocky confidence that he could talk his way out of his predicament. "I don't remember," he told Piers. "Like this is just like a dream, all this."

It was a reply Piers would hear more than once over the next ninety minutes. The list of things that Robert Barrett didn't remember was longer than his criminal record. He didn't remember who had travelled to Toronto with him; the phone calls to and from London charged to his hotel room; sending a message from Toronto to Helmuth at the London airport; meeting Helmuth at the airport; going to his van and receiving money from Helmuth; flying from London to Toronto on the night of July 6; getting arrested for cocaine possession at Pearson airport; boasting about setting up the Hanna Buxbaum murder during a card game in the Westbury Hotel; telling anyone he had been offered money to arrange Hanna's death; shouting at his mother for calling the Buxbaum residence to express her condolences; or calling Helmuth on the days following Hanna's murder. Piers had almost had enough.

"What are you sure of?" he asked.

"My name," Barrett chortled.

"It's not funny."

"Oh, I know it's not funny . . . Like this is pretty wild."

"You're very close to a murder charge."

"I didn't kill anybody," Barrett soberly replied.

"I didn't say you did . . . Why did you receive calls from London at the Westbury Hotel —"

"I don't know."

"– the day of the murder."

"I don't know."

"*Half an hour* after the murder?"

"I don't know."

"You don't know . . . Did you tell anyone back in February or March that you were offered money to kill Mrs. Buxbaum?" Piers asked, recalling what he had learned from Debbie Barber.

"No, I don't, I don't think I did."

"You don't *think* you did?" Piers asked incredulously.

"No."

"You mean to tell me if somebody offered you money to kill their wife, you wouldn't *remember*?"

"If I was a normal person I probably would."

"Aren't you a normal person?"

"I'm a cocaine addict," Barrett declared with a smile. "I don't remember things like anniversaries and shit."

"Well there's quite a bit of difference between an anniversary and having someone ask you to kill their wife, wouldn't you agree?"

"Oh yeah," Barrett replied.

Piers decided to test Robert Barrett's memory a final time.

"Okay. Did Mr. Buxbaum offer you money to kill his wife?"

"No."

"At any time?"

"Not that I can recall."

"Did you ever *tell* anybody that he offered you money?"

"Not that I can recall."

"Did you ever *brag* to anybody that he offered you money to kill his wife?"

"Not that I can recall."

"Does that mean that you could or you don't remember?"

"Right."

"Okay. Why would you tell anybody –"

"I don't know."

"You don't know why you would tell anybody that he offered you money to kill his wife?"

"Well I don't know if he did or he did not, but I'm saying if he did, I don't see why I would go around telling people about it."

It was the last obfuscation of the night.

"Okay Mr. Barrett, you can consider yourself officially under arrest."

"Okay."

"You are charged with causing the death of Hanna Buxbaum."

Piers read the young man his rights, and then asked him if he had anything to say. Barrett shook his head.

"Put your cigarette out," Piers said. "Stand up, you're gonna be lodged in the cell block upstairs."

After the required body search, Barrett was placed in the cell next to Helmuth. Forty-five minutes later, Barrett was taken to the guardroom, where he held a one-minute telephone conversation with his lawyer. Back in his cell, Barrett asked Constable Linker if Helmuth Buxbaum was in the next cell. The policeman nodded and went back to his desk. "Helmuth, Helmuth!" Barrett cried, whistling loudly when he got no answer.

At 8:54 P.M., Helmuth was taken from his cell to a private room where a man named Arthur Fish explained that Del McLennan had retained the high-profile Toronto lawyer Eddie Greenspan to act on his behalf. Fish, a law student articling with Greenspan, advised Helmuth not to talk to anyone and told him that he would see him in the morning. "After the phone call, I went back to my cell," Helmuth said later. "I saw Barrett on the way back to the cell. Barrett winked at me. Barrett also put his fingers to his lips. He made a 'be quiet' gesture."

Squirrel, it seemed, had divined that the walls had ears.

13

CLOSING THE NET

"Gary broke down and was crying. He said he'd really done
it this time. He said that she said, 'Please, honey, don't do it'
and that she directed it at Helmuth. That's when [Gary] told
me he looked at Helmuth, pointed the gun at him, and said,
'You bastard, it should be you.' He showed me the gun and
said, 'I killed her.'"

— *Robin Foshay to Const. Bart Linker, August 10, 1984*

Police wiretaps are never more productive than when the kingpins fall in a
major investigation. That's when other suspects start phoning each other,
and those involved in the Buxbaum murder were no exception. From the
evening of July 23 onward, the remaining conspirators lived beneath the
shadow of their own imminent arrests — arrests they inadvertently
hastened with a string of desperate telephone calls triggered by the news
that Helmuth Buxbaum and Robert Barrett had been imprisoned.

Six hours after Helmuth was put behind bars, the man who had murdered Hanna Buxbaum called Anita Pitcher at Janet Hicks' apartment to
set up a meeting. Although Gary Foshay put up a breezy front, news of
the sudden arrests had left him badly shaken. He knew that his fate was
now in Robert Barrett's hands. Whether the cocaine addict would keep
their secret, or crack under police pressure and make a deal to save his own
skin, remained to be seen. Well aware of Barrett's character, Foshay
regretted not having silenced him when he had had the chance.

"Well, listen, I'm at the pay phone right now. Did you hear the news?"

"No," Pitcher nervously replied.

"Rob got caught, and the old man got caught, and they're charged for
conspiracy."

"Are you serious?" Pitcher said, her knees going weak.

"Yeah, so listen, I would like you to get a hold of Doug [Hunter, a friend of Hicks]. Tell him to pick you up an c'mon down here. I'm at the Well [Wellington Tavern] an' I'll wait right here for you."

"We're just gettin' ready. We're comin' down there anyway."

"Well then hurry up. I wanna talk to you, okay, kiddie?" Foshay said. He was anxious to get his plans for leaving the country in place before the inevitable knock came on *his* door.

"Yeah, no problem," Pitcher said.

"All right. Who's 'we'?" Foshay asked, displaying the paranoia that would build to murderous levels over the next few days.

"Uh, Trish," Pitcher answered, referring to Patricia Kinsman, a friend who had just gotten out of jail after failing to pay a fine.

"Tell her zip."

"No, no problem."

"Tell Doug if he wants to see me, to come down here. We got some talkin' to do and some things to get fixed."

"Yeah, he said he was going to drop down there."

"All right, sweetheart, I'll wait right here for you."

Pat Allen, who had been drinking so heavily since the murder that he had started throwing up blood, was still asleep when his phone rang at 8:30 A.M. on July 24. It was Brian Challis, one of his friends from the Wellington, who had some bad, if cryptic, news.

"Is there anyway you can go to Florida?" Challis asked.

"Is there [any]way I can go to *Florida*?" Allen repeated sleepily.

"Yeah."

"Yeah, I can go to Florida if you want me to."

"Ah, have you been down to the coffee shop yet?" Challis asked.

"The *where*?"

"The coffee shop."

"Why?" Allen asked, momentarily forgetting that his friend was too experienced to answer directly on a line he suspected was bugged.

"Uh, just to spend twenty-five cents," Challis replied. Allen finally snapped wide-awake.

"Newspaper?"

"Yeah . . ."

"Where are you?" Allen asked.

"Ah, I'm around about four blocks," Challis answered, carefully disguising his whereabouts.

"Come on over."

"Okay."

"Bring me a paper," Allen ordered.

"I got it."

There was no doubt that Pat Allen's furtive caller made his delivery. That afternoon, Const. Malcolm Lees received a call from a well-placed informant who told him that Allen was "freaking out" over the arrests of Buxbaum and Barrett.

Janet Hicks had managed to insulate herself from the rising temperature of the murder investigation by leaving London to spend a few days in the country. Teena Vanderwal, who had met Hicks in Kelly's Bar nine months earlier, had rented a cottage in Grand Bend for the week starting July 21 and invited her friend to tag along. The two women had been relaxing in the cottage on the evening of July 23, when word of the arrests came over the radio. Hicks quickly silenced Vanderwal, straining to catch every word of the newscast. When the rock music resumed, she told her friend that Squirrel had been with her in Toronto at the time of the murder – a less than earth-shattering reference to Vanderwal, who, for the time being, was out of the loop.

Their Grand Bend retreat on Shady Lane soon attracted a crowd. While Vanderwal was barbecuing hamburgers on the afternoon of July 24, Pat Allen and a group of friends rolled up. Allen and Hicks borrowed Vanderwal's car, saying they were going to the store. Once he was alone with Hicks, Allen stressed the need for absolute silence about the events of July 5 and 6, and told Hicks that she might have to help Gary Foshay come up with an alibi. Back at the cottage, they joined in the party, carefully avoiding any mention of either the murder investigation or the arrests.

After a few drinks for the road, the others returned to the city, leaving Allen, Hicks, and Vanderwal to spend the night in Grand Bend. Allen drank so much that night he passed out. The following afternoon, the three drove back to London, where they picked up Gary Foshay at the Wellington Tavern. An impromptu party was soon in full swing, with Foshay buying the drinks and displaying the same swaggering largess he had shown since the Buxbaum murder.

At one point, Rick Diorio showed up packing a gun, and told Foshay that he was on his way to Vancouver. Vanderwal thought Diorio looked terrified. Word on the street was that Barrett's former bodyguard didn't know whom to be more afraid of, the police or Gary Foshay. A little knowledge, he had finally realized, *was* a dangerous thing.

Later that night, Vanderwal, Hicks, and Foshay returned to Grand Bend. The next day, the Buxbaum murder was once again the principal topic of conversation. Hicks and Foshay both expressed surprise that Helmuth had met Barrett in so public a place as an airport just hours after his wife's murder. The conversation turned to the events of the three-day trip to the Westbury Hotel in Toronto. Vanderwal listened bemusedly to their account of throwing syringes into the hotel room walls. But she didn't know what to make of it when they said someone had made the mistake of "signing their real name" at the Westbury.

The threesome went out to dinner at a nearby restaurant, where they talked about the Toronto trip, which Vanderwal still didn't connect to the Buxbaum and Barrett arrests. But when Foshay left to use the washroom, Hicks finally let her friend in on the truth about the man who was buying their dinner.

"I'm sorry I couldn't tell you before," she said.

"What?" Vanderwal asked.

"Haven't you figured it out yet?" Hicks teased. "Gary said you were a smart girl and would have figured it out a while ago."

"Figured what out?"

Hicks glanced to either side of their table, before whispering her secret.

"Gary is the one who pulled the trigger."

"Pardon?" Vanderwal asked incredulously.

"The 402. Gary is the one who pulled the trigger. It was supposed to be a kidnapping and it went wrong and Gary feels really bad about it."

After dinner, they drove back to London, where they attended Boys' Night at the Wellington. For the rest of the week, they would shuttle between their favourite tavern and their Grand Bend retreat, bringing back a fresh crowd of revellers to the cottage on each trip. Events hurtled along on the slippery rails of drugs and liquor. On Friday night, July 27, Doug Hunter, Hicks' friend, rolled Teena Vanderwal's car. Compared to the predicament the young university student would soon find himself in, the accident was a mere trifle.

Towards the end of their stay in Grand Bend, Hicks unfolded a T-shirt and showed Vanderwal a silver .45-calibre pistol that she claimed to be keeping for Foshay. That night, when the two women went for a walk on the beach, Hicks tucked the .45 into the back of her bikini. Early the next morning, Vanderwal noticed the gleam of the .45 from the waistband of

Foshay's jeans as he got into the boat to go fishing. But she wasn't about to say anything to the man she now knew had murdered Hanna Buxbaum – particularly since he had been so generous to everyone over the past several days, spending the proceeds of his work. As Janet Hicks said, he *did* feel really bad about what had happened.

By the time their brief vacation was over, Gary Foshay's murder money had run out and it was back to business as usual. On the afternoon of Tuesday, July 31, the unemployed welder turned hitman showed up at his younger brother's door in London, wondering if his welfare cheque had arrived.

With the remaining conspirators spooked, the OPP refined the focus of its extensive surveillance. Investigators were granted an authorization from County Court Judge J. Winter to install a probe at Janet Hicks' apartment, a place where three suspects lived and two others, Foshay and Allen, regularly visited.

Despite their interest in the conspirators still at large, investigators did not forget about Helmuth Buxbaum. As the wiretaps came down at the Buxbaum cottage on July 24, Corp. Ken Allen and Const. Andy Fotheringham visited the Elgin-Middlesex Detention Centre (EMDC), where Helmuth was remanded in custody until August 28. After getting another authorization from Judge Winter, the officers installed a microphone in the inmate interview rooms at EMDC. Police were aware that, since his arrest, Helmuth had been seeing Pastor Paul Fawcett regularly. In case the accused man confessed to the murder, something that might happen if Fawcett was even partially right about his former benefactor, they were anxious to tape their conversations.

"My opinion, from what I hear," the clergyman told police after half a dozen private visits with Helmuth, "is that he is either guilty, framed, or insane."

After days of trying to find Randy Leslie, the man who claimed to have been told about Barrett's part in the Buxbaum murder during a card game at the Westbury Hotel, the OPP got lucky. Leslie, who had disappeared after his first interview with the Metro Toronto Police, had been re-arrested on drugs and firearms charges.

On July 24, Const. Bart Linker drove to Toronto, where Leslie repeated his claim that Barrett had boasted about arranging Hanna Buxbaum's murder during the card game. He said that Barrett had told him he had been paid $14,000 for the hit by the victim's husband, who wanted to collect "a lot of money" in an insurance claim, and that a final payment on the contract killing was still due. "I got the guy's address and everything up the fucking street. The guy that so-called set her up," Leslie crowed, not realizing that Barrett was already under arrest.

With the reels of the OPP's hidden tape recorders busily spinning, detectives began interviewing people whose names they had picked up on wiretaps or who had called to volunteer information. Dawn Watson told police about Helmuth's cocaine habit and kinky sexual preferences, vices she claimed Robert Barrett had eagerly pandered to for the last six months. To back up her story, she gave constables Aspden and Edwards the name of Terry Gallagher, another prostitute who had been paid $300 by Helmuth to perform lesbian sex acts with Dawn for his titillation. The next day, Gallagher confirmed Watson's story, adding that she had been with Helmuth and Barrett on at least one occasion when they had purchased cocaine.

In a strange twist, a guard at the EMDC told investigators that his son's wife, Joanne Bottaro, had received letters from Helmuth after sleeping with him more than twenty times during her stint as a part-time prostitute on the Pearson International Airport strip in late 1983. Although her husband now needed the letters for a custody suit with his estranged wife, he was willing to share them with police.

After subsequent interviews with other young prostitutes who had spent time with Helmuth, detectives were struck by a common feature of his relationships. In nearly every case, he had complained about his sex life with Hanna and told the girls he wanted out of his marriage. Police got an idea of just how anxious he was to do something about his unhappy home life when Debbie Schaeffer, Helmuth's former mistress and travelling companion, provided an additional fact: "He offered me $5,000 and to be set up in California to have his kid," she told constables Brady and Edwards. "I refused. He offered up to $20,000. I still refused."

The fuzziest outline of a motive for Hanna Buxbaum's slaying was beginning to emerge. If Schaeffer was telling the truth, the unhappy husband had been prepared to begin a new family with a younger woman months before events had made him an eligible widower. Such unseemly haste betrayed an impatience that might well have turned murderous.

One of the most important interviews police conducted was with Lenny Peltier, a shadowy figure who stood on the periphery of London's petty underworld. Peltier's home phone number had shown up on Bell Canada tolls detectives had obtained from the telephone in Robert

Barrett's suite at the Westbury Hotel. When asked about the two-minute conversation Peltier had had with Barrett on the afternoon of July 6, he confirmed what Barrett had all but admitted to Inspector Piers on the day he had been arrested – that Peltier had been his drug connection at the London airport that night. Peltier, who neglected to tell police that he had also sold cocaine to Barrett, Diorio, and Pitcher on July 4, said that Squirrel had paid him with $1,700 in crisp, new fifty-dollar bills that he noticed were consecutively numbered. When Peltier had asked about the source of the money, Barrett had dropped a none-too-subtle reference to the Buxbaum murder before flashing his hallmark smile.

While Piers was interviewing Peltier, the wiretaps on Helmuth's two residential lines at Komoka came down, and police prepared to execute search warrants at all the banks and trust companies where the wealthy businessman had accounts. The next day, July 27, Const. Bill Harlow of the Grand Bend OPP called to say that he had an informant who claimed that Hanna Buxbaum's killer had just spent a few days in the area and had talked about the crime to a local waitress, Kim Smith – a tip constables Brady and Edwards were assigned to check out. Smith told police that she knew nothing about the murder.

Police got some bad news on July 30, when Finn Nielsen from the Centre of Forensic Sciences filed his report on the exhibits he had been given from Hanna Buxbaum's body and the crime scene. The .32-calibre lead slug removed form the victim's skull was so badly damaged that the firearms examiner couldn't tell investigators much about the weapon that had fired it, except that the revolver's bore had likely been in poor condition. Nielsen noted that the results of the tape lift from Hanna's left cheek revealed "close range firearms discharge residues," indicating that the weapon had likely been less than two feet from her head when it had been fired. Finally, Nielsen reported that no projectiles had been found in the section of wooden post removed from the guardrail at the murder scene, eliminating the theory that a hole in it had been caused by a bullet.

The next day, constables Karen Brady and Paul Edwards conducted the OPP's first official interview with Debbie Barber, whose apartment had been under physical and electronic surveillance for nearly three weeks. Compared to what they had learned from the wiretap, and from Barber's interview with Sgt. Bob Cann of the London police, her first statement was meagre, revealing little more than that she wasn't yet ready to talk. When constables Gentle and Aspden interviewed her again a month later, it was a different story.

While his colleagues were getting nowhere with Debbie Barber, Const. Bart Linker was filling in an important part of the puzzle. Linker returned to the Rent-A-Wreck office where Anita Pitcher had hired the blue Nova and showed employee Keith Jones photos of various people in a line-up. Jones positively identified Pat Allen as the man who had been with Pitcher when she rented the car on the afternoon of July 4. It was a powerful piece of evidence to take into the interview with the young woman who, knowingly or not, had rented the murder car.

For days now, Inspector Piers had been preparing for the first big move in the murder investigation since the arrests of Buxbaum and Barrett. When he received word on July 31 from Corp. Ken Allen that a probe had been successfully planted in Janet Hicks' apartment, he decided to throw a second big scare into the remaining conspirators. The time had come to acquaint Anita Pitcher with the consequences of consorting with killers, and to let the others know that the hour of reckoning was drawing ever nearer.

The single most important interview of Project Angel to date began at 11:49 A.M. on August 1 in the conference room at London Detachment. From the moment Anita Pitcher opened her front door to find Ron Piers and Greg Calcott on her doorstep, she knew she was in trouble. For days now, the people involved in the murder conspiracy had been giving her the same advice; no matter what happened, she wasn't to tell the police *anything*. But on the ride back to London Detachment, Pitcher realized that that would prove easier said than done.

For the first fifteen minutes of their interview, which was secretly recorded, Piers listened as patiently as he could while Pitcher spun out a fantasy to protect her friends. She told Piers that she had rented the blue Nova to spend a weekend at Canada's Wonderland with a male stripper called Free Rise, whose real name she couldn't remember. Out of the goodness of his heart, her "brother," Pat Allen, had given her the money for the car, which Anita had returned to Rent-A-Wreck on Sunday, July 8, after driving it all weekend in Toronto.

For two weeks, police had known from the description they had been given by chauffeur Charles Downswell that Pitcher had been one of three people who had travelled by limousine with Robert Barrett to the Westbury Hotel on the night of July 4. If anyone had been driving the blue Nova in Toronto that weekend, it hadn't been Anita Pitcher. Still not certain about how deeply Pitcher was involved in the conspiracy, Piers let her know that he didn't have time for her well-intentioned but transparent lies.

"Okay," he abruptly said, "Maybe we'd better start from the beginning again."

"Why? Am I lying?" the startled woman replied.

"Yes."

"I'm scared, that's why," Pitcher said shakily.

"I'm going to read you something before we go through this again," Piers replied.

"My rights, right?" Pitcher ventured.

"No. It says, 'Everyone who commits first degree murder or second degree murder is guilty of an indictable offence and shall be sentenced to prison for life' . . . This is a murder investigation and you're deeply involved . . . Tell me the story from the beginning again, and this time, tell me the truth."

"Yup. I will. I swear to God I will," Pitcher replied, a promise she more than kept during the next hour and a half.

Pitcher quickly exchanged her story about a weekend in Toronto with a male stripper for something far more fantastic – the truth. She explained how she had gone to the Westbury Hotel with Barrett, Diorio, and Janet Hicks on the night before the murder to party and shop. Although the detectives already knew that from their own investigation, nothing had prepared them for what she told them next. Pitcher stunned Piers and Calcott with her description of a meeting in a parking lot on the afternoon of July 4 that included Barrett, Allen, and a man in a brown station wagon, a meeting that had taken place *before* she had set out for Toronto with the others.

"Who was driving?" Piers asked, referring to the other car.

"It looked like Mr. Buxbaum, from the description I can remember, compared to the paper," Pitcher replied.

She told police that she watched the brown station wagon follow the Nova out of the K-Mart parking lot and disappear into the late afternoon traffic. An hour later, when Barrett and Allen returned to pick her up, they had a fur coat which they jokingly told her to try on – unprompted corroboration of Debbie Barber's story that Buxbaum had gotten rid of a mink coat the night before the murder because it might connect him with Barrett.

Before asking his next question, Piers reflected on a grim possibility: if Pitcher had it right, Helmuth Buxbaum had not only met with Robert

Barrett shortly *after* his wife's murder, but hours *before* as well. Where, the detective wondered to himself, had the three men gone after leaving Pitcher at the K-Mart?

Although Anita Pitcher didn't know it, she held the key to a far more important question: who had actually been present on the two July 5 encounters with the Buxbaums on Highway 402? From conversations overheard at the Westbury Hotel the day after the murder, Pitcher knew there had been a morning attempt on Mrs. Buxbaum's life by Pat Allen, Gary Foshay, and a third man whose existence police were learning about for the first time, a man she would only refer to as "Terry." (In honour of their weekend at the Seaway Motel, Pitcher had developed a case of romantic amnesia about Terry Armes, protecting him as much as she could throughout the interview.)

"I just heard the three of them talking about it, that Gary, Terry, and Pat, tried this beforehand . . . and that they should have left it at that and not gone through with it," she said.

Piers was struck by the parallel between Pitcher's story and the account Debbie Barber had given to Sgt. Bob Cann of an abortive morning attempt on Hanna's life, including the crucial fact that Pat Allen had bailed out. But unlike Barber, who hadn't known the identity of Allen's confederates, Pitcher was able to name Hanna Buxbaum's executioners. The bombshell revelation came when Piers asked her a question about Hanna Buxbaum's still missing purse.

"What about the purse?"

"I don't know," Pitcher honestly replied.

"When was the last that you heard anything about the purse?"

"When we were still in Toronto . . . They just said 'Did you get the purse and the jewellery?' And they said 'No, just the purse.'"

"Who was talking about it?" Piers probed, trying to break through the shield of Pitcher's anonymous pronoun.

"Pat asked Gary and Terry if they got the purse and the jewellery; Gary said, 'No, we didn't get the jewellery, we just got the purse.'" Pitcher replied.

Piers drew a deep breath. If Pat Allen was asking about which of Hanna's personal effects Foshay had taken, then Allen, it seemed, hadn't been at the murder scene. More importantly, it looked like Hanna's killers were Gary Foshay and his mysterious partner, "Terry."

Before the interview ended, the detective gleaned other valuable information. Although Robert Barrett had had no recollection of getting anything but drugs at the London airport, Pitcher told police that when he returned to the Westbury with Janet Hicks, he talked about having received a "large sum" of money from Helmuth Buxbaum. Pitcher also said that she had picked up the Nova in London and had returned it to Rent-A-Wreck. She had received the keys from a pretty, curly-haired young woman named Robin, the same woman who had passed on instructions from Terry Armes to wash the Nova before returning it to Rent-A-Wreck. After returning the car, she had had to pick it up again, when Janet Hicks told her that Pat Allen wanted 300 miles put on the odometer. Finally, Pitcher told detectives that Gary Foshay had hidden a weapon in Hicks' apartment, a handgun he had been carrying ever since the Buxbaum murder.

It may not have been the .32 revolver that killed Hanna Buxbaum, but Ron Piers wasn't taking any chances. When the interview ended, he instructed Mel Getty to get a search warrant for Hicks' apartment. In the meantime, he and Calcott had more talking to do. After returning Anita Pitcher to her apartment with the advice to keep what she had told police to herself, the officers picked up her temporary roommate, Janet Hicks. The full court press was on, and Ron Piers had no intentions of letting up.

When Hicks began talking she gave Piers and Calcott hope that this witness more than most might want to help them catch Hanna Buxbaum's killers. "My mother was murdered," she told them. "I know what it feels like and I felt sorry for those kids . . . If I knew Rob had done it, or anybody else who'd done it, I would have turned them in because I do not believe in killing."

But the noble sentiment was a sham; it soon became obvious to the detectives that Janet Hicks was ready to go to the wall for her homicidal friends. Over the next two hours, she told police as many lies about the case as Anita Pitcher had given them facts. Even when confronted with the possibility of spending twenty-five years in prison for the privilege of protecting Pat Allen and Gary Foshay, she refused to tell police what she really knew about the events of July 4, 5, and 6.

Instead, Hicks claimed that she'd gone to Toronto at the invitation of Robert Barrett "to do some shopping and party around." While Rick Diorio and Barrett spent July 4 and 5 on a cocaine binge, mainlining every fifteen minutes, she and Anita Pitcher had bought a few things at the Eaton Centre and walked Yonge Street. Disgusted by Barrett's drug excesses, she had then called her sister, Karen, on Thursday evening, telling her to have Pat Allen and Gary Foshay pick her up in Toronto and take her back to London. They had dutifully arrived around noon on July 6, but before returning to London with them in a cab, she flew to the same city with Robert Barrett to pick up more drugs. In relating her false story, she made no mention of picking up money at the London airport, or of having paged the man who supplied it, Helmuth Buxbaum, from Pearson when their flight was delayed – telling omissions that Piers noted.

Apart from the difficulty he had with the idea of Allen and Foshay as knights errant and Janet Hicks as a maiden in distress, Piers had a fundamental problem with her story. If, as she claimed, she had been turned off by Barrett's cocaine binge, why had she flown back to London with him to pick up more drugs, leaving her rescuers behind? And why hadn't she mentioned the wad of money she had had in her purse when "Mr. and Mrs. Barrett" flew back to Toronto on the night of July 6 after the airport meeting with Helmuth Buxbaum? Building on her half truth that Barrett had travelled to London to pick up drugs, Piers proceeded to catch Hicks in a major lie.

"He also picked up some money, isn't that right?" he asked.

"No, 'cause –"

"A lot of money. You ought to know, you carried it off the plane," Piers declared, putting Hicks on notice that the detectives weren't without their own sources of information.

"I don't know how much was there," Hicks replied, quickly retreating from her initial story. "All I seen is the first numbers."

"Now let's start again when you get to the airport, and let's have *all* the truth."

Investigators encounter many suspects who won't volunteer the facts, but who readily acknowledge them when they come from the police; Janet Hicks wasn't one of them. The tactic of contradicting her lies with detailed information from the investigation simply led to sudden memory loss or more lies. Hicks denied knowing how much money Barrett had slipped into her purse on the evening of July 6, or that Helmuth Buxbaum had been the man they had met at the airport – even after Piers told her that the entire episode had taken place under the watchful eye of the RCMP. "As far as I knew," she said, "I was taking money for a coke deal, to buy some coke in Toronto."

It was a strange statement for a woman who had just finished telling police that she had asked her friends to get her out of Toronto because of Robert Barrett's drug excesses. And if the money was, in fact, to buy drugs in Toronto, why had Robert Barrett bought twelve grams of cocaine in London, when he knew he had to run the gauntlet of RCMP security at two airports?

"You already went down there to buy coke," Piers said. "Why would you come down and get money and buy coke in Toronto, when you already bought it in London and you're on your way back?"

"'Cause he bought a little bit in Toronto – I mean London – I'm getting all screwed up," Hicks protested. She tried to say that she didn't know Barrett had purchased drugs in London, a glaring contradiction of her earlier claim that buying drugs had been the sole purpose of their quick trip. Piers seized on the growing absurdity of her story.

"So he flies all the way to London to buy coke, and flies all the way back to Toronto to buy coke. That doesn't make sense . . . I suggest that if your memory doesn't improve, you're gonna be in serious trouble."

"I have a very bad memory," Hicks replied, something she proceeded to demonstrate graphically when Piers began asking about what had happened at the Westbury Hotel after she and Barrett returned to Toronto.

Hicks flatly denied that either Foshay or Allen had received any of the money she and Barrett had picked up in London; denied knowing that Pat Allen was involved in a murder conspiracy; failed for the second time to mention the presence of Terry Armes at the hotel; and claimed not to know who had made phone calls to the Westbury from her apartment shortly before and shortly after the murder.

"I didn't know anything about this murder till I got back and read the paper on Saturday morning," she protested. "Most of the time I was in the other room reading a book."

"How come Anita does, and you were in the same building with Anita?" Piers replied.

"I don't know."

Again using information supplied by Pitcher as a lever, Piers tried to pry out more details about the mysterious "Terry," who had apparently been Foshay's partner on the day of the murder.

"When did Terry and Gary come to Toronto with Pat?"

"No Terry there that I know of," Hicks stonewalled.

"Was Terry there?"

"No Terry that I know of," she stubbornly repeated.

"Well Anita knows Terry was there. Why wouldn't *you* know?"

"Maybe Anita knows Terry."

"So in other words, you want to be charged. Is that what you're telling me?" Piers asked as bluntly as he could.

Unable to get Hicks to admit that Gary Foshay's accomplice had been in Toronto, Piers confronted her with another part of her roommate's story.

"Why wouldn't you produce the gun over at the apartment?"

"I don't know there's one there," Hicks calmly answered.

"Foshay brought a gun in there about five days ago."

"If he did, I didn't see it."

"Well, Anita saw it."

"Maybe Anita saw it. *I* didn't see it," Hicks coldly replied.

"Why would Anita tell us you had a gun?"

"Don't ask me."

"Why is Anita staying at your apartment?"

"'Cause Anita's not working right now . . . She's staying there until she gets a job and then she's moving out."

"You know as well as I do that Anita rented the car that was involved in the murder and *that's* why she's staying at your place," Piers declared.

"No, I don't."

"You don't know a lot."

"I know a lot about a coke deal and that is all."

"And you're gonna stick to the coke deal?"

"Yes . . . I don't know nothin' about a murder."

Piers was prepared to arrest Hicks if the gun was uncovered by the four-man team that began searching her apartment that afternoon. But apart from newspaper clippings about the Buxbaum murder, the search came up empty. Knowing that time was on his side, Piers let the frightened woman go, fairly certain that he could learn more about Hanna Buxbaum's murder with Janet Hicks at large than in jail – particularly now that a probe had been installed in her apartment.

Following up on the bonanza of information gleaned from Anita Pitcher, Piers gave instructions to get the necessary authorizations to intercept phone calls at Robin Foshay's house, where he now knew the blue Nova had been parked some time after the murder. By August 3, the wiretap would be operational.

The Hanna Buxbaum murder investigation was coming down to the short strokes.

It didn't take long for the panic created by the police interviews of August 1 to heat up the telephone lines at Janet Hicks' apartment. At 9:19 P.M., she left the message at Pat Allen's apartment that it was "very important" he meet her that night at the Wellington Tavern. When he finally showed up, Allen was too nervous about the surveillance team that was dogging his every step to speak to her in public.

Intermediaries were pressed into service. Teena Vanderwal conveyed a message to Allen from Hicks: the police now knew that he had a key to Hicks' apartment, the origin of telephone calls to the other conspirators at the Westbury Hotel on the day of Hanna's murder. Rattled by the day's developments, Allen wondered aloud to Vanderwal if Hicks could be trusted. At 3:33 A.M., the OPP listened in on Allen telling a male caller that the phones were tapped, the police had raided Hicks' apartment, and most important of all, that "someone has talked."

It was the same story with Gary Foshay. When the conspirators and their friends gathered at Doug Hunter's large house the day after Pitcher and Hicks were questioned, betrayal and murder were in the air. In a series of meetings there on Friday, August 3, Foshay, Allen, and Hicks discussed what to do about the traitor in their midst, Anita Pitcher.

"All hell broke loose," Hunter, who was at the meetings, later said. "Everybody was mad at Anita. They felt that Anita had ratted to the police . . . Everyone was planning on wasting Anita that day. Gary Foshay said he was going to do it . . . Then they cooled off 'cause I was getting too scared."

It was not the first time that his shady acquaintances had given the middle-class university student a bad moment. Shortly after Doug Hunter had started seeing Janet Hicks, she had shown him the contents of a blue tote bag she kept in her closet. Cradling the KK9 submachine gun and smiling up at him, Hicks asked if he knew anyone who would be interested in buying it. The terrified young man told her that he "wasn't into stolen weapons" and began to have second thoughts about his new friend.

But Hunter was a moth to the flame of these urban desperados. On the night before Hanna Buxbaum was killed, he had been in Hicks' apartment when Pat Allen dropped by and left with the blue tote bag. After the police search of her apartment, Hicks had called Hunter to do her a favour. When he arrived, she explained that the OPP had overlooked Gary Foshay's gun in the bottom of her laundry hamper; handing it to Hunter, she asked him to hide it at his place. "The gun I took to the house was put in the east outside wall of our sunroom, between one of the boards, in a Miracle Food Mart bag," Hunter said later. "The night they were talking about killing Anita, it was taken away."

Over the next few nerve-racking days, the conspirators fine-tuned their latest murder plans – and expanded them. Anita Pitcher was to be drowned at Grand Bend on August 10. Janet Hicks was to arrange additional contracts on several others who knew too much and couldn't be trusted: her niece, Tracy Larocque; Gary Foshay's estranged wife, Robin; and even Hicks' own sister, Karen. (When police were tipped to the impending slayings, Ron Piers took the information seriously and provided immediate protection to the proposed victims.)

Terrified that his friends meant business, Hunter raced to Hicks' apartment and warned Anita Pitcher. The two ended up spending the night together. During their pillow talk, Pitcher gave Hunter a complete rundown of the murder, including the fact that Janet Hicks had played a key role in the rapidly unravelling conspiracy.

When the group once again gathered in his house the next night, Hunter confronted Hicks, demanding to know if she had, in fact, been involved in the murder. She insisted that the whole mess revolved around a drug deal, a story she tried to back up by getting Teena Vanderwal to tell him the same thing. Then the conspirators began fretting that Hunter might be siding with Anita Pitcher, and toyed with the idea of silencing him, too. The young man who had opened up his mother's house and backyard pool to murderers suddenly felt the deadly antagonism of his old friend, Janet Hicks.

"I said, 'What's wrong with you? Do you think I've ratted?' And she said, 'If the shoe fits.' I went downstairs and had four beers and shut the door to my party room . . . Gary walked in. He gave me a jab. I was sitting in the dark with only a candle. I think I said, 'Fuck off, Foshay . . . If you don't trust me and you think I ratted, then just blow me away or give me a gun and I'll do it myself.'"

As angry as Gary Foshay was, there wasn't much he could do to Doug Hunter besides what he actually did – kick in the sliding door of his rec room, and tear one of the fluorescent lights from a fixture in the ceiling and smash it against the wall. For one thing, if Foshay was going to kill everyone who knew what he had done, he would have to borrow Pat Allen's KK9 for the job. The list included his wife, his brother, his sister-in-law, his uncle, and a rapidly increasing number of female acquaintances.

Doug Hunter, a world-traveller by the standards of the denizens of the Wellington Tavern, figured in Foshay's dream of escape. For days, the gunman had been planning to flee to Bermuda, where he would "hook up with some rich girl" and live off the money Janet Hicks would collect from Helmuth Buxbaum when the rich businessman was let out of prison after the OPP's case collapsed. After a seven-year exile in the sun, which would turn the Buxbaum affair into a faded memory, Foshay would return to Canada to be reunited with his latest love, seventeen-year-old stripper Tracy Larocque. Like it or not, Doug Hunter, a former resident of Bermuda, would be his sidekick throughout his exile. If there was one thing the killing business inspired, it was fear.

"Gary said, 'I took Mrs. Buxbaum out of the car. I was going to shoot her.' She looked at her husband and said, 'No honey, don't.' And he shot her in the head and the back section blew off." He went on about 'If you don't co-operate, your Mom and Heidi [Hunter's girlfriend] are dead' . . . So I said I would co-operate and go to Bermuda."

Foshay's lust to silence potential witnesses gradually gave way to theatrical preparations for his escape. He got Tracy Larocque to peroxide his greying hair, and then began gathering money for Bermuda from various young women. His girlfriend Debbie Trollope gave him a $200 cheque, which he promptly signed over to Teena Vanderwal in exchange for a $500 loan from her Visa card. Pat Allen and Janet Hicks tried to persuade him to slip into the United States by boat, but Foshay sullenly stuck to his plan to fly out of Toronto for Bermuda with his reluctant travelling companion on August 9.

Before he left, Foshay paid a final visit to his brother, Trent, and his common-law wife, Donna LeBlanc. Doug Hunter witnessed the emotional farewell and Gary Foshay's remarkable confession. Foshay told the startled couple everything about the murder on Highway 402, except the fact that he had pulled the trigger on Hanna Buxbaum – a detail filled in by Hunter when his desperate friend disappeared into one of the bedrooms to have a private word with Debbie Trollope. Trent Foshay couldn't quite believe what he had heard.

"I talked to Gary. He said something about twenty-five years, people were after him. He had made out a will. Gary was hugging and kissing everybody. I figured he was on a drug trip."

That evening, Trent called his sister-in-law, Robin Foshay. He explained that Gary had just come by and "spilled his guts" about the Buxbaum murder. During the call, both of them uttered the words "Gary is the shooter." Before hanging up, they agreed not to admit to anyone that they had talked, a pact that amused the police officers who were listening to and recording their conversation.

On the eve of his escape, Foshay was at Hunter's house watching television with friends. Hunter had already gone to bed in preparation for their trip to Pearson International Airport in the morning. He and Gary had reservations on Air Canada flight 942 to Bermuda under the names D. Hunter and M. Hunter. They were set to depart at 10 A.M.

After the others had turned in, a restless Gary Foshay sat on the floor and romanced Tracy Larocque, a girl half his age. The two had met four days earlier at Doug Hunter's swimming pool. The young woman had been attracted to the baby-faced tough guy with the mysterious way about him. Although she knew something was going on, she wasn't quite sure what until she went dancing with Foshay at the Junction and asked him how long he would be in Bermuda. "He said a long time, until things cool down," she said later.

That wasn't all Foshay told her: "Gary said 'Me and my friend committed the murder.' We had a couple of dances and I felt the gun in his pants . . . I asked Gary if he was involved . . . Gary replied 'Squirrel met Buxbaum. They were discussing about the murder. Squirrel said he would do it.' He told me that Squirrel asked him because he was good with guns and knew how to pull the trigger. He said, 'I killed her.'"

That night, when they had returned to Doug Hunter's for a swim, Larocque had been ordered upstairs by her aunt, Janet Hicks. Hicks bluntly asked her how much she knew, neglecting to specify exactly what she was talking about. The teenager told her she didn't know anything. Hicks then turned out the light and pressed something cold into her niece's hand. It was a gun. Larocque dropped it, and Hicks put it into her hand a second time, never explaining if it was cheap theatrics or a macabre warning. Like everything else that had been happening to Tracy, the moment had been both fascinating and unreal, and the young stripper abandoned herself to the deadly affair.

Three days later, she had fallen hard for the handsome fugitive. Sitting alone with him now in Doug Hunter's living room, she was mesmerized by his deep voice and the drama of their imminent separation. He told her that he didn't want all his friends to "go down" and that they should "stick together." But even though he tried to heighten her lovestruck mood by giving the teenager his wife's diamond ring, talking all the while about a reunion in Bermuda, it was clear that fear of capture, not Tracy Larocque, was the biggest item on Gary Foshay's mind. "Gary kept looking out the window, because he didn't think he would make it to Toronto," Larocque said later.

As it turned out, making it to Toronto wasn't the problem, but making it to Toronto on time. The man who bitterly complained that his accomplices in the Buxbaum murder had been amateurs, missed his own getaway flight to Bermuda and had to book another through New York. Before Tracy Larocque left for London, Foshay gave her his last remaining coin as a man of the street – a gun and a gram of hash oil. The couple said their goodbyes, and Foshay and Hunter proceeded to U.S. customs and immigration. But it proved harder to get their escape plans off the ground than they'd thought. Foshay was refused entry to Bermuda on an immigration technicality, and they had to re-book their flight for the following morning.

From the airport, Hunter and Foshay took a bus to the terminal at the Royal York Hotel in Toronto and called Heather Roper, a friend of Hunter. The threesome "got sloshed" in a succession of downtown bars and ended up back at Roper's apartment with a bottle of champagne provided by Gary Foshay. Hunter called Teena Vanderwal and Tracy Larocque in London to see if they wanted to come to Toronto to party, but couldn't reach them. He also called Janet Hicks' apartment and talked to her sister, Karen, about their travel plans. Although Foshay looked "very down" to Roper, she didn't know why until Doug Hunter made a bizarre suggestion: "Doug suggested we change Gary's appearance, dress him up like a woman . . . When Doug kept at it, he [Gary] said, 'I've already changed my hair colour four times and shaved off my moustache.'"

Roper asked what was going on, and Foshay said that two people who had been picked up for a murder were trying to put the blame on him. Roper was saved from learning more about Foshay's problems when he was called to the telephone just after midnight. But her relief turned to fear when she heard him ask the other party, "How's Uncle Smith and Aunt Wesson?"

Hunter then suggested they cash in their tickets to Bermuda and buy Foshay a ticket to western Canada. Reluctantly, Foshay agreed. But at 6:30 the next morning, when Heather Roper awakened her guests, Doug Hunter told her that they had changed their minds again; they would be leaving for Bermuda at the appointed time after all. The young woman didn't feel at ease again until she watched the two men getting into a limousine in front of her house for the half-hour drive to Pearson airport.

At 9:20 A.M. August 10, 1984, the daily meeting of detectives working on the Hanna Buxbaum murder investigation was dominated by Corp. Ken

Allen. Allen informed his colleagues that a telephone call intercepted the previous night at Janet Hicks' apartment between Karen Hicks and Doug Hunter revealed that Gary Foshay was planning to flee the country.

A check with Air Canada confirmed that Foshay and Hunter indeed held reservations on a flight scheduled to depart for Bermuda at 10 A.M. Allen immediately contacted the RCMP at Pearson International Airport, instructing them to detain Foshay and Hunter until OPP investigators arrived. If they refused to be voluntarily detained, Foshay was to be arrested for first degree murder.

At 9:50 A.M., Wayne Harris and Susan Lockhart of the RCMP met with ticket agents at gate 105 of Terminal 2. After checking the flight coupons for Air Canada flight 942, they discovered that D. Hunter and a "Miss" Foshay had already boarded the aircraft, which was due to depart for Bermuda in ten minutes. The plainclothes police officers boarded the jet and asked the people in seats 24A and 24B if they were Gary Foshay and Doug Hunter. The two men acknowledged that they were. Harris and Lockhart then flashed their identifications and discreetly asked the men to accompany them off the plane.

"Does this mean we are going to miss our flight?" Hunter asked.

"Yes," Harris replied, guiding his charges down the aisle of the jet while curious onlookers craned their necks over the tops of their morning newspapers.

After searching the men, the officers took Foshay and Hunter to the RCMP office in the basement of Terminal 1. Doug Hunter asked what it was all about, and Harris told him that officers of the London OPP wanted to talk to them. Although Foshay said nothing, Harris noticed that as he lit his cigarette his large hands were shaking.

Four hours later, Gary Foshay was on his way to London Detachment in the back of an unmarked OPP cruiser. The only thing that travelled to Bermuda was the killer's luggage.

Robin Foshay was more relieved than surprised when Const. Bart Linker called her early Friday to arrange an interview about her estranged husband's involvement in Hanna Buxbaum's murder. A police wiretap had picked up the young woman's intention to visit a lawyer, and the detectives decided to talk to her before she was silenced by counsel. Robin called her mother and asked her to babysit Melissa and Aimee while she talked to police.

It was the interview Ron Piers had been waiting for, a kind of Rosetta

Stone for deciphering what had actually happened that night on Highway 402 and in the critical hours after the murder. Robin told constables Linker and Gentle how Foshay and his accomplice, Terry Armes, had arrived at her house at 7:30 P.M. on July 5 driving a blue Nova. Gary had immediately asked for cleaning supplies. While Armes had gone to work on the interior of the Nova, her husband emptied out the contents of an ivory-coloured woman's purse. In the cascade of personal effects, Robin had noticed a driver's licence belonging to a Hanna Buxbaum of Komoka.

With his wife holding open a white garbage bag, Foshay had sorted through the contents, removing any valuables he could find, including a number of foreign coins which Hanna had brought back from the Buxbaums' European vacation. Before leaving that night, Armes had buried them in the back of the Foshay property. The purse had later been loaded with bricks and thrown in the Thames River behind 1 High Street, the woman claimed.

Robin told police that Foshay had broken down while still at the house and confessed to murdering Hanna Buxbaum. She had listened in horror as he described how the doomed woman had pleaded with her husband, who had financed the hit, not to do it. "That's when he [Gary] told me he looked at Helmuth, pointed the gun at him, and said 'You bastard, it should be you,'" Robin Foshay told Bart Linker.

For more than a month the young woman had been tortured by Hanna's murder; now that she could finally talk about it, the devastating information just kept coming. Robin said that after the Nova had been backed into the rear of the driveway and an orange tarpaulin thrown over it, Foshay told her that someone would remove it the next day. The following morning Pat Allen, who told Robin that he was the "go-between" in the Buxbaum murder, had dropped in to pick up a pair of shoes he had left there. Robin saw her husband and Terry Armes waiting outside in a car, ready, apparently, for the trip Gary had told her they would be making to pick up the murder money in Toronto.

Then on Sunday, July 8, Armes had called to tell Robin that Anita Pitcher was on her way from Toronto to remove the Nova from her driveway. When police added their knowledge of Janet Hicks' incessant phone calls to Robin's home looking for Gary Foshay, it completed the circle: almost every part of the murder conspiracy had in one way or another touched Robin Foshay. Thanks to the single mother with the conscience, police now knew the identity of the mysterious "Terry." Best of all, her information might lead to the recovery of the first physical evidence that would connect the killers to their victim – the glass jar of Hanna's coins, and the dead woman's purse.

When he heard what Robin had said, Piers immediately obtained a search warrant and dispatched Const. Mel Getty and four members of the Tactical and Rescue Unit to search for the jar of coins. Five minutes after the team arrived, they unearthed the jar from its hiding place under a raspberry bush. Robin Foshay also turned over the pair of earrings Gary Foshay had taken from Hanna's purse and given to his daughter on the night of the murder – earrings Esther Buxbaum later identified as the ones she had given to her mother for safekeeping during their trip to Europe.

Gary Foshay was arrested and charged with first degree murder and conspiracy to murder at 3:53 P.M., just eight minutes after his arrival at London Detachment. On the advice of his lawyer, he refused to be interviewed by police. An hour later, Pat Allen, looking casual in a red muscle shirt and navy blue sweat pants, was led into the station by two members of the physical surveillance team. Greg Calcott charged Allen with the same offences as Gary Foshay and locked him in a holding cell beside his friend. Like Foshay, Allen refused an interview.

A third man, Terry Kline, was arrested in Calgary that same day. The name "Terry" had turned up on police wiretaps in frequent and guarded conversations with other key suspects, and Kline was mistakenly confused with the "Terry" Anita Pitcher had implicated in Hanna's murder.

When Inspector Ron Piers released the names of the men who had been arrested to a packed press conference at 9:30 P.M., his sense of satisfaction was less than complete; five were down, but there were still two to go.

The next day, Karen Hicks drove a few more nails into the coffin that her sister, Janet, had been busily constructing for herself. She told constables Brady and Edwards that Janet had called from Toronto at 7:30 A.M. on July 5 to tell her that she was staying in suite 1404 of the Westbury Hotel. Hicks had instructed Karen to write down the information and leave it on the hutch for Pat Allen – a fact Janet Hicks had somehow neglected to tell Inspector Piers during their two-hour interview on August 1. A few moments later, Pat Allen had called Karen at the Hicks apartment and been given the message, just before he and his associates drove out to Highway 402 to kill Hanna Buxbaum. That afternoon when she got home from work, the radio was blaring, and Karen knew that someone had been in the apartment. That someone, the police knew, had spent quite a bit of time on the telephone to the Westbury Hotel.

Karen also confirmed that Robert Barrett had called on the evening of July 6 from Pearson and asked her to page Helmuth Buxbaum at the London airport. She was to give him the message that Barrett would be arriving late from Toronto, and that Helmuth should wait for him. A few minutes after she called the airport, Buxbaum returned the call and Karen, thinking he was there to drive Barrett and her sister home, relayed the information.

Karen Hicks handed over stubs of the airline tickets her sister and Robert Barrett had used on the night of July 6. She then described an encounter she had had with Pat Allen on August 1, just after police had searched her apartment. Karen had asked Allen if it were true that a gun had been hidden in the apartment. His reply, as she related it, had the officers reaching for their notebooks: "He said that there was a gun, but it was not the one used in the murder; the gun that *was* used was no longer in existence."

While the police were interviewing Karen Hicks, motorists driving over London's Wellington Street bridge couldn't figure out what all the men were doing in the Thames River. Since 10:26 A.M., members of the OPP's Underwater Search and Recovery Unit, led by dive master Const. K. W. Aitchison, had been scouring the Thames for Hanna Buxbaum's purse. They started their search from the shadow of the bridge and gradually worked their way westward, swimming parallel to a 100-foot line that had been run from the bank to the middle of the river. Although that stretch of the Thames was only four feet deep, the current was strong, and the river, a debris-strewn sewer. Whenever the divers stood up to talk, they sank more than a foot into toxic goo before hitting the solid river bed.

Two hundred feet west of the bridge, Constable Aitchison was swimming in two feet of water when he spotted the white purse in a pool ten feet from shore. It had been weighted down with two bricks. Inside the purse, the diver found several pieces of identification belonging to Hanna Buxbaum.

Folded neatly in the bottom of her water-logged purse was Helmuth's still unsigned application to a Michigan psychiatric hospital.

The police had hoped that Foshay's and Allen's arrests would convince Janet Hicks to tell the truth about the Buxbaum murder, but the frightened young woman persisted in protecting the killers' interests. After visiting Gary Foshay in jail, Hicks repeatedly tried to arrange an alibi for the accused man, begging Teena Vanderwal, Bonnie Holt, and Patricia Kinsman to tell authorities that they had been having dinner with Foshay on the night that Hanna Buxbaum was murdered. All three refused. Judging from a comment she made to Holt, Hicks seemed to understand exactly where her loyalty was taking her: "She told me that she had been questioned, and that if she didn't talk, she would be charged."

Before doing that, Ron Piers dispatched constables Brady and Edwards to take Janet Hicks through her story one last time. In a variation on the good cop, bad cop routine, Brady conducted the first part of the August 16 interview, noting down the suspect's answers without challenging what she said – even when the policewoman knew she was lying. Except for minor variations, including the fact that the mysterious "Terry," whose existence she had denied to Inspector Piers, *had* been with Allen and Foshay when they showed up at the Westbury on July 6, her statement remained unchanged from her earlier interview with Piers.

It was now the turn of Const. Paul Edwards to tighten the screws. He got Hicks to admit that Gary Foshay had, in fact, left a gun at her apartment, something she had lied about to Piers. She also admitted that Terry Armes had been to her apartment on the night of July 8, looking for Allen and Foshay. But when it came to anything touching Pat Allen, Hicks flatly refused to implicate her friend in the murder. She told Edwards that she had never relayed instructions from Allen to Anita Pitcher about putting 300 miles on the Nova before returning it to the rental agency, even though police knew from Pitcher that she had. And, although she admitted calling her London apartment from the Westbury Hotel early on the morning of July 5, she concealed the fact that the purpose of the call had been to let Pat Allen know her whereabouts, something police had known about since their interview with Karen Hicks five days earlier. But it was Janet Hicks' insistence that she didn't know how much money Barrett had slipped into her purse in London Airport, and her stubborn claim that the money had been for a drug deal, that brought the interview to its dread conclusion.

"I am not satisfied with your explanation," Edwards told the rattled woman. "I've been told you had a large amount of money on you in the airplane. You couldn't make change for a drink because you didn't have any small bills. I don't understand the drug deal when you would come to London and get both the drugs *and* the money. That doesn't wash at all."

It was Janet Hicks' last chance to come clean, but she didn't take it.

"I'm trying to figure it out," she stammered.

"Why, Janet? There's one explanation that I could come up with. You were involved in that murder," Edwards said.

"No I wasn't," she protested, her voice beginning to crack.

"I'm arresting you now for conspiracy to murder Hanna Buxbaum," Edwards informed her. After reading Hicks her rights and giving the standard police cautions, the detective asked the accused woman if she had anything to say. "I don't know what to tell you," Hicks wailed.

As the detectives led her upstairs to the holding cells, Janet Hicks began to cry.

While his co-conspirators had remained in London, seemingly powerless to act as the police investigation tightened around them, Terry Armes had taken his experience in the building trade to Winnipeg, where he moved in with his brother and landed a job as a sales representative for Westhome Industries. In early August, the company hired Armes to market their home-improvement and building products throughout the Prairies and north-western Ontario.

Armes quickly fit in with the other canvassers and siding installers who worked for Westhome. Every Friday on their day off, the men gathered at Fingers restaurant to have a few beers over lunch and talk shop. During an August 3 session, Armes told the others that he had left London because the siding business had gone soft. Before the men had finished their meal, Armes suddenly "turned really white" and blacked out. When he came to, he explained to fellow salesman Jim Rutledge that he had hypoglycemia. "He told me the blackout was from bad nerves, which have been worse in the past couple of weeks," Rutledge said later.

As they travelled the country selling siding together, Rutledge and Armes developed a rapport. During an August 7 sales trip to Kenora, Ontario, the two men were having dinner one night when Armes confided that there had been other reasons for his decision to leave London. He told Rutledge that he had wanted to get away from his wife and children, and had even broken up with his girlfriend. The other man listened patiently to Armes' story, but had the feeling that there was more on his mind than he was willing to say.

Their next conversation took place on August 10, in a Miami bar – Miami, Manitoba. Even though it was their day off, Rutledge wanted to make some sales calls in the small community, leaving Armes in a motel bar while he knocked on doors. On their way back to Winnipeg that night, Armes began asking Rutledge about how thorough the Manitoba authorities were in checking someone out for bonds and licences – documents Armes would need to keep his job. Rutledge assumed Armes had a wallet full of unpaid traffic tickets or other fines and told him they could prevent him from getting his bond. If there was anything like that, Rutledge advised, it was best to tell their boss, because as things stood, Armes was only covered by the blanket company bond.

"Jim, it's worse than that. You don't know how bad it is. I was in the wrong place at the wrong time with the wrong people," Armes nervously replied. When Rutledge tried to find out more, his friend irritably broke off their talk.

A few days later, a group of company salesmen were playing pool in the beverage room of a motel in Stoughton, Saskatchewan, when Armes excused himself to make a telephone call. In high spirits before the call, Armes returned to the table looking "really pissed off." He told the others that he was going to walk back to his motel room, a mile and a half away. He had good reason to want to be alone. Janet Hicks, who had already told him about the arrests of Foshay and Allen, had just finished telling Armes that Anita Pitcher was talking to police. Hicks herself expected to be arrested at any moment.

The next day, August 16, Armes showed up at Rutledge's house "upset and sort of crying." He told his friend that he could no longer stay at his brother's house, and would be moving to a new address in downtown Winnipeg. Rutledge drove Armes to his new quarters and waited while Armes took three women who lived there into another room. When they came out half an hour later, Rutledge overheard a snippet of conversation between two of the young women: "Isn't that harbouring a fugitive? Could we get in trouble?"

Rutledge asked his friend what was going on. Armes told him that a good friend of his had just been arrested, and warned Rutledge not to call him at his brother's house or to use his telephone. As Rutledge got ready to leave, Armes stopped him, his dark eyes wide with fear: "They're getting closer to me."

His instincts were sound. On July 20, Ron Piers decided that he had enough information to arrest Terry Armes. During the past week, Anita

Pitcher had added to her already detailed account of the conspiracy, telling police that Armes had been paid $3,500 for the murder. She also positively identified her former lover from a photo line-up. In combination with Robin Foshay's information, the evidence against Armes was overwhelming.

Piers called the Winnipeg City Police and told Det. Ken Biener to place surveillance on Armes' brother's apartment, where the OPP believed Armes might be staying. He also dispatched Mel Getty to RCMP headquarters in Toronto to fax his western colleagues a photo of the suspect. If Winnipeg police spotted Armes, they were to arrest him on the spot and charge him with the first degree murder of Hanna Buxbaum.

With the help of a change of address and the Manitoba telephone company, Terry Armes managed to elude police for a few more days. On the afternoon of August 21, his former girlfriend, Valerie Maxwell, called the OPP and told them that Armes had called her at 3 A.M. from an unknown location. When Const. Andy Fotheringham tried to put a trace on the call to see if it had originated in Winnipeg, he was informed that he would have to deal with Manitoba Telephone, which was not part of the Bell Canada system. The provincial phone company was happy to co-operate, but it would cost the OPP $400 – no small sum in an investigation where every hour of overtime had become the subject of major bureaucratic wrangles. Ron Piers authorized the expenditure.

Armes, meanwhile, avoided his brother's place and tried to lie low. On Friday, August 24, he was drinking at the bar of the Airport Hotel with some friends from work when he told Jim Rutledge he wanted to talk. He asked Rutledge if he had ever wanted to make a lot of money. When the other man replied that everyone did, Armes philosophised that the greater the risk, the more a person could make. He himself had made a grab for the brass ring once, but had severely underestimated the risk. Even though Armes was "pretty juiced," Rutledge sensed that he was finally ready to reveal whatever it was that had been bothering him since the day they'd met. "I asked him if this had to do with drugs, and he said, 'No, I wish it was.' He said he wanted out now but it was too late. He said, 'They got the last one, and they're coming for me next,'" Rutledge said later.

Floundering in alcoholic paranoia, Armes suddenly told Rutledge he wanted to leave the bar, pointing to a table of strangers he claimed were policemen because they hadn't been drinking for the past hour and a half. Tiring of his friend's hysterics, Rutledge told him not to be so silly. On the way out of the bar, Armes began to scuffle with his unhappy confidante. "He started pushing me, so I gave him a slap. I called him a dizzy bastard. I told him if there is something he wants to tell me, tell me. And to stop talking in riddles."

As the two men drove aimlessly around Winnipeg, Armes made an oblique approach to Rutledge to help him hide out for a while. Still not understanding the other man's predicament, Rutledge once again accused Armes of beating around the bush. If he had any outstanding tickets or warrants, he should go to a lawyer and get it "straightened out," Rutledge advised. But he *had* to stop talking in riddles. "'That's all I can tell you,' he says. He says, 'I hope I haven't mixed you up, this isn't like me normally. They're coming to get me next. I'm too tired, you'll probably understand this later on.'"

Two days later, Jim Rutledge finally understood, when he picked up the *Winnipeg Free Press* and read that his tormented friend had just been arrested for first degree murder.

14

CAGED

"My visions, my terrible headaches, and the voices I started
to hear almost drove me to insanity . . . I told
[Superintendent] O'Brien in tears that I had had the vision of
my wife and my parents calling me . . . For several months I
thought that a definite attempt was made to drive me insane."
— *Helmuth Buxbaum on his early imprisonment*

It was a long way from the imperial suite of Vienna's Biedermeier hotel to
the segregation cells of Elgin-Middlesex Detention Centre. For Helmuth
Buxbaum, who had lived in luxury for most of the past decade, "the
hole" was purgatory in cement and steel.

On July 24, 1984, as inmate 929455B made the short ride up Wellington Street to Queen's Avenue in an unmarked police cruiser, he hadn't
known what to expect from his first court appearance. The drab courtroom inside the five-storey, faceless Ministry of Transportation building
was perfectly suited to an event that was as brief as it was perfunctory. Provincial court Justice of the Peace Len Obokota remanded both Helmuth
and Robert Barrett in custody; with that terse ruling, constables Linker
and Aspden turned their prisoners over to court security officers.

The guards put Helmuth in the front cage of the paddywagon for the
ride to EMDC. Barrett, who was riding in the back, shouted to his old
friend, but Helmuth pretended not to hear him. Undeterred by their dire
circumstances, Barrett would later approach Helmuth in the prison yard
and ask for money to buy a decent suit for his court appearances. As for
Helmuth, he would tell his lawyers that he had assumed that Robert Barrett's presence at the OPP detachment on July 23 had been nothing more
than sheer coincidence, the result of an untimely drug bust.

Helmuth was still reeling from the morning's revelation that Barrett was the co-accused in Hanna's murder when warders at EMDC finger-printed, photographed, and strip-searched their newest inmate. After his personal information was entered into the prison computer, guards escorted Helmuth into the bowels of the London jail. Their destination was the cells where dangerous, disturbed, or imperilled prisoners were held for weeks on end without companionship or the simplest amenities.

There were no windows in his latest cage, just piercingly bright fluorescent lights that burned night and day. Helmuth had not experienced anything like it since the war years, when his mother, Luise, and the younger Buxbaum children had slept for three weeks on the floor of the Vogtland station in Saxony, ill-fed and unable to wash, waiting for a train to take them to Austria.

"I was immediately placed in the punishment cell," Helmuth recalled. "Some people call it the hole, others call it segregation. That's really a fancy name for a horrible place. . . . Basically, [it's] just a concrete box with a smaller concrete box with a steel sheet on it to sleep on," Helmuth said later. "I had no pillow, no towel, no toothbrush, no comb . . . The first twenty-four hours I spent just crying and praying."

He prayed for that divine variety of forgiveness that transcends merely human concepts of crime and punishment, washing sinners clean.

The next day, Helmuth demanded and got a meeting with the EMDC's superintendent, complaining bitterly that as a wrongfully charged, wrongfully detained, and innocent citizen, he shouldn't be subjected to such primitive tortures as sleeping on a pillow made out of the only soft thing in his cell – a roll of toilet paper.

"I told him that I could not take these conditions. He said, 'Why? What do you need?' I said, 'Sir, I have no shoes, no pillow, no soap, no sheets, no towel, no comb, no pen and paper, and nothing else to read other than the Bible.' He said, 'So!' I said, 'Sir, do you want me to lose my mind? You are dehumanizing me!' . . . I said, 'Will you at least let me have a small bar of soap so I can wash my hands after a bowel movement?' He said, 'You could make a dangerous weapon out of a bar of soap . . . You could put the soap into a sock and hit a guard with it.'"

Unmoved by the new inmate's rantings, the Superintendent explained that Helmuth had been placed in isolation for his own protection, noting that Robert Barrett was in the same institution and might make an attempt on Buxbaum's life. Unconvinced, Helmuth went on a six-day hunger strike to protest his segregation from the other prisoners. His self-imposed privations kindled little sympathy, as a remark he would later attribute to a guard clearly showed: "Buxbaum you may have been somebody outside, but in here, you are nothing but a goddamn fucking asshole."

Buxbaum's early behaviour in segregation convinced authorities that he was a high risk for suicide. He had begun talking about wanting to be with Hanna and the Lord. On August 1, just over a week after his arrest, Helmuth was handed a visiting slip with the abbreviation "Dr." written on it. He was taken to a private room, where he was greeted by Paul Gatfield, a psychiatrist from University Hospital, who had been asked by prison administrators to assess the new inmate. Gatfield questioned him about his personal medical history and any "psychiatric problems" in the wider family. Helmuth told him about a brother's suicide attempt and their mother's clinical depression, prompting a direct question about Helmuth's own state of mind. "If you had a gun in your cell, would you have killed yourself?" Gatfield asked. Although Helmuth didn't answer the question directly, he admitted that he felt like starving himself to death.

Before leaving, Gatfield asked Helmuth how an apparently religious man like himself could have become involved in so desperate a situation. Helmuth replied that it must be part of God's plan for his development as a Christian, adding that "many famous people [have] also gone through a lot of suffering."

Dr. Gatfield later recorded his impressions of the interview: "Has been sending out unusual, religiously oriented letters and has [an] inappropriately optimistic outlook on his predicament . . . He suggests a heavy alcohol and drug intake . . . There is massive denial of import of present events. He is innocent – God is paying him back for his alcohol and drug transgressions . . . No significant depression. No treatment indicated. If events force him to see himself realistically, he may become depressed and run risk of self-harm. Should just be watched for now."

Although the psychiatrist concluded that Helmuth wasn't in a dangerous state of mind, that wasn't the impression Paul Fawcett was left with after a subsequent visit. Once again, the troubled man expressed his desire to die. He gave the pastor a letter listing his transgressions over the past six months, asking that it be read aloud to the congregation at West Park Baptist Church. "I said that I had fallen into sin. I said I was visiting places where there were nude dancers. I said I drank and finally took drugs. I asked the congregation to forgive me."

At the end of his letter, Helmuth wrote that he had had no part in

Hanna's murder. Whether his fellow Baptists ever heard the contents of the letter or, as Helmuth claimed, Fawcett simply tore it up, they dispensed their own form of justice long before the accused man was ever tried. On Wednesday, August 8, the Elders of West Park Baptist Church voted unanimously to expel him from the congregation.

After repeated complaints of maltreatment from their new prisoner, correctional authorities finally removed Helmuth from solitary confinement. If anything, his misery intensified. Once he abandoned his hunger strike, he couldn't seem to get enough to eat and supplemented his prison diet with grass he picked in the yard; in the first six weeks behind bars, he lost fifty pounds. Every morning, he woke up shivering, his single blanket no match for the icy breeze that blew from the cell's malfunctioning air-conditioner. Warders ignored his frequent pleas for extra bedclothes, prompting another outburst from the man who was having a hard time adjusting to the profound change in his status: "I pay every year, personally and through my companies, in excess of $500,000 in taxes (not including property taxes) and would be glad to buy my own blanket," he declared.

No one cared. A week after his admission, he broke a molar while eating dinner. When he asked to see a dentist, he was told that the prison dental office had been defunct for some time and that he would just have to wait. Six miserable weeks later, the tooth was finally repaired.

The man who was accustomed to buying whatever he wanted soon learned that his simplest request now had to pass through a complex net of institutional regulations. Like all new inmates, Helmuth thought the prison rules were maddeningly petty. When Pastor Fawcett brought him a picture of Hanna for his cell, it was seized by prison officials who explained that since the inmate already had the six photographs permitted by the rules, it would be a violation of the regulations to have a seventh, even if it was of his deceased wife. "I have six children, but also had a wife," Helmuth lamented. "I had to make a choice which child's picture I didn't want."

The inmate who had found solitary confinement such an agony discovered that life in the general population had torments of its own. Ten hours a day, from 6:30 A.M. until 4:30 P.M., heavy rock music pounded from a speaker in the day room, its decibel level far exceeding the normal pain threshold for Helmuth's ears. To the amusement of other inmates, Helmuth complained incessantly about the noise, having to shout his complaints to his warders to be heard above the din. When he requested permission to return to the relative quiet of his cell, he was informed that he would need a special doctor's order, which, as a healthy prisoner, he couldn't get.

Occasionally, the frustrations were more exquisite. On August 11, Helmuth received a postcard from Cindy, the stripper he had slept with in Lucerne, during the family trip to Europe. Helmuth had given her his business card, and now the young woman told Helmuth she would like to come to North America and wondered if he still wanted to see her.

Helmuth found it was hard enough to adjust to life in the general population, but the task was made even more difficult by the prison authorities constantly shifting him from one unit to another. Even though he appeared to understand that he was being moved for his own protection, Helmuth resented having to adjust to a new environment every two or three weeks. His mind started playing tricks; at night disembodied male voices began telling him to masturbate and to hide. The troubled man poured out his woes to any prison official who would listen: "My visions, my terrible headaches, and the voices I started to hear almost drove me to insanity . . . I told [Superintendent] O'Brien in tears that I had had the vision of my wife and my parents calling me . . . For several months I thought that a definite attempt was made to drive me insane."

Torment turned to fascination for Helmuth the day he was jogging in the prison gym and found himself face to face with Gary Foshay. One look into the inmate's cold eyes was enough to persuade him that they were the same eyes that had blazed from behind the stocking mask Hanna's killer had worn on the night of the murder. Trembling, Helmuth followed Foshay into an exercise room, where he was lifting weights and kibitzing with other inmates. "When I heard his voice," Helmuth later wrote, "I recognized it as the gunman's voice."

A few days later, Foshay approached Helmuth in the yard.

"Hi, Bucky," the killer said.

"Hi," Helmuth answered.

"It's too bad I never met you earlier, I could have really fixed you up with some beautiful chicks."

"What do you mean?"

"I had two chicks working for me. You would have really liked them."

Helmuth said nothing, so Foshay changed the subject: "You know, I am a *real* man of action, not like Barrett and Allen. They will never find the gun. I put it where nobody will *ever* find it."

Although he complained to authorities about not having a toothbrush, Helmuth neglected to let them know that he had found his wife's killer.

By August 19, 1984, Helmuth was so upset about the conditions of his incarceration that he was ready to seek help from a source that would do little to endear him to his keepers. In the first of nineteen letters to Ontario's Ombudsman, Helmuth complained with some justification that he was being treated like a convicted murderer, even though he had yet to be tried. He outlined several violations of his human rights by prison authorities, and bitterly denounced Superintendent O'Brien for failing to supply him with a German edition of the Bible, even though he had been requesting one for over a month. How long, he wondered, could the prison chaplain be on holidays? After urging the government watchdog to launch a full-scale investigation into the institution, Helmuth closed the letter, "God bless you! Thank God for the Ombudsman!"

By late summer, prison authorities had branded Helmuth Buxbaum a garrulous troublemaker. On the morning of Sunday, September 2, a fight erupted between a female guard and Helmuth's cell mate, Colin Grey. The Roman Catholic inmate wanted permission to attend a Protestant service at the prison chapel, but the guard refused; mass for Catholics, she reminded him, was held on Saturday evenings. Incensed that his friend was confined to the cellblock while others were free to worship, Helmuth accused the guard of violating the young inmate's human rights.

As he emerged from the Protestant service, Helmuth was stopped by the commander of the guards, who briskly escorted him into a meeting room next to the church to deliver an ultimatum. If he persisted in his troublemaking ways, he would be "buried" in the hole.

Everywhere he turned, Helmuth was reminded of the dark valley into which he had stumbled.

On September 6, after forty-four days behind bars, Helmuth Buxbaum watched optimistically as his best hope of freedom strode into a York District courtroom in stern and commanding silence. The London millionaire had never heard of Eddie Greenspan, but luckily for him, his corporate attorney, Del McLennan, had. Immediately after Helmuth's arrest, McLennan had hired the renowned criminal lawyer to do what he could to help his friend and client. The first step along the obstacle course to acquittal was getting inmate 929455B released on bail. The courts had done the same for Peter Demeter and John DeLorean, similarly high-profile, wealthy men charged with serious crimes, and Greenspan was confident he could persuade Mr. Justice William Maloney to do no less for his well-heeled client.

Although Greenspan had drafted an ostensibly impressive case for securing Helmuth's release, it had not been an easy job. Given Helmuth's longstanding generosity to West Park Baptist Church, the Toronto lawyer had expected little trouble in finding people to act as surety for his client. Instead, Greenspan was surprised to discover that most of the congregation, including the church's powerful Board of Elders, couldn't put enough distance between themselves and the accused man.

"It is simply shameful that the church is not helping this man," Greenspan's assistant, Arthur Fish, wrote. "He has given hundreds of thousands of dollars to church related causes over the years, and has essentially single-handedly supported the Christian Academy of Western Ontario . . . One of the reasons which church members have given for not acting as surety is that the Bible, in Proverbs, chapter 6, verses 1–5, appears to say that you shouldn't go surety. This is utter bullshit." The law student's enthusiasms were understandable. Fish's knowledge of Helmuth's tidal personality was so far restricted to the view from the high-water mark.

In the end, the TD Bank provided the support Helmuth's friends wouldn't, approving an irrevocable letter of credit for one million dollars. But there were stringent conditions, including the replacement of Helmuth's personal stake in Treugott Management with an independent trusteeship. The result was the highest bail ever posted in a Canadian court. Helmuth also consented to such severe bail restrictions that, had the court smiled on his application, he would have voluntarily undergone the closest thing to house arrest that is permitted under Canadian law.

After much arm-twisting, Greenspan finally came up with a superficially impressive list of business associates and close family members who signed affidavits assuring the court that Helmuth Buxbaum was a devout Baptist, a model father, an outstanding businessman, and a law-abiding citizen. The wily lawyer even came into court armed with an inventory of the religious pictures and artifacts in the Buxbaum home, hoping that the show of piety might be taken for piety itself. Helmuth could only look on admiringly. What else, he wondered, could any judge possibly require to authorize his release from prison?

But Mr. Justice Maloney had scarcely settled into his chair to consider

Greenspan's affidavits when Crown prosecutor Michael Martin jumped to his feet to argue that the counsel for the defence was trying to deceive the court. "I have gone through those affidavits and frankly, sir, I disagree with the veracity of the information," Martin declared.

After weeks of reading police reports that painstakingly delved into Helmuth Buxbaum's bottomless appetite for illicit sex and illegal drugs, the prosecutor wasn't about to accept Greenspan's glowing testimonials to the accused's Christian principles. To illustrate that his misgivings were well-founded, Martin asked the court for the right to cross-examine everyone who had certified Helmuth's morality.

Annoyed by the unconventional request, Greenspan protested that Martin could have assuaged his doubts by privately interviewing the affiants before court convened. The Crown, Greenspan insisted, was just prolonging the bail hearing out of "sheer orneriness." Martin begged to differ, and Maloney sided with the elegant Crown prosecutor with the shock of silver hair. "I can see your point," the judge said. "I suppose any scoundrel could find somebody to take an affidavit that would set forth some redeeming qualities about him." The relentless prosecutor was given permission to bring out the dishonesty, infidelity, and drug abuse that had lain beneath the surface of Helmuth and Hanna Buxbaum's idyllic marriage.

"The problem," Martin commented after questioning several signatories of the affidavits, "was that Mr. Buxbaum kept company with other women. He frequented places known as dating bureaus, escort services in London. He consorted with prostitutes. He maintained a woman in a home that he owned, who in effect was a prostitute. He is a member of a Fundamentalist Baptist Church. As a result of these carryings-on, he was, in effect, criticized by the elders in the church."

The astonished judge interrupted the prosecutor in full flight. "My God," he gasped, "the affidavit material, it paints the man as being a living saint, the finest man I had ever encountered . . . Certainly in the affidavits he makes me feel . . . humble."

Eddie Greenspan's dwindling patience with the devastating attack on his bail argument ran out when Paul Buxbaum took the stand and was bluntly confronted with embarrassing questions about his parents' sex life. "I wonder if I might make a submission," Greenspan said, sourly accusing the Crown of using the court's time to conduct a "fishing expedition" for lurid details about Helmuth Buxbaum's personal life.

It was Greenspan at his theatrical best. In truth, the lawyer for the defence was already aware of Helmuth's drug addiction and womanizing. And his familiarity with the bizarre contradictions in Helmuth's character was not only based on what he had been told.

Acting on Helmuth's instructions just four days after his arrest, Arthur Fish had retrieved two of Helmuth's briefcases from Komoka. Their contents revealed a man whose interests were considerably broader than Christian philanthropy. They included a loaded Colt .45; forty-five ounces of gold; a large amount of cash; a spoon and syringe; a vial of amber liquid bearing Chinese characters; a cellophane bag of pills; a bottle of vitamin E cream; Hanna's $1,000,000 life insurance policy naming Helmuth as her sole beneficiary; a membership card in the Bizarre Video Club; a price list from an English pornography company; and a copy of *Dominance*, a kinky magazine with glowing articles on the pleasures of incest, humiliation, and adult baby experiences.

The contents of the briefcases posed a ticklish problem for Greenspan. As a passionate believer in the absolute privilege of the solicitor–client relationship, he adamantly maintained that his job was to defend his clients, not to judge them. But he also knew that the law drew the line at hiding evidence, as he made clear in his memoirs: "It goes without saying, that the law does not permit the suppression of evidence – physical evidence or evidence of any other kind. You can't stab someone, then go to your lawyer, saying: 'Here, put this knife in my file.' A lawyer who concealed potential evidence would risk not only disbarment but criminal charges for interfering with the administration of justice."

Realizing that there was a possibility, however slim, that the gun in Helmuth's briefcase might be the murder weapon, he told Fish when he called from Komoka that under no circumstances was it to be removed from the house. He then dictated a letter over the phone that he insisted Helmuth sign before Fish took possession of the briefcases. The letter authorized the law student to retrieve from the Buxbaum home "potential evidence with respect to the criminal charges against me, conspiracy and first degree murder." The items were to be held by the law firm of Greenspan, Rosenberg.

Not all of the items in Helmuth's briefcase left Komoka that day with Arthur Fish. Although Greenspan's only specific instruction had been to leave behind the Colt .45, Fish and Paul Buxbaum decided to remove other items from the briefcase as well, including the spoon, syringe, vial of amber liquid, and the pills in the cellophane bag.

As for the $33,000 in cash and gold in Helmuth's briefcase, it was eventually applied to Greenspan's legal bill. Before accepting the money, the cautious lawyer had his client sign a separate undertaking that the monies had nothing to do with the charges against him. Eddie Greenspan was no more anxious to be accused of spending evidence than of hiding it.

Even though he knew that the picture of Helmuth painted by the affidavits he had solicited was flatteringly one-dimensional, it was in keeping with Greenspan's reputation for championing the client's cause even in the most doubtful of circumstances. He insisted that the millionaire's sexual conduct was irrelevant to the bail hearing, and asked the judge to curtail the Crown's line of questioning. He was about to be hoisted on his own petard.

"That picture in that affidavit is of a man who is a model of virtue," Mr. Justice Maloney replied. "Now he has got a drug problem and he is an adulterer. For goodness sakes, how can you say that this isn't relevant? You made it relevant."

By the time the bail hearing resumed on September 17, Greenspan had decided to abandon his attempt to admit the affidavits. Instead, he advanced the argument that Helmuth Buxbaum qualified for freedom on the basis of his $1-million bail ticket and acceptance of virtual house arrest. But when he went on to dismiss the disparate views of his client as nothing more than the quarrelling aspects of an "extremely complex man," the flabbergasted judge cut him off in mid-sentence.

"How can the two pictures stand side by side?" Judge Maloney asked. "Mr. Greenspan, the way I was brought up, you could not say of a philanderer and a drug user, a person who engages in unlawful conduct and with undesirable people, you could not say of him that that is a good, God-fearing Christian. I say that the two concepts are incompatible. You call this a complex man?"

"On the evidence," Greenspan stoically continued, "you have a man who has set up a corporate structure to maximize the charitable donations that he can give and goes way beyond it . . . He is a man who, as Nick Potocska talked about yesterday, he is a man who has established a Christian academy. He is a man who has paid for a home for unwed mothers, and he is a man who makes extensive contributions to missionaries around the world."

"The Ayatollah in Iran prays to a god," the judge shot back, "but where is clerical rule when you shoot people at sunrise?"

Buoyed by Judge Maloney's acceptance of his argument that the affidavits were transparently misleading, Michael Martin gave the judge a host of other reasons for keeping the accused behind bars. As a free man, Martin argued, Helmuth would likely commit other criminal offences; in particular, there was a good chance that he would return to his former cocaine habit. But most importantly, according to Martin, granting bail to Helmuth Buxbaum might easily allow the accused murderer to escape justice. The London millionaire, he noted, had stashed more than $250,000 in cash and an unknown quantity of precious metals in a Swiss bank. And on July 23 (the very day Helmuth Buxbaum was arrested for his wife's murder), a police wiretap recorded Helmuth making "definite and immediate" plans to leave the country and take up residence in Germany.

"What is the inducement for him to go?" Mr. Martin rhetorically asked. "Well, he is a forty-five-year-old man facing twenty-five years in prison, a minimum of twenty-five years in prison. He would be seventy years old when he gets out, if he gets convicted."

As for the million-dollar bail offer, Martin was openly contemptuous: "In effect, the rich man is able to buy his way out of jail," he sneered. The only way to serve justice in the Hanna Buxbaum murder case, Martin insisted, was to keep her widower behind bars until he faced the charges against him.

Mr. Justice Maloney accepted the prosecutor's arguments and denied Helmuth's bail application. For the first time, but not the last, the prosecution had bloodied the nose of a barrister not used to getting worked over on the legal ropes. But Eddie Greenspan's emphatic rebuff at the bail hearing would soon be overshadowed by the stunning actions of his own client, moves he would later find difficult to defend as the behaviour of an innocent man, or, for that matter, a rational one.

Helmuth was shattered. For weeks he had lived on the hope that his ordeal in prison would soon be over; instead, he found himself getting back into the paddywagon for a sombre trip back to EMDC. Alone in his cell, and unaware of the extent of the massive police investigation into his recent past, Helmuth spun fanciful theories to account for the court's decision. He was denied bail because the Crown had lied to the judge; it hadn't helped that Mr. Justice Maloney was, in Helmuth's opinion, inebriated during part of the hearing. His basic rights as a Canadian citizen were in tatters, he mused, and that could only mean one thing: the system had already made its mind up about his guilt and the rest was just an elaborate charade until they made their arbitrary decision official.

His growing paranoia was fanned by the intense media coverage of every development in the sensational case, publicity that Helmuth saw as uniformly negative and, more importantly, highly prejudicial to his right to a fair trial. Helmuth grew sullen and unco-operative. He complained to Pastor Doug Dakin that he had been thrown in the hole for twenty days after being caught with a comb, an article that qualified as contraband under prison regulations. When Dakin looked into the matter with Superintendent O'Brien, he was informed that Helmuth had also been placed in segregation because he had flung his food tray out of his cell, spraying a guard with his unwanted breakfast. The prison official noted that "Helmuth's attitude and discipline have deteriorated substantially over the last few weeks."

They were about to get much worse. Faced with the prospect of what he was now convinced would be a show trial if his case went forward, Helmuth decided to arrange his own bail. The troubled inmate was poised to finance the first of ten attempted jailbreaks that his own lawyer would later characterize as "harebrained schemes."

With his preliminary trial just ahead, Helmuth could not have chosen a worse accomplice for his first attempted escape: his co-conspirator in the Hanna Buxbaum murder, the ever-opportunistic Pat Allen. During one of their daily thirty-minute walks in the prison yard, Allen told Helmuth that if he contributed $10,000 to an escape plan, he would be included in a break-out attempt engineered by two men on the outside using plastic explosives. Suspicious of Allen, Helmuth insisted on dealing with the man he was told was the mastermind of the scheme, Ray Isler. After a single, brief conversation, he wrote a $10,000 cheque to Isler, who unfortunately for Helmuth, failed to get paroled in time to either arrange the jailbreak or cash his cheque. Unable to buy freedom, Helmuth opted for the next best thing – cocaine.

"Nicholson [one of the conspirators in the escape plan] told me that he could get some cocaine for me through his girlfriend, Melinda," Helmuth said later. "I filled out a request for a $400 withdrawal from my account to Melinda Van Pater for two grams of coke.

"About two weeks later, Nicholson came back from court and slipped about twenty-five hits of acid under the door of our day room. I had never taken acid before in my life and did not know the effect. Nicholson told me that Melinda had been unable to get any cocaine. I took two hits (very small, round, whitish pills) and did not feel any effect. So I took ten more and had to lie down because I was starting to hallucinate."

Having met Melinda Van Pater through the unsuccessful drug buy, Helmuth gave her one of his monthly income-equalizing cheques for $8,496.41, hoping to build up a travelling fund for his imminent escape. But when he sent one of his sons to collect the money for his planned flight to Brazil, the woman refused to turn it over, knowing full well that Helmuth wouldn't denounce her to the police for pocketing his getaway money.

The next break-out plan looked like a comparative bargain. Weeks after the explosives scheme fizzled, another inmate offered Helmuth a $5,000 ticket to freedom. Bob McKenzie claimed that he had hired two men from Montreal to cut through the jail's chain-link perimeter fence and free their client by taking blow torches to the glass windows of the day room.

But before his liberators set foot near the jail, Helmuth entered a more tantalizing escape plan with a man he met at Bible class. Jim Nespalon was a pious murderer who had spent most of his life behind bars for a string of serious crimes. One day, as a female Salvation Army officer straightened the room where the two men had just completed their Bible studies, Nespalon struck up a conversation with Helmuth. His loving descriptions of his wife and his son led Helmuth to conclude he was the epitome of a good Christian. "I showed him a European game called Mil and he and I spent many hours playing the game," Helmuth said later. "We became intimate friends."

During one conversation, Nespalon, who would soon be eligible for parole, suggested he might have a way of easing Helmuth's righteous anguish. He proceeded virtually to repeat Bob McKenzie's break-out plan, adding the twist that after their rescuers had cut through the day room windows with welding torches, the Christian fugitives would flee to Northern Ontario and hide out in a friend's cottage until the multimillionaire could arrange to flee the country.

"I gave him $10,000 and promised him a job when he got out," Helmuth said later. "He made me promise him that officially this was only a loan from one Christian brother to another."

The parole board, however, didn't think Christian Jim was quite ready for the street. Instead of approving his parole, they transferred the hardened criminal to an even more secure institution; Helmuth quickly learned that there were no refunds on the black market of jailbreaks. From his new cell in Millhaven, Nespalon wrote that his "expenses" had exhausted the $10,000 and that he wouldn't be able to repay Helmuth the loan in the foreseeable future.

The subsequent flurry of escape attempts made James Bond movies look like *cinéma vérité*. One enterprising inmate promised to charter a helicopter that would pluck Helmuth out of the yard to freedom. Another, known as the Polack, had a brother in Sarnia who was prepared to drive a bulldozer through the wall of the jail's day room. Two members of a motorcycle gang would be standing by to spirit Helmuth out of the rubble, and whisk him to a rendezvous with Phillip Buxbaum, who would be waiting at a prearranged location with the necessary passports and money. Inmate Jim Elliott received $5,000 from Helmuth to hijack the paddywagon that shuttled him back and forth to his many court appearances. Finally, an older inmate who called himself Varga, and who claimed to have worked for British Intelligence during the Second World War, devised a break-out plan premised on getting Helmuth transferred to the Clarke Institute in Toronto. He explained that it would then be a relatively easy matter to escape from the psychiatric institution. Despite his later claims that he had always realized that the schemes were obvious scams, Helmuth Buxbaum kept planning – and paying for – his escape, to the tune of nearly $30,000.

Helmuth's compulsive shadiness finally began to rattle the confidence of the people who still supported his claim of innocence, including Doug and Louise Dakin, who had been named guardians of the Buxbaum children. Late one November evening, Dakin arrived home to find a message waiting for him to call a Jim Elliott in Windsor, Ontario. The stranger said that Helmuth Buxbaum had issued him a $5,000 cheque, but that the Royal Bank in Byron was refusing to honour it. The ex-convict wanted Dakin to help him get his money.

Curious about the mysterious Mr. Elliott, Dakin asked Helmuth about the call. He explained that he had given Elliott the cheque to arrange a jailbreak. Confronted by the pastor's speechless reaction, Helmuth quickly added that he had never really taken Elliott's proposition seriously; he had only given him the money to rid himself of the pesky inmate – a less than convincing explanation considering that Elliott received the cheque shortly before he was paroled.

When he discovered that Helmuth's schemes threatened to compromise young Phillip, Dakin finally decided to do something about them. The last thing any of the children needed, their guardian decided, was more grief from their father. The loss of Helmuth's financial support had forced the closure of the Christian Academy of Western Ontario in late August, and Dakin had been having trouble finding a new school for the Buxbaum children. When he tried to place Esther and Danny at Central Baptist Christian School, he was bluntly informed by its principal, Wes Clough, that "no Buxbaum children could be enrolled in the school" by the express decree of the Board of Elders. Even Saunders Secondary School, a local public high school, had balked at accepting Phillip because of the "notoriety of his father's case." Publicity over a jailbreak involving one of the children, Dakin thought, might be just the thing to send the already traumatized family over the edge.

Dakin had learned about Phillip's proposed part in one of Helmuth's escape plots after he and the teenager visited Helmuth at EMDC. The pastor noticed that Phillip looked "very nervous" and asked him if anything was wrong. The boy reluctantly admitted that his father had sent him $5,000 to arrange his escape. Phillip was to use the money to buy a boat and then meet his father at an appointed time and place. As one of Helmuth's lawyers later wrote after interviewing Phillip, the teenager claimed he was also instructed to buy a gun and "kill anyone who got in his way."

After a shouting match with Helmuth over involving his own son in such dangerous plots, Dakin persuaded Phillip to tell the police about his father's escape plan. After informing the OPP, Phillip made an emotional plea to Helmuth to face his accusers in court: "Dad, let's fight this one through, let's be men and let's try to be honest in our pursuits," he pleaded. Whether it was his son's earnestness or the fact that prison authorities wouldn't let him have any more cheques, Helmuth's escape attempts came to an end.

"Yeah, let's try to win this battle" he said. "I know I am innocent, I should prove it in a court of law."

Thanks to the eleventh-hour manoeuvring of Robert Barrett and Pat Allen, that would very shortly become a much harder thing to do.

By December 5, the Helmuth Buxbaum murder case had become the toughest ticket in London. Hours before the seven people charged with slaying Hanna Buxbaum began their preliminary hearing, spectators waited in line to get one of the few available seats. One woman had planned her vacation around the scandalous affair, returning from her first week off in Las Vegas to spend her second watching the courtroom drama unfold. Although opening day was slowed down by a series of procedural wrangles between the Crown and the defence, there was one surprise development. The Crown decided to give Gary Foshay, the man police believed had actually executed Hanna Buxbaum, a separate preliminary from the others, setting his hearing for December 18.

Although very few people knew it, two of the accused, Robert Barrett and Pat Allen, already had a good idea of how their day in court was likely to turn out. Just before noon on August 27, guards at EMDC had intercepted a note that was being passed from the cell block housing Pat Allen to the one where Barrett and Foshay were being held. Allen, the note's author, despite poor spelling, made clear what he thought was about to happen, and what the conspirators ought to do about it: "You guy better start getting your shit together. Jan wrote a statemean on everyone and I know this to be true. Tell Gary she told everything about him and I mean a lot. So how do you guy feel now. Ask you lawyer. Some of us are in big fucking trouble . . . Just get your shit together because she has did enough to burn you to . . . Fucking women. Annette [Anita] has wrote one to on you."

Although they didn't know it for sure, most of the conspirators suspected that Terry Armes had also talked to police. He had. On September 19, 1984, Armes told constables Getty and Edwards how Gary Foshay had disposed of the .32-calibre revolver on their way to the Wellington Tavern just hours after the murder. The next day, OPP divers recovered the badly rusted weapon from the Thames River, almost exactly where Armes had told them it would be – ten feet east from the Rideout Street bridge, fifteen feet from the north bank. Desperate to get his charges reduced, Terry Armes would keep on talking about the intimate details of the Hanna Buxbaum murder right up to securing a deal for the reduced charge of second degree murder on September 13, 1985 – a month before Helmuth's trial began.

Barrett and Allen were also quick to realize the advantages of co-operating with the Crown by giving evidence against Helmuth Buxbaum. Allen had been mulling over that possibility with his lawyer, Fletcher Dawson, for weeks. The way he would later describe his decision to help the prosecution was simple; if he pleaded guilty to conspiracy to murder, and agreed to testify against Helmuth, the Crown would drop the first degree murder charge against him – a deal whose strongest proponent was Crown attorney Alasdair MacDonald. By agreeing to this, Allen could shave as many as fifteen years from the sentence he could expect if he were convicted on both charges. He was overheard telling his mother and common-law wife at EMDC that September, "Don't be surprised when I plead guilty to conspiracy. My gut feeling is I am going to get somewhere for this plea of [between] seven to ten years."

Despite their inclination to make a deal, the two men had had enough experience with the judicial system to assess the Crown's case against them before changing their original stories. For the first week of their preliminary hearing, neither Barrett nor Allen had felt particularly threatened. But everything changed on December 14, when Anita Pitcher took the stand and inextricably tied them to the murder. Barrett had also been shaken by the RCMP's detailed surveillance evidence documenting his meeting with Helmuth at the London airport the night after Hanna's murder. As Helmuth would put it when he found out about the deals, the stage was now set for the Crown "to join hands with murderers to get Buxbaum."

That weekend, Barrett and Allen negotiated the terms of their deal. As Barrett wrote later, "The Crown Attorney approached Pat & I and said if we testified against Buxbaum, they'd drop the 1st degree charge. We said that we would only if Terry [Kline] was released and Jan [Hicks] received no more than two years. They said OK and before anything was said, we got it in writing. It sounds shitty, I know, but instead of everyone getting found guilty of 1st degree murder, now only Buxbaum, Foshay, and Armes [will]."

Both inmates gave new statements to police in which they recanted their earlier stories. They now fingered Helmuth Buxbaum as the man who had ordered, helped plan, and financed the murder of his wife. Over the informal objections of the police who favoured proceeding against all seven accused, the Crown dropped the first degree murder charges against Barrett and Allen, and guaranteed that they would be allowed to serve their sentences outside of Ontario. The Crown also arranged the legal calendar so that they would testify against Helmuth at his preliminary hearing *before* they were sentenced on January 17, 1985.

When dealing with Barrett and Allen, Michael Martin wasn't about to leave anything to the honour system.

Christmas 1984 was a season of misery for Helmuth Buxbaum. Cut off from his family, spurned by his church, and betrayed by his co-conspirators, he told Dr. Paul Gatfield that he wanted to die. Racked by migraines, but deprived of the Fiorinal that had once helped him cope with the sickening pain, Helmuth prepared to spend his first Christmas in the hole. It was the only place that prison authorities could be sure that he would be safe from predatory inmates and his own apparently uncontrollable compulsion to escape. But by now, the greatest danger Helmuth Buxbaum faced was from himself.

On Christmas Eve, he took a paper clip he had been hiding and broke it into sharp slivers, using them to mutilate his wrists, forearm, neck, ankles, and penis. Bleeding from several small wounds, he was finally ready to send season's greetings to his tormentors. "I put my finger in blood and I wrote on the wall, 'Merry Christmas, [Superintendent] Lockhart,' and then I put a heart around it with an arrow through it. I thought I'd be dead and they'd find me like this."

Deliverance was not that easy. Helmuth survived his ultimate jailbreak attempt to take the tragic lead in a trial by twelve of his peers. On April 23, 1985, the last of the Crown's seventy-five witnesses at the preliminary hearing had been heard from and it was time for Mr. Justice Alan Baker's decision. Helmuth listened impassively from the dock as the judge committed him to stand trial for the first degree murder of Hanna Buxbaum.

He was headed for that dread place described in Psalm 57, where his soul would be amongst lions, and men's teeth would be as spears and arrows, and their tongues sharp.

15

THE CRUEL MIRROR

"What I listened to in court was not my life at all. It was as if
all the good things had been taken out and all the bad things
compressed to make it appear that my life was one continued
lewd string of infidelities."
— *Helmuth Buxbaum on his 1985-86 murder trial*

Helmuth Buxbaum's trial for arranging the murder of his wife began on
October 15, 1985, approximately 200 miles from the spot where she was
shot down by the side of Highway 402. Ontario's Chief Justice Gregory
Evans, whose lawyer-son was part of the prosecution team, had agreed to
move proceedings to St. Catharines in the interests of a fair trial, something Eddie Greenspan successfully argued would not be possible if
Helmuth was tried in London. Fifteen months after the slaying, feelings
in that city were still running high.

Despite the change of venue, people came from all over southwestern
Ontario, including London, to take in one of the oldest forms of live
theatre in the world. Two hundred of them lined up every morning, hoping to get one of the 150 seats in Courtroom 10 where one of the most
sensational murder trials in Canadian history would unfold. Their preparations were occasionally as outlandish as some of the evidence they
would hear.

One woman took her nine-year-old daughter to a day-care centre
before the regular school day began, so that she herself could get in line by
7 A.M. On their days off, a group of women who worked part-time at the
Buxbaum's Komoka nursing home travelled back and forth from London
to take in the trial of their former boss. A St. Catharines oral surgeon
showed up every day to stargaze, describing Eddie Greenspan, Michael
Martin, and Mr. Justice John O'Driscoll in terms that the baseball-loving

defence attorney would appreciate: "I think here we have three Wayne Gretzky's – or at my age, maybe three Mickey Mantles – and it's not very often that you get a chance to watch Mickey Mantle perform."

Batting practice and the pregame stretch went on for three days, a procedural warm-up during which twelve jurors were picked from fifty-five nominees and various pretrial submissions were tendered. Judge O'Driscoll finally threw out the first pitch, outlining for the jurors how his court would work. Displaying the respect and courtesy he would show them throughout the lengthy trial, the judge instructed the jurors to listen carefully to each witness, suggesting that they even scrutinize body language for the subtle signs that give testimony the ring of truth or the stamp of falsehood. He also told the ten men and two women who would decide Helmuth Buxbaum's fate that there were really thirteen judges in the court: twelve judges of the facts and one judge of the law.

Some members of Ontario's defence fraternity would express it a little differently: when Judge John O'Driscoll was on the bench, there were really two Crown prosecutors on the case. Although Judge O'Driscoll would be the first to admit that his reputation as a hard-liner was well deserved, he rarely talked about the conviction it was based upon – that "human life is pretty special," and that any society that forgot this in its administration of justice was in deep trouble.

Whatever personal animosities his judicial sternness stirred up, no one could say that Judge O'Driscoll was unfamiliar with the world that people like Eddie Greenspan inhabited. For sixteen years, he had been a defence counsel himself and was no stranger to controversial cases. It had been John O'Driscoll who defended rock legend Jimi Hendrix after his arrest at Pearson International Airport on a narcotics charge in the early 1970s. With 17,000 screaming fans waiting for their idol at Maple Leaf Gardens, he had negotiated a speedy deal with the Crown that allowed Hendrix to perform as scheduled; in return, he posted bail for his celebrity client out of the night's gate receipts. If he had hardened since those days of rock and roll justice, the endless flow of human misery that passed through his courtroom was to blame.

As he listened to the judge's opening remarks and remembered the bitter wars of the bail and the preliminary hearings, Eddie Greenspan knew that he had his work cut out for him. The guilty pleas of Barrett, Allen, and Armes, and their decision to testify against his client had made the Crown's case daunting. But if anyone could successfully defend Helmuth, it was Greenspan.

Called to the bar in 1970, he had rapidly become one of Canada's top criminal lawyers, using the media as effectively as he did the courtroom to advance his reputation. In his capacity as junior defence counsel to Joe Pomerant in the Peter Demeter trial, Greenspan came out of the celebrated case with a national reputation – even though Demeter was convicted of murdering his wife, Christine, and sentenced to twenty-five years in prison. Win or lose, Greenspan was a formidable opponent, throwing himself into the cases he took like Ty Cobb played baseball – spikes up and always trying to steal second base. As those who knew him observed, although the eminent lawyer loved his wife, spectator sports, gambling, and the city of Paris, his passion was the law – Eddie Greenspan-style. The courtroom legend would be hard pressed to win with the defence Helmuth himself had chosen – not guilty. But if he did, it would be well worth his while. The contract he had with Buxbaum included an unprecedented $250,000 bonus for a clean acquittal.

A few days before the trial started, Greenspan was thrown a slow curve by the Crown. In early October, the prosecution had told him that the first six people to testify would be "motive witnesses" – Dr. Avinoam Chernick and some of the women that Buxbaum had slept with. For a courtroom natural like Greenspan, this was not an overly demanding way to begin his cross-examination, and he was left with ample time to prepare. But at 2 P.M. on Friday, October 11, just four days before the trial began, the Crown informed him that it now planned to begin its case with its star witness, Robert Barrett. The game had just been changed from baseball to boxing, and Michael Martin was leading with his best punch.

Greenspan immediately cried foul, protesting that the Crown's change of plans had been relayed to him so late in the day that he had been able to prepare just five of twelve defence areas necessary for the crucial cross-examination of the trial's most important witness, and then only by working eighteen-hour days. He explained that he was also in the middle of setting up an office in St. Catharines and that everything, including his firm's typewriters, was still in boxes. Nettled by the Crown's calculated lack of consideration (as well as by missing his beloved World Series), Greenspan wanted Barrett's appearance postponed until Monday, October 21. "I am not happy about it at all, nor am I happy about the last four days of my life," he growled.

Enjoying their colleague's predicament, the Crown argued that Greenspan had had plenty of time to prepare, pointing out that Barrett had testified for two days, January 8 and 9, at Helmuth's preliminary hearing, and then again on April 23 at the same proceeding as a defence witness. He had also given evidence at Gary Foshay's separate preliminary.

Unfortunately for Greenspan, Judge O'Driscoll did not see the Crown's action as unfair, discourteous, or professionally incorrect. He advised defence counsel that he knew of no rule compelling the Crown to call witnesses in a specific order. "I do not want to listen to interminable whining as this trial goes on," the judge warned in making his ruling.

Michael Martin opened the trial by painting a broad picture of the case the Crown was about to present. He had much more to go on than his celebrated adversary. One detective who had worked on the investigation claimed that police had collected so much damning information against the accused that it was the first murder trial where the Crown actually had "throw-away" evidence. Martin gave a brief history of the Buxbaums, explaining how Helmuth wanted out of his restrictive marriage in order to submerge himself in the world of cocaine and prostitutes inhabited by people like Robert Barrett. In clear, unemotional tones, Martin described how the plot to murder Hanna had been entered into by Buxbaum and Barrett, who later hired others to carry out the actual execution. The jurors sat silently as he described the roadside slaying of the mother of six, while Barrett and some of his friends conducted a wild drug party in a Toronto hotel. Despite the fact that Gary Foshay had been Hanna's executioner, Martin left no doubt where he believed the ultimate responsibility for the crime rested: "Now, although Helmuth Buxbaum himself did not pull the trigger of the gun which killed his wife, I expect the evidence will show that he paid a killer to do so and drove her to the place of her death."

On Monday, October 21, the man who held the key to the Crown's case was sworn in as the trial's first witness. Thanks to the delays caused by jury selection, discussions about models built for the proceedings, and photo exhibits, Eddie Greenspan had, despite Judge O'Driscoll's ruling, won the extra time he needed to prepare for Barrett. Martin's associates, Alasdair MacDonald and B. P. Evans, drew out the bizarre train of events from the emaciated young man. Barrett had lost 14 pounds from his 140-pound frame during his year and a half in prison, most of it in the final weeks before his appearance at the Buxbaum trial.

Barrett outlined his dealings with Buxbaum: the cocaine sales, the pimping, and the drug parties at various London hotels. He testified that by the end of April 1984, Buxbaum, who described his wife as a "pain in the ass," approached Barrett to have Hanna killed. The fateful decision to proceed with the contract killing was taken after the Buxbaums returned from their trip to Pine Rest Christian Hospital, and Hanna independently fired Barrett from his landscaping job at Komoka. Barrett explained that he was given a first payment of $5,000 to expedite the plot, which was to have Hanna "kidnapped" and then murdered.

To draw suspicion away from Helmuth, the killers were to have sent a ransom note from the United States along with Hanna's jewellery. Barrett testified that Helmuth had promised him a $10,000 bonus if her body was not found for at least a year. He also claimed that he had been offered a new beginning for himself and his family in the form of a house and a job at the Buxbaum's nursing home on Prince Edward Island. By the time he had finished his seamy tale, the prosecution had well and truly thrown its gauntlet down.

On day two of Barrett's testimony, Eddie Greenspan cross-examined on behalf of his wealthy client. For three and a half days, he would joust with Helmuth's most damaging accuser. His first task was to draw the jury's attention away from the dread content of Barrett's testimony, and refocus it on the kind of person it had come from. (It is one of the ironies of the criminal justice system that, while it is strictly forbidden to lead character evidence against an accused, no such protection extends to witnesses whose careers as thieves, prostitutes, pimps, and frauds are regularly used to impugn their evidence.) Greenspan thoroughly worked through Barrett's criminal record, pointing out his multiple convictions for break-and-enter and drug-trafficking.

Having established that the accusations against Helmuth hadn't come from a Sunday school teacher, Greenspan hammered away at the inconsistencies between what Barrett was now claiming and his various statements and testimony at the preliminary hearing. It was a classic defence tactic designed to present the witness as unreliable. From there, it was a short jump to another unflattering conclusion; that Barrett and Pat Allen had had plenty of time in jail to make up a false story against Helmuth, in order to strike a plea bargain with the Crown and save their own skins.

From the Crown's perspective, Greenspan's tactics went too far in his questioning of Barrett. Alasdair MacDonald objected to defence counsel repeatedly marching up to the witness and thrusting papers in his face. "Not only is that antagonistic, but in my view it is unfair and tends to intimidate," he complained. Judge O'Driscoll agreed, ruling that

Greenspan had to stay behind the counsel table unless he had something to hand the witness.

Surprisingly, Barrett wasn't overly rattled by Greenspan's tactics. By the third day, he was feeling sufficiently comfortable to land a few jabs of his own. When Greenspan depicted him as a "night person" – a junkie and drug pusher the jury couldn't see for what he actually was because he had been in prison for some time – Barrett replied that the other side of his own client was equally invisible: "It's the same with Helmuth Buxbaum . . . There's two people to Helmuth Buxbaum. You don't even know the other side of Helmuth Buxbaum, Mr. Greenspan. There's no possible way you could know. I have seen it."

At times, the exchanges grew heated – on Barrett's side because he didn't appreciate his entire life being denigrated by Helmuth's hired gun, and on Greenspan's because his belief in his client's innocence gave his cross-examination a passionate edge. It was one of the fundamental tenets of his approach to the law: a defence lawyer is obliged to give the benefit of even the slightest doubt to his client, as long as it is an honest doubt and doesn't run counter to the facts. Aside from the accused's mother, Greenspan believed, his lawyer should be the one person in the entire world "who starts with the assumption the authorities must be mistaken." The corollary to that view is that it is often necessary to rough up people like Robert Barrett in the clinches.

"You are a sly, very cunning, very manipulative person," Greenspan snapped.

"That's part of your opinion as well, Mr. Greenspan. You are just doing what you get paid to do," Barrett jabbed back. He insisted he wasn't lying, or worried about a perjury charge, and instead protested that Greenspan was trying to intimidate him. "How many times yesterday did you call me a pimp? Whether or not that is the truth or not, it doesn't matter; I don't have to be addressed like that, and if that is not trying to intimidate me, I don't know what is."

The collision between Greenspan and Barrett illustrated what was to become a concern of both the prosecution and the defence throughout the trial; the enormous and, at times, prejudicial interest of the media in a case that featured maximum titillation: murder, money, sex, and drugs, with a generous helping of Christian hypocrisy thrown in for good measure. Sensitive about the Crown's deal with Barrett and Allen, Martin complained in a *voir dire* about a *Toronto Star* article published on

October 23 under the headline, "DRUG-DEALING PIMP SAYS HIS MUR-
DER TESTIMONY IS A TRADE FOR LENIENCY." He wanted Judge
O'Driscoll to instruct the jury not to be swayed by inflammatory newspaper reports. Enjoying his opponent's discomfort, Greenspan pronounced
on the dilemma from temporarily higher ground: "Everyone knows the
problem of escalation of sensationalism, but how one stops it is a matter
that . . . a responsible press has to work out for itself."

Exhibiting some savvy of his own, Judge O'Driscoll, who knew how
the press works, observed that the problem was not usually with reporters,
but rather the rewrite desk, which was always able to add a little flavour to
the story without the troublesome impediment of having actually taken
in the proceedings.

When the jury returned, Judge O'Driscoll dispensed some wise
advice: "I think I would be foolish and you would think I were silly, if I
were to ask you not to read a newspaper or not to watch television or not
to listen to a radio until the trial is over. I am not asking you to do that.
What I do ask is this, though; that you listen with a certain amount of cir-
cumspection, a certain amount of reservation, and when you read, say to
yourself, or when you listen or watch, say to yourself, 'I was there, I heard
it, I saw it.' What we have here is a trial by jury. What we don't have, and
what we don't want, is a trial by media. So you are mature adults and I am
sure that even without me reminding you of this, you would have already
come to the same conclusion."

When the cross-examination resumed, Barrett was not feeling well
and asked for permission to sit down. When the judge asked the nature of
Barrett's complaint, he softly replied, "I am just a little nervous." It was the
understatement of the trial. As a Crown witness, Barrett knew that his
prison peers now had him pegged as a rat. By May 13, 1985, within a
month of being moved to protective custody at Laval penitentiary, Barrett
had been placed in solitary confinement because he feared another
inmate would kill him. But even when protected from the rest of the
prison population, he hadn't felt secure. In a May 29, 1985, letter to Insp.
Ron Piers, Barrett claimed that a lot of people inside knew they could
earn a big pay cheque if Allen and Barrett didn't testify. His cry for help
was crystal clear: "I hope to hear back from you as soon as possible and
please, do whatever you can as fast as you can; the hours are like days in
solitary."

To back up his complaint, Barrett had attached a letter from an enterprising inmate who was pressuring him for details about the case, so that

the man could sell his testimony to Eddie Greenspan and plot an escape attempt if he were called to give evidence. Barrett claimed that inmates Billy Germa, Justin McKenna, Peter MacDonald, and Daniel Borland had all approached him with the same scheme. On June 19, Inspector Piers had paid Barrett a visit, and, satisfied that the prisoner's fears were justified, arranged for his transfer back to Ontario on September 11, 1985.

Throughout his court appearances, Barrett remained convinced that a contract would be put out on his life by either Helmuth or Gary Foshay. At one point during his testimony, he thought he saw a spectator in the gallery pointing a camera at him. Afraid that someone might soon be turning his picture over to a hit man the way he alleged Helmuth had once given him Hanna's, he refused to continue until the spectator in question was checked out. (The offending object turned out to be binoculars.)

Despite his nervousness, Barrett held up reasonably well under Greenspan's abrasive cross-examination. The best the feisty lawyer was able to do was trip him up on the sequence of events surrounding Helmuth's June 7 visit to Florida, when they had met at the Gateway Inn, and the timing of the $1,500 wire Helmuth later sent Barrett from Canada. When Greenspan tried to discredit Barrett by pointing out discrepancies between his trial and preliminary testimonies in minute detail, the scrawny witness simply replied, "I'm not as good with words as you are, Mr. Greenspan."

Regardless of the effect of Greenspan's cross-examination of Barrett on the jury, there was one person in court who thought that he was doing a superb job. At the end of the first week of testimony, Helmuth couldn't say enough about the quality of his defence: "Thank you Eddie for what you have done for me so far. I cannot tell you the gratefulness that wells up inside of me when I think of you. I know that so far, you could not have defended your own father or brother better than you did me. For this I will be always thankful as long as I live. . . . Please convey to your staff my heartfelt thanks. May our God Jehovah continue to bless you with wisdom and discernment."

When Eddie Greenspan first heard about the involvement of Paul Ringuette and Brigitte McCurdy, his reaction was swift and dismissive: Robert Barrett had made up a self-serving story to buttress his claim that Helmuth Buxbaum had given him money to go to Florida to arrange Hanna's murder. Regrettably for the defence, the couple was all too real.

Shortly after absconding with the money Barrett had given them to kill Hanna Buxbaum, Ringuette had been arrested for shoplifting in Calgary and sent back to prison in Quebec on outstanding warrants. During the Buxbaum investigation, Debbie Barber had told detectives about the Barretts' all-expenses-paid trip to Florida. Kelly Barrett later confirmed the story, explaining to police how her husband had tried to hire fellow vacationer, Paul Ringuette, to carry out the murder contract. To back up what she was saying, Kelly showed the detectives photographs of the Barretts sightseeing at the Epcot Centre with their new-found friends, Ringuette and McCurdy.

Noticing the tattoo on Paul Ringuette's arm, the detectives had one of the photographs blown up, and then tried to match Ringuette's unique tattoo with booking details stored on the Canadian Police Intelligence Computer. With the help of the Montreal Urban Community Police, they hit the jackpot. The detectives matched the tattoo with Ringuette and discovered that he was an inmate of Laval Institution, where they subsequently interviewed him and learned the whereabouts of his girlfriend. The couple's independent statements corroborated Barrett's claim that he had been sent to Florida to arrange a murder, not to set up a reliable cocaine connection for Helmuth. Coming as it did from disinterested parties with nothing to gain by lying, it was bombshell evidence.

McCurdy testified first. She haltingly outlined her days on the run with Paul Ringuette, when the pair had been supported by Paul's friend in the Hell's Angels. She then described their week-long trip to the Gateway Inn in Florida, where they had met Rob and Kelly Barrett. The jury sat motionless as McCurdy testified that Barrett had wanted to hire her boyfriend to kidnap and kill Hanna Buxbaum. She claimed that Barrett had even given them photographs of Hanna and the Buxbaum family car, as well as a map showing the way to the couple's Komoka estate. After murdering his victim, Ringuette was to return her jewellery to Barrett. Once in possession of the proof that the deed had been done, Barrett would then pay them with Helmuth's money.

At the end of her first day of testimony, Martin, who couldn't help noticing the young woman's beauty, asked Brigitte if she had enough money to look after herself. Knowing how damaging her testimony had been, Eddie Greenspan sarcastically suggested that the prosecution tell her about the good restaurants, too.

French-speaking Paul Ringuette used an interpreter when he followed his girlfriend to the stand. His story was basically the same as McCurdy's.

He remembered being offered $10,000 to carry out the contract killing, with a promise of more money in a year's time. He also testified that Barrett had instructed him to get to London as quickly as possible to complete his deadly task – orders that may have reflected Barrett's knowledge that the Buxbaums were set to depart on a European vacation in four days' time.

Although Greenspan conducted a vigorous cross-examination, he was unable to shake the couple's story. Making matters worse for the defence, Kelly Barrett followed Ringuette and McCurdy to the stand, confirming various elements of their story, including the fact that her husband had given the Ringuettes some Polaroid photographs. She also added the damaging new fact that, after meeting Helmuth on the day before the murder, her penniless husband had returned with a substantial bankroll.

October 30 was spent on submissions with the jury absent. Greenspan's previous readiness to let the press govern its own excesses was now replaced by a formal request to Judge O'Driscoll that he instruct the jury not to read or listen to stories about the case, since they might be influenced by the media's mistakes. Greenspan's concern was raised by the fact that Nafisha Somani and some of the other prostitutes who had had dealings with Helmuth were about to testify.

The judge frostily told Greenspan that it was "silliness" to tell a group of adults not to read papers or watch television in this day and age. If it ever got to the point where the accused was not receiving a fair trial because of media distortion, Judge O'Driscoll declared, then and only then would he take action and sequester the jury.

In his submissions about the admissibility of "bad character" evidence, Greenspan worried that testimony about lesbian sex, vibrators, and his client's alleged preference for adolescent virgins, would prejudice not only the jury but also everyone else against Helmuth. He was surprised when MacDonald announced that the Crown would not lead evidence about prostitutes from the Taurus Escort Service before the defence was called. In other words, if Greenspan called witnesses to attest to Helmuth's sterling character, as he had at the bail hearing, the Crown was prepared to call rebuttal evidence.

But that didn't mean that Martin wouldn't be calling any prostitutes to give evidence. It was Martin's position that three women, Nafisha Somani, Dawn Watson, and Susan Ambrose, had information about matters beyond their professional relationship with Helmuth that was relevant to the murder charge.

As Const. Mel Getty took Helmuth back to jail that night, they chatted about the day's proceedings. Apparently under the illusion that it was his entire life that was being judged, not just a single, momentous act, Helmuth complained that the Crown was trying to "throw mud" at him and vowed to fight back. "If you want a long fight, you can have a long one. If you bring fifty bad ones [witnesses], we will bring a hundred good ones, even if it takes to the end of March, if that's what you want."

When court, and the interminable submissions, resumed the next day, the Crown gave notice that it didn't intend to elicit from Nafisha Somani anything about vibrators or the young girls Helmuth allegedly craved. Despite the assurance, Greenspan continued to recite case law in an effort to keep out as much of the potentially damaging testimony as possible.

Judge O'Driscoll was not impressed. He found, in effect, that Greenspan himself had made sex and drugs an issue during his testy cross-examination of the "pimp," Robert Barrett, who had been upset with Hanna Buxbaum's threat to report him to police for selling cocaine to her husband. He ruled that keeping company with prostitutes was relevant to motive because it shed light on the state of the Buxbaums' marriage during the period leading up to Hanna's murder. The judge also cautioned against any attempts "to pretty up, or to sanitize the evidence," an approach he warned would have the undesirable effect of distorting the facts.

After Nafisha Somani testified about her relationship with Buxbaum, including his strange offer to pay her if she would have his child, it was clear from the faces of the jurors that the prosecution had followed the judge's instructions to the letter.

Dr. Avinoam Chernick then told the court what he knew about the state of the Buxbaums' marriage, a story that included the sex counselling, Helmuth's cocaine use, and the fact that the accused didn't find Hanna sexually appealing. As was his daily habit, Helmuth kept detailed notes, some of which he shared with his lawyer. Listening to Dr. Chernick, he wrote: "When I was cheating on Hanna, as well as abusing my body with cocaine, I had terrible guilt feelings and was anxious to speak to someone about it. I knew that to continue this way would eventually destroy my family. I should have gone to Pastor Paul [Fawcett] and confessed, but I did not trust him. He would have taken me before the Church – probably thrown me out of the Church, or sent me away to some shrink. Paul B. [Buxbaum] had already moved out when he found out about Monica Taylor and I did not want to hurt my children and

Hanna any more. When I said, 'start over again', I really meant getting back to a clean living – no cocaine, wholesome, family life. I do not have any real close friends, so I talked to Dr. Chernick, who misinterpreted what I was talking about. When this ordeal is all over, I still have to go before the Church to be disciplined."

After Dr. Chernick finished on the witness stand, Anita Pitcher added her testimony to a Crown case that was growing stronger by the day. She told the court about renting the blue Nova with Pat Allen, and then described driving it to a London McDonald's outlet where Barrett and Allen had met Helmuth on the afternoon of July 4.

Greenspan began his cross-examination of Pitcher according to the pattern he would follow when dealing with the prosecution's star witnesses, making sure the jury knew all about her fourteen fraud convictions, and her drug use, before turning to more relevant matters. In one of his best performances, he effectively highlighted various discrepancies in her many accounts of the parking-lot meeting at MacDonald's. In her August 1, 1984, statement to police, she claimed that there were three people in Helmuth's brown station wagon when she arrived with Allen and Barrett, and she wasn't sure if the accused was one of them. Ten days later (after the arrests of Foshay and Allen), she claimed that there was only one person in the car and that person looked like Helmuth Buxbaum. At Helmuth's preliminary hearing, there were again three people in the Buxbaum station wagon, and by the time of the actual trial, Helmuth was in the car with two "figmentations" or shadows!

In a submission, Greenspan argued that Pitcher had no choice but to say that Helmuth was there, unless she wanted to be charged as an accessory to the murder. He observed that she was a "simple girl" who had difficulty with questions. Martin agreed that she didn't have the mental ability to respond to complex questions, prompting the judge to observe in Pitcher's defence, "I would think that anyone of great ability would have trouble following it all."

Judge O'Driscoll and Greenspan rarely agreed. In fact, the two men had recently crossed each other's path in the aftermath of a trial by judge, in which Judge O'Driscoll had sentenced a policeman to nine years in prison after finding him guilty of raping a fourteen-year-old schoolgirl. Greenspan, who took the case on appeal, convinced the appellate court to order a new trial at which the policeman was acquitted in 1985. Although both men were far too professional to let past run-ins affect their dealings in the Buxbaum case, there would be many subtle collisions between

Greenspan's robust defence tactics and the authority of a judge who was very much in control of his court. These were not doubles partners.

Susan Ambrose followed Anita Pitcher to the witness stand. From the perspective of the police, Ambrose was crucial to the Crown's circumstantial case against Helmuth, both because of what she had to say and the fact that she had voluntarily contacted investigators with her information. The attractive young woman, whom Helmuth now described as "a cockroach on a wedding cake," testified that Buxbaum had told her that he wanted to get rid of his wife, but that the normal solution – divorce – ran against her religious beliefs and his financial interests. Ambrose had then "jokingly" suggested he kill her with poison herbs, a frivolous idea that Helmuth had appeared to take seriously. If Ambrose would get the herbs, Helmuth had said he would give them to Hanna in her tea while they were in Florida in February 1984. Afterwards, Ambrose would move into the Buxbaum mansion, where, in time, the children would accept her as their stepmother. (Interestingly, Ambrose's admission that she, in fact, not Helmuth, had suggested poisoning Hanna wasn't made until the time of the trial, when she found out for the first time that two chambermaids from the Golden Pheasant Motel had overheard her playful seminar on deadly herbs.)

Greenspan outdid himself in his assault on Ambrose's character; not only was she a liar, a prostitute, and a welfare fraud, she was even a messy housekeeper! In a valiant attempt to limit the effect of her devastating testimony, he introduced bills to show that repairs to the couple's Volvo, which Ambrose said was the only reason she turned to table-dancing, and very soon after, to prostitution, had cost much less than the $1,500 she had claimed. But the only thing Greenspan was able to demolish was the alleged cost of Ambrose's car repairs, not her story that Helmuth had tried to recruit her to murder his wife.

Judge O'Driscoll repeatedly cautioned Greenspan about arguing with the witness. At one point during his cross-examination of Ambrose, Greenspan declared a little grandly that he wanted the jury out. Judge O'Driscoll firmly reminded him just whose court it was: "Mr. Greenspan, I will put the jury out, not when you want to." Greenspan apologized, but after the second day of Ambrose's testimony, it would be Judge O'Driscoll who had the red face.

On Tuesday, November 5, the judge told Ambrose that under the provisions of the Canada Evidence Act, she didn't have to testify about a conversation that she had had with her husband, Ron Ambrose, because they were married. The next afternoon when court resumed case law was presented by the defence, and the judge graciously admitted that he had been wrong, since the conversation in question had taken place before the couple was married on February 15, 1984.

Upset by Greenspan's style of questioning, at one point the exasperated woman finally exploded: "Mr. Greenspan, I don't know what you expect from me. You repeat your questions to me endlessly . . . I'm not trying to play games with you, Mr. Greenspan. Smirking at me isn't the answer."

Helmuth was delighted with what he saw as the total destruction of Ambrose's credibility. "What a superb day! Again, thanks to all of you, especially to you Eddie!" he wrote. But his note also contained some strange confabulations. Working from the fact that she was now in the photography business in Vancouver, and claiming that Vancouver was the porno-capital of Canada, Helmuth wondered if Ambrose was planning to star in pornographic movies. His surmises became much darker. Having "heard" that Ambrose's father had died, he wondered, "was it a heart attack after drinking some medicinal herbs from his daughter Susan!!!"

In a sunny mood, the result, in part, of the hot lunch that his guard had been able to get him that day, Helmuth dispensed some advice to his defence team. Owing to his son Paul's "attitude of confusion" he didn't think it was a good idea to call him as a defence witness. But there was a tactic that could help their cause: he wanted Greenspan to tell the judge that the accused wanted to direct a question to the bench. "My question will be: My Lord, I have been sitting in the prisoner's box for a long time. It is very difficult to sit here and listen to all those lies. My Lord, we could shorten this trial considerably if I could be permitted to take the stand."

Greenspan declined Helmuth's helping hand. However happy his client may have been with his cross-examination of Ambrose, Greenspan knew that the tactic of discrediting witnesses was becoming less and less effective as the sheer number of people he tried to depict as liars increased. Despite the many points he had scored against Ambrose, he knew that her powerful testimony was unshaken. The Crown had produced a witness who had come forward from beyond the reach of the police investigation and testified about a plot to murder Hanna that predated the Barrett conspiracy – and Hanna's $1-million life insurance policy. The credibility of her story was corroborated by the testimony of Betty Case, and two of her chambermaids at the Golden Pheasant Motel, Elizabeth Davis and Joyce Black. Even if Ambrose had done most of the talking about poisoning Hanna, why, the jury was entitled to ask, had Helmuth remained in the room, arranged to see the woman again, and even given her a job application for his Komoka nursing home?

If the Crown kept producing witnesses who testified that they had had discussions with Helmuth about murdering his wife, Greenspan would soon be faced with the nightmare of all defence attorneys: the indefensible proposition that, in a world of liars, his client was the only honest man.

On the eighteenth day of the trial a witness whom Helmuth himself was worried about took the stand. Early in the proceedings, he had asked his defence team to request a publication ban on any detailed evidence of sexual deviation, "for example – Dawn Watson giving me oral sex and putting a finger on my anus behind the service station on Highway #401. I think evidence like that would only add to the injury of my children's emotional trauma."

Helmuth had considerably more to worry about than Watson's recollections of service station sex. Faced with yet another witness who was set to testify that his client had approached her about having his wife murdered, Greenspan tried to find out exactly when Watson had spoken to police, and precisely what she had said on each occasion. In its submissions the day before Watson testified, the Crown revealed that she had spoken to the police on three occasions, but that only once had her information been taken down in statement form. The other interviews had merely been recorded in the officers' notebooks.

Greenspan particularly wanted an account of the third and final police interview, in which she claimed Helmuth had brought up the subject of murdering his wife. He also wanted the dates of the second and third conversations, and the names of the officers involved. Martin agreed to give the dates, times, and names, but balked at handing over the notebooks. Judge O'Driscoll ordered that Greenspan be given Watson's written statement, and the relevant portions of the officers' notebooks, clearing the way for the former prostitute, who now worked in the kitchen of a London smorgasbord restaurant, to take the stand.

Watson testified about the trip to Toronto when Helmuth had talked to her under the influence of cocaine about various ways to get rid of his wife: a boating accident, poison, perhaps a robbery and kidnapping if the children were away. Complaining that Hanna incessantly badgered him about his new life style, and claiming that a messy divorce would scar the children, Helmuth had then asked her if she knew anyone who might be willing to take on a contract killing.

After describing her European vacation with Helmuth a little more than a month before the murder, she told the court about something much more damaging than Helmuth's sexual proclivities. She said that when Robert Barrett had first introduced her to Buxbaum at the Park Lane Hotel in February 1984, Pat Allen had been there – a damning piece of evidence if true, since it would mean that Helmuth would have recognized Allen during the Buxbaum's stop behind the disabled blue Nova on the morning of July 5. And if that was so, why hadn't he passed that information along to the police?

Once more, Greenspan resorted to character assassination in his attempt to discredit Watson's testimony, pointing out that she had been into drugs of every description, and prostitution, by the age of seventeen. There was also the matter of her criminal convictions for theft and assault.

Greenspan drew out the fact that Watson hadn't told police about Helmuth's murder plans until her third interview on November 30, 1984 – the day Ron Piers and Mel Getty had subpoenaed her to testify at Helmuth's preliminary hearing. According to Watson, the policemen hadn't taken notes as she talked. Trying to explain away Watson's highly prejudicial evidence, Greenspan theorized that she had concocted her story to help her friend Robert Barrett, since there were rumours on the street that Squirrel was trying to negotiate a deal with the Crown.

Watson vehemently denied Greenspan's allegation, insisting that she had come to court to tell the truth. She explained that as Helmuth's former girlfriend, she hadn't wanted to inform against him in July and August, in case it turned out that the police had no case – a comic fabrication given her July 17 "anonymous" call to the police denouncing Helmuth as Hanna's killer. If her testimony was true, the more likely reason for her original evasiveness was that Watson had simply not wanted to get involved in a murder case.

This time there was no jubilation in the Buxbaum camp after the witness left the stand. Though disheartened, Helmuth tried to show a stiff upper lip. "Well, not every day can be a terrific day. We maybe lost a battle, but we will win the war," he wrote to Greenspan, and his associate Chris Buhr. Privately, Helmuth insisted that Allen had not been present when Barrett had introduced him to Watson, and suggested that a good investigator "could find out a lot of goodies about her [Watson]."

When Helmuth and his guard left after court that night for the ride back to the detention centre, he saw Watson walking with Inspector Piers. "When she saw me, she threw kisses at me. I just raised my hands to show her my handcuffs," Helmuth wrote. Despite his show of bravura, he was feeling bone tired and depressed. "When I read the newspaper articles, I get sick. They report mostly what is led in-chief, but very little of what comes out during the cross-examination."

What Helmuth didn't understand was that reporters only dwell on the cross-examination when it refutes a witness's testimony; the absence of detail in press reports reflected the fact that, although Greenspan had scored a lot of minor points, he had landed very few heavy punches. Unscathed after nearly three weeks of evidence, the Crown continued to dominate the ring.

The next morning, in a *voir dire*, a tireless Eddie Greenspan argued strenuously against admitting Corinne Willoughby's evidence. She hadn't testified at Helmuth's preliminary, and her name hadn't surfaced during the two lengthy pretrial meetings between the Crown and the defence, at which the contentious issue of character evidence had been discussed. Martin submitted that Willoughby's evidence had not been relevant until Greenspan had made the point during his cross-examination of Barrett that he had been the one who introduced Helmuth to the practice of mainlining cocaine – a fact that was then used to present the accused as a "naive babe in the woods" who had innocently strayed into Kelly's Bar. The Crown was anxious to make the point that Helmuth had, in fact, already been injecting cocaine as early as September 1983, the date of his last meeting with Willoughby. Once again, Judge O'Driscoll ruled in Martin's favour.

Greenspan was upset because he thought that he had been given all of the statements of the prostitutes who had been interviewed by the police; now he learned that the Crown had not, in fact, practised full disclosure. Agreeing with Greenspan, Judge O'Driscoll ruled that Willoughby's evidence had to be postponed until the defence had a chance to properly prepare.

Ever helpful, Helmuth tried to assist Greenspan with his research. He wrote, "Corinne is basically a scared, shy kid who will say anything the police will suggest to her because of the possible threats of losing her illegitimate child, [and] being charged for prostitution and drugs. Oh, Eddie and Chris, I am so very tired of hookers and prostitutes, I don't want to see another one for the rest of my life . . . Martin is obviously bent on opening the flood gates of bad character to salvage his case. I don't know what you can do other than to warn him that we will bring 3 good witnesses for every bad one."

Helmuth's army of good character witnesses was never mustered.

According to the Crown's theory, Helmuth's bankbook was as important as his marriage bed in understanding why Hanna Buxbaum had been murdered. Through his next witness, Michael Martin wanted to establish that Hanna's $1-million insurance policy represented a significant amount of money relative to the Buxbaums' net worth – a case that was easier to make when viewed in light of the large amount of money that had disappeared from the company in the year and a half before Hanna's murder. In presenting this evidence, the Crown prosecutor hoped to give the jury a motive for the murder.

The intimate financial details of the Buxbaums' business empire were unveiled in the chiaroscuro of a *voir dire* through the testimony of Duncan Findlay, the chartered accountant who had prepared the annual audits of Treugott Management since March 1983. Findlay, who was also Pastor Doug Dakin's brother-in-law, had been one of the members of West Park Baptist Church who had initially agreed to sign an affidavit vouching for Helmuth's good character, but who changed his mind after a meeting of the church's Board of Elders.

Findlay explained that Treugott Management was now owned by the family trust (i.e., the six children), not by their parents. Helmuth owned 58 per cent of Canadianna Nursing Homes Ltd., the balance belonging to Hanna. Other specific nursing homes, such as Grace Villa, were owned entirely by Helmuth. Findlay estimated that Helmuth's personal shares were worth approximately $4 million, Hanna's roughly $2.5 million. In other words, as of March 1985, the nursing homes were worth a total of $5.5 to $6.5 million dollars to their owners, compared with their value of approximately $10 million in the year before Helmuth was charged with murder. (As a subsequent witness, Nick Potocska, explained, the depreciated value was also the result of other business factors, not just the scandal.) He emphasized that the real value of the Buxbaum business was as an operating chain of nursing homes, and that the homes would be relatively worthless without their annual government licences.

Findlay testified that in 1983 and 1984, the Buxbaums personally drew out more than $2 million in cash from the business, without accounting for where $1,094,000 had gone. The accountant also confirmed that he had advised Helmuth to get life insurance to cover the capital-gains tax of approximately $2.25 million that would be owed by their heirs in the event that he and Hanna died. Because the assets were in a spousal trust, the taxes would not be payable if only one of the Buxbaums died. In other words, should Hanna alone die, the tax problem Duncan Findlay was worried about wouldn't materialize, and any life insurance benefits would go unencumbered to her sole beneficiary, Helmuth.

Judge O'Driscoll reserved his ruling on the admissibility of the evidence.

After court that day, Ron Piers and Helmuth traded small talk as they rode back to the detention centre. Helmuth's notes to his defence team for November 8 were neatly printed out under the heading, "Mr. Piers Tries to Make Up," and included his recollection of their conversation:

"Well it looks as if this trial will be over by Christmas," Piers observed.

"It sure would be nice to be at home with the children," Helmuth answered.

"That's for the jury to decide," Piers replied.

"Yes, but if you bring any more hookers it will take a lot longer," Helmuth shot back.

"Well, I am sure glad this case is out of my hands now."

The conversation had then turned to Gary Foshay. When Helmuth told Piers that he had identified Foshay in prison as his wife's murderer from his voice and blazing eyes, the Inspector asked why then he hadn't testified at Foshay's preliminary.

"I was so fed up listening to all those lies and watching perjury after perjury," Helmuth wrote, "that I did not want to swear on the Bible which they had sworn on to speak the truth."

When Piers reminded him that he could solemnly affirm to tell the truth, rather than swear, Helmuth replied, "That's what I will do when I testify."

At the bottom of the note to his lawyers, Helmuth requested that the prison psychiatrist be sent to see him. "He seems to understand what I am going through," the troubled man wrote.

On Friday, November 8, CBC news reported that when court resumed on the following Tuesday, the Crown was expected to introduce evidence that Helmuth took out a $1 million U.S. life insurance policy on his wife just five months before her death. The information was accurate, but one of the basic rules of court reporting had been violated – testimony given in the absence of the jury had been published. The legal integrity of the trial had been shattered, or at least it had in the opinion of Eddie Greenspan. He immediately asked for a mistrial. (It turned out that the report had been inadvertently aired by one of Greenspan's friends in the media, who hadn't been at the trial, and didn't realize that the testimony had come out in a *voir dire*.)

Judge O'Driscoll dismissed Greenspan's application. "There has never been a perfect charge to the jury and there has never been a perfect trial . . . an accused is entitled to a fair trial not a perfect trial." The judge also ruled that the Crown could lead Duncan Findlay's evidence of Helmuth's financial situation to shed light on their contention that Hanna's $1-million insurance policy provided a partial motive for her murder.

Martin submitted that the February 7, 1984, life insurance application was significant, following as it did so closely on the heels of Helmuth's January 23 conversation with Susan Ambrose about poisoning Hanna. To a person worth $4 million, $1 million U.S. was a considerable sum of money, particularly since the Buxbaums had been withdrawing funds from the company so freely in recent years.

Eugene High, the friend and insurance agent who had sold Helmuth Hanna's policy, followed Findlay to the stand. His evidence merely backed up information already supplied by Buxbaum's financial adviser; when Duncan Findlay had advised the Buxbaums to buy life insurance, he had recommended policies for both Hanna and Helmuth, since the estate-planning advantages would kick in only if both spouses died. In other words, by buying a policy only on Hanna's life, the corporate threat Duncan Findlay had been trying to neutralize had not been addressed. As things stood now, the insurance money would be paid directly to Helmuth as the beneficiary, and the Buxbaum children would still be facing the same $2.25-million tax bite if anything happened to their uninsured father.

Still, both sides took comfort from Findlay and High's testimony. The prosecution claimed that Helmuth's decision to place a million-dollar policy on his wife's life went to motive, since Duncan Findlay's advice had not really been followed. The defence countered that Hanna's life insurance was not a motive because it had been purchased at Duncan Findlay's suggestion, not Helmuth's. It would be up to the jury to decide if the fact that the policy was taken out such a short time before Hanna's murder by the man now charged with the crime was innocent corporate planning or part of the motive for a cold-blooded crime.

With the argument over Hanna's life insurance policy behind him, Greenspan was immediately confronted by another headache. The Crown recalled Corinne Willoughby, but the defence still insisted it needed more time to investigate her relationship with Helmuth. Greenspan didn't get it. He was also turned down in his attempt to hear Willoughby's evidence in a *voir dire*, but did manage to get an undertaking from the Crown that it wouldn't lead evidence of the accused's penchant for observing lesbian sex. Despite this minor victory, Helmuth recorded his disappointment at Judge O'Driscoll's ruling: "I must admit that this judge is *not* giving me a fair trial. I would continue to make more mistrial motions until we get it!! Would I be able then to get bail until the trial starts??"

On November 13, the twenty-first day of the trial, Corinne Willoughby finally took the stand and described her escapades with Buxbaum as a teenage prostitute. She testified that she had started seeing him in August 1982, and along with another young prostitute, went to the Bahamas with him two months later. They then planned a December 4, 1983, trip to Cancun in Mexico. Corinne estimated that the arrangements for the holiday were discussed at the end of September 1983, but she testified that she had later decided not to go on the trip because Helmuth planned to take two other women along. She claimed that the last time she had seen him was the day they had discussed the travel plans. It was on that day, according to the witness, that she had seen him inject cocaine at the Ramada Inn in London. The last contact she had had with Buxbaum was when he called her looking for a doctor's note saying she had been unable to make the Mexican trip because of her child's illness, a ruse that would enable the millionaire to get a refund for her ticket – a refund he picked up the day after his wife's murder.

While Eddie Greenspan was preparing for one of the trial's most important witnesses, Pat Allen, Chris Buhr led the defence and made concerted efforts to push Willoughby off her story. He suggested that she had in fact seen Helmuth for the last time on January 23 or 30, 1984, which would place their final farewell *after* Helmuth had met Robert Barrett. Willoughby refused to budge, and her damaging testimony was on the record; before he met Robert Barrett, Helmuth was already injecting

The Buxbaums during their pilgrimage to Oberammergau to see the famous Passion Play. Eleven days later, on July 5, Hanna would be murdered.

Twelve-year-old Danny viewing Paris from the Eiffel Tower during the family's trip to Europe, June 1984.

Hanna and Mark in Europe, just days before her murder.

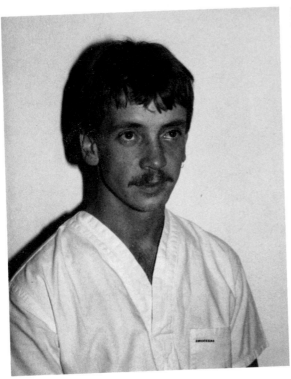

Robert "Squirrel" Barrett, the drug dealer who supplied Helmuth Buxbaum with women and cocaine and who later arranged the murder contract.

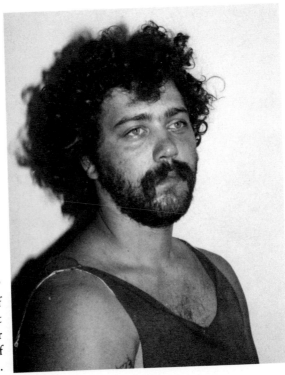

Patrick "Speedo" Allen at the time of his arrest in August 1984 as a conspirator in the murder of Hanna Buxbaum.

Gary Foshay, the gunman in the Buxbaum slaying.

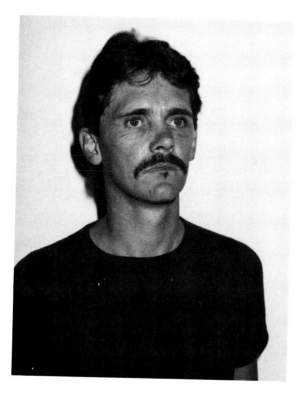

Terry Armes also took part in Hanna's execution. Later he claimed his only crime was in getting drunk with the wrong people.

Janet Hicks, a conspirator in the Buxbaum murder, at the time of her arrest.

Det. Insp. Ron Piers (now Deputy Commissioner of the OPP), who headed up the OPP's investigation into Hanna's murder and personally charged Helmuth Buxbaum.

Jurors leaving the St. Catharines courthouse after finding Helmuth Buxbaum guilty of first degree murder. They sat in one of the longest criminal trials in Canadian history. (*The Standard*, St. Catharines, Ont.)

A dean of the Ontario Bench: Mr. Justice John O'Driscoll, who brought his reputation as a tough judge to the trial, which he presided over in 1985-86. (*The Standard*, St. Catharines, Ont.)

The prosecution team toasting its victory with coffee: Crown Attorney Michael Martin is flanked by Assistant Crowns Brendan Evans and Alasdair MacDonald. (*The Standard*, St. Catharines, Ont.)

Edward Greenspan, Buxbaum's trial lawyer, reacts to the verdict that sent his client to prison for twenty-five years. Although he talked about challenging the verdict on forty-nine grounds, he never handled the appeal.
(*The Standard*, St. Catharines, Ont.)

Clayton Ruby, Buxbaum's lawyer on appeal, who believes the verdict was a major miscarriage of justice.
(Paul Orenstein)

Helmuth Buxbaum in Kingston penitentiary in 1990 after spending seven months in solitary confinement for an escape attempt.
(Bill Becker, Canapress)

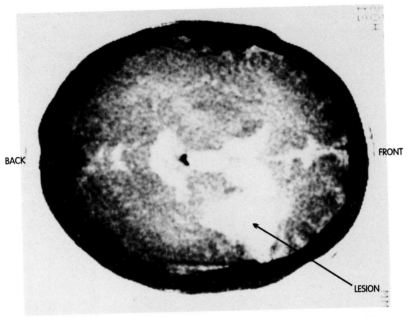

BACK

FRONT

LESION

A CAT-scan of Helmuth Buxbaum's brain taken after his 1982 stroke. The illustrations (below) indicate the area of dead tissue in the right frontal and parietal lobes. Several medical experts have diagnosed Buxbaum as suffering from Organic Personality Syndrome as a resuslt of his extensive brain damage.

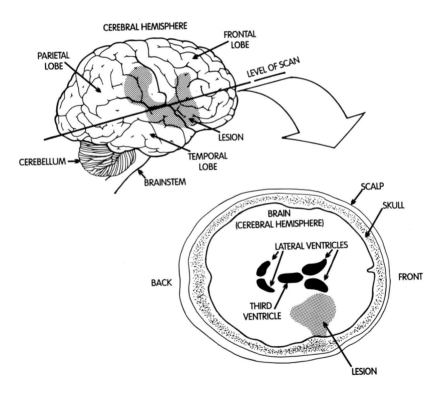

CEREBRAL HEMISPHERE

FRONTAL LOBE

PARIETAL LOBE

LEVEL OF SCAN

LESION

CEREBELLUM

TEMPORAL LOBE

BRAINSTEM

SCALP

SKULL

BRAIN (CEREBRAL HEMISPHERE)

LATERAL VENTRICLES

BACK

FRONT

THIRD VENTRICLE

LESION

cocaine. The innocent lamb, it appeared, had had a few strands of black wool before he strayed into the fold of the bad shepherd.

In notes to his lawyers, Helmuth insisted that to call Willoughby at this time was highly unfair, no more than another cheap attempt on Michael Martin's behalf to plant damaging ideas in the minds of the judge and jury. "To my knowledge I have *never* taken cocaine in front of Corinne and *certainly never* taken a needle of cocaine in Corinne's presence. Quite the contrary; Corinne's sister, Rosanne Willoughby, told me that Corinne was shooting cocaine and speed with her girlfriend Lisa Finn, and that she had broken off with Finn because she had gotten Corinne hooked on chemicals. Finn herself told me one time that she and Corinne were doing chemicals and [asked] if I was interested to try. I told her that I was *not* interested."

A week later, Helmuth again wrote to his defence team about Corinne and his use of cocaine, but his recollection had begun to change. "I am still very sure that I never took an injection of cocaine in front of Corinne, but we may have snorted some coke together with Lisa Finn."

By November 19, 1985, the defence team had a much more important subject to deal with than Helmuth's belated recollections of exactly how he had taken cocaine with teenage prostitutes. The jury was about to hear from the most damaging witness, next to Robert Barrett, in the Crown's crowded stable: Patrick Allen.

Shortly after noon on Wednesday, November 13, Alasdair MacDonald began leading one of the principles in the Hanna Buxbaum murder through the details of his involvement, including the abortive morning attempt on the doomed woman's life. Pat Allen described how he and Helmuth had held a conversation at the front of the blue Nova, while the woman who was already supposed to be dead waited for her husband to return to their station wagon.

Allen testified that after he had told the older man that the hit was off, Helmuth said that he would get in touch later in the day. Back in London, Allen had called Barrett at the Westbury to tell him that Helmuth had been late for the morning murder attempt. When he finally had shown up, so had the OPP, aborting the deadly ambush. After considering his position, Allen had called Barrett back and bailed out of the contract killing, which was then taken over by Gary Foshay.

When Martin had finished with this witness, Greenspan stood up to begin his cross-examination, knowing that what he did over the next few days could make or break his case. He quickly let the jury know that they were listening to a man who willingly acknowledged that he was capable of accepting a murder contract to kill an innocent woman without blinking an eye. Allen bluntly informed Greenspan that such sang-froid was not unusual when a person was "speeding."

Allen admitted that, at the time of the murder, he had had a $2,000-a-week speed habit, which was aggravated by the cocaine Robert Barrett began lavishing on him in January 1984, courtesy of Helmuth Buxbaum. On July 5, he had been coming to the end of one speed run and just beginning another, Allen claimed, which accounted for his "schitzy" state of mind. At times like that, he confided, an addict could even forget what he had done.

It wasn't long before Greenspan raised the witness's self-serving deal with the Crown, a trump card he would play at every opportunity in the trial. Even though Allen believed he was only 85 to 90 per cent guilty of conspiracy to murder (a notion based on his eleventh-hour decision to hand the deadly task to Gary Foshay), he explained why he had ultimately agreed to a plea bargain: "I was waking up at night in cold sweats and dreams I never had before, and I couldn't handle it any more." Whether it was conscience or simple fear, the ordeal had clearly taken its toll on Allen. Since his arrest, he had lost forty-five pounds. As his fellow inmate Robert Barrett well knew, a rat got a lot of exercise inside just looking over his shoulder.

Most of what Allen had to say was devastating to his client's interests, but Greenspan was particularly worried about Allen's contention that he and Buxbaum had held a brief conversation on the morning of the murder around the time Const. Philip Medlyn had shown up. Greenspan was entitled to his concern. If that conversation had taken place the way Allen described it, then Helmuth would have been conspiring to murder Hanna. From the defence point of view, the story simply had to be knocked down.

Hoping to skewer Allen on the details, Greenspan asked the witness to take him through exactly what had happened. Allen testified that he and Buxbaum were at the front of the Nova when the policeman asked from the side of his car if he could help them. After the officer left, they had held their brief discussion about getting in touch later, and then Buxbaum had returned to his car. Greenspan glared at Allen and flatly accused him of lying. When the lawyer began to repeat his comment in response to a request from Allen, Judge O'Driscoll interrupted him: "Mr. Greenspan, we've been through this many times before. You can ask the witness what he said or what he did, or you can make suggestions to him, but we are not going to get into, 'You're lying'; 'No, I'm not'; 'Yes, you are.'"

Greenspan protested that he was entitled to call Allen a liar because Constable Medlyn had testified at the preliminary hearing that when he called to the person at the front of the Nova, Buxbaum was already back at his car. The merit of that observation would soon be tested when the officer himself took the stand. In the meantime, Greenspan could only hope that his blunt denunciation of Allen would somehow weaken the import of his otherwise damning evidence.

Shortly after the man he had accused of lying had answered the last question of his two-and-a-half day cross-examination, Eddie Greenspan got an unwelcome surprise. As part of the ongoing preparation for the trial, Chris Buhr and Robert Sheppard were talking to Helmuth about the details of the murder day, when their client informed them that he *had* recognized Allen as Robert Barrett's friend during the morning stop on Highway 402. Even more devastating, Helmuth went on to claim that while they were talking in front of the disabled Nova, Allen had, in fact, suggested to him that he get in touch with Robert Barrett at the Westbury Hotel. Rocked by these disclosures, Buhr and Sheppard reported Buxbaum's revelations to Greenspan, who was fresh from having called Allen a liar based on Helmuth's earlier version of the highway meeting.

Greenspan was on the horns of a dilemma. When Arthur Fish had visited Helmuth at the EMDC the day after his arrest, he had told the accused man that he was hiring the best law firm in Canada, but that they had one rule; "they do not lie." Although Greenspan firmly believed that it was a defence lawyer's duty to defend, not to act as an investigator for the prosecution, he would never assist any client in misleading the court. In his memoirs, he wrote, "It is a lawyer's duty to put the Crown to the most rigorous test, but no lawyer can assist a client in the commission of perjury. Accused persons are always presumed innocent, but, even beyond this general presumption, if a lawyer leads an accused's denial of guilt in the witness-box as part of the defence's evidence, then the lawyer himself, in his own mind, must be in a state of doubt about the defendant's guilt . . . No lawyer can knowingly allow a client to state falsehoods or deny true facts under oath."

The theoretical had suddenly become stunningly real. The question of whether Buxbaum had contact with Barrett on the day of the murder was central to the case. Greenspan had attempted to discredit Barrett during

cross-examination by vigorously denying any such contact. With Buxbaum now claiming that he recognized Allen as Barrett's friend, his earlier
claim that he left the morning scene feeling uneasy about the man made
little sense. The additional fact that there now appeared to have been a
friendly conversation by the side of the road, in which Barrett's name was
mentioned, clearly supported Allen's version of events and made a mock-
ery of Greenspan's cross-examination and Buxbaum's claim of innocence.
The question was, what to do about it?

The next morning before court, Greenspan, Buhr, and Sheppard met
privately with their client. Greenspan explained to Helmuth that if what
what he had told Buhr and Sheppard was true, it would appear that he had
been involved in the death of his wife. If that were so, Greenspan wanted
his client to give him immediate written instructions to negotiate a guilty
plea to a charge of second degree murder, or to raise a defence of insanity.

It was the one time during his trial that Helmuth fumed at his own
lawyers. Buxbaum refused to give his counsel instructions to plea bargain,
and insisted that the trial proceed based on his total innocence. Faced
with Greenspan's alternatives, he quickly reverted to his previous story,
insisting that his bombshell revelation was not true. That night, he followed up his retraction with a remorseful letter.

"Dear Eddie, I feel terrible [about] what has happened and I want to
apologise for it. My natural instinct is to find an excuse why I was so foolish to try, but I know that won't do any good at all. So, all I can say, please
forgive me, and it shall not happen again."

When Greenspan returned to the fray with his case once more intact, it
may have been with his own, rather than his client's words, ringing in his
ears. "A defence lawyer, unlike a jury, need not be in a state of *reasonable*
doubt," he declared in his memoirs. "He has a duty to give the benefit of
even the slightest doubt to his client, as long as it is an honest doubt and
does not run counter to his factual knowledge."

Constable Philip Medlyn took the stand on November 18 and testified
that as he was getting out of his car on the morning of July 5, 1984, to
assist what he thought were motorists in distress, he saw Helmuth Buxbaum walking back to his brown station wagon. Medlyn's account was
consistent with Pat Allen's testimony. The police officer testified that the
hood of the Nova was up when he stopped, and two men, Allen and Buxbaum, were standing by its right front fender. Their brief conversation

had taken place in the few seconds it had taken Medlyn to put on his hat, get out of his squad car, and walk back towards the Nova.

(Helmuth's own version of the event, as described to Corp. Leo Sweeney two days after the murder, squared with Medlyn's testimony. He had told the OPP officer that he and the "other guy" were both looking under the hood when the police car pulled over in front of the Nova. "The officer got out, put his hat on and started walking to the car. The other guy by the hood started waving to the officer. By that time I was walking back to my car. I heard the guy say something like 'Everything is okay, fine.'")

Chris Buhr, who handled Medlyn's cross-examination, made sure that the jury heard that the police already knew about the Buxbaums' morning stop from Helmuth, hours before Medlyn identified him as one of the men he had stopped to help on July 5. What the jury didn't hear was that Helmuth hadn't volunteered that information; the question about the morning stop had been put to him after Medlyn phoned investigators about his encounter with Buxbaum on the highway.

The Crown's increasingly detailed picture of Helmuth Buxbaum's actions and demeanour on the day of his wife's murder was further refined by the testimony of his hated brother-in-law, Heinz Wagner. Wagner told the court about Hanna's biweekly visits to her mother, Ottilie Schmidt, at Millwood Manor Rest Home in Kitchener, noting that Helmuth accompanied his wife perhaps once or twice a year. He then spoke about Helmuth's surprise visit to the Wagner's home on the day of the murder, his first appearance in a long time. Wagner testified that his unexpected caller had been very nervous and appeared to be in a great hurry – exactly the bearing that might be expected of a man who had to rearrange the details of his wife's imminent execution, or so the Crown wanted the jury to believe.

Roy Buxbaum, now sixteen, filled in some of the crucial blanks of what had happened on the terrible evening of July 5. Refusing to swear on the Bible because of the prohibition contained in James 5:12, the young man affirmed to tell the truth and described his stop at McDonald's with his aunt and uncle on the way back from the Toronto airport. He testified that after they had finished their snack, Helmuth took over the driving from Hanna. Tired from his long flight from Vancouver, Roy curled up in the backseat and went to sleep.

As they approached the Komoka exit, Roy was roused from his nap by the sound of his aunt and uncle talking about stopping to assist a disabled car Helmuth believed might be their neighbour. (Having been asleep, he hadn't heard all of their conversation.) After Helmuth had pulled up behind the blue car and turned off the ignition, a masked man had suddenly appeared and thrust a pistol within an inch of Roy's right eye. From his prone position in the backseat, Roy could hear his aunt, who had been dragged out of the car, pleading with her assailant: "Please, I have five children at home!" Moments later, he made out the words, "I have her purse, let's go!"

As chilling as Roy's account of the murder had been, it was his recollection of events after the shooting that had the jury shaking its collective head. The teenager testified that when he had rushed to his wounded aunt's side after her attackers had fled, his uncle had hung back on the other side of the guardrail – hardly the reaction one might expect of someone whose wife had just been brutally attacked.

Roy couldn't say where his uncle had been while the attack was taking place, but the Crown's next witness, Robert Mitchell, could. The trucker testified that as he approached the murder scene on the evening of July 5, he had seen two men standing by the guardrail, and a third on the opposite side near the ditch. Mitchell observed a puff of white smoke rise near the two men by the guardrail, then saw the older, heavy-set man move around the two cars parked on the shoulder of the highway and start toward the driver's side of the brown station wagon. If Mitchell had it right, the jury had just been told something that could keep them awake at night: Helmuth Buxbaum had calmly witnessed the execution of his own wife. Try as he might, Chris Buhr failed to poke any major holes in the trucker's testimony on cross-examination.

The next morning, Buhr was once again on his feet making submissions about unfair press articles, which the defence believed could improperly influence the jury. Judge O'Driscoll wanted to know if Buhr was contending that the press had prejudiced the accused's right to a fair trial, a view the judge made clear he did not share: "So far the press has been very responsible in their reporting of what happened in this courtroom." Like many people who find themselves losing in a public debate, Greenspan and company were beginning to blame the messenger.

Terry Armes' testimony filled the newspapers with more sensational information about the accused. As the killer's accomplice, one of two assailants who had actually been present at the murder, Armes had more potential than any other witness to drive nails into Helmuth's legal coffin. Before he even testified, the defence made lengthy submissions aimed at preventing the jury from hearing the phrase they believed would have deadly consequences for their client: "Please, honey, no, not this way." According to Armes, these were Hanna Buxbaum's pathetic last words.

Buhr argued that if the phrase had indeed been spoken, the sentiments expressed had simply been Hanna's opinion; there was no factual basis for asserting that the terrified woman knew that her husband was involved in the conspiracy to take her life. Buhr also argued that the words were not admissible as a dying declaration, since a robbery and only a robbery was taking place at the moment that Hanna was said to have uttered them. In other words, there was no reason for her to believe that her death was inevitable – the prerequisite of having a person's words legally deemed to be a dying declaration.

Judge O'Driscoll saw it differently, ruling that the evidence was admissible as an exception to the hearsay rule on the basis of *res gestae* – a spontaneous exclamation made under the stress, nervous excitement, or pressure of the moment.

The faces of the jury registered the full impact of Hanna's final words when Alasdair MacDonald led Terry Armes through her last, terrified moments on earth, eliciting a description from him that was almost word for word what he had already told police: "Hanna Buxbaum was trying to pull away from Gary Foshay and she is looking up at Helmuth and said, 'No, honey, please not this way', and she mentioned something about her children, and he didn't even blink an eye, he just stood there."

Armes also testified that he had overheard Buxbaum and Allen at the front of the Nova agreeing to get in touch with Barrett, or "Squirrel," as he referred to him, although he thought that their conversation had taken place after Constable Medlyn had left the scene. Sipping water as he testified, Armes remarked that the murder had been so badly planned that he didn't even know that Roy Buxbaum was in the car until the boy sat up to see what was going on. It wasn't until the following day, July 6, that Armes found out from an account of his crime in the *London Free Press* that Roy was Helmuth's nephew. Before the jury was removed to hear *voir dire* evidence, Armes testified that Foshay had been clutching Hanna's ivory-coloured purse when he scrambled up from the ditch.

With the jury out, Armes recounted a very damaging conversation he claimed to have had with Helmuth in a holding cell at the London courthouse during Gary Foshay's preliminary hearing. "The only thing I said in my statement," Armes said he had told Helmuth, "was that you went off the highway and come back on." Helmuth was not pleased. "You didn't do *that*," Armes claimed Helmuth replied, "That's really incriminating. You have to get that withdrawn out of your statement."

Armes first mentioned the jailhouse conversation with Buxbaum to constables Mel Getty and Paul Edwards just days before he was to testify at the Buxbaum trial. Alasdair MacDonald, who was also told about it, offered to bypass the evidence in his questioning of Armes if Eddie Greenspan thought that it was the kind of evidence for which disclosure was essential. Greenspan accepted the offer and the problem evaporated, marking the beginning of a new civility that would gradually supplant the previously sour relationship between the prosecution and the defence.

Not everyone, though, had been schooled in the gentlemanly arts. Greenspan commenced his cross-examination of the witness with the usual reminder that the man who had just fingered Helmuth Buxbaum had done so in return for reduced charges from the Crown.

"In dropping a first degree murder charge against you, your parole eligibility has gone from the time you are sixty years of age to the time that you are forty-five years of age."

"If you look at it my way, I was not guilty of murder in my heart," Armes complained. "I got to do a fucking life sentence because I'm drunk."

"Mr. Armes," Judge O'Driscoll chided, "you may get excited, but there is no real need to be using that kind of language in here."

Much of Greenspan's effective cross-examination focused on his contention that Armes had given the police what they wanted to hear in exchange for a lesser sentence. He noted that there had been no reference to any conversation between Buxbaum and Allen at the front of the Nova when Armes gave his first statement to police on August 29, 1984, shortly after his arrest. Armes explained that the statement had been rushed because the police had wanted to get him lodged in the EMDC. What was the hurry, Greenspan cynically countered, pointing out that Armes' 165-page statement had taken several hours to complete. Armes insisted that he was told to say everything he had to say before going to prison, because if the police interviewed him at EMDC, the other prisoners would know he was a rat.

Ignoring the witness's answer, Greenspan persisted in his pet theory, noting that there was still no talk of a conversation between Buxbaum and Allen in Armes' second statement on September 19, 1984 – and still no deal with the Crown. Dismissing Greenspan's inference, Armes stubbornly repeated that he had indeed heard the two men talking about getting in touch with Barrett. Undeterred, Greenspan reminded Armes that he had finally gotten his deal for a guilty plea to a lesser charge only after his third and final statement to police on November 28, 1984.

For once, Armes could correct his relentless inquisitor, explaining that the deal was arranged with Michael Martin *before* Ron Piers came to see him that day. Piers and Getty informed him of the offer when his final interview was three-quarters over. As for the fact that Armes had mentioned the damning conversation at Gary Foshay's preliminary trial on February 25, 1985, the witness explained that he had simply had a lot of time to reflect on what had actually happened in the solitude of his jail cell.

(Police records would ultimately shoot down Greenspan's contention that Armes' recollection of the conversation was a recent fabrication to help him negotiate a deal. In a December 9 Crown submission, Const. Mel Getty's notes of August 29, 1984, recorded the fact that Armes had told him that day about a conversation between Buxbaum and Allen in which he had heard Helmuth use the words, "I'll get back to you later.")

Dismissing Armes' explanations, Greenspan contended that Armes' memory improved the further he got away from the actual event, and the closer he got to making his deal. He pointed out, for example, that there had been no mention of the word "honey" when Armes first described Hanna begging Helmuth for her life. Nor was the word "honey" mentioned in either of his two subsequent statements. Only when he testified at Gary Foshay's preliminary hearing in February 1985, had he used the word for the first time in relating Hanna's last words.

When Greenspan suggested that someone else had put that word in Armes' mouth, the witness readily agreed, admitting that a police officer had asked him if that was what Hanna had in fact said with her last breath. After thinking about it, Armes agreed that "honey" was exactly the word Hanna had used to address her husband.

After a full day of dogged questioning, Greenspan had clearly demonstrated that Armes had been involved in a long and determined effort to make a deal with the Crown that would give him a more lenient sentence. But the only discrepancy the defence could lay bare between the otherwise damning evidence of Terry Armes and Pat Allen was which of the two men had actually dangled Robert Barrett over the fourteenth-storey balcony of the Westbury Hotel. On the momentous issue that had brought them all together in the St. Catharines courthouse, the Crown's three key witnesses had now all made the same accusation: the conspiracy in which they had participated to murder the mother of six had been driven by the man sitting in the prisoner's dock taking notes, her husband, Helmuth Buxbaum.

At one point during Greenspan's cross-examination of Armes, the strain of five weeks at trial, including, no doubt, his client's stunning if short-lived revelations earlier in the week, showed on the battling defence attorney. Hearing something behind him, Greenspan suddenly swung around and addressed a barb at Michael Martin, who had just finished a noisy and unselfconscious yawn at the Crown table: "Bored? Bored, Mr. Martin?"

Greenspan asked for the jury to be removed. In a hasty submission, he got a complaint off his chest that had been bothering him for days. "My lord, I am only raising this now because it has been going on for some time, and I really think it is utterly rude and improper; Mr. Martin – he yawns loudly all the time, and – I don't mean twenty-four hours a day – but, in my respectful submission, it is a bad tactic, and it is wrong. It is loud and I can hear it when I am standing over by the jury, and I don't know why it is necessary for him to do that."

Greenspan's injured sensibilities fell on deaf ears. Martin preferred not to dignify his thin-skinned colleague's "whining complaint" with a reply. Greenspan protested that he was not an over-sensitive soul, but the Crown's bad manners had been displayed on several occasions and enough was enough. Judge O'Driscoll used the occasion to remind the offended party that lawyers who practise in glass courtrooms shouldn't hurl accusations:

"There are a lot of things that go on that shouldn't go on, such as throwing down transcripts of evidence when you get an answer that you don't like – and that shouldn't go on, but it does." Greenspan, who knew the judge was referring to him, pointed out that the difference was that Mr. Martin hadn't objected to his theatrics. Weary of the exchange, Judge O'Driscoll made a final, withering comment: "Lots of things happen during the course of the trial that shouldn't happen. Surely, when you have been in a courtroom for as long as you and I have, you develop a bit of hide and we move on."

Judge O'Driscoll ordered the jury back and the long grind began again.

The following week began as inauspiciously for the defence as the one that had just ended. In a submission on November 25, Greenspan objected to the introduction of a colour photo that showed a large pool of Hanna's blood at the site of her murder. He argued that it was unnecessarily inflammatory, since the court already had a scale model of the scene that clearly showed the location of the victim's body. Judge O'Driscoll ruled against him, admitting the photo because it showed the precise position of the dead woman's head in relation to the pillar of the overpass.

Meanwhile, Greenspan was wrestling with another disturbing matter. Rattled by Corinne Willoughby's damaging testimony about his client's drug habits, which weakened the important defence argument that Robert Barrett had led Helmuth into new vices like mainlining cocaine, he began to worry that the Crown might be planning to sandbag him with evidence from several other prostitutes. If more of them were, in fact, set to testify along the lines of Willoughby, it would put the defence in double jeopardy; not only would it become implausible to maintain that Barrett had led his client astray, but the evidence of the prostitutes would be a sly way for the prosecution to introduce evidence of bad character that would further alienate the accused with the jury. Greenspan simply had to know what the Crown knew.

In a note hand-delivered to Martin on November 19, he asked for full disclosure on the subject of Helmuth's drug activities in the company of prostitutes. The matter ended up in front of the judge. Martin explained that police had interviewed 400 people during their investigation, including 100 prostitutes. But the Crown had been interested in what Buxbaum had told them about his relationship with his wife, not what they did with syringes or their bodies. The prosecution was unable to give Greenspan the information he wanted for the simple reason that they didn't have it.

As a sign of good faith, Martin offered to let the defence go through the statements of all the prostitutes, including those of girls who hadn't been called to testify. Satisfied that such an arrangement would prevent him from having to deal with another surprise witness like Corinne Willoughby, Greenspan accepted the offer. But there was a limit to how much reassurance the Crown was prepared to offer; when Greenspan asked for a firm list of witnesses the prosecution intended to call, Martin turned him down, pointing out that since the police investigation into the murder was still active, any list he might provide could change as the trial proceeded.

The Crown's next two witnesses supplied more details about the accused's behaviour on the night of his wife's murder. Truck driver Colin Lawrence testified that the accused waved him over and told him, "My wife has been shot. Two guys shot my wife." Moments later, as they had headed over towards the guardrail, Helmuth added, "She has been shot in the head." The jurors exchanged looks as Lawrence testified that the fallen woman's husband never approached her body. "I couldn't understand the calmness. It is not normal," he said, noting that he had stopped at hundreds of roadside accidents over the years and had never seen a close relative of a victim display such cool detachment.

According to Dr. Robert Anthony, Helmuth's demeanour hadn't changed much by the time he reached the hospital later that night to check on the condition of his wife. Anthony testified that Helmuth had shown little emotion when he was informed of Hanna's death. "He just shook his head and said, 'It can't be, it can't be.'" Although Anthony admitted that reaction to a loved-one's death could range from violent emotion to stonefaced denial, Helmuth's reaction had been so flat that, after he was gone, both Anthony and the attending nurse remarked on its strangeness.

At the end of an effective cross-examination, in which he got Anthony to admit that Helmuth's reaction wasn't quite as flat as he had portrayed it, Greenspan asked the doctor if he knew anything about "Organic Brain Syndrome." He proceeded to draw out that such a condition could, in fact, account for Helmuth's emotional flatness on the night of his wife's murder. It was the first mention of the personality disorder that qualified as a disease of the mind under the Criminal Code's insanity provisions, but it wouldn't be the last.

The next day politics and the press cast a shadow over the judicial proceedings. Greenspan informed Judge O'Driscoll that a newspaper story had appeared in the *London Free Press* attributing some highly derogatory remarks about the accused to Bob Rae, the leader of Ontario's New Democratic Party. Although Greenspan had only heard about the contents of the article from one of the Buxbaum children, the Crown was ready with a copy of the story for the judge to peruse.

In the context of a remark about Ontario's nursing-home system, Rae had said that millionaire nursing-home operators like Helmuth Buxbaum should become extinct. Judge O'Driscoll found the article innocuous, but Greenspan persisted in his attack. "To mention Helmuth Buxbaum in the fashion he does, in the middle of a trial for murder, is a terrible thing for somebody to do." Arguing that the opinion of a leader of a political party could seriously influence the trial, Greenspan insisted that the judge admonish the jury. In words that showed Judge O'Driscoll thought

Greenspan's point was trivial, the judge complied. "You are sensible, fair-minded people who can separate the wheat from the chaff . . . I am sure that you will toss it aside, the same as you would when you read about this trial and you come across a typographical error."

At the end of November, there was still more than two weeks left in the Crown's case, and everyone realized that the trial would drag on into in the new year. The proceedings had settled into their own rhythm, and Judge O'Driscoll observed that it would be wrong to hurry the process along. He took a couple of days off to attend the annual Supreme Court judges' meeting in Toronto, and then announced that there would be a sixteen-day recess from December 20, 1985, to January 6, 1986.

As the days wound down towards the Christmas break, the Crown called the remainder of its witnesses. A long line of police officers was followed to the stand by Brian Richardson, the neighbour Helmuth had claimed he thought might have been having car trouble on the night of his wife's murder.

Richardson's testimony helped both the prosecution and the defence. He testified that he owned a full-size, medium-blue Chrysler Newport with a black roof – hardly the kind of vehicle that could be mistaken for a mid-size, dark-blue Chevy Nova. But, demolishing a theory held by the police, he also testified that the Richardsons were not close friends with their wealthy neighbours, so the Buxbaums would not have known that they were away in Florida on July 5. It was a small boost to Helmuth's credibility, and the hard-pressed defence team was grateful.

More damaging testimony was on the way when Phil Conley took the stand to give his circumstantial evidence. Conley recounted how he had overheard a telephone call at Needham's Funeral Home on July 8 in which Helmuth told a male caller, "I told you I would phone you at 10 A.M. on Tuesday." Conley testified about his concern over Helmuth's explanation at the time. It simply hadn't added up that someone named "John" would be calling him for money when Helmuth was at a funeral parlour grieving for his wife. As Helmuth's testimony would soon prove, he had lied to Conley at the time; it had been Robert Barrett on the line asking for more money. Since the cocaine deal had already gone down, the question was very simple; what had the money been for?

When the Crown attempted to lead Conley through a description of what he and Paul Buxbaum had subsequently found when they searched Helmuth's fallout shelter, Greenspan strenuously objected; the last thing he wanted was more evidence of bad character in the form of testimony about the syringes and pornographic videos the pair had found there. Martin countered that character had already been made an issue by Greenspan's own cross-examination of Robert Barrett and Dawn Watson.

It was an important juncture in the trial. If Judge O'Driscoll ruled in favour of the Crown, it had serious implications for what witnesses Greenspan might call for the defence, including the question of whether to put Helmuth himself on the stand. The crucial issue was temporarily shelved when the defence asked Judge O'Driscoll to defer his ruling on character evidence until the last prosecution witness had testified. By that time, at least, Greenspan would know with a certainty whether or not the Crown intended to sandbag the defence, and blacken the accused, with more evidence of bad character. If he could be reassured on that point, perhaps a compromise would be possible.

The next witness was Nick Potocska, who backed up Duncan Findlay's financial testimony regarding Helmuth's net worth after debt, liabilities, and the amount owing to employees were subtracted from the value of the businesses. Chris Buhr argued for the defence that Potocska's complicated *voir dire* testimony about the financial workings of the Buxbaum business empire would only distract the jury from the real issue — whether Helmuth had engineered his wife's death. Once again, Crown prosecutor Alasdair MacDonald argued that only by establishing his personal net worth could it be shown that $1 million U.S. was a significant amount of money to the accused and, therefore, a possible motive for the crime. The judge agreed that Helmuth's need for cash was relevant and admitted Potocska's evidence. In passing, he noted that one of the jurors was a corporate vice-president who could lead the others through the complexities of Buxbaum's financial statements.

Though the trial was far from over, Helmuth had reached his own verdict on John O'Driscoll. On December 3, he handed a curt note to his lawyers: "With the experience in court so far, I think you should move for a mistrial and start over again with a different judge."

On the afternoon of December 3, the accused watched from the dock as the man who had arrested him for the murder of his wife took the stand. With two appearances sandwiched between the testimony of other policemen, Insp. Ron Piers was the last witness for the prosecution. His surprisingly abbreviated evidence commenced in a *voir dire*, and moved in and out of the presence of the jury as legal arguments emerged and were dealt with during the course of his testimony.

He described the visual test police had conducted at the murder scene with a car similar to the Chevy Nova used by Hanna's killers, and testified on other matters, but the lion's share of his time on the stand was devoted to recounting the precise circumstances of Helmuth Buxbaum's arrest.

After minor edits to the July 23, 1984, tape recording of Helmuth's final statement to police that lead to his arrest that same day, the tape was played in open court for the benefit of the jury. The recording of the interview between Piers and the accused spoke for itself, and Martin quickly turned the witness over to Eddie Greenspan for cross-examination.

Over the next few hours, the two men played courtroom cat and mouse. Greenspan tried to get the detective to admit that before Helmuth uttered a word after identifying the Nova as the murder vehicle, Piers had already decided to arrest him. If he were able to wring that admission from the witness, Greenspan knew he could have the damaging statement ruled inadmissible on the grounds that Piers had failed to inform the suspect that he had the right to retain and instruct counsel.

But Piers had been around too long to fall into a procedural trap. Over and over again, he insisted that the decision to arrest the suspect had not been made until Helmuth had refused to answer further questions after consulting his lawyers. As for what might have happened had Helmuth not asked to see a lawyer and merely terminated their interview, Piers was characteristically succinct: "I believe I would have let him go and made a further appointment."

Having failed to shake the testimony of the policeman who had directed the investigation into Hanna Buxbaum's murder, Greenspan made a submission on December 9 against admitting a police reenactment of what a driver could actually see from the exit to County Road 14 looking west towards the murder scene just over a third of a mile down Highway 402. He argued that, at best, the experiment would yield mere opinion evidence due to lighting conditions and differing individual visual powers. Greenspan contended that the only way to test the truthfulness of Helmuth's claim that he had been able to see the colour of the blue Nova on the night of the murder was to conduct a proper scientific test.

Judge O'Driscoll dismissed his argument and admitted the police reenactment into evidence. The prosecution would now be able to claim that at a distance of 1,800 feet, the approximate distance Helmuth had been from the murder car on the night of the murder, the colour and shape of the blue Nova would have been completely indistinguishable.

To the man in the prisoner's dock, the substance of the judge's rulings no longer mattered; the pattern was all too clear: "I know this judge does not intend to give me a fair trial. Please do a mistrial motion."

After nearly two months in court and the testimony of sixty witnesses, the Crown was ready to close its case. Before it did, Eddie Greenspan asked for a ruling from Judge O'Driscoll on the important question of whether character had become an issue in the trial as a result of earlier cross-examination of Crown witnesses. If it had, Greenspan claimed that he might be forced to forgo calling Helmuth to testify in his own defence.

As it turned out, Judge O'Driscoll never had to rule on the matter. Greenspan gave the Crown an undertaking that the accused would be his last witness, which took care of Martin's worry that the defence would carefully avoid leading any character evidence in his examination of the accused, and then call a string of witnesses to attest to Helmuth's sterling reputation. Since the Crown would be limited to cross-examining Helmuth on matters raised in Greenspan's examination-in-chief, the wily defence lawyer could then conceivably apply two coats of whitewash to the accused before the matter was turned over to the jury, without the prosecution being able to do anything about it.

One person, however, remained obsessed with the issue of character. Convinced that Crown prosecutor Michael Martin was out to get him for purely personal reasons, Helmuth carefully noted down what he saw as the base motives of his tormentor: "[Martin's] whole thrust has been to get a conviction! He joined hands with well known . . . criminals. He associated himself with criminals to finish the job they started! They wanted to destroy my family and Martin is helping them to finish the job. They made my children into half-orphans . . . He wants to make them into full orphans!!"

The next morning Judge O'Driscoll did rule on another very unusual motion: Eddie Greenspan's request that the judge himself call witnesses. Greenspan was unhappy that the Crown had chosen not to call people like Janet Hicks, who could contradict certain testimony from the prosecution's most effective witnesses. Arguing that the defence should not be forced to call conspirators as witnesses (Hicks was actually an accessory after the fact), Greenspan cited an interesting case in his effort to persuade Judge O'Driscoll to make this rare move.

The case, *Regina v Talbot (No. 2)*, was a murder trial in which the Crown called a psychologist who testified that the accused could avail himself of the defence of insanity under Section 16 of the Criminal Code. But the accused man had emphatically instructed counsel not to raise an insanity defence. Persuaded by the psychologist that the matter required independent testing, the judge intervened and called psychiatrists as his own witnesses. Both the case cited by Greenspan and Judge O'Driscoll's response were deeply ironic given the future course of the Buxbaum saga. In reminding Greenspan how rare it was for the court to call witnesses and denying him his motion, Judge O'Driscoll made it clear that he wouldn't have hesitated to resort to the little-used power if he had thought it necessary. "I would exercise that right if the interests of justice required such action. In this case, there is no need for such action. I see no injustice taking place."

Just before noon on Thursday, December 12, 1985, Martin advised the jury that the Crown's case was closed. Greenspan requested an adjournment until Monday, sensitive, perhaps, about beginning the case for the defence on Friday the thirteenth. That night, with the shadows of paranoia dancing a devil's jig on the walls of his cell, Helmuth recorded his thoughts about the progress of his trial. "In my opinion, there is no question anymore that the Crown does not only have an 'oblique' motive, but a desperately sadistic or satanic motive to totally destroy a beautiful family. Their motive, simply expressed in one word is: Hate!"

16

THE MAGICIAN

*"There is an old magician's trick in which, as the theatre
audience watches, the magician makes an elephant
disappear . . . The essence of that trick, and it is a trick, is to
distract all of the audience's attention while the elephant is
simply led off the stage."*
*— Crown prosecutor Michael Martin on Eddie Greenspan's defence
of Helmuth Buxbaum*

The case for Helmuth Buxbaum's defence began on Monday, December
16, day forty-two of the marathon murder trial. Before the first defence
witness was sworn in, and long before the jury uttered its verdict, the
accused man's life had already changed forever. The fountainhead of his
fortune – one chronic-care hospital, two rest homes, and six nursing
homes – was sold by Hanna's estate for just over $19 million, $11 million
less than Helmuth believed his empire to be worth. If he were now
acquitted, the squire of Komoka would have a healthy bank account but
no business. It had taken just seventeen months to wipe out the fruits of
twenty years of hard work. It was a bitter pill to swallow for someone who
was supposed to be presumed innocent until tried and found guilty.
Helmuth's sole consolation was that his home, at least, had not been sold
to his colleague in the nursing-home business (and one of Hanna's pall-
bearers), Norbert Schuller.

Such merely private agonies were of little concern to the dynamo who
now took the field on behalf of his disconsolate client. Eddie Greenspan
was fighting for something far more important than real estate: Helmuth
Buxbaum's freedom. It was an uphill battle. Marshalling all of the personal
magnetism that had so often mesmerized juries in the past, Greenspan
announced that Helmuth would be taking the stand in his own defence.
In making the dramatic disclosure, he stressed that the accused would be
testifying not because he had to (the right to remain silent, he reminded

them, was a fundamental principle of Canadian law), but because he wanted to – a fact Greenspan hoped the jury would take as a sign of his client's honesty.

Pacing the courtroom as he spoke, Greenspan vowed to discredit the damaging evidence of Susan Ambrose and to remove Hanna's life insurance policy as a motive for the murder. Several medical experts would be called to testify about the effects of Helmuth's 1982 stroke, testimony designed to explain but not excuse his prurient indulgence in sex and drugs. Greenspan also promised to account for the telephone call that Helmuth had made from the Toronto airport just hours before Hanna's death, declaring that his client had not been trying to reach Robert Barrett at the Westbury Hotel, but a woman by the name of Lucy Addis.

Most important of all, he promised to lay bare significant contradictions in the evidence of Robert Barrett and Pat Allen that would help the jury to assess their otherwise damning testimony in a new light. In true Perry Mason style, Greenspan told the jury that he would be producing a witness who would testify that Robert Barrett had confessed to him that he and he alone had been responsible for Hanna Buxbaum's death, and that Helmuth was totally innocent. He made no bones about the fact that his surprise witness, Daniel Borland, was a hardened criminal serving time in the same prison where Robert Barrett had been lodged while awaiting Helmuth's trial. Greenspan hoped that in the circumstances, the jury would understand; since his arrest and imprisonment a year and a half earlier, Barrett hadn't been rubbing shoulders with many law-abiding citizens.

Two hours after he began his opening remarks, Eddie Greenspan was ready to go to work, but not before reminding the jury that he didn't have to prove his client's innocence as Michael Martin and company had been obliged to prove Helmuth's guilt; the job of the defence was merely to undercut the evidence that the Crown had brought against Helmuth Buxbaum with another version of events that *might* be true. Fanning the damp kindling of minor inconsistencies, inconsequential facts, and exotic possibilities into the flame of reasonable doubt is the role of a defence attorney; no one was better at it than Eddie Greenspan.

His first target was Susan Ambrose, whose independent corroboration of Helmuth's intention to murder his wife had been especially damaging to the accused, as it had originated beyond the police investigation with a voluntary call from the young woman. To reinforce his effective cross-examination of Ambrose, Greenspan produced a witness prepared to portray her as a pathological liar. Glen Nevin, a General Motors dealer from Lucan, Ontario, testified that the bill for repairing the Ambrose Volvo had actually been $295.17, a far cry from the $1,500 Ambrose had claimed on the stand.

To bolster his point that Ambrose couldn't be trusted, Greenspan planned to call two other witnesses. He wanted Jack Pescod, a neighbour of the young couple, to talk about the violent arguments they had had during January 1984 – flare ups that Ambrose had testified never took place. Contrary to Ambrose's claim that she had cleaned up her apartment before fleeing to Toronto, Pescod was also prepared to describe the filthy condition in which he had found the hastily vacated rooms – ubiquitous garbage, unwashed towels, dirty bed linen. Finally, Greenspan intended to call a witness who would verify that Ambrose had, in fact, listed Choice Entertainment, a Vancouver-based escort service, as her last employer on an application for B.C. Hydro – despite her indignant denials on the stand that she had returned to her career as a stripper and prostitute after leaving Ontario. But Judge O'Driscoll refused to hear these last two defence witnesses because their evidence was too peripheral to the matter on trial.

Even so, Greenspan was still able to demonstrate that Susan Ambrose had told a number of lies in her sworn testimony; unfortunately for the defence, her conversation about herbs with Helmuth Buxbaum at the Golden Pheasant Motel wasn't one of them. With the testimony of the two chambermaids who had overheard it firmly on the record, the best Greenspan could hope for was that the jury would decide that Susan Ambrose was a kind of tin-plated Lucrezia Borgia, and that she, not the accused, had proposed poisoning Hanna Buxbaum. Why Helmuth had stayed with her after listening to her proposition was one of those bizarre events that Greenspan had forewarned the jury simply had no explanation.

Duncan Findlay, the Buxbaums' financial adviser who had already given evidence in a *voir dire*, testified in front of the jury that Helmuth Buxbaum had approached Eugene High to purchase life insurance on his wife only after being advised to do so by Findlay. At the time, Findlay had recommended that the policies be made payable to the Buxbaums' estate or to their corporations. In response to a later question from Helmuth, Findlay had informed his client that life insurance premiums could not be written off against the business.

Anxious to preserve Hanna's large insurance policy as a possible motive for her murder, Michael Martin brought out on cross-examination that Helmuth had not believed in life insurance at an earlier date and had, in fact, cancelled a number of policies. More to the point, he drew out the fact that Helmuth had chosen to have Hanna's policy made payable to him rather than to his corporations, once again reminding jurors that there would be no tax liability to the business if only one spouse died.

Eddie Greenspan's theory of the case was that Robert Barrett, for reasons of his own, had hatched and executed the plot that cost Hanna Buxbaum her life. The Buxbaums' groundskeeper, Ken Surette, testified that while Barrett had worked briefly at Komoka, Hanna had confronted him over the cocaine he had been supplying to her husband. Surette described how agitated and surprised Barrett had been to learn that Hanna knew about his drug dealings with her husband.

After the Buxbaum's housekeeper, Gizella Toth, loyally testified that during the five years she had worked at Komoka she had never seen the Buxbaums quarrel, Greenspan called another witness who was crucial to his theory. Janet Hicks, who was already on parole from her eighteen-month sentence for being an accessory after the fact to Hanna's murder, testified on December 18 that Barrett and Allen had shown up at her apartment at 10 A.M. on July 4, the day before the murder, not late in the afternoon as the conspirators had claimed in their evidence.

Since Hicks also said that, during that morning encounter, Pat Allen had offered her $1,000 to go to Toronto with Barrett, Greenspan thought he had found an important inconsistency in the Crown's theory that Helmuth was actively involved in planning his wife's death. Since Barrett had only been able to reach Helmuth by phone for the first time since the Buxbaums' return from Europe at around noon on July 4, and their well-documented meeting hadn't taken place until early afternoon on the same day, Hicks' testimony could be used to advance the proposition that Barrett and Allen had been working on their plot to murder Hanna Buxbaum independent of the accused.

Impressive on first glance, the argument lost its force when Alasdair MacDonald got Hicks to admit on cross-examination that not as much had gone on in her morning meeting with Barrett and Allen as she had claimed in her examination-in-chief.

"The first time you heard about going somewhere with Rob Barrett and Pat Allen, you did not know where it was that you would be going to, correct?"

"That's correct."

"It wasn't until late in the afternoon that you finally found out you would be going to Toronto?"

"Yes."

"Rather than Florida or somewhere else?"

"Yes."

With those answers, Janet Hicks had deprived the defence of one of its few arguments, which perhaps was why Greenspan would neglect to mention her evidence on cross-examination when it came time to address the jury.

That night, Helmuth thanked his lawyer for his "superb" presentation for the defence. Having chafed under what he saw as highly damaging press coverage during the Crown's case, Helmuth noticed that the media reports were better for him now that Greenspan was calling the witnesses. The prisoner also felt a new friendliness in Inspector Piers "Clouseau," evidenced by the fact that the detective had allowed Helmuth to see – and hug – his son Phillip that day.

On the way to the Niagara-District Detention Centre after court, Piers asked Helmuth if the "Lucy" Greenspan had referred to in his opening remarks to the jury was a real person. It wasn't an exercise in small talk. The police were convinced that his July 5 call from the Toronto airport had been to Robert Barrett at the Westbury Hotel to arrange the time and place of Hanna's execution, exactly as Barrett had testified. Piers knew that it would damage the Crown's case if Greenspan could produce a witness to explain away the crucial call.

Helmuth replied that Addis was an Irish immigrant who was staying with her brother in Toronto and claimed that he would have provided police with that information on the day of his arrest if Piers had allowed him to retrieve his diary from his briefcase in Komoka. Without asking any further questions, Piers assigned Mel Getty to find and interview the young woman and her brother. Getty found out that Helmuth had, indeed, called Addis, though not on the day of the murder as Greenspan apparently intended to claim. The call had actually been placed more than a week before, a detail the Addises remembered because they had been vacationing in Northern Ontario during the week of July 5. Piers informed Michael Martin, who suddenly found the prosecution's case significantly strengthened.

Unaware of the hole he had punched in his own defence, Helmuth asked Greenspan to consider a proposition that demonstrated the extent of his heady, new optimism. "*If* the Crown drops the charge against me on Friday [December 20], I will be willing to give them an undertaking that I will not sue them personally. This way I could still be with my children at home for Christmas. If they don't want to consider this, I will sue every one of them."

Helmuth continued to fume at the alliance he believed the Crown had entered into with thieves, drug pushers, and prostitutes who were prepared to convict him in an effort to save their own skins. "If it were not so serious, it would be humorous how Martin . . . has to rise to the defence of well-known criminals; how he . . . has to defend their trustworthiness, their reliability and their honour. A true association of his hypocrisy with his scammers!"

As the Christmas break drew near, the fatigue of the beleaguered defence team began to show. When court resumed on the morning of December 19, Judge O'Driscoll asked if there were any changes to the scheduled appearance of witnesses because of a snowstorm the day before. "No," Greenspan quipped, "unfortunately they are here."

Everyone was looking forward to a respite from the proceedings except the man who had tried to take his life during his first Christmas behind bars, and who now faced his second with no end in sight to his agonizing incarceration.

Dr. Thomas Feasby, a neurologist, began the last day of testimony before the Christmas break, supplying the background to Helmuth's 1982 stroke in order to set up the defence's most important medical witness, neuropsychiatrist Dr. Andrew Malcolm. Feasby was followed to the stand by Dr. Gary Nancekievill, who read from notes he had taken about Helmuth's dramatic mood swings less than two months before Hanna's murder.

Through Nancekievill, the court learned that Helmuth had planned to check into Pine Rest Christian Hospital, a psychiatric institution in the United States, and that he had even gone so far as to ask his family doctor if Ontario's medical plan would cover part of the cost. Dr. Nancekievill testified that another doctor, psychologist Ken Nichols, had warned him that Helmuth might be suffering from a cyclothymic personality disorder.

The prosecution was interested in Dr. Nancekievill's evidence for reasons of its own. Michael Martin asked for permission to examine the portion of the doctor's notes that suggested that Helmuth had given his wife venereal disease, information he argued would provide the jury with an important insight into the true state of the Buxbaum marriage. It was important to the Crown's case to show that the Buxbaums' marital discord clearly predated Helmuth's 1982 stroke. "The stroke was not something that changed an unhappy marriage, it was simply another episode in it," Martin declared, "which ended with the murder of Hanna Buxbaum."

Ever on guard against attempts by the Crown to slip in evidence of the accused's bad character, Greenspan countered that only those parts of Nancekievill's notes that were considered by neuropsychiatrist Dr. Andrew Malcolm ought to be ruled admissible.

To get a better sense of the issue, Judge O'Driscoll sent the jury out and listened to the doctor's evidence. Nancekievill testified that urethritis was a bacterial or viral infection that can be contracted through sexual intercourse. Non-specific urethritis, though, was normally sexually transmitted. (First Helmuth, and then his wife, were treated for both varieties in the late 1970s.)

During cross-examination, the Crown inquired about a streptococci bacterial infection that Nancekievill had diagnosed in Helmuth after a urethral swab in February 1978. Knowing that the particular bacteria was normally found in the rectal area, Martin asked if this was consistent with anal intercourse. Possibly though not necessarily, Nancekievill replied, pointing out that anal perspiration could infect the urethral area.

Despite its inconclusive nature, Martin asked that the medical testimony be admitted, while Greenspan insisted that it be kept out because Nancekievill's information was as much as six years old. As for the doctor's memories of trouble in the Buxbaum marriage, the defence wanted the reference ruled inadmissible on the grounds that Nancekievill couldn't remember any details of the alleged "marital maladjustment" he referred to in his *voir dire* evidence. Once more, Judge O'Driscoll was persuaded by the prosecution's arguments.

On December 20, Martin cross-examined Nancekievill on his medical notes in open court. The Crown prosecutor made sure that the jury understood that the accused had been treated for urethritis a total of fourteen times. They also heard about Helmuth's bad nerves and his growing concerns about nuclear war. Finally, Martin brought out details about the aftermath of Helmuth's severe stroke, including the details of his remarkable recovery – although Nancekievill testified that, just three weeks after the traumatic event, Helmuth had complained to him that his family had imposed too many controls on him.

There was one final matter. Martin and the entire Crown team had suspected from the beginning of the trial that Greenspan might try to introduce evidence of insanity as an alternate defence to the murder charge, if it looked as though his client were going to lose the case on the merits. So when Nancekievill had testified about Helmuth's cyclothymic condition, the prosecution table had been all ears. Martin was quick to bring out that in Nancekievill's opinion this was a personality description, not a mental illness. The last thing the Crown team wanted planted in the jury's mind was the notion that Helmuth Buxbaum hadn't been responsible for his actions.

That night in the solitude of his cell, Helmuth wrote a poem that expressed some thoughts of his own about the drama unfolding in Courtroom 10:

"He's cyclothymic," says the doc,
I listened keenly in the box . . .
"He's cyclo-something," Martin shouts,
Thymic, cycloned, he has gouts . . .
He points his spindly fingers in my eye,
My heart it pants, I breath a sigh;
But Martin carries on his song,
And hurts me in that courthouse all day long . . .
Mr. Martin, have you been to jail,
Lost all your family, friends, sent no mail?
If you had 17 months in jail endured,
You'd have all of clino-rethra-ics for sure!
This will I now tell to thee:
You hate this man, I surely see:
When sins of past his eyes now see,
When memories chill and his friends flee. . . .
When now at Christmas his heart aches,
With wife and children far away,
When this day seems the worst of days . . .
Accusations you have learned,
A hanging prosecutor you have earned
Far worse a disease you have got:
Hater of men, and that is that!
What happened to you my dear man,
That you moved into "hatred land"?
Martin, MacDonald, Evans too,

Go spend a fortnight in that zoo,
And you will understand him too!
If your brother's sins you not forgive
Then with your own sins you must live!
The judge he stops his sombre tone,
$12,000 poorer I go home.
Getty even wishes a goodnight,
And quickly disappears from sight.
But as my eyes fill up with sand,
And I drift into no man's land
My thoughts they wander, think it through,
I know a man, you know him too . . .
He also lived in this here zoo;
And moneychangers felt his whip,
His anger made their tables tip;
He healed the sick, he healed the lame,
His love, compassion was to all the same;
"Forgive them Lord," he cried when he died,
Our Saviour, Lord, the crucified!
Lord if you were now in this here zoo,
They'd call you cyclothymic too!

When court resumed on January 6, 1986, it didn't take long for Eddie Greenspan to realize that he was in for a difficult finish to the trial of his life. In an ill-fated attempt to refute Dawn Watson's damning testimony, namely that she had told Terry Gallagher about Helmuth's desire to kill his wife, Greenspan called Gallagher as a defence witness. But instead of repeating her evidence from Helmuth's preliminary hearing, where she had flatly denied any such conversation, Gallagher now said that she couldn't remember what Watson had told her. The only thing she seemed interested in revealing to the court was her body, ample amounts of which were on display beneath a diaphanous pink dress. She became so difficult to handle, an exasperated Greenspan asked for and was granted the right to cross-examine his own witness. But she stubbornly stuck to her new and unhelpful story; she simply couldn't remember if Watson had told her about Helmuth's murder plans.

With appalling speed, Gallagher turned into a witness for the prosecution under Michael Martin's pointed cross-examination. Raising precisely the kind of bad character evidence Greenspan had laboured so mightily to keep off the record, Gallagher testified that the first time she had met Buxbaum he had wanted her to inject cocaine. Instead, she had taken him up on his offer to snort the drug through a $ 100 bill. Gallagher also testified that she knew that Helmuth was unhappy with his wife, a fact that took on even greater force when she added that she had had a session with him just before the Buxbaums' pilgrimage to Oberammergau and was even to have seen him the day after his return from Europe.

The next witness to blow up in Greenspan's face was John Barrett, though this time, at least, the lawyer knew that the fuse was lit before he ever called him to the stand. John was important to the defence because he could testify that his brother, Robert, had been upset after Paul Buxbaum, acting on behalf of his mother, had fired him from his job with the Buxbaums. It was Greenspan's intention to use that information to advance the defence theory that a furious Robert Barrett, faced with the threat from Hanna that she would turn the drug pusher over to police if he didn't keep away from her husband, had acted alone in plotting the victim's death. But John Barrett could testify about a lot more than his brother's reaction to being fired, as the jury would soon find out.

On December 17, the day after he announced that John Barrett would be called, Greenspan was at the Parkway Inn, the home away from home for so many of the trial participants, when he was handed Barrett's new twenty-four-page statement taken earlier that day after a five-hour session with police. For once there would be no complaints about the timeliness of the Crown's disclosure; the explosive document was delivered to the defence as soon as it was typed.

The next day, as planned, Greenspan proceeded with his examination-in-chief of John Barrett, bringing out that his brother Robert had indeed been "down in the dumps" after being fired from his temporary job at Komoka. Having extracted the information he wanted the jury to hear, Greenspan then contended that there was fresh information in Barrett's new statement that ought to be ruled inadmissible. This time he wanted both the witness and the jury sent out, while he made arguments to have the offending material excluded.

"I thought you were going to suggest you wanted me to leave, too!" Judge O'Driscoll remarked.

"It never once entered into my mind," Greenspan innocently replied, before adding one of his hallmark quips: "I have often thought that *I* wouldn't mind leaving."

Given the contents of Barrett's new statement, Greenspan's move was understandable. The so-called defence witness was set to testify that Helmuth preferred young girls because they were sexually naive, and that he had injected cocaine into his penis and made homosexual advances towards the witness during a trip to Detroit. Knowing that such evidence could easily overshadow the useful testimony Barrett had to give as a defence witness, Greenspan asked for a ruling on examples of bad character that he claimed would seriously hurt his client if they were admitted. Though "highly disgusting," these activities were totally irrelevant to the murder trial.

The defence was particularly worried about the effect on the jury if Barrett was permitted to describe how, during a trip to Detroit, Helmuth had dipped his penis into the plum sauce while in the washroom of a Chinese restaurant and then watched as Nick Potocska, unaware of what his employer had done, ate the tainted goods. Struggling to find words to describe the incident, the normally loquacious Greenspan got some help from an unlikely quarter. Michael Martin suggested "misapplied" might aptly describe what Helmuth had done with the plum sauce before Nick Potocska had used it on his egg rolls. Greenspan agreed, but insisted the episode be kept from the jury. "Other than it would turn this jury off Chinese food . . . I can't imagine what other possible probative value it would have to the issues before them and can only be calculated to inflame the minds of the jurors against Mr. Buxbaum . . . to truly hate this man."

The Crown was willing to make a compromise on evidence touching bad character because it had a far more important use for the witness's testimony. Martin wanted to bring out the fact that John Barrett's brother and the accused had had a conversation about arranging a murder contract on Hanna *before* Robert had gone to work at Komoka – testimony that, if believed by the jury, would demolish Greenspan's main defence contention that Robert Barrett killed Hanna on his own after being fired to protect his lucrative business association with Helmuth. With such bigger game in mind, Martin could afford to be magnanimous about Helmuth's shortcomings as a dinner companion. "I do not propose to elicit from the witness any description of the plum sauce episode," he said.

Judge O'Driscoll issued a detailed ruling on bad character evidence that gave limited comfort to both sides: the Crown could ask about Helmuth testing the cocaine and sending John for syringes because it demonstrated Buxbaum's knowledge of that world. The witness could also be asked about cruising for prostitutes and injecting Fiorinal. On the other hand, evidence about requests for young girls and boys during his trip to Detroit and whatever may have happened when he was lying on a motel room bed with John Barrett was inadmissible.

But on the most explosive issue raised in Barrett's new statement, the prosecution was the clear winner. Noting that the Crown was arguing that Buxbaum had hired Robert Barrett to kill Hanna, and the contention of the defence was that Barrett had acted alone, Judge O'Driscoll ruled that John Barrett's evidence relating to Robert telling him about the murder plot before he went to work for the Buxbaums was admissible. It not only shed new light on the main plank of the defence theory, it also affected Eddie Greenspan's allegation that Robert Barrett had made up the conspiracy story to get a reduced sentence by delivering Helmuth's head to the Crown.

It was a bad moment for the defence, and once more Helmuth was ready with some tactical assistance. That night, he asked his lawyers to enter his thirty-one Bible course certificates as exhibits in the trial. Greenspan contained his enthusiasm for the suggestion.

Martin's cross-examination of John Barrett continued the next day. Barrett testified that Helmuth complained to him that Hanna had a "fat ass" and that he preferred young, skinny, sexy women. He also claimed that Helmuth told him that he was sick and tired of his family badgering him about his drug use. Barrett told the court that he had heard rumours of his brother's involvement in the murder plot before Robert had ever gone to work for Helmuth.

Furious, the defence asked that their own witness be declared hostile. Under section 9 (2) of the Canada Evidence Act, Judge O'Driscoll ruled that Greenspan could cross-examine Barrett on the issue of when he had first learned of Robert's involvement in the murder plot. At Helmuth's preliminary hearing, John Barrett had testified that when he and Robert had been in Florida, he had been under the impression that the money Helmuth had given his brother was for cocaine. He now admitted that that was untrue, explaining that he had lied at his previous court appearance to protect his brother. Greenspan pointed out that John's testimony at the preliminary came three and a half months after Robert had pleaded guilty to conspiracy to murder and been sentenced to ten years in prison. How, Greenspan wondered, could John's testimony have possibly hurt a man who had already been convicted?

Ignoring the logical hole the defence had just punched in the witness's

350 THE PRODIGAL HUSBAND

explanation for his sudden change of heart, Martin used his final questions to John Barrett to reinforce the effect of his new testimony. He got Barrett to repeat that Robert had clearly told him during their trip to Florida that Helmuth had paid him to arrange the murder of his wife. Although Robert had accepted the contract, he assured his brother that he had no intention of actually carrying out the murder, and was only scamming his mark. Barrett ended his testimony with the claim that he had heard rumours about the murder contract on at least two occasions before the Florida trip.

Relieved to see the last of John Barrett, Greenspan called Dr. Dennis Profitt, an associate professor with the departments of Psychology and Biomedical Engineering at the University of Virginia. Dr. Profitt was an expert in the field of human visual perception and was called to discredit police theories about what could and couldn't be seen at the murder site from County Road 14.

Profitt testified that it was impossible to impose a standard on what a particular person might be able to see for a number of reasons, including the angle of the sun, and the immediate background behind the murder car on the day in question. Even the bend in the road would allow a person to see more of the side of a car (and therefore its colour). The only way to conduct a valid test would be to replicate the exact conditions of the July 5, 1984, murder scene, a virtually impossible task.

(Independent corroboration of Dr. Profitt's expert opinion was provided by another witness, Barbara Noble, who testified that at a distance of 2,100 feet, she had been able to identify a blue car at the murder scene parked under the overpass, and from 1,700 feet had picked out two men standing beside that car.)

Greenspan had successfully challenged the accuracy of the OPP's unscientific re-creation at the murder scene, but at this point in the trial, what Helmuth had been able to see as he approached County Road 14 on the night of July 5 was a trivial matter. It would take the next defence witness to deliver the first serious blow to the so far unshakable case for the prosecution, or so Eddie Greenspan was hoping.

With a lengthy criminal record dating back to 1975, including convictions for theft, attempted prison break, possession of stolen property, armed robbery, and mischief, Daniel Borland was an unlikely candidate to ride to Helmuth Buxbaum's rescue. But for the hard-pressed defence team, he was the closest thing to a trump card they had. Borland was prepared to testify that Robert Barrett had admitted that Helmuth Buxbaum was innocent of any involvement in his wife's murder, and that he and he alone had engineered the crime.

From the beginning there were problems, including the security risk represented by the star witness for the defence. In a submission, Chris Buhr asked permission to address the issue in the privacy of the judge's chambers. But Judge O'Driscoll ruled that the matter would be dealt with in court in the absence of the jury, citing his aversion to conducting any official business in chambers unless it was absolutely necessary.

At issue was Greenspan's strong objection to the Crown's proposal that Borland's feet be shackled to the chair during his testimony. He pointed out that another convict-witness, Paul Ringuette, hadn't been shackled, even though he had a longer criminal past and had twice escaped custody, a formidable record compared to Borland's lone successful jailbreak. There were also metal detectors at the courtroom doors that would be tripped by the leg irons, an alarm that would adversely affect both Borland's credibility and his demeanour. He should, Greenspan argued, be permitted to walk in and out of the courtroom unshackled, as Barrett, Allen, and Ringuette had when they had testified for the prosecution.

What Greenspan didn't say was that Borland's escape from a Barrie jail while awaiting trial for armed robbery in 1982 had been a study in determination. After someone tossed a rope over the prison wall, Borland scrambled straight up the twenty-foot cement barrier with warders dangling from his ankles. He had then wriggled through the razor wire at the top of the wall, inflicting serious lacerations to most of his body. Borland had remained at large for ten days, even making a trip to hospital, where he managed to get his wounds stitched up without arousing suspicion.

Crown prosecutor Michael Martin was in favour of the shackles not because he wanted the witness treated any differently from other convicts who had testified, but because he had received information that the brazen Mr. Borland was planning yet another escape attempt. The police had been told by another prisoner-witness that Borland had talked about using his court appearance as a pretext for granting himself full parole. Martin coolly reminded the judge that he would be separated from the agile witness by a mere three-foot wooden barrier. "It is not the first time I have thought of that, quite frankly," Judge O'Driscoll observed.

In ordering the precautionary leg irons, the judge said that there was nothing novel about prisoners being shackled at trials, explaining that he had once presided over a case in which the four accused had been shackled by the ankles in the prisoners' box for the entire proceeding. "I suppose I can put it no better than Shakespeare did: discretion is the better part of valour," he added.

To Eddie Greenspan's dismay, Daniel Borland was sitting in the witness box shackled to a chair when the jury returned.

The twenty-six-year-old inmate testified that a few months after he had been transferred to Laval penitentiary in March 1985, he had described in a letter to Eddie Greenspan how Robert Barrett had confessed to him that Helmuth had had nothing to do with his wife's murder. It had been Barrett himself who had issued the death sentence to avoid being turned in to police for selling cocaine to the accused. Borland claimed that Barrett was concerned that if he told the truth at Helmuth's preliminary, he would be charged with perjury, or even murder. The bottom line, Borland maintained, was that Helmuth was "innocent."

During all trial submissions, the jury and, occasionally, the witnesses are required to leave the courtroom. In Borland's case, this presented a problem, since court had to recess to allow security personnel time to unshackle and then reshackle the witness before taking him away every time the judge listened to arguments from counsel. When Greenspan grumbled that this was an even better argument for not shackling Borland, Judge O'Driscoll glanced soberly at the defence counsel and said, "Mr. Greenspan, we have an extra set, so don't you go too far away."

Because of the gravity of Borland's allegations, the Crown took pains with his cross-examination. Using Greenspan's tactic of discrediting Crown witnesses with evidence of bad character, Martin brought out the details of Borland's seamy past, a history pathetically similar to that of many other prisoners who testified at the trial. He had begun his institutional life at age eight, when he was placed in the Sacred Heart Children's Treatment Centre. By thirteen, he had launched his criminal career, stealing cars and adding machines. As a juvenile he was sent to the John Boscoe Residence for Boys, and then to the infamous St. John's Training School in Uxbridge, Ontario, in 1975. He soon escaped and ran away to Las Vegas, Nevada, where he supported himself with a series of petty thefts. After his recapture, his next escape was from Guelph Reformatory.

During some of his capers, the career criminal had exhibited remarkable presence of mind. When he and an accomplice were surprised during the robbery of a Becker's milk store, eighteen-year-old Borland had calmly stepped behind the counter and served customers, pocketing their money while his partner held the terrified female clerk at knifepoint in a refrigerated room at the back. In time, he had graduated to more ambitious projects, robbing a bank and a jewellery store with a sawed-off shotgun. Since his fourteenth year, Daniel Borland had been at liberty for less than twelve months.

The professional prisoner had been transferred from Kingston to Laval after his involvement in a sit-down strike and an escape plan with four other inmates in the late fall of 1984. In Laval, there were only seven inmates who spoke English: Borland, Billy Germa, Raymond Kenton, Peter McDonald, Justin McKenna, Pat Allen, and Robert Barrett. Under cross-examination, Borland denied knowledge of a scheme at Laval to discredit Barrett in order to help Buxbaum, who would then become a "meal ticket" for his knights in tarnished armour.

After receiving Borland's letter, Greenspan had visited him in Laval penitentiary on August 6, 1985. Unsure at first about whether he would be prepared to testify, Borland finally decided to do the right thing: "Mr. Barrett told me this man is innocent, and I don't want to see anyone go to prison who is innocent."

Eddie Greenspan was ready now to play his favourite instrument; the jury's heartstrings. By summoning several of the Buxbaum children to the stand, he hoped to replace the image of Helmuth's crumbling and crisis-ridden marriage with a more flattering portrait: that of an essentially loving relationship in which the foibles of the philandering husband had been known and forgiven by his wife.

Eighteen-year-old Phillip Buxbaum testified that his parents "loved each other very much," providing an eyewitness account of the hugging and kissing that was a routine feature of their relationship. He claimed that his parents had always worked as a team, totally depending on one another.

At this point in the trial, Greenspan knew that he couldn't completely ignore the dark side of Helmuth's personality. He brought out that Phillip had learned about his father's drug use in April 1984, when he saw the tell-tale bruises and needle marks on his body. The teenager described how in May 1984, Helmuth's cocaine habit had sparked a family conference where various solutions to the crisis were discussed, including the possibility of turning Robert Barrett over to police if he persisted in leading their father astray.

One thing Greenspan didn't want to hear about was Helmuth's ill-fated plan to escape prison and flee to Brazil, a bid for freedom in which Phillip was to have played a pivotal role. He argued in a submission that he didn't want evidence about the July 1985 plan to be called by the Crown this late in the trial, since it would leave the jury with a superficial impression of his client's guilt. "We are almost at the end of a three-month trial," Greenspan pleaded with the judge.

Unmoved, Judge O'Driscoll ruled that the Crown could cross-examine the defence witness on the escape plan. By way of compensation to the defence, he also directed that, even though it stretched the rules of hearsay evidence, he would allow Greenspan to elicit further details about the Buxbaum marriage from their clearly sympathetic son, who punctuated his testimony with smiles directed at the accused.

Phillip testified that his mother had told him about Helmuth's womanizing in 1984. Although she hadn't liked it, Phillip said that his mother accepted her husband's infidelities because she believed that marriage was for life. "She would forgive him for anything he would do, and continue on trying to make the best of the marriage," he said. "She accepted that because she loved him unconditionally."

After bringing out damaging details about the escape attempt in which Helmuth had involved his own son, Michael Martin made clear he wasn't buying the airbrushed portrait of the Buxbaum marriage painted by the defence. Under cross-examination, he asked sarcastically if Phillip's father had hugged his mother when he was on his way to meet one of his prostitutes. The flustered witness replied that he couldn't say because he hadn't known about his father's debauches in places like the Golden Pheasant Motel. Phillip had made exactly the point the prosecution wanted to establish: the Buxbaum children weren't the best judges of the state of their parents' marriage because they simply had not known how bad the situation was.

Before moving on to his next witness, Greenspan re-examined Phillip about the damaging jailbreak plan. In particular, he wanted to bring out the reason Helmuth had felt it necessary to flee the jurisdiction before his trial. Phillip explained that his father wanted out because he believed he wouldn't get a fair trial and because he was already being treated to unusually harsh punishment as an accused person. Helmuth also felt that the press and the public had turned against him long before court was ever convened. Rounding out the picture of an innocent man in turmoil over injustices he had already suffered, Phillip testified that other prisoners were making Helmuth's life hell by terrorizing him for money. As Phillip left the stand, Greenspan hoped the jury would see that there was more to

Helmuth's otherwise damning break-out attempt than a tacit admission of guilt.

Mark Buxbaum added to the rosy picture of his parents' relationship with reminiscences of his own. "It was very good. It was a very open and honest relationship, and there was a deep, calm respect that I could see." Mark explained that his father had always insisted that the children treat their mother with the utmost respect, an ironic observation in the circumstances. The young man also described the relaxed circumstances of his mother's last breakfast with the family, hardly the rushed affair one might expect if Helmuth had indeed been plotting the imminent demise of his wife, or so Greenspan hoped the jury would believe.

When Martin objected to what he considered to be self-serving statements about the Buxbaum marriage being allowed in as evidence, Greenspan witheringly reminded the prosecutor that such comments had at least as much relevance as some of the remarks the Crown had elicited from Helmuth's rented ladies. "I am not going to say it will necessarily win or lose the case, but it might have as much significance as telling some prostitute his wife is fat," Greenspan said.

The next phase of Greenspan's defence was more expert medical evidence to explain some of his client's admittedly bizarre behaviour. Dr. Joseph Marotta was associate dean of the Faculty of Medicine at the University of Toronto with impressive credentials as a neurologist. On Saturday, December 7, 1985, Marotta had done a neurological examination of the accused and now reported to the court that Helmuth had a parietal lobe lesion of the brain and damage to his motor control system. The CAT-scan done at the time of Helmuth's 1982 stroke also indicated damage to the frontal lobe of his brain, he testified.

On September 12 and 24, 1985, noted psychologist Dr. Ruth Bray had conducted independent tests on Helmuth designed to uncover any residual effects of his stroke. Bray looked at the accused's previous medical history only after she had completed her own testing, reducing the possibility of being influenced by anyone else's findings. Bray found it noteworthy that Helmuth made no attempt to gain her personal sympathy, a response markedly at odds with most people accused of crimes, who usually try to make a good impression on the clinician. Helmuth went through the tests without the slightest attempt to exert any social charm.

At one point, when a guard had brought Bray a cup of tea, Helmuth protested that he should have it. From the very beginning, it had been obvious to her that she was dealing with a brain-damaged individual with a potential defence under the Criminal Code's insanity provisions. "I know at the time, that's what first came into my mind and what I, when I originally saw him, assumed would be the defence . . . I had never seen such a clear-cut case," she later said.

Beyond that subjective impression, Bray found that Helmuth showed a serious deficit in abstract thinking: his ability to think creatively, to solve problems, and to exhibit normal mental flexibility were nowhere near the level of his other skills. The prestroke Helmuth had functioned in an intellectually superior range; his performance in non-structured tests was now abysmal. His Minnesota Multiphastic Personality Inventory test (MMPI), 566 true or false questions that the courts regularly rely on to give a personality profile of an accused, indicated that Helmuth was not trying to make himself look sicker or better; in answers that were often against his own interests, he was, in the doctor's opinion, responding honestly. He admitted, for example, that he was attracted to young girls.

Bray depicted a man who was feeling distressed and inadequate, too confused to analyse and deal with life's normal problems. She noted that Helmuth had always been an "overcontrolled" individual, and that one of the ways he coped with unpleasant situations was to simply deny or repress them.

Bray also found that Helmuth suffered from a host of other mental deficiencies. He was introverted, exhibited lamentable social judgement, and had a poor ability to assess how others were feeling towards him. In particular, she testified about an unusual response from Helmuth to the Rorschach, or ink-blot test, that has been a staple of psychological assessments since the 1920s. In Bray's experience, male patients usually do not mention the sexual images they see in the blots in the presence of a female examiner. In this case, Helmuth had described in vivid detail the very things she would have expected him to repress. Normal adult inhibitions seemed to be curiously absent.

At one point in his cross-examination of Bray, Michael Martin asked the doctor if Buxbaum was suffering from a neurosis or a mental illness, clearly aware of the possibility that Greenspan might be setting up a Section 16, or insanity defence. Bray replied that a neurosis was not actually a mental illness, but more of a thoroughgoing misinterpretation of day-to-day situations. She explained the distinction by pointing out that neurotic people have trouble dealing with reality, not with being out of contact with it. She had not really answered the prosecutor's question, but it was an effective way of keeping her testimony in line with Buxbaum's chosen defence. Martin didn't pursue the matter.

When Martin ventured into the particulars of Helmuth's answers to explicit sexual questions from the MMPI test and his sexual history questionnaire, Greenspan jumped to his feet. Having already been burned on previous occasions, he didn't want any more evidence of bad character coming from the mouth of another defence witness. Bray, Greenspan contended, was there to give evidence about a "psychological condition consistent with a post-stroke frontal lobe lesion," not Helmuth's deviant sex with prostitutes. The judge overruled him, finding the cross-examination proper because it helped the jury to weigh their opinion of the witness's testimony.

To Greenspan's consternation, Bray went on to testify that Helmuth had admitted to her that he played out his sexual fantasies with prostitutes, exploring his interest in oral and group sex in a way that would spare Hanna's involvement in practices she would have loathed. Although cocaine gave him vivid fantasies about sex, he was often unable to perform sexually after he had hired willing partners. In the accused's defence, Bray pointed out that, based on his sexual questionnaire, Helmuth certainly hadn't "tried everything," as the prosecution had laboured to make out. When Martin suggested the word "kinky" would describe Helmuth's sexual adventuring, Bray told the straight-laced prosecutor, "Certainly that depends on what you think of as 'kinky.' My understanding in this day and age is that unless you belong to a fundamentalist religion, most people don't consider oral sex kinky."

Bray noted that a lot of stroke-free men try to work out their mid-life crises in bed. The difference in Helmuth's case was his colossal lack of judgement: while other men used prostitutes with a certain amount of control and autonomy, he had carried on a high level of indiscriminate sexual activity that was clearly self-destructive.

Before she left the stand, Bray observed that Helmuth had answered questions in ways that were truly unusual for a person with a high-normal IQ – a characteristic of schizoid, drug-addicted, or even psychotic subjects. The doctor testified that some of Helmuth's mental processes, particularly in uncontrolled situations, "were very similar to psychotic thought patterns." He responded quickly and confidently, even though his answers were invariably shallow. In particular, he would quickly drop topics that aroused strong reactions, and his own emotions swung back and forth very quickly. The tests she had run told Bray that Helmuth was either under a great deal of stress, or brain-damaged, or both. "Somewhere along the line," she testified, "he has lost the capacity for abstract thinking and logical planning and analysis."

Although she didn't quarrel with Eddie Greenspan's professional duty to conduct his client's chosen defence, Dr. Bray left the stand remembering a pre-trial conversation she had had with Dr. Andrew Malcolm: "We thought if we got up and said what we were going to say, that somebody might raise the question, 'Hey, how come this isn't a Section 16?' as in similar cases, in fact, in less *obvious* cases I've had. Even thought it wasn't raised by the defence, judges have raised the question of a Section 16."

Paul Buxbaum took the stand between the appearances of two of the most important medical witnesses for the defence. Like his brothers, he told the court that his parents had loved each other, and that Hanna had been his father's closest friend. He admitted that Helmuth's infidelities and drug use had created tension in the marriage, but used the parable of the Prodigal Son to illustrate their relationship: Hanna was always waiting with open arms for the man she had married to come back to her.

Alarm bells went off at the prosecution table when Greenspan began to lead Paul through the changes that had come over Helmuth after his stroke. As Paul described the new aloofness in his father, his uncharacteristic irrationality and flagrant indiscretions, Martin wondered again if the defence was about to raise the issue of insanity. With the evidence of the next witness, neuropsychiatrist Andrew Malcolm, they would get their answer.

The famous expert in organic diseases of the mind was the last witness to testify before the accused himself took the stand. Dr. Malcolm's credentials were impeccable: a fellow of the College of Physicians and Surgeons, a celebrated author, and a clinician, he had testified in many august forums, including an appearance in front of the United States Senate. His special field was organic diseases of the brain, but he had also spent a great deal of his clinical time studying the effects of drug use.

Malcolm had visited Helmuth on four occasions after his arrest to conduct a battery of tests. In addition to his own work with the accused, he had attended court to listen to the evidence of doctors Bray and Marotta and had reviewed the 1982 medical records documenting Helmuth's stroke. The doctor testified that physical evidence gathered at the time of the stroke showed an unmistakable infarct (dead brain tissue) in Helmuth's parietal lobe. A CAT-scan also revealed an infarct in the right frontal lobe of that "very mysterious organ," the brain.

Malcolm testified that a standard book in his field, *Psychiatric Aspects of Neurologic Disease* by Benson and Blumer, had a chapter on frontal lobe disorders precisely like the one Helmuth was suffering from. The classic example of the condition was the 1868 case of Phineas Gage, who had undergone a striking personality change after sustaining damage to the frontal lobe of his brain. The physician who attended him noted that although he had made a physical recovery from his injury, the balance between his "intellectual faculty" and his "animal propensities" had been destroyed. The once sober and accomplished businessman became fitful, lecherous, and impatient of restraint or advice when it conflicted with his desires. The changes were so radical, according to Dr. J. R. Harlow, that his patient was "no longer Gage."

In Malcolm's expert opinion, Helmuth Buxbaum showed "very clear evidence from a psychiatric point of view of frontal lobe disorder." The doctor explained that the personality change associated with the disorder could be blatant or barely perceptible. In Helmuth's case, Malcolm believed that the change had been very dramatic, a conclusion backed up by Paul Buxbaum's observations of his father in the months following his stroke. The doctor also pointed out another bedevilling subtlety of the condition; frontal lobe lesions like Helmuth's worked their mysterious alterations in the victim's personality while leaving intellectual functions largely intact. In other words, the changeling could appear to be quite normal to the unprofessional eye.

Malcolm testified that hypersexuality was another common trait in patients suffering from frontal lobe damage. Referring to the Phineas Gage case to illustrate his point, he explained that as a frontal lobe patient regresses to a more primitive level, he loses the fine-tuning of his adult responses and often becomes crude and uninhibited. In Malcolm's opinion, Helmuth's already considerable sex-drive clearly became pathological after his 1982 stroke.

Greenspan was scrupulous in pointing out that Helmuth hadn't been a paragon of virtue prior to April 17, 1982. Through Malcolm, he brought out the fact that the accused had had at least seven affairs before his stroke, none of them simultaneously. But throughout his adulterous relationships, he had always felt guilty and craved Hanna's forgiveness; after the stroke, he had become an amoral satyr – a transformation Malcolm told the court that could be traced directly to his frontal lobe damage. "He lost his tact and restraint and he became disinhibited with regard to sexual expression, and he began to be risk-taking and he allowed himself to appear in places where ordinarily he wouldn't let himself be."

The most recent literature on frontal lobe damage of the kind Helmuth was suffering from included a paper by Dr. Bruce Miller of the Harbour Medical Centre attached to University College Los Angeles. Although the paper was presented to a learned society in Dallas, Texas, in late 1985, Judge O'Driscoll ruled against allowing Greenspan to cite the work, "Hypersexuality or Altered Sexual Preferences Following Brain Injury," as part of the defence. Since Miller was not yet recognized by the medical profession as an authority in the field, his reputation was, in effect, ahead of him, Judge O'Driscoll explained. Frustrated as he was, Eddie Greenspan saw the pale humour in the ruling:

"My Lord, I would like to postpone the trial for five years."

"I guess it's similar to a bottle of good wine that hasn't aged yet," the judge replied.

When court resumed the next day, January 15, 1986, the jury heard some remarkable evidence, though it was unclear if they realized it. Dr. Malcolm testified that the accused satisfied the criteria laid out in the *Diagnostic and Statistical Manual of Mental Disorders*, the bible of his profession, to be diagnosed as suffering from Organic Personality Syndrome.

The intensity of this well-documented condition varies widely from patient to patient, but its two phases are clear: during the first or "pseudo-depressed" stage, the patient appears to have lost all initiative. Compared to his prestroke condition, he comes across as apathetic, indifferent, even vegetative. The appearance of what looks like clinical depression, a "flat-tening and dulling of the emotions," is, in fact, just the physical "slowing down" of a stroke victim in the aftermath of his attack.

The second or "pseudo-psychopathic" phase is a regressed state in which sexual inhibition and social judgement can be greatly diminished. According to the professional literature, "erotic behaviour, sexual exhibi-tionism, or lewd remarks are not rare" in a patient who enters this phase of the condition. Like a classical psychopath, the now self-centred and often obsessive patient begins to behave "indiscreetly" and may become "strikingly promiscuous." His new personality traits can be completely foreign to his previous experience, but are frequently monstrous exagger-ations of prestroke behavioural patterns. Unlike the classical psychopath, whose anti-social behaviour springs from mysterious sources, the pseudo-pathological behaviour of the patient suffering from Organic

Personality Syndrome rests on a well-known cause – irreversible brain damage.

The court had just been advised that the man it was trying was mentally ill, and at least one party to the proceeding immediately realized the implications. As Dr. Malcolm once again described the irrefutable evidence of a right frontal lobe infarct that in his opinion had caused the accused's "pseudo-psychopathic behaviour," Michael Martin decided to find out exactly what Eddie Greenspan had in mind.

"I'm wondering if my friend is trying to establish, or is about to establish, a Section 16 defence through this witness?" For days, the "rumble" around the courtroom had been that there was going to be a pitched battle on the insanity issue. Judge O'Driscoll, who had heard the rumours, wondered if the opening shot had finally been fired. In scarcely a heartbeat, he had his answer from Greenspan: "I'm not even thinking about it."

For the second time in the trial, once in the privacy of a defence interview room, and now again in open court, the issue of insanity had been raised and brushed aside.

It was a crucial point in Helmuth Buxbaums' defence. Eddie Greenspan knew he was walking a fine line with his own medical witnesses. If he went too far in using their testimony to account for his client's moral sleaziness, he knew that the Crown could call rebuttal evidence to show that Helmuth had exhibited similar behaviour before his stroke. Similarly, if Judge O'Driscoll saw evidence of Buxbaum's insanity in the testimony of any defence witness, he could order a psychiatric assessment of the accused even though he was not pleading insanity. But after what he called Greenspan's "flatfooted" repudiation of the insanity defence, it became very difficult for the judge to intervene – especially when such an intervention from the bench would so directly undermine the right of an accused to choose his own defence. Had Michael Martin inquired of Dr. Ruth Bray or Dr. Andrew Malcolm if they thought Helmuth Buxbaum was insane, instead of asking Eddie Greenspan if he were about to raise a Section 16 defence, the sensational trial might have taken its most spectacular turn. As Greenspan would later put it in a letter to Dr. Ruth Bray thanking her for her trial testimony: "The entire psychiatric and psychological evidence was a potential mine field but we seem to have crossed the mine field relatively unscathed."

At 2:35 P.M. on January 15, 1986, day fifty-four of his trial, Helmuth Treugott Buxbaum took the stand in his own defence. True to his religious beliefs, he refused to swear on the Bible, affirming instead that what he was about to tell the court was the truth. Having listened as the Crown blackened his client with a one-sided account of the vices of his later years, Greenspan set out to give the jury a more complete picture of the man whose life would soon be in their hands.

To accomplish that, he needed the Buxbaum story from its genesis, not just the escapades of the prodigal husband. He guided Buxbaum through his early years in Europe, his emigration, the marriage to Hanna, and the opening of their first nursing home in 1967. Step by step, he conjured up the picture of a man and a woman who had achieved their version of the American dream with hard work, thrift, and self-denial, partners in life as well as in business. Greenspan deftly wove occasional strands of testimony about the affairs, the prostitutes, and the drugs into the broader cloth of their spectacular financial success. With his client's foibles presented in context, Greenspan offered the jury the portrait of an extraordinary man who had succumbed to some very ordinary weaknesses – a husband in love with his wife everywhere but the marriage bed from which he had repeatedly, and ignobly, strayed.

The liaisons with Cathy Russell and Monica Taylor were presented along with Helmuth's heroic work to free Georgi Wiens, unworthy acts mixed with admirable ones in the lawyer's line of questioning, exactly as they are in the real life of every human being.

One of the tactics of Greenspan's approach was to have Helmuth himself candidly admit to and describe the tawdry vices he had succumbed to in later life. In a bland monotone that conveyed not only the facts, but the air of a man who would be easy to manipulate, Helmuth told the court how he had been drawn to the sociable and ever-smiling Robert Barrett from the moment the two had met in Kelly's Bar in late 1983 or early 1984. Through Barrett, cocaine had become his new god. He told the court that he took the drug at home, in various London motels, and in the apartments of people like John Barrett. He even admitted to injecting cocaine with Robert Barrett when the young man was supposed to be working as a landscaper at Grace Villa nursing home after his confrontation with Hanna in the spring of 1984.

Although Helmuth admitted to using cocaine with Cathy Russell, he contradicted the evidence of Corinne Willoughby, insisting that Barrett had introduced him to mainlining that first afternoon in Kelly's. The experience had been magical; instead of the fifteen minutes it normally took for the cocaine to take effect, he experienced immediate relief from the pressures and problems that filled his life.

When his wife finally stumbled across some of the drug in his clothes, Helmuth described how Hanna had flushed it down the toilet. Even though at an urgent family meeting he had agreed to get treatment Helmuth simply enjoyed the drug too much to give it up. Cocaine had come between the debilitated patriarch and his once all-important family.

One of the most damning parts of the Crown's case against Helmuth was the flurry of financial transactions at critical points in the alleged conspiracy to murder Hanna Buxbaum. Incriminating as they might seem to a casual observer, Greenspan now offered another explanation. Helmuth described the economic theories that both he and Hanna had subscribed to that recommended frequent withdrawals from banking machines to prevent the government from knowing what a person was doing with his money. As suspicious as his withdrawals on May 24, July 4, and July 6, 1984, may look to the average bank customer, they were in fact nothing more than Helmuth's usual banking routine.

He also testified about other elements of the economic-survivalist and hard-currency theories that governed his life, from buying gold and building a fallout shelter, to using Swiss bank accounts to divide his wealth between Europe and America in the event that one government seized his assets. Strange as his dealings might seem to ordinary people, Greenspan wanted to make sure that the jury had the opportunity of assessing those actions against something other than Hanna's murder.

Greenspan was poised to rebut some of the detailed allegations that faced his client, including why he had given Robert Barrett $5,000 on May 24, 1984. Helmuth told the court that he had gone to see Barrett that night because he had felt badly that the young man had been fired from his job at Grace Villa. According to Helmuth, Barrett had been so furious that he had wanted to stab Paul Buxbaum. After the drug-dealer calmed down, the two men had talked about finding a steady supplier of cocaine. Barrett suggested that Florida would be the best place to set up a reliable connection, and for that reason, not a murder contract, Helmuth had given him the first $5,000 payment in late May.

After Barrett's trip to Florida and the Buxbaums' pilgrimage to Europe, Helmuth had agreed to the meeting at a London McDonald's outlet on the eve of his wife's murder because Barrett had needed more money. Contradicting the testimony of Barrett, Allen, and Anita Pitcher,

Helmuth claimed that Barrett had shown up alone for their parking-lot rendezvous. The two men had then driven to Komoka to retrieve a stolen fur coat that Barrett had earlier sold to Helmuth and now wanted to sell to another customer for some badly needed cash.

"And did you say anything further to him?" Greenspan asked, leading up to his client's denial of the Crown allegation that he had then accompanied Barrett and Allen to the 402 to select the spot for his wife's murder.

"Well he wanted me to follow him and I told him no. I said, 'My wife, I promised my wife I would be home for supper and I cannot go anywhere with you.' He wanted me to follow him out to the 402 and I said, 'There's just no way.'"

Whatever may have been going through Eddie Greenspan's mind at that moment, he continued with his examination-in-chief as if nothing had happened. But the prosecution was electrified by Helmuth's answer, a stunning slip of the tongue they would later use to suggest that the accused man had convicted himself out of his own mouth by temporarily lapsing into the truth. After all, what did a trip to the 402, the place where his wife would be murdered in a little over twenty-four hours, have to do with a cocaine connection in Florida, or the sale of a fur coat? Martin decided not to raise the damning statement in cross-examination, depriving Helmuth of the chance to explain it away. Because the accused had been called to testify, Martin would be speaking last in the trial. He decided there was no better place to refer to the accused's fatal stumble than in his summation – a final word to which the defence could make no reply.

Having heard about Hanna Buxbaum's last hours from a host of Crown witnesses, the jury finally got the chance to hear an account of the murder from the man who was charged with arranging it. Helmuth described the family's leisurely breakfast on the morning of July 5, the pleasant visit to Hanna's mother and the Wagners, and the drive to Toronto Airport to pick up Roy Buxbaum. He explained that the telephone call he placed from the airport had been to Lucy Addis, a young woman he had met while travelling.

That night on their way home from the airport, Helmuth testified that he had seen someone frantically waving from further down the highway under the CN overpass. Thinking it might be a neighbour, he decided to go to their assistance, swerving off his exit ramp at the last minute and heading back out onto the highway. Awakened by the sudden change in direction, Hanna had lifted her head and allegedly said, "You missed the turnoff, aren't we going home?" But after looking down the road herself, Helmuth claimed she had agreed that the disabled vehicle looked like the Richardson's car. The Buxbaums continued down the 402 and stopped behind the blue Nova.

With all eyes in the jury box riveted on the stand, Helmuth launched into his description of his wife's brutal murder, an event he noted had taken place with breathtaking speed. One minute they stopped to offer assistance, and the next a masked gunman appeared demanding Hanna's money and jewellery. Helmuth drew a pathetic picture of his wife pleading for her life and trying desperately to get her rings off, while the masked gunman with the wild eyes pressed his pistol to her right temple. When Gary Foshay ordered his victim out of the car, Helmuth and Hanna's eyes met: "Do what he wants," Helmuth claimed he told her.

As the gunman dragged Hanna out of the front seat of the station wagon, the witness described how he had slipped out of the driver's seat and stepped onto the highway to flag down help. Just before a truck sped by without stopping, he heard three shots. Returning to his car, he saw a white cloud of smoke floating above the ground. In the blink of an eye, the gunman was running from the scene shouting to his accomplice, "Let's go, I've got her purse, let's go."

After the blue car left, Helmuth explained that he and Roy had gone over to the guardrail to see what had happened to Hanna. "Oh, my God, they shot her," Helmuth claimed he said. "We have to get some help right away." After failing to flag down one passing truck, they managed to get help from the driver of a second one, Colin Lawrence.

Helmuth described his feeling of utter disbelief when Dr. Anthony advised him on the evening of July 5 that his beloved Hanna had been pronounced dead in a London hospital. After asking to see her, he was horrified at the callousness of the hospital personnel: "They didn't even have the decency to wash her face before they showed her to me."

Helmuth began his fifth day of testimony trying to explain the call he had received from Robert Barrett at Needham's Funeral Home the day after Hanna's murder. He claimed that Barrett had been in a panic because he didn't have the money to pay for the cocaine he had arranged to buy from Florida; unless he came up with it, he would be killed. Helmuth agreed to deliver a substantial sum of money to Barrett that night at the London airport, explaining to the court that he had just lost his wife and "didn't want to get Robert Barrett killed."

Another dark cloud over the accused was his sale of a gold bar to Chris

Brooker the day after Hanna's death, a transaction that the prosecution had convincingly presented as part of Helmuth's attempt to collect the murder money for Hanna's killers. With a straight face, the accused claimed that the market value of gold had been decreasing, and that he had been anxious to sell some of his holdings before the price dropped even further. It was an explanation that required the jury to believe that less than twenty-four hours after his wife was murdered, he would be watching the precious metals market with his usual eagle eye.

Greenspan then led Helmuth through one of the deadliest parts of the Crown's case, the accused's well-documented meeting with Robert Barrett at the London airport on the evening of July 6. Once again, Helmuth claimed that the money he had given to his terrorized friend had been for drugs. After completing the transaction in the Buxbaum van, where the two men agreed on the price of $100 per gram for a 200-gram order of cocaine, Helmuth had hurried home, afraid that his family would be worried about him.

As for the two overwhelmingly suspicious stops on Highway 402 on the day of Hanna's murder, Helmuth told the court that he hadn't told the police about the morning encounter with a blue Nova because he hadn't thought it was significant at the time. His words must have conjured up memories for Eddie Greenspan of Helmuth's mid-trial revelation to the defence team that he had, in fact, recognized Pat Allen during that first stop and even talked with him about contacting Robert Barrett at the Westbury Hotel. In keeping with his quick retraction of that story, Helmuth now testified that it had only occurred to him a few days later that the first stop might have been significant, at which point he had brought it to the attention of the police.

The stress Helmuth was under was beginning to show. In response to Greenspan's questions, he denied using cocaine on either July 6 or 7, explaining that his supply had run out. He had apparently forgotten that he had already testified that he bought $2,000 worth of the drug from a London pusher on the afternoon of July 4, just before his meeting at McDonald's.

Helmuth admitted to receiving a second telephone call at Needham's funeral home from Robert Barrett, allegedly seeking more drug money on Sunday July 8 – the same call he had lied about to an eavesdropping Phil Conley. He explained to the court how he had then travelled to Toronto where he cashed in $16,000 worth of gold bars, not to hand over to Robert Barrett, but to take his children to school in Germany.

Strangely, he had somehow neglected to tell them about his momentous plan. Even though he had tried to call Robert Barrett that same day, July 12, from a phone booth on his way to the family cottage, it had only been to tell him "to make sure that he didn't use or sell" Helmuth's 200 grams of cocaine. It was left to the jury to ponder why anyone would entrust a treasure trove of cocaine to an uncontrollable drug addict like Squirrel.

Greenspan next got his client to explain away a potentially incriminating detail from his final statement to police on the day of his arrest. At the end of his July 23, 1984, interview with Insp. Ron Piers, the detective had asked about the purpose of Robert Barrett's trip to the Gateway Inn in Florida. Once Piers had made clear that he knew that Helmuth had financed the junket, the suspect had replied, "You know I think you're trying to put me into something here." Helmuth now explained that with almost daily reports about the infamous DeLorean drug case all over the newspapers and television, he simply hadn't wanted to talk himself into charges of conspiring to import cocaine.

Concerned about the negative impression that might be created by Helmuth's escape attempts, Greenspan argued in a *voir dire* that the accused's state of mind was important to understanding his desperate actions. Under questioning by his own lawyer, Helmuth testified that he had come to the conclusion that he wouldn't get a fair trial after going through a bail hearing where the emphasis had been placed on cocaine and women, not factors relevant to his alleged plan to murder his wife. That impression was reinforced for him when he was denied bail despite having no previous criminal convictions, twenty-one character witnesses, and the offer to post bail of a million dollars. As press reports depicted him as first a nursing-home operator, then a multimillionaire, and finally a tycoon, more and more inmates had begun pressuring him for money. Faced with injustice and extortion, escape had seemed like the only answer for someone with as strong a "consciousness of innocence" as Helmuth.

At one point in the *voir dire*, Greenspan asked his client if there was anything else that made him think he wasn't going to get a fair trial. It was a classic example of one question too many. "Well, I don't know, I don't want to pass judgment, but to me the judge [at the bail hearing] looked somewhat inebriated," the accused replied.

It was not the first time Greenspan had elicited a damaging reply from his own witness. During the preliminary hearing, he had asked his client who his best friend was in each of the months leading up to the murder. In every case, Helmuth gave the desired answer: Hanna. But when Greenspan got to July, the accused man thought long and hard before answering that in the month of the murder, Rev. Paul Fawcett had been his best friend. Const. Mel Getty had a bird's-eye view of Greenspan's anger. "On the way back to the defence table, Eddie asked me if I had a gun with me. When I told him I did, he asked if he could borrow it for a moment."

In the first recess after accusing a judge of drunkenness, Helmuth must have thought that he was back in the clutches of Herod, his childhood music teacher. Although his furious lawyer didn't twist his ear, he certainly bent it.

Michael Martin began his cross-examination of the witness immediately after the *voir dire* about Helmuth's numerous escape attempts. Now that Eddie Greenspan had tried to make the jury see the accused through rose-coloured glasses, the Crown prosecutor was determined to present them with what he believed to be a truer picture of Helmuth; an adulterous hypocrite with a history of prestroke drug use who had coldly turned to murder to rid himself of his loving but unwanted wife.

Before he paraded the dark side of Helmuth's life before the court, he lingered over the accused's numerous jailbreak attempts. Greenspan had hoped to present them as the desperate schemes of a man worried that he was about to become a victim of frontier justice. Martin was betting the jury would see them as the actions of a guilty man.

Martin also asked Helmuth if he had a complaint about the judge at his bail hearing, a subject the accused wasn't anxious to pursue, given Greenspan's fury at his remark. "I would rather not repeat it," the witness feebly protested. The relentless Martin finally made Helmuth say that he had said the judge was drunk, a statement the prosecutor suspected would sit as well with the jury as it had with the presiding judge of the murder trial, John O'Driscoll.

Concerned that Greenspan's medical witnesses might have created the impression that Helmuth had become a changed man after his stroke, Martin reviewed the accused's prestroke affairs, including his backseat encounter with a seventeen-year-old kitchen helper from his Komoka nursing home. The faces of the jurors grew sterner as he outlined Helmuth's relationship with his secretary – a deception that went on intermittently for a year and a half during the months Hanna and the children were living in their winter quarters in Boca Raton, Florida. Martin tried to make Helmuth admit that he had, in fact, suggested group sex to Cathy Russell in the mid-1970s, long before frontal lobe damage could be used to account for his hypersexuality. Greenspan vigorously challenged the relevance of the question, and after listening to submissions from both sides, Judge O'Driscoll drew a line in the legal sand: "We have travelled a long way in this trial and we have virtually been in and out of every motel and hotel in North America . . . There will be no more questions on this topic."

Martin did, however, get Helmuth to admit that he had snorted cocaine with Cathy Russell on three or four occasions – drug use that clearly predated his contact with Robert Barrett, the man the defence wanted the jury to believe had led its innocent client astray.

Undeterred by Judge O'Driscoll's mounting fatigue with matters sexual, Martin continued the onslaught, leading Helmuth through his infidelities with Monica Taylor and then with the women he met through a Toronto telephone club, a feature of his prestroke sex life he had somehow neglected to mention to Dr. Andrew Malcolm. To emphasize his contention that Helmuth had been a dedicated lecher long before his stroke, he confronted the witness with an advertisement Helmuth had placed in the *Kitchener-Waterloo Record* for travelling companions. Although the accused couldn't remember this particular episode, the police had already provided Martin with the name of Deborah Goodall, a woman who had answered the ad, and whose sister had subsequently gone on a trip with Helmuth to Martinique.

Martin then turned his attention to Susan Ambrose's allegation that Helmuth had wanted her to kill his wife as early as January 1984. Eddie Greenspan had realized that he couldn't deny the incident or explain it away because of the testimony of the two chambermaids at the Golden Pheasant Motel. So he had done the next best thing: blamed the entire plot on Ambrose herself. The Crown prosecutor proceeded to draw out the logical inconsistency of Greenspan's defence. Why, he asked the witness, had he had sexual intercourse with Ambrose, paid her, and even brought her an employment application the following week, if, in fact, she had proposed poisoning Hanna? Why hadn't he simply picked up the telephone and called the police? "I don't know why I didn't," Helmuth lamely replied. "I should have, I guess."

Then there were all those telephone calls in mid-June 1984 between Helmuth in Komoka and Robert Barrett at the Gateway Inn in Florida, communications the accused insisted had been about establishing a reliable cocaine connection. With the devastating evidence of Barrett, Ringuette, and McCurdy firmly on the record, Martin undermined Helmuth's testimony with a different line of questioning. If Helmuth had been caught trafficking in cocaine, wasn't it true that he would have little chance of getting the necessary government licence renewals for his 1,000-bed nursing-home empire? In other words, was he really asking the jury to believe that he had been willing to throw away a $25-million business empire to guarantee himself a supply of his favourite drug?

Martin then turned his attention to the morning stop behind the blue Nova. Hadn't he found it strange that although the man claimed that he wanted to fix something in the car's motor, the hood of the Nova wasn't up? Or that the man had shouted that everything was fine to the OPP officer, even though he hadn't used Hanna's panty hose, or anything else, to make repairs?

Talk of the murder day led Martin to a telling discrepancy between what Helmuth had told the police and his testimony in court about Hanna's reaction to stopping for a disabled blue car on the evening she was murdered. During his defence testimony, Helmuth said that his wife had agreed to stop in case the car did, in fact, belong to the Richardson's. Yet in his statement to Inspector Piers, Helmuth had told a different story: "And she didn't want me to, she said, 'No, no, don't stop.'"

The witness attempted to cover the contradiction by saying that he had been heavily drugged during the police interview, and that the sedatives had made him dizzy. "Well," came Martin's dry reply, "those pills don't stop you from telling the truth." Crown witnesses, he wanted the jury to realize, weren't the only people whose memories improved the further they got from the events they were describing.

As Martin led Helmuth through the sequence of events just before the deadly attack on Hanna, the jury was presented with other oddities in the accused man's story. He hadn't noticed that the licence plate of the blue Nova was covered with green felt, and despite the fact that he didn't know if the people needed his assistance, he switched off the ignition of his car when he pulled onto the shoulder. His explanation was unconvincing: "Even if I come to an intersection and the light turns . . . I shut off my engine," he said.

Martin then paraded the litany of lies Helmuth had told in the course of giving his version of events. When the police had first questioned him about the Florida telephone calls to and from Robert Barrett, he had denied any part in Barrett's alleged plan to make a major cocaine connection; he had lied to Roy Buxbaum about the person he was calling from Pearson Airport on the day of Hanna's death, telling him it was a business call; he had lied to Cal Stiller at the London airport when he said he was waiting for his nephew; he had lied to Phil Conley about the call from Robert Barrett to Needham's funeral home, telling him it was a man named John. Why all the lies?

On the last day of his testimony Helmuth admitted to Martin that Pat Allen might have attended one of his drug parties at the Park Lane Hotel in January 1984. As unforgettable as the menacing speed dealer was, Helmuth maintained he couldn't be sure if the man at one of the parties had indeed been Allen. Martin next asked if Allen had been the man the accused had spoken to during the morning stop on Highway 402 on July 5. Helmuth admitted that he had been, but added that he had only realized that after seeing Allen in prison. Helmuth's qualification to one side, the prosecutor had made his point: Pat Allen had the kind of face a person wasn't likely to forget. If he had been at the Park Lane party in January 1984, why hadn't Helmuth recognized him by the side of the highway on the day of his wife's death? And why hadn't he told police to go looking for a creepy-looking denizen of Kelly's Bar instead of sending them on a wild goose chase after someone he claimed had stolen Hanna's purse?

Throughout his questioning, Martin had worked hard to show that, time after time, Helmuth's actions had not been those of an innocent man. He now tried to close his cross-examination with a final, striking example of Helmuth's guilt. After getting the accused to admit that he had recognized Gary Foshay as Hanna's murderer while in prison, an event that had taken place in the fall of 1984 before his own preliminary hearing, Martin intended to ask Helmuth why he had never taken that information to the police.

Before the prosecutor got the question out, Eddie Greenspan was on his feet objecting to the Crown's line of questioning. He argued that Martin was straying into the sacrosanct ground of solicitor-client privilege that guarantees that discussions between an accused and his lawyer remain strictly confidential. Although he never said it in so many words, Greenspan implied that Helmuth, on his lawyer's advice, had three times refused to testify at Gary Foshay's preliminary. After a discussion between counsel and the judge, in which the Crown prosecutor voluntarily agreed to stop this line of questioning, Greenspan tried to get the judge to make a formal ruling: "It's a very interesting little point. Definitely worth it for the law reports," he prompted. Judge O'Driscoll didn't bite. "Well, Mr. Green-span, I learned a long time ago as a judge you never say anything unless you *have* to say something."

The Crown was finished with the witness, and after a brief re-examination by Eddie Greenspan, the accused stepped down for the last time. The trial that had begun with Robert Barrett had ended with Helmuth Buxbaum. What happened next depended largely on which of the two men the jury believed.

As it had with its the decision to put Helmuth on the stand, the defence took a calculated risk with its summation. His associates handed Green-span a 624-page script, banking on his legendary powers as a courtroom performer to overcome the jury's exhaustion and to sway them with a final emotional plea for the accused. Though the special effects were daz-zling, the plot was decidedly thin.

Greenspan again attacked the Crown's case through the cast of disrep-utable characters that had been used to make it. He portrayed Barrett, Allen, and Armes as the true villains of the piece, petty criminals who had turned to murder and who were now implicating Helmuth Buxbaum to avoid spending twenty-five years in prison. Anita Pitcher had lied about the July 4 meeting at McDonald's between Buxbaum, Barrett, and Allen to avoid being charged as an accessory. Dawn Watson's story about Hel-muth wanting his wife murdered was the product of a memory shorted out by heavy drug use. Susan Ambrose, not the accused, had proposed the plan to poison Hanna during her tryst with the millionaire. Implicit in the entire defence position was the unspoken allegation that the Crown and the police had connived with Hanna Buxbaum's killers to convict Hel-muth for reasons that would never be explained.

Greenspan was on firmer ground with his insights into human nature than he was with the facts of the case. He reminded the jury that marriage is only perfect in romance novels, and that the Buxbaums, like every couple, had had their problems. At least Hanna had known about Hel-muth's adultery, and had made the conscious decision to forgive him. "We would all wish for a spouse so tolerant of our individual frailties," he cooed, hoping to strike a sympathetic note with every juror who had ever had reason to be forgiven for an unworthy act.

With the wand of his rhetoric painting the air, Greenspan admitted that his client was an "ignorant and immoral man," but then plucked the sting from the words by depicting Helmuth as a child-like stroke victim, whose fixation with prostitutes and cocaine was best understood against the backdrop of his medical history, though he was very careful to point out that insanity was not an issue in the trial. "What you see is what he is," he said. "He is a man with no subtlety." A man, that is, without the guile to enter a murder conspiracy and then try to conceal it.

The lack of a motive, Greenspan contended, was one of the weakest points in the Crown's case. The Buxbaums had more than enough money from their highly successful companies, and the much-talked-about insurance policy on Hanna's life had only been taken out on the recommendation of financial advisers. Nor was sexual unhappiness a motive for something as drastic as murder, particularly for a man who was being so well serviced by prostitutes. Hoping that if he could make the jury laugh, he could make them doubt, the portly counsel added a flourish at his own expense: "If being overweight is a reason to be killed, then a lot of us are in serious trouble."

The very length of the marathon summation led to inevitable stumbles. In his zeal to make his case, Greenspan's arguments were occasionally inconsistent. At one point, he urged the jury not to believe Anita Pitcher when she claimed to have been at the July 4 meeting at McDonald's with Barrett, Allen, and Buxbaum, a meeting Greenspan had already insisted was attended only by Robert Barrett and the accused; at another, he used testimony from the young woman about that event to back up a defence claim that Allen and Barrett were lying about the length of time it had taken them to get back to London after their jaunt to Komoka and the 402 with Helmuth on the night before the murder. As Michael Martin would later put it: "Now, on the one hand, he argues that it took sixty-five minutes because Anita Pitcher looked at the clock in the K-Mart plaza . . . But, on the other hand, he says Anita Pitcher wasn't there. Well, how could Anita Pitcher know that it took sixty-five minutes if Anita Pitcher wasn't there?"

Another weakness in Greenspan's presentation was his unsatisfactory explanation of why he hadn't, as promised, produced the woman he claimed Helmuth had actually telephoned from Pearson airport on the day of his wife's murder. With the comment that he wasn't "entitled" to explain his change of plans, Greenspan posed a self-serving question to the jury designed to have them accept the evidence of a witness who had never testified: "If Helmuth Buxbaum had not called the sister-in-law of Lucy Addis as he said, don't you think the prosecutor would have called that woman to tell you that?"

The Crown table could only smile. Why would they call reply evidence when the defence witness in question had never been put on the stand by Greenspan? Far better to leave the record as it stood, with Robert Barrett claiming that Helmuth had called him from the airport on July 5; Helmuth Buxbaum admittedly lying to his nephew Roy about making a business call; and Eddie Greenspan breaking his vow to produce the woman he wanted the jury to believe the accused had really telephoned.

On the vital issue of the two stops Helmuth had made on Highway 402 on the day of his wife's death, Greenspan adopted an approach that was a little like the defence argument used by his former law partner, Joe Pomerant, in the Christine Demeter murder trial. In defending her husband, Peter Demeter, Pomerant had seriously advanced the theory that the massive trauma to the back of the young woman's head had come as the result of a fall – a ludicrously improbable explanation that Greenspan, as Pomerant's assistant, had found embarrassing at the time in light of overwhelming medical evidence that someone had clubbed her to death.

But his only reply to the fact that his client had stopped behind the same car twice on the same day was as jarringly unbelievable: "I suppose the Crown will suggest to you that, by stopping twice in one day, Mr. Buxbaum should be convicted for that coincidence alone." Unlike Pomerant, Greenspan at least had the good sense not to beat a dead horse.

At one point in the defence summation, Judge O'Driscoll interrupted Greenspan in full flight with a frightening observation. "Excuse me, Mr. Greenspan, there's seems to be something awry. I am not sure what it is. The building is shaking." During a hastily called recess, it was learned that an earthquake measuring five on the Richter scale had just rocked Toronto, St. Catharines, and Hamilton. Court resumed after a seventeen-minute break and Judge O'Driscoll asked a question that was understandable in the circumstances:

"What is the wish of counsel? Do you wish to carry on, or do you wish to stop?"

"I am content to carry on," Greenspan replied. "For my next trick, I'm going to part the waters of Lake Ontario," he joked.

When this incident was related by George Jonas, the co-author of Greenspan's memoirs and a good friend, it was portrayed in a different light: "It occurred to him that bringing the jury back immediately might not be a good idea. He couldn't be sure if the jury was in any mood to listen to suggestions about Buxbaum's innocence even under ideal circumstances, let alone following an earthquake. But Mr. Justice O'Driscoll wanted the proceedings to continue right away, so Greenspan had no choice."

Although the defence was under no burden to prove the accused's innocence, Greenspan presented the jury with his theory of what had really happened to Hanna Buxbaum. The heart of his argument was that Robert Barrett, and Robert Barrett alone, had hatched the murder plot. If true, Greenspan knew that the jury would be entitled to wonder how Barrett had been planning to pay Hanna's killers the substantial sum of money he had promised, a major problem for the chronically broke drug addict. Greenspan's answer was that Barrett intended to send a fake ransom note to Helmuth accompanied by Hanna's wedding ring after Paul Ringuette had disposed of the victim and given Barrett her jewellery. Once the distressed husband sent him money for the release of his beloved wife, Barrett would then use the ransom money to pay Ringuette for the murder.

As convenient as the ransom theory had been to explain how the penniless Barrett had intended to pay for Hanna's murder, it later became equally inconvenient for the defence when Barrett testified that he and Helmuth had discussed the kidnap plan on the way to pick out the murder site on the night of July 4. Abandoning his previous theory, Greenspan now argued that Barrett had been lying about the kidnap plan, citing Pat Allen's testimony that he had never been asked to make the murder look like a kidnapping when he had been hired to do the job. Assuming that Barrett would still have to come up with the money to pay the killers, the only thing Greenspan's bedazzled listeners knew for sure was that ransom money wouldn't be paying Pat Allen's bill. It was left up to the jury to resolve the inconsistencies in the defence's logic.

In one of many ironies in the long trial, Greenspan closed his plea for his client with the testimony of Daniel Borland, the man he claimed destroyed Robert Barrett's credibility. The jury could be forgiven for giving little weight to what Borland had said; after all, Eddie Greenspan had devoted most of the last three months to the fine art of discrediting Crown witnesses on the basis of their disreputable characters. Somehow the claim that the defence's low lives enjoyed a higher pedigree than those of the prosecution hardly seemed like a winning argument, particularly when it was remembered that what Barrett, Allen, and Armes were saying had earned them lengthy prison terms.

After four and a half days of non-stop conjuring, the magician withdrew, hoping to return for a final bow.

Michael Martin's final accounting of the Crown's case began with welcome news; he would deliver his summation in one day. The prosecutor sensed that Greenspan's marathon summation had numbed the jury rather than persuaded it, leaving them vulnerable to a brief and elegantly argued reply from the Crown.

A masterpiece of simplicity, Martin's address, which he wrote, focused on the fanciful theories of the defence and six crucial questions: How had Foshay, Allen, and Armes known that the Buxbaum car would stop on the morning of July 5, 1984? Why hadn't they been concerned about being identified in the morning, when there had been no attempt to disguise themselves or mask the licence plate of the Nova? On the evening of July 5, 1984, how had they known that the Buxbaum car would stop at about 7:15 P.M.? When Hanna was removed from the car to be shot, why had Roy been ordered to put his head down, while Helmuth was permitted to roam freely outside? Why had Helmuth been reluctant to admit that the car in the morning and in the evening was the same one? If Helmuth had never crossed the guardrail to comfort his wife, and was, as he had testified, on the road trying to flag down a passing truck when Hanna was shot, how had he been able to tell trucker Colin Lawrence that the victim had been shot in the head?

Promising to deal with each of these dark questions in the course of his remarks, Martin turned his attention to Eddie Greenspan's allegation that the Crown had called a host of prostitutes to blacken the accused's character, rather than dealing with facts relevant to the murder charge. Dispatching that contention with a single statistic, Martin pointed out that only four had testified, none of them to recount the accused's sexual proclivities: Susan Ambrose had been called to give evidence about Helmuth asking her to poison Hanna; Dawn Watson to testify that he had asked her to find someone to kill Hanna in a fake drowning, a staged robbery, or a kidnapping; Nafisha Somani because Helmuth had told her he was unhappy with his wife and wanted the prostitute to have his child; and Corinne Willoughby because she could show that Helmuth's mainlining of cocaine had begun before his friendship with Robert Barrett.

Much of the defence case rested on depicting the post-stroke Helmuth as the unwitting "sucker of all time," who was led into the netherworld of drugs and prostitutes by the calculating Robert Barrett. Martin once again strongly challenged that picture, reminding jurors that the accused's adulterous ways had begun in 1967, and that he had, in fact, been as promiscuous before his stroke as after it, a man who had taken out his sexual urges "on teenage kitchen maids in the backseat of a car at a drive-in movie theatre."

Like his adultery, Helmuth's drug use had also predated his stroke. Martin pointed out to jurors that he had used cocaine with Cathy Russell and Corinne Willoughby before he had ever laid eyes on Robert Barrett. He also reminded them that Helmuth had eventually developed at least four drug contacts in London, a heavy blow to the defence contention that the accused had been totally dependent on Robert Barrett for cocaine. As his actions became more depraved, his life of hypocrisy had taken a deadly turn. The accused had gone from a man who complained to a bevy of prostitutes and pushers about his fat and sexually unappealing wife, to a cold-blooded schemer bent on arranging her death.

Martin bluntly told the jury that Helmuth's $5,000 payment to Robert Barrett on May 24, 1984, had simply been part of a $25,000 murder contract on Hanna Buxbaum's life. As for Helmuth's story that the money had been paid to arrange a cocaine connection in Florida, Martin was convincingly contemptuous. Barrett had headed off to Orlando with $3,500 in his jeans, not "*Miami Vice*-type Florida big-time money." Who would ever take him seriously as a major cocaine buyer when all he had was the kind of drug money that normally changed hands in Kelly's Bar?

More to the point, Martin asked, where had the photographs of Hanna and the family car that Barrett had given to Ringuette and McCurdy come from? If, as the defence claimed, Barrett had decided to kill Hanna after he was fired, he would no longer have had access to the house. There could only be one answer: the photographs had been given to him by Helmuth Buxbaum.

The time had come for Martin to use what the Crown team saw as Helmuth's self-incriminating slip during his examination-in-chief by Greenspan. Quoting Helmuth's reply to his own lawyer's question as to whether there had been any further conversation with Robert Barrett after the accused had given him the fur coat at Komoka on the late afternoon of July 4, Martin hoped to strike a fatal blow for the prosecution. He quoted Helmuth from the transcript: "He wanted me to follow him out to the 402 and I said, 'There's just no way.'" What, Martin, thundered, did the 402 – the highway where Hanna Buxbaum would be murdered twenty-four hours later – have to do with the exchange of the fur coat?

After a luncheon recess, Martin made the most devastating comment of his summation when describing the Buxbaums' morning stop on Highway 402. "Contract murderers," he told the jury, "do not go out on the highway and wait, hoping that their innocent victim will innocently stop in order to be killed. Buxbaum stopped because he knew the Nova with the killers would be there, and he stopped behind them so that the killers could do their murderous work."

The point was a deadly one. If Helmuth were telling the truth when he claimed not to be involved in the murder plot, then the jury would have to believe that the killers had coincidentally positioned themselves on the route the Buxbaums would take both that morning and evening with absolutely no assurance that their victim could be induced to stop – in effect, murder by wishful thinking. As Martin proceeded to argue, the fact that the killers were at the right spot at the right time was no more of a coincidence than that they hadn't been disguised in the morning – an unnecessary precaution then because Helmuth had been the only other person in the Buxbaum station wagon.

The defence had dismissed as lies testimony from Allen and Armes that there had been a conversation with Helmuth about getting in touch with Robert Barrett after the abortive morning attempt on Hanna's life. In Armes' case, Greenspan had argued that he had concocted the story to get a deal with the Crown, a supposition Martin exploded by reminding jurors that Armes had first mentioned the damning conversation to Const. Mel Getty before he had even given his first formal police statement on August 29, 1984. The proof of that claim was contained in the constable's notebook.

Martin contended that, before the next attempt on Hanna's life, the accused and his fellow conspirators had had to communicate the change in plans, and invited the jury to accept Robert Barrett's testimony that Helmuth had called Barrett at the Westbury Hotel from Pearson Airport. Their only other option was to believe Helmuth's story that he had, in fact, called Lucy Addis, a call he had admittedly lied about to his nephew. And although the defence had promised to produce the woman the accused had allegedly spoken to that day, Greenspan hadn't kept his promise. It would be up to the jury to decide what that meant.

The jurors were presented with more unanswered questions when

Martin took them through the ghastly details of Hanna's execution. If Helmuth had really believed that the disabled car belonged to his neighbours, the Richardsons, why had he turned off the ignition when he realized his mistake? Since he testified that he had been out on the highway when the fatal shots rang out, how had he known that Hanna had been shot in the head? Finally, why hadn't he gone to his wife's side after her killers had fled the scene? As for Helmuth's claim that his behaviour at the scene had been influenced by his 1982 stroke, Martin was openly derisive: "Now, people with strokes still love and care for their spouses."

The portrait of Helmuth's guilt took on darker tones as Martin reviewed his actions in the days following Hanna's death. It seemed strange, Martin said, that the accused had not remembered the morning stop behind the murder car until July 7, two days after the crime. And if it was true that Robert Barrett had been facing death unless he could come up with $20,000 for 200 grams of cocaine, why had Helmuth, with a line of credit of $600,000, given him only $13,000 gathered from a suspiciously secretive variety of sources on July 6? And if Barrett had really needed the money as a matter of life and death, why would he spend $1,700 of the desperately needed funds on drugs at the London airport when there were supposed to be 200 grams of cocaine waiting for him in Toronto? Only if the jury believed in carrying coals to Newcastle could the preposterous story be believed, or so Martin argued.

Daniel Borland's evidence of a jailhouse confession from Robert Barrett was dismissed as the false testimony of a man hoping for a reward from the wealthy accused. Why, Martin wondered, would Barrett tell a perfect stranger such dangerous secrets, and then ask him not to tell Pat Allen, Barrett's "joint partner" and closest associate? Nor did Borland's testimony square with evidence from at least four other witnesses who claimed that Barrett had told them of Helmuth's desire to dispose of his wife as early as January 1984 – long before he ever decided to carry out the plot. Eddie Greenspan had argued that Barrett had lied to people like Ringuette and Pat Allen about Helmuth's involvement to convince them that they would be paid for the hit. But what possible reason would Barrett have for telling Debbie Barber the same story in January 1984?

In considering the reason behind the crime, Martin philosophized that human actions are seldom directed by a single motive. In the Buxbaum murder, there were a number of possibilities: What would happen to Helmuth's nursing-home licences if the government found out that he was "a womanizing cocaine addict," as they surely would have had Hanna lived long enough to denounce Robert Barrett to the police? What would happen to him at the psychiatric hospital the family was pressuring him to check into after their European vacation? A contested divorce would have been unpleasant for the children and sparked serious financial problems for the accused. Helmuth's debauched life style required large amounts of cash, making Hanna's life insurance policy an attractive side benefit of the murder.

In the end, Martin offered the jury the law, instead of an easy answer about what had triggered Hanna's murder: "Much of the behaviour of Buxbaum which has been described in the evidence is bizarre. Befuddled actions of a frightened man: a millionaire flying to Europe on People's Express with a prostitute from London, Ontario; a businessman hanging out in Kelly's Bar with teenage women and drug addicts; a church-going husband asking prostitutes to bear children. We may never be able to unravel the twisted thoughts of Helmuth Buxbaum. It is not necessary to do so."

The jury, Martin reminded the twelve men and women in front of him, could convict the accused without the Crown proving a motive for his crime. And convict him they should given the alternative of believing that Barrett, Allen, Armes, Pitcher, Barber, Ringuette, McCurdy, Watson, and Ambrose were all lying whenever their testimony conflicted with Buxbaum's.

Martin ended his address with an elegant comparison: "There is an old magician's trick in which, as the theatre audience watches, the magician makes an elephant disappear . . . The essence of the trick, and it *is* a trick, is to distract all of the audience's attention while the elephant is led off the stage. Well, in this case, the elephant is the guilt of Buxbaum . . . The distraction is provided by Mr. Greenspan when he condemns Barrett, Allen, Armes, Susan Ambrose, Dawn Watson, the Crown, the police, and in effect everybody; everybody lies if they conflict with Buxbaum . . . Therefore, I submit to you that you shouldn't lose sight of the elephant, which is the guilt of Buxbaum. Look upon the conduct of Helmuth Buxbaum for what it is, the conduct of a guilty man."

With Michael Martin's final words, Judge John O'Driscoll adjourned proceedings until February 11, a week-long recess during which he would fashion his charge to the jury out of the thousands of pages of notes he had taken while trying to absorb a mountain of information from 89 witnesses and 160 exhibits.

When court reconvened, Judge O'Driscoll asked the jury to keep their minds focused on a single question: had the Crown proven beyond a reasonable doubt that the accused had arranged the murder of Hanna Buxbaum? In offering that direction, he cautioned them not to pass judgement on Helmuth Buxbaum's morals or his sexual predilections. Deflating Eddie Greenspan's sinister interpretation of the plea bargains the Crown had negotiated with certain witnesses, Judge O'Driscoll advised the jury that it was a commonplace of the system. He also defined the section of the Criminal Code dealing with insanity before dismissing its application in the matter under consideration, despite the evidence of doctors Bray and Malcolm. "In this case, there is no evidence of, indeed there is no suggestion of, any insanity."

After he summarized the evidence of both the Crown and the defence, Judge O'Driscoll made a dramatic request of the jury. Telling them to assume that everything about the accused's testimony was true, that he had not accompanied the killers to select a murder site on July 4, that the morning stop on Highway 402 had been mere coincidence, and that he hadn't recognized Pat Allen or the blue Nova from any previous dealings, the judge wanted them to reflect on something of such fundamental importance to the case that its understanding might clarify the dread matter before them:

"When you are deliberating, perhaps you can consider this question. It is a question that I have considered many, many times and I always come up with the same answer . . . How is it that two out of three of those same 'creeps' just happen to be on the side of 402 Highway some ten hours later when Helmuth Buxbaum is returning home, and they are situated where they are situated and they lured him to drive past his exit in order that he could render assistance to the two of them, two of the same people in the very same car? I ask you, is there more than one answer to that question?"

Greenspan was flabbergasted. Judge O'Driscoll had clearly meant exactly what he had said in denying an eleventh-hour defence motion aimed at preventing him from expressing an opinion on the evidence before the court. With the defence team in shock at the judge's devastating intervention, some of the most powerful words of the entire proceedings now came down from the bench. If the jury accepted the Crown's version of events, Judge O'Driscoll soberly observed, then the accused had delivered his wife up, "not only once, but twice on the same day to her executioners."

At 1:14 P.M. on the afternoon of February 12, the weightiest task of the criminal justice system fell to two machine operators, two teachers, a retailer of cake decorations, an engineer, a corporate vice-president, a transmission inspector, a quality-control operator, a millwright, an electrician, and a housewife.

Judgement day was at hand.

17

LIFE

"I asked the psychiatrist to kill me . . . One time, I lost the
ability to speak at one of the sessions I had with him . . . I hit
my head on the wall of my cell which resulted in a cut on my
forehead, a broken nose and a cut lip (I was taken to
hospital) . . . I wrote 10 poems, some of them rather weird. I
mutilated myself by trying to cut off my penis."
– *Helmuth Buxbaum, from the hole in Millhaven penitentiary*

Justice dealt a swift blow to Helmuth Buxbaum at 1:53 P.M. on the
afternoon of February 13, 1986. It had taken jury just twelve and a half
hours to boil down sixty-eight days of sensational evidence, conflicting
testimony, forensic tests, psychiatric assessments, and legal jousting to a
single word: guilty. Helmuth sat emotionless in the prisoner's box, staring straight ahead as jury foreman Keith Hancock, a General Motors
worker, announced the accused man's conviction on the charge of first
degree murder. A disappointed Eddie Greenspan lowered his eyes,
clasped his hands in front of him, and quietly asked the court clerk to
poll the jury. The disbelieving convict turned his head towards the jury
box, and peered into the faces of the men and women who would not
meet his gaze as, one by one, they repeated their unanimous verdict.

Mr. Justice John O'Driscoll asked Helmuth if he had any final remarks.
"My Lord, I am not guilty of the charge," the convicted man whispered.
Since conviction for first degree murder carries an automatic prison term
of twenty-five years with no possibility of parole, Judge O'Driscoll immediately pronounced sentence. Before removing the prisoner, Const.
Mel Getty told Helmuth to put his arms behind his back to be hand-
cuffed.

"Why? You never did that before?" he asked.

"You were innocent before. Now you're a convicted wife-killer." the
police officer replied.

Moments later, Helmuth Buxbaum was hustled through the crush of reporters waiting outside the courtroom and driven back to the detention centre, where he would spend the next month awaiting assignment to a federal penitentiary. Weary of the reflected glare of their father's notoriety, none of the Buxbaum children had attended court to hear the verdict.

"I would say in the back of their minds, they didn't know which way it was going to go," Pastor Doug Dakin told journalists after he telephoned Komoka to advise the six children of their father's conviction. (He was too late; a reporter had already called.) "They heard [things] that they haven't heard before in their lives during this trial, and they had to learn to understand and care for their dad. They didn't know what to do if he got out, and they didn't know what to do if he [stayed] in."

There was no such ambivalence in the stern face of Eddie Greenspan as he emerged from Courtroom 10 after losing the biggest case of his career. Long before the jury had finished deliberating, the veteran defence counsel was marshalling the arguments he planned to use to win his client a new trial: "Round one and *only* round one is over," he declared. "Round two begins now."

Throughout the trial, Greenspan had repeatedly objected to Judge O'Driscoll's willingness to let Crown prosecutors delve into his outwardly pious client's double life of tawdry sex and illegal drugs. Though irrelevant to the murder charge, that salacious evidence had been used with devastating effect to poison the minds of the jurors against the accused man, or so Helmuth's lawyer argued.

Greenspan had, in fact, wasted little time before locking horns with the judge. Immediately after the jury had retired to consider its verdict, he harangued the court for two hours over what he saw as Judge O'Driscoll's one-sided charge, a judicial intervention he believed had voyaged well beyond the points of law at issue to an expression of support for the Crown's position. "You made it clear to the jury that you feel Mr. Buxbaum is guilty and should be convicted," he said. "The words Your Lordship has put to the jury can leave no reasonable person with any other view."

After hearing the jury's verdict, the flamboyant lawyer vowed to appear on the steps of Ontario's Court of Appeal at ten the next morning with a customized valentine for the Crown and the judge: a list of the forty-nine grounds he would use to begin the process he hoped would lead to a new trial for his now convicted client.

It was a promise Eddie Greenspan never kept.

✦ ✦ ✦

Helmuth Buxbaum's troubles quickly multiplied. In the wake of his conviction, he was inundated by painful lawsuits. Isbrandt Buxbaum was the first family member to seek damages from the millionaire-convict. In his statement of claim, Isbrandt sought compensation for the "severe and traumatic mental and emotional upset and nervous shock" Helmuth had inflicted on Roy Buxbaum by exposing him to Hanna's execution.

The civil suit also claimed compensation for Roy's sister, Karen. Isbrandt's lawyers argued that Hanna Buxbaum had promised to finance Karen's university education by providing her with free lodging at Komoka and paying her tuition at the University of Western Ontario. All told, the unemployed former taxi-company owner was asking for $405,000 in damages and medical expenses.

As bad as it was to be sued by the brother he had once idolized, the worst was yet to come for Helmuth. On June 27, 1986, three of the people closest to him – his eldest son, Paul, his most trusted business associate, Howard Johnson, and the guardian of his children, Pastor Doug Dakin – petitioned the Supreme Court of Ontario to have him declared legally dead. The bizarre but not unprecedented procedure of "disentitlement" would prevent Helmuth from benefiting from the will of the woman he now stood convicted of having murdered. (In her February 1981 will, Hanna Buxbaum left $200,000 to twenty-three charitable, relief, and missionary organizations; $3,000 apiece to each of her nieces and nephews; and the balance of her multimillion dollar estate to her husband. In the event of his death, the assets of the estate were to be divided equally among her six children.)

In their statement of claim, the three men, who were the administrators of Hanna's estate, laid out the cold calculation that their case rested on. "Buxbaum was in poor health at the time of the death of Hanna Buxbaum, having suffered a stroke in 1982 and having developed dependency upon dangerous and life-threatening drugs. Had Buxbaum not arranged the murder of Hanna Buxbaum, he would likely have predeceased her."

Their civil suit required a final act of penance from the still wealthy convict. The Buxbaum family wanted Helmuth to pay $100,000 in damages for arranging Hanna's slaying, another $500,000 in punitive damages for the pain and suffering he had inflicted on his own family, and a further $1,000,000 to replace the monies he had already drained from his wife's estate.

Even Christian Mutual Life, the New Hampshire insurance company that had arranged the $1-million policy on Hanna, got into the act. Lawyers for the firm asked the courts to declare the policy null and void so that Helmuth wouldn't be able to profit from the death of his victim.

Then came the most bitterly ironic suit of all – Helmuth's own civil action against the man who had so passionately pleaded his cause during his sensational criminal trial, tough-talking Eddie Greenspan.

The professional relationship between Helmuth Buxbaum and his counsel broke down the morning after the millionaire was sentenced to life imprisonment. Eddie Greenspan did not carry through on his promise to enter round two of the fight to free Helmuth. A spokesman for the law firm of Greenspan, Rosenberg explained that the appeal had been delayed by a procedural hitch; because Mr. Buxbaum was a federal inmate, his jailers at the Thorold Detention Centre had to pass the notice of appeal to the high court.

When a document was later filed with the court on February 20 saying that Helmuth would represent himself in the appeal, Greenspan dismissed the puzzling information as a "mere formality." He explained to the press that his firm was in the process of negotiating an appropriate fee for conducting the appeal and that he would be representing the millionaire convict before the appellate division of the Supreme Court of Ontario as soon as that process was complete. "In the event that a resolution was not reached between us within thirty days, I wanted to make sure that [notice] was filed," Greenspan added.

But there was more on the table than the $125,000 Greenspan wanted for handling Helmuth's appeal. There was also the matter of the unpaid balance of $165,259 owing on his invoice of $1,329,133, the largest bill ever presented by a lawyer for a criminal case in Canadian history. Helmuth refused to remit the unpaid balance and headed into court to find out why he had been charged so much in the first place. There were many red faces and raised eyebrows in Ontario's legal community as the press followed the controversial action with nearly as much alacrity as they had exhibited during the murder trial.

In an affidavit filed in the Supreme Court of Ontario in the summer of 1986, Helmuth claimed that one of the country's most outstanding lawyers had taken advantage of his client's vulnerable position and healthy bank balance. "He told me that I had the best lawyer in the country and that he does a better job when he is well paid," the unhappy convict complained, a remark that was denounced as fantasy by Robert Sheppard, one of Greenspan's law students who had worked on the case.

Helmuth acknowledged that he had initially agreed to pay Greenspan a retainer of $30,000, and fees of $275 an hour, or $2,750 a day. Shortly after his preliminary hearing, Helmuth had approved increases in Greenspan's hourly rate, and ultimately agreed to pay his lawyer's firm as much as $10,000 a day to handle his defence. He had also agreed to a bonus clause that would give Greenspan a separate payment beyond the normal fee for an acquittal. Their contract stated: "In the event of an acquittal, it is agreed that an additional sum of $250,000 (due to acquittal, and for no other reason) shall be paid forthwith to the firm of Greenspan, Rosenberg."

In a somewhat unusual move, Helmuth had agreed to have Greenspan's bills taxed (reviewed and approved) by an assessment officer with the Supreme Court of Ontario taxing office in Windsor. Every month from the beginning of the legal preparations until the end of the murder trial, Helmuth had signed a form consenting to the fees levied in the previous thirty days, waiving his right to have Greenspan justify the account in any other way. "Any concern I had over the mounting expenses was squelched by my feeling that a confrontation with Mr. Greenspan would have made him angry and perhaps caused him to abandon me," Helmuth claimed.

By the time the St. Catharines jury had brought in their verdict, Helmuth Buxbaum had paid his lawyer $1,106,730.78 – specifically, $971,600.50 in legal fees and $135,130.28 for hotel bills and other disbursements.

Helmuth's civil lawyer, J. J. Carthy, later said in court, "[Mr. Greenspan] should have said that 'no one has ever seen a published report of fees as high as I'm going to charge you' . . . He should have said, 'You should know I'm charging you top-of-the-line fees for losing this case.'"

In a subsequent affidavit, Helmuth added that he had been "like jelly in [Greenspan's] hands. I would have signed my death sentence if they had put it in front of me. I didn't know what I was signing."

The awe-struck innocent of Helmuth's affidavit was not the Helmuth Buxbaum that Eddie Greenspan knew. Buxbaum, Greenspan insisted, was acutely aware of what was happening in his case, and had formally agreed to it: "Every step of the way was authorized and approved by

Mr. Buxbaum, all of it in writing," Greenspan declared in his own affidavit. The Komoka millionaire had shown considerable "business acumen" in their dealings and had clearly understood that his account would be closed to further appeal after it was reviewed by the tax officer in Windsor.

Adamantly denying allegations that he had bullied Helmuth into the lucrative deal, Greenspan said his client had repeatedly declined to follow his advice that he obtain an independent legal opinion on their fee arrangement. That decision, Greenspan insisted, showed that Helmuth was "independent and was neither intimidated nor overpowered by me." As Greenspan's lawyer, future Supreme Court of Canada justice, John Sopinka, put it, "The brain damage [Helmuth's cerebral infarct] had nothing to do with his business acumen."

Greenspan took particular objection to the suggestion that he had had the taxing done in Windsor rather than in Toronto or London to ensure that his large bills would escape public attention and, perhaps, public opprobrium. The move, he claimed, had been designed to protect Buxbaum's best interests, not his lawyer's.

"Buxbaum agreed with me that it would be preferable if the taxations and approval proceeded in Windsor rather than Toronto or London because the fact of the taxation and approval, if discovered by the media, would be highly publicized and might be harmful to his defence," Greenspan swore. "Buxbaum and I believed the media would present Buxbaum as a rich man paying large sums to defend himself." Given what had happened at Helmuth's bail hearing, when the Crown effectively depicted Helmuth's offer to post a $1-million bail as a rich man's attempt to abuse the courts, the lawyer's point was well taken.

But Greenspan saved his best for last, noting that Buxbaum had never complained about fees or disbursements prior to his conviction; in fact, he had praised the handling of his case even after the defence had failed and the final bill had been tallied. In one of his many letters to Greenspan, Helmuth concluded that the defence counsel "did far better beyond expectation and the time spent in the courtroom was . . . of the highest level of professionalism and competence, even though we lost. Your greatful [sic] client and friend, Helmuth."

Ultimately, it was monies owing, not arguments offered, that created the legal technicality that put Helmuth Buxbaum's civil action against his former lawyer in limbo. Mr. Justice Samuel Hughes, the veteran of two complex royal commissions in Ontario, was not entirely persuaded by

Greenspan's comments about the fee dispute. Mr. Greenspan, Hughes observed, "blows hot and cold," a reference to the lawyer's depictions of convenience of his former client's mental abilities. At the criminal trial, Greenspan argued that Helmuth Buxbaum was a "mental cripple" who could not defend himself from small-time criminals in London – the sucker of all time; but when the venue shifted to the civil hearing, he was asking the judge to believe that the same Helmuth Buxbaum was a shrewd businessman who knew exactly what he was doing when he signed the complex legal documents authorizing his million-dollar defence.

Nevertheless, Hughes rejected Helmuth's bid to review his former lawyer's docketing practices, ruling that the challenge of the defence bill was premature because it hadn't been paid in full. If he paid the remaining $165,259 owing to Greenspan, the judge concluded, Helmuth would be entirely free to renew his challenge.

Uncertain about his finances pending the outcome of the other civil actions against him, Helmuth licked his wounds and dropped the case. Although he would soon find himself a new white knight to conduct his appeal, he had a more immediate problem to take care of – staying alive at Millhaven penitentiary.

To the men and women who ran Canada's correctional service, Helmuth Treugott Buxbaum was their worst nightmare. A quick glance at his previous institutional record showed both a suicide attempt and several jail-break schemes, harassment from other inmates bent on extorting money from the millionaire-convict, and a case that had become a national sensation. Worst of all, the problem he represented was long term; if his appeal failed, he wouldn't be eligible for full parole until July 23, 2009. For the lucky institution that drew him, inmate 929455B was a potential twenty-five-year headache.

Placed in super-maximum security, Helmuth began his sentence at Millhaven with a list of goals that provided his new keepers with a measure of comfort. Although he denied his guilt, he made clear that he wouldn't be taking out any frustrations he felt towards the justice system on prison authorities. He informed Millhaven personnel that he wanted to pursue his education with special emphasis on Bible studies. He also wanted to learn how to play a musical instrument and to indulge his passion for chess.

When he learned about the institution's private family visiting program, he enthusiastically enrolled, unaware, it seemed, that his children would not be nearly as anxious for a trailer visit with the man who had arranged their mother's murder as he was. As a correctional officer wrote after travelling to Komoka and interviewing one of his sons, "It seems unlikely . . . despite the size of the Buxbaum family that they will tax the visiting facilities in the institution. If Mark Buxbaum is indeed representative of the attitude of his brothers and sisters, visits may indeed be few and far between."

The first inkling Helmuth gave that he had more on his mind than becoming a chess-playing Bible student, who planned to spend his evenings watching educational TV until his conviction was overturned, surfaced in questions he asked about conjugal visits. The particular love interest he had in mind was Liza Dikih, a thirty-three-year-old mother of two from London, who had been visiting him in various prisons since the spring of 1985. Dikih had first met Helmuth at her brother's London jewellery store shortly before the Buxbaums left on their European trip. After his arrest, she visited him at the Elgin-Middlesex Detention Centre in the company of Mark Buxbaum.

During the course of their discreet prison visits, a romance blossomed, and Helmuth immediately requested trailer visits. Since inmates had to prove that a common-law relationship existed for at least six months prior to their most recent conviction before they were eligible for a conjugal visit, Helmuth's request was almost certainly doomed to fail. Everyone in Correctional Service Canada (CSC), including Helmuth's prison chaplain, Ian Davis-Young, had serious reservations about the wisdom of bending the rules.

"Mr. Buxbaum states that while he and Mrs. Dikih are very much in love and wish to marry, they wish and need to confirm their sexual compatibility before making a final decision. It seems to me that any relationship that has sexual functioning as its ultimate basis is asking for trouble. It also seems to this observer that Mr. Buxbaum's request is incompatible with his faith stance. Mr. Buxbaum is part of what may be termed conservative Protestantism, one of the strong beliefs of which is that sexual behaviour is to be reserved for a relationship of loving fidelity *within marriage* – sexual intercourse is not to be practised outside of the marriage bond. Therefore, in my opinion, Mr. Buxbaum's request compromises his own stated beliefs."

When Helmuth was officially informed that his request had been turned down, his new lawyer, Clayton Ruby, fired off a letter to Andrew

Graham, Ontario's Deputy Commissioner of CSC, pointing out certain inanities in the regulations and asking that the decision be reconsidered: "Helmuth Buxbaum is serving 25 years with no parole as a minimum penalty on a possible life sentence. He was convicted of murdering his wife! To suggest that a regulation ought to be applied to him which prevents a common-law relationship unless it has existed for a minimum of six months immediately prior to his conviction, is, in *his* case, to mean that he will never have a trailer visit . . . The content of the rule itself is a bit of moralistic nonsense. I suspect its object is to prevent prostitutes from plying their trade in institutions. That may be a laudable objective. But the rule goes far beyond what is necessary to achieve that limited purpose. On the present rule, Mr. Buxbaum could have a long-standing, close, intimate relationship of a non-sexual nature with Ms. Dikih for twenty years and still not be allowed to have sex with her."

The system held fast. Helmuth next asked Dikih to make a matrimonial application to the Attorney-General, much to the consternation of his children and their guardian, Pastor Doug Dakin. When word of the proposed nuptials leaked out, Helmuth Buxbaum was once again front-page news. Editors were captivated by the fact that he was remarrying just five months after being convicted of murdering his former wife. A story on the front page of the *Toronto Star*, which was carried under pictures of Helmuth and Hanna, featured quotes from staffers in the Attorney-General's Office commenting on the proposed marriage.

If anyone in custody wants to marry, approval must first be sought from the Attorney-General, to guard against manipulation of the justice system. If investigation showed, for example, that a convict awaiting appeal planned to marry a prosecution witness, the wedding bells wouldn't be permitted to ring. In Buxbaum's case, the investigation produced no reason to deny the marriage application. The only thing open to public debate was whether Liza Dikih had been smitten with Helmuth or his bank balance. But when then Attorney-General Ian Scott gave Helmuth the go-ahead to marry, a barrage of letters to the editor lambasted his decision:

One man wrote, in a letter typical of the public's response, "When this abomination becomes a reality, this convicted murderer and his wife will have conjugal visits of three days every three months at a trailer on the prison grounds. Well why stop there? Why not just let the poor man go, he could come back to the penitentiary on weekends – if it wouldn't be too inconvenient. This damn lunacy must really stop. Instead of receiving the death penalty for premeditated murder, this convicted wife-slayer is given something he deprived his first wife of – another chance. The inmates are running the asylum." – Walter A. Blunt

It was precisely the kind of media attention that prison authorities abhor. Fearful that repeated accounts of Buxbaum's marriage plans, which always included prominent reference to his fortune, would lead to fresh extortion attempts at Millhaven, prison officials suddenly found themselves confronted by something far worse than bad publicity – the first attempt on the celebrity inmate's life since his transfer to a federal penitentiary.

The August 16, 1986, attack took place while Helmuth stood outside the locked gym waiting for the doors to open. The man standing immediately in front of him suddenly wheeled around and drove a piece of straightened wire from a chain-link fence into Helmuth's abdomen. At the same time, a second man standing behind him plunged a syringe filled with battery acid into Helmuth's back, puncturing his liver. When the stabber tried to withdraw his weapon, the wire snagged on Helmuth's rib-cage. Every time his attacker tried to pull it free, all he managed to do was drag his victim closer to him. Luckily for Helmuth, the sudden, forward jerks prevented the other man from emptying the entire contents of the syringe into his liver.

After recovering their weapons, his assailants had fled, confident that the well-known consequences of breaking the inmate code of silence would be enough to keep Helmuth from exposing them. When the wounded man sought medical attention, personnel at the nursing station called the prison's chief of security. Helmuth refused to identify his attackers and was immediately placed in solitary confinement in the prison hospital.

A spokesman for CSC, Dennis Curtis, explained to a curious press that Buxbaum's silence was not surprising. "Under these circumstances, it is usually better for one's health to keep quiet."

Alone yet again, Helmuth slipped into deadly despair. "I asked the psychiatrist to kill me," Buxbaum wrote on December 14, 1986. "One time, I lost the ability to speak at one of the sessions I had with him . . . I hit my head on the wall of my cell which resulted in a cut on my forehead, a broken nose and a cut lip (I was taken to hospital) . . . I wrote 10 poems, some of them rather weird. I mutilated myself by trying to cut off my penis."

During his five-month hospital stay, authorities at Millhaven struggled to develop a plan for dealing with Helmuth Buxbaum. It was now out of the question to return him to the general population, where they feared he might be murdered. But segregation, it seemed, was no longer a viable alternative to a risky existence in the general population.

Just two weeks before the attack, guards searching Helmuth's cell had found two paper cups filled with sixty assorted tablets, a cache they had concluded he may have been hoarding for another suicide attempt. Since Helmuth wasn't far enough into his sentence to qualify for anything less than an s6 security level, even a transfer to Warkworth Institution was out of the question. Needing to be in Ontario to have any chance of family visits, the only alternative appeared to be protective custody at Kingston penitentiary.

Complicating matters even further, Helmuth himself opposed such a move, calling Kingston "unsanitary, rat-infested, and dilapidated." Other inmates had warned him that "KP" was well known in the system as the institution of choice for informers, who later ran the risk of becoming targets of prisoner justice when transferred to other penitentiaries. Even after authorities informed Helmuth that the dreaded Gary Foshay would soon begin serving his fifteen-year sentence for second degree murder at Millhaven (Hanna's executioner was convicted on October 10, 1986, after a six-week trial) he begged to be allowed to stay in segregation rather than be moved to Kingston. "I have gotten use to solitary now and I am content to stay where I am," he wrote. "I am safe here and have all [the] things that I need."

The warden wasn't persuaded. He ordered prison psychiatric and medical personnel to assess the controversial inmate as part of an inter-disciplinary CSC team tasked with examining a proposal for his *involuntary* transfer to Kingston Penitentiary. A new CAT-scan carried out at Kingston General Hospital confirmed the results of Helmuth's 1982 test: he was suffering from a brain lesion that extended into the frontal lobe. "The findings at this time show the extension of the tissue loss that has occurred, involving primarily the basal ganglia and the parietal lobe, both in the right middle cerebral territory. As a consequence of the loss of tissue, some atrophy which involves primarily the frontal and parietal lobes on the right side is evident."

When the staff doctors had finished their work, Millhaven's warden wasn't the only person they informed about the results of their probing into Helmuth Buxbaum's damaged brain. Dr. D. G. Workman was so disturbed by what he found that, on October 20, 1986, he wrote to Clayton Ruby, voluntarily sharing some disturbing information.

"I am writing to you in connection with my position as the physician at Millhaven Prison and my interviews and review of the laboratory and other investigations on Mr. Helmuth Buxbaum. Although I am neither a neurologist or a psychiatrist, and I am not well versed in the definition of legal sanity, I am concerned that Mr. Buxbaum's condition may certainly be one which would render him incapable of being responsible for his actions. Briefly, the neurological findings and CAT scan have shown damage which could make him incapable of forming rational judgments or having normal feelings in terms of guilt, et cetera. I have briefly discussed this with the prison psychiatrist, Dr. George Scott, who states that certainly Mr. Buxbaum is a 'primitive man.' I have not discussed this matter with Mr. Buxbaum and would not intend to raise it, but I thought you should be aware of my concerns in this matter."

For months, Clayton Ruby had been strangely troubled by his new client and Dr. Workman's unsolicited professional concerns finally made him realize why: what if Helmuth Buxbaum were insane?

18

THE OTHER ELEPHANT

"In my opinion, Helmuth Buxbaum was insane at the time of the offence . . . The evidence is overwhelming that he has, and had, Organic Brain Disease . . . Whether something was legal, right or wrong, was not something which his brain could address."

— *Dr. Robert Hill, psychiatrist, December 13, 1988*

Since the day he was arrested in Harvard Square for joining a Congress of Racial Equality picket line, Clayton Ruby has burned with a public passion for social justice. Twenty-five years after the *enfant terrible* of Toronto's Forest Hill village had his encounter with rifle-butt justice in Lyndon Johnson's America, Ruby had become one of Canada's high-profile champions of human and civil rights, a kind of Superman in bencher's robes to a cast of rebels, outcasts, protesters, tragic figures, and libertarian zanies, who for one reason or another had run afoul of the law.

Some said his concern for the underdog came from the way his own father, Lou Ruby, had been rebuffed by the anti-semitic Toronto establishment of his day; others claimed that his mistrust of the system flowed from the his realization that historically the most dangerous occupation in the world was being a Jew. Whatever drove him to tilt against the system that liked to claim him as one of its own, it was clear that he operated with a wider humanity than most. The father who gently taught his daughter, Emma, that Jews were sometimes punished merely for being Jewish was also the lawyer whose firm had defended the Canadian immigrant and former terrorist, Mahmoud Mohammad Issa Mohammad.

Helmuth Buxbaum had found the perfect replacement for Eddie Greenspan – a knight who passionately entered the lists on behalf of the dispossessed and despised, and whose lance, if anything, was even sharper.

Long before Ruby received Dr. Workman's disturbing letter, he had been puzzled by his new client's unpredictable nature. At times, Helmuth Buxbaum seemed perfectly in touch with reality, expressing himself articulately (especially over the details of Ruby's fees) and responding swiftly to sound advice. He had, for example, immediately withdrawn his application to marry Liza Dikih in 1986 after Ruby had pointed out that the wedding would not be in the best interests of his pending trip to the appeal courts.

At other times, it was as if Helmuth were in psychological combat with the world as it was, a child rearranging toy soldiers on the dishevelled bedclothes of his life. The first casualty in the convict's on-again, off-again quarrel with reality was his judgement. In particular, Ruby had been struck by Helmuth's uncritical zeal to blame his conviction on a justice system that had failed him spectacularly at every step of the process – the same frontal assault on the facts that had suggested to psychiatrists at Elgin-Middlesex Detention Centre that he was exhibiting "massive denial" of his situation.

No one in the judicial system was spared the prisoner's bitter denunciations in the daily letters he wrote to Ruby from solitary confinement in Millhaven and Kingston penitentiaries. Eddie Greenspan was now the most tactless, egotistical, money-grubbing person Helmuth had ever met, "a pompous, pouting, pussy pimple on the behind of the press."

The client who had once written that his lawyer's performance had exceeded his highest expectations, now complained that he had been the victim of professional neglect. Greenspan had been careless in his preparation of witnesses, allowing them to fall prey to "police tricks," he claimed. Even his lawyer's marathon address to the jury now became part of the reason Helmuth had been convicted; the judge and jurors had been "annoyed" by Greenspan's lengthy speech and took out their displeasure on the accused. He wrote, "I believe that Eddie does not see that . . . since he says he wants to die during a jury address . . . He made me die instead."

Helmuth had also suffered at the hands of ruthless police officers and scheming Crown prosecutors who padded the case against him with titillating stories about prostitutes and illegal drugs to secure his conviction – and the promotions they lusted after. Using the same elastic logic that characterized his rants, he argued that it had been a violation of his basic right of freedom of religion even to raise his private vices, since the Lord had long since wiped those black marks from Helmuth's moral ledger. If the courts themselves were not so essentially ungodly, they would not have so badly misunderstood the Christian doctrine of forgiveness.

"After my affairs (adultery)," he wrote. "I always confessed to Hanna (whom I had sinned against) and she forgave me. Now, according to my religion, when the offended person forgives, and God also forgives (because I repented my sins and asked God to forgive me) then . . . no man (and that includes any . . . level of civil or criminal court) can hold a sin against me according to the Bible."

His religious insight prompted him to offer some advice to his new counsel. "You could call one or two 'expert theologians' as witnesses who would confirm this. Since the Charter of Rights guarantees that my religious beliefs will be respected by any Canadian court of law, my trial, filled with accusations of adultery and abuse of my body with cocaine, was violating my constitutional rights of freedom of religion. Just for this reason alone, the court should set aside the past trial and order one without smear tactics where I truly get a fair trial . . . I can back up my opinion with many scripture references if you wish to know them."

If there had been any doubt that the Crown attorney was out to get him, Helmuth insisted, it had been swept away with Michael Martin's damning, post-verdict interview with reporters: "The penny really dropped when, after the verdict, Martin carelessly told the reporters that he really wanted Buxbaum and Foshay; he did not really care about getting Allen and Barrett."

After reading a book about Donald Marshall, Helmuth sent $2,000 to the Micmac who had been wrongfully imprisoned for eleven years by Nova Scotia's tainted justice system. "*Justice Denied* reminds me a lot of the Crown's witnesses used at my trial. So many testimonies were the result of police coaching – lies which had been placed in their mouths. The public inquiry with Donald Marshall will demonstrate how low the police is [sic] willing to lower its ethical standards if they want to get a conviction."

The Crown's handmaiden, Mr. Justice John O'Driscoll, had coaxed the jury into returning a guilty verdict, or at least he had according to the convicted killer. After rereading the judge's charge, Helmuth was enraged at what he saw as Judge O'Driscoll's misrepresentation of the evidence and influence of the jurors to convict an innocent man, all to even an old score with Eddie Greenspan and to get promotions for the Crown team. Although his own accusers had never supplied any motives for his murder of Hanna, Helmuth expounded on more than a few to account for what he saw as their sinister manipulations of justice:

"The whole trial did not produce any motive on my part for the murder of Hanna. The judge said that they could have the cake (evidence) without the icing (motive). I think the hanging judge knew that all the Crown would get promotions (and they did) if they got a conviction . . .

"All of man's actions are motivated. But in my case, the judge told the jury that even though there was no motive at all on my part (Barrett had a lot of motive) the murder did not have to have a motive. Now that is ridiculous!! I suppose he implied that I habitually went around murdering?!? His address to the jury left me almost breathless. How could a highly educated man, given the ultimate authority over Canadian citizens, be so unfair, callous, and unlogical [sic]? . . . Perhaps it was just a way of telling Mr. Greenspan that he [Judge O'Driscoll] was the final authority and that he was displeased with his [Greenspan's] bluffing, and expressions of anger; or perhaps it was a way to settle an old vendetta between the two."

But even if all else in his trial had been handled properly, Helmuth contended, the incompetence of his jury of amateurs would likely have resulted in the wrong verdict in any case. It would have taken a panel of lawyers, he argued, to properly consider the mountain of detail in the complex trial; instead, he had been saddled with people who didn't even know how to take proper notes, and who lacked the intelligence to draw the correct inferences from the testimony they had listened to uncomprehendingly for sixty-eight days. "For court lawyers, it probably is easy to follow, but to say that an average intelligence jury could put the pieces together is like expecting a parapelegic [sic] to climb Mount Everest!!" he bristled.

In the end, it had been easier for the jury to grasp the salacious accounts of the media and the Crown's day-long address, than to follow Eddie Greenspan's often complex line of questioning and epic summation. Helmuth admitted that he himself had often been confused by Greenspan's questioning of witnesses on cross-examination, so what could he expect from a group of people that took their task so lightly that during *voir dires* the jury room was often filled with the sound of prolonged laughter? "The jurors were a very insincere group of people . . ." he wrote. "The behaviour of the jury alone should guarantee me a new trial. Perhaps someone should check how much my jury consumed in alcoholic beverages during their deliberations on Feb. 12, 13/86!!"

Incompetent defence lawyers, corrupt police, ambitious prosecutors, a vindictive judge, simple-minded and possibly inebriated jurors, and a scandal-mongering press – the sorry gang, according to Helmuth, that had stripped him of his freedom after his day in kangaroo court. By the end of 1986, he had become so overwrought by the stunning injustice he had suffered, he began to think that he was slipping into insanity. "Sometimes I feel that mentally I am starting to split away from my soul," he wrote to Clayton Ruby. "The suicide rate this year is three times what it was during '84 and '85 in Millhaven Pen'. It was on the news; I don't want to be one of the statistics."

To Helmuth's lawyer, the only thing more disturbing than his client's analysis of how he had been convicted was his peculiar notion of who might be able to get him out of prison. The flip side to Helmuth's unshakeable conviction that the outside world and, in particular, the justice system was run by corrupt officials was that the prisons were filled with ministering angels like convicted killer Peter Demeter.

The Crown's case against Buxbaum was based entirely on "rehearsed perjuries," Demeter wrote to Ruby on October 21, 1986. The one-time Toronto real-estate mogul, who was serving a life sentence for the 1973 murder of his wife, claimed that he had learned about the miscarriage of justice during a pair of jailhouse conversations with Robert Barrett in 1984. "A slight, young man, The Squirrel (R. Barrett), searched me out within a few minutes of his arrival on our range," Demeter wrote, adding that the meeting had occurred before he was placed in segregation on November 4, 1984. "He seemed to know all about me and my case, [and] wanted to know everything about Eddie Greenspan."

Barrett had just heard that Helmuth had retained the crack criminal lawyer, and knowing that Greenspan had unsuccessfully assisted in Demeter's murder defence, wanted to find out all he could about his courtroom style. For nearly two hours, the young inmate paced the prison range listening to everything the experienced lifer had to say.

Demeter claimed that, at a second encounter, Barrett opened the conversation by saying that the Buxbaum case was "completely identical" to his own prosecution eleven years earlier; just as Demeter had done no wrong, neither had Helmuth Buxbaum. "He said Buxbaum knew nothing, had no part in his wife's murder," Demeter reported. But in what promised to be a sensational case, police investigators and Crown prosecutors were "dead set to hang that blame" on Helmuth.

According to Demeter, Barrett explained that force of circumstance had driven him, and him alone, to plot the murder of Hanna Buxbaum. Demeter recalled Barrett saying, "I had to get rid of the old scumball. She threatened to finger me to the police after I spent months getting Helmuth hooked on drugs." According to Demeter, Barrett simply couldn't afford to let that happen. "He mentioned how his entire lifestyle changed on account of Helmuth's money and largess. He made a bloody killing on the whores alone. 'You sir, as a businessman yourself, can appreciate that I had to protect my investment. On the coke alone, I made exactly double on each and every delivery, charged for half the weight the full price, then sold the other half [at] the going rate again.'"

Barrett said that he and his associates were prepared to reveal the truth to the authorities, but only if Buxbaum paid them $250,000, Demeter reported.

A man with complaints of his own against the Canadian justice system, Demeter concluded that Robert Barrett and the other conspirators had simply cut self-serving deals with the Crown when Helmuth Buxbaum's preliminary hearing began the following autumn. He also believed that daily reports in the *Globe and Mail* clearly demonstrated that the Crown's chief witnesses had crafted a complex but transparent set of lies to frame the Komoka millionaire: "All the Barrett-Gang with their sweetheart deals [were] singing the total fabrications that the Crown wanted from them . . . I was never more convinced of their rehearsed perjuries than when Mrs. B. allegedly spoke English to Helmuth Buxbaum just before her execution."

Neither the Hungarian-born Demeter, nor his Austrian wife of six and a half years, Christine, had spoken English as their first language, a fact that had conferred a singular habit. "I never spoke a single word in any other language but German in times of heightened anxiety, like driving situations, fights, urgent messages on the phone," he explained. He was convinced that the German-speaking Buxbaums shared the same practice: "It is utterly inconceivable for that German-born-raised-educated-married-to woman to utter any other last appeals but in her native, accustomed, between-them-only, language of endearment."

Demeter had begun by detailing his own theory about the Buxbaum trial in letters to Eddie Greenspan and Ontario's Attorney-General, Ian Scott, in mid-December 1985. The inmate was horrified when his former lawyer's office responded that they couldn't decipher his handwriting, so they would send an associate to visit him *after* the trial. Eddie

Greenspan had apparently seen enough of Peter Demeter to realize his value as a character witness. Demeter was outraged: "The H. B. trial would have an entirely different outcome since I know what happened, crown witnesses-wise, illegal deals, prepaid perjuries-wise, as I was already through all that and more – much, much more over the last 13 years + . . ." he wrote to Clayton Ruby. "My evidence is not *new* evidence as far as your appeal is concerned! It was the strongest piece of exonerating material the defense had available at trial!"

Demeter insisted that his offer to help Helmuth was based on nothing more than a simple desire for justice: "I never knew about H. B., let alone met him in my entire 53 years until his sad situation got similar headlines. (July is gurken season for the media!) I have zilch interest in his trials and tribulations; (I lost my father and two adult brothers in the last six weeks of Hitler's war in Jan./Feb. 1945 – I have minimal love for East Prussians to begin with. But I set down and did the following out of my needs of fair play (if there is any such animal in Canadian courts)."

Demeter wasn't the only saviour behind prison walls. Patrick Kelly, a former RCMP officer who steadfastly maintained his innocence after his own 1984 conviction for murdering his wife, promised to get Buxbaum confidential police reports, which he claimed would outline the real story of how the wealthy businessman had been falsely convicted. Despite his suspicions that Kelly was just another fraud artist or, worse, an undercover plant working for the police, Buxbaum excitedly pursued the inmate's offer to access the police reports for a fee: "He knows a lot about government and its workings . . . I think he has some pretty creative and stimulating ideas, most of which I concur with," he told Clayton Ruby.

And then there was Peter Dale MacDonald. In a series of letters to crime reporters and a number of Ontario lawyers, the convicted thief insisted that he, too, knew the tawdry details of Robert Barrett's monstrous perjury, information Barrett had allegedly shared with him while the two men were lovers in Laval penitentiary. "Barrett told me that he felt extremely bad for what he was doing and that if he knew for certain that he wouldn't get recharged and that the deal would still stand with the police, then he would change his testimony," MacDonald wrote to one journalist. But ultimately, MacDonald claimed, Barrett had been too afraid of what would happen if he reneged on his deal. Instead, he had asked MacDonald to discredit *him* as a Crown witness by testifying for the defence at Buxbaum's trial about their jailhouse pillow talk.

In making his bizarre claim, MacDonald had indignantly denied allegations by Crown prosecutor Michael Martin that he and other inmates of Laval were simply trying to swindle Helmuth Buxbaum:

"A few of us guys were blamed for starting a conspiracy while at Laval to discredit Barrett, yet Barrett approached me with the idea . . . Barrett . . . wrote me several letters afterwards, little cards, when I was in Cowansville, and one of those cards said, 'Pete, please don't get in touch with Greenspan after all, okay, because I'm scared that the police, Piers, will make it hard for me.'"

Acting on his own initiative, MacDonald, like Peter Demeter, had first contacted Eddie Greenspan's office and attempted to expose the deceitful trap that London junkies and Crown prosecutors were supposedly laying for Helmuth Buxbaum. But the police "spread acute propaganda to the defense personnel so they couldn't and wouldn't deem me creditable enough to help their client, Helmuth Buxbaum . . . As a result, important facts were never presented . . . It is highly likely that a person accused of involvement in a murder is not guilty," he wrote in a letter to CTV's current affairs program, "W5."

Predicting that a guilty conscience would soon persuade Robert Barrett to make a full confession of his self-serving treachery, MacDonald offered to repeat his story while patched into a lie detector. "Take notice also that down the road a major Crown witness that lied for his personal benefit, may turn around and come forward with the truth. This is highly likely . . . because an innocent man, Mr. Helmuth Buxbaum, was sent to jail because of a deal that the OPP made with certain well known people."

Enthused by the letters from Demeter and MacDonald, Helmuth became convinced that Robert Barrett wanted to confess his lies, but that the authorities wouldn't let him. When he discovered that Barrett had agreed to undergo a behaviour modification program in British Columbia as part of his pre-release plan, Helmuth concluded that it was a sinister plot to erase all vestiges of the truth from his false accuser's mind: "I think we have arrived at the Soviet Psychiatric Hospital System. What they are really doing is to change his mind on coming clean with his conscience; he wants to confess, but they are now 'professionally altering his mind.' (Brainwashing him.) When he gets out, he will be so brainwashed that he will be useless in court!!"

Helmuth's schemes to undo his conviction knew no bounds. Obsessed with the notion that the Crown had, in effect, "purchased" Barrett and Allen's testimony, he instructed Clayton Ruby to "outbid the Crown's bid." In return for the two perjurers confessing to their lies, he would set them up in businesses in Columbia or Brazil, where they would be beyond the reach of Canadian authorities. As the lead perjurer, Barrett was to receive monthly instalments totalling $50,000 to recant. "This whole thing may turn your stomach," he wrote to Ruby. "I, at least, hate to have to pay for the truth, but if it is the only way . . . so be it!"

Like many other prisoners, Helmuth habitually watched shock TV shows like "Geraldo," "Donahue," and "Oprah," thrilled (and reassured) by their unlikely stories of innocent men sent to prison by perjured testimony, police cover-ups, and scientific tricks. He became convinced that the key to proving his own innocence might well be revealed in one of these weird cases, where premenstrual syndrome and even sleepwalking had been successfully used as defences to murder charges. Helmuth was always ready to believe the unbelievable, provided it gave him a glimmer of hope. At times, his credulity was stunningly irrational.

"A prisoner told me of a case in the U.S.A.," Helmuth wrote to Ruby, "where a woman was shot, [her alleged killer] was convicted of murder and served many years in prison when another postmortem autopsy was done and it was found that the woman had actually died from a heart attack . . . If Hanna were exhumated [*sic*] and an autopsy performed by qualified pathologists, it is possible that they could find the possibility of coronary infarct. The pathologist from the forensic department of the Ontario coroner's office was either on drugs or very drunk when he testified for the Crown during my trial and prelim'. I don't think he would have been interested in finding the true cause of death nor is he (as an alcoholic) able to!!"

Helmuth even began advertising in newspapers to find potential witnesses for his appeal. Then, losing his patience with the entire judicial process, he gave instructions to his lawyer that he hoped would allow him to bypass a justice system that was too blind or too corrupt to recognize and correct its horrible mistake:

"I have thought about this for several days and hereby direct you to write a registered letter to Mr. Kurt Waldheim, Chancellor of Austria and to advise him:

"1. That I was an Austrian citizen since the 2nd World War . . .

"2. That I became a Canadian citizen in 1963 not knowing that I could have retained my Austrian citizenship.

"3. That I was wrongfully arrested, detained, had my bail denied and now am wrongfully convicted of murder.

"4. I am asking him to receive my Austrian citizenship back again and allow me to return and retire in my home country."

Kurt Waldheim never smiled on Helmuth's retirement plans and Hanna's body was never exhumed. Although he dutifully wrote to the Austrian chancellor, Clayton Ruby did his best to discourage Helmuth from pursuing the more mercenary salesmen of false hope. He pointed out that the dozen people who answered Helmuth's newspaper ads tended to be hardened criminals who were of no use to his appeal.

Ruby also advised caution when assessing the claims of Helmuth's other jailhouse defenders: "Mr. Demeter is perhaps the most notorious murderer and liar in the country, and his evidence, no matter what it is, is unlikely to be helpful. I will write to him but I don't think it's worthwhile spending a lot of money chasing him down."

Ruby's most contemptuous backhander was reserved for Peter Mac-Donald: "MacDonald is a swine . . . I am telling you that everything he is saying to you is a lie." The lawyer reinforced his point by quoting one of Eddie Greenspan's associates on the Buxbaum case, Robert Sheppard: "He says he [MacDonald] is a 'wacko' and unreliable . . . Barrett had told him that you only wanted your wife kidnapped, and not killed, so that you could look heroic by paying the ransom and thereby improve your sex life . . . The story is pretty implausible, and was probably a lie. The conclusion is reinforced by the next development which was, [according to] Mr. Sheppard, that MacDonald went directly to the Crown . . . and told the Crown that Mr. Sheppard had offered him a $5,000 bribe to lie about the case! . . . In the light of this conduct, it seems to me that Mr. MacDonald is untrustworthy and unreliable and not helpful."

Helmuth soon had independent proof that people like Peter Dale MacDonald had more on their minds than rebalancing the scales of justice. Shortly after the millionaire-convict's transfer to Kingston penitentiary, MacDonald mailed a telling letter to Helmuth's fiance, Liza Dikih:

"H. must come to grips with the fact that I am the only one who can help him with the help that he requires . . .

"H. must also pull his mind together and make some fucking sense regarding my situation. Does he want a good percentage chance for a release, or does he want to continually fantasize about Ruby as his saviour?

"He hasn't got a fiddler's prayer going with idiots like G & B. They weren't believed before and without the Squirrel, they won't be believed again. Clay Ruby is a great lawyer, but only God can acquit H. now; and Squirrel, in this case, is God."

When his demands that Helmuth co-operate with him were ignored, the threats began. MacDonald explained that he had saved a number of letters which could prove devastating to Helmuth's appeal. Those letters, he warned, would be turned over to police unless his mother received "fifteen" every month from the Buxbaum family. "It's but a small token of his sincerity to me," MacDonald wrote. "I'm going to wait until the end of the month, Liza, and if my Mom hasn't been blessed, then I will go and put in to see Piers. She should be seen each month regularly with fifteen blessings and without delay, because a delay will make me go to where the welcome is . . . Let's hope that January is good to my Mom."

After learning about the outrageous correspondence, Clayton Ruby wrote a letter of his own to the would-be blackmailer. "No client of mine will pay any extortion. If you write to Ms. Dikih again, or contact her in any way, I will take criminal proceedings against you. Nor will I stand by if you contact Mr. Buxbaum's family again . . . On the basis of the one attempt you made, I am prepared to accept that perhaps this was mere childishness. But do not be foolish."

On the same day that he wrote to MacDonald, Ruby sent a letter to Helmuth that shattered his fanciful belief that Robert Barrett wanted to confess his alleged perjuries at the trial. Ruby reported that, through Barrett's lawyer, Wally Libis, the quarterback of the Hanna Buxbaum murder had made his feelings crystal clear. "Mr. Barrett indicated that reports of his wishing to change his testimony were fictional and fantasy. Indeed, [Mr. Libis] indicated that Mr. Barrett was worried that you would hire someone to kill him."

Helmuth, who was being treated for a case of suspected hepatitis, was devastated. From a hospital cell in Kingston penitentiary, he began to complain that prolonged sensory deprivation had damaged his mind. He was experiencing unfounded panic attacks, olfactory misinterpretations, and "psychotic-like" episodes. "After considering this hospital stay (since Aug. 16/87) for several days, I have come to a conclusion (which I hope is not the result of my tendency to be paranoid): I am the subject of a psychological experiment . . . Sometimes I really worry, thinking that they might be doing some criminal psychological tests (experiments) with my teenage children."

Delusion wafted through Helmuth's suspicious mind like smoke, obscuring reality and creating in its place a shadow-world filled with menacing figures. He began to suspect that Liza Dikih was a conspirator in the state's psychological plot against him. He worried that hospital nurses were taking blood samples from him with used needles, a handy way of infecting him with hepatitis. Reflecting on his attempted suicide at EMDC, he now theorized that it had been nothing less than a murder plot by the authorities who had wrongfully charged him with Hanna's murder.

He wrote, "I believe that after I was charged in the London court-house, it dawned on the Crown (Mr. Martin) and the OPP (Ron Piers) that they had indeed made a very bad mistake. As they started to investigate, they realized that I was cocaine-addicted and that without medical help, I would go into a very deep depression. When they realized that, they decided to kill me by suicide. When the warden of EMDC refused to go along with it, he was quickly transferred and a man who was willing to do it was put in his place. John Lockhart, a criminal psychologist, had me thrown into the hole for no apparent reason and then managed to smuggle a large paper clip to be put on an Ombudsman letter form. What they did was attempted murder!! And it almost worked."

Still convinced that he had been wrongfully imprisoned, the inmate bitterly observed that the justice system, despite its pious declarations, did not really prefer to let ten guilty men go free rather than send one innocent man to prison, "unless I am part of some intentional, monstrous experiment to see if our system is failproof! When I think of Judge O'Driscoll, the idea is not so crazy after all."

In prose that swaggered to the stately measure of the American Constitution, he concluded that the only answer to his predicament was to ask his lawyer to launch yet another unconventional effort to secure his release: "I know that I have said this to you before, but I repeat: I hold the religious belief that I have been given the inalienable right by my creator to be treated as a human being and not to be caged like an animal!!!! The government has the right to punish and even execute, but they have never been given the right to cage human equals, created in the image of God!!! Even the pilgrim fathers of the United States knew that. I think this truth is indeed self-evident; I don't understand your reluctance to speak to a constitutional lawyer about this."

Clayton Ruby's inaction had nothing to do with reluctance; rather, it was based on the growing suspicion that help for his tortured client lay in a very different direction.

Clayton Ruby knew that the February 21, 1986, appeal filed by Eddie Greenspan on Helmuth Buxbaum's behalf was unlikely to succeed. Although Greenspan had gathered forty-nine separate grounds to challenge his client's conviction, most were too inconsequential to lead to the original verdict being overturned. Even though Ruby would add a few new grounds of his own after reading the voluminous trial transcript, he was sceptical that an appeal on the merits alone could get his client a new trial.

The only real hope was an alternative argument on appeal under Section 16 of the Criminal Code, which holds that no one can be convicted of an offence that was committed while that person was insane – a concept the law examines in all its forms from natural imbecility to organic amnesia. Fortunately for Helmuth's new lawyer, he had been able to persuade his client at their very first meeting on July 29, 1986, that if Greenspan's modified grounds of appeal failed, Ruby could raise an insanity defence should the circumstances warrant it. Helmuth may not have liked it, but the eminent lawyer made clear that it was the only way he would agree to take the case. In view of what he now knew, Ruby was glad that he had written instructions that, potentially at least, gave him far greater leeway with Helmuth's appeal than Eddie Greenspan had ever had with his defence.

Armed with Dr. Workman's concern about Helmuth's brain damage and a correspondence file from his client that would pass any layman's test for delusional thinking, Ruby decided to investigate further the possibilities of raising an insanity defence on appeal. With Helmuth's lukewarm co-operation, he arranged for a battery of experts, including two doctors who had appeared at the original trial as defence witnesses, to assess his client.

Over the next few months, seven eminent psychiatrists and psychologists travelled to Millhaven and Kingston penitentiaries to examine inmate 929455B. The list, by careful design, was impressive: Dr. Frank Ervin, a neuropsychiatrist from Harvard and McGill universities and former director of the Stanley Cobb Laboratories for Psychiatric Research at the Massachusetts General Hospital; Dr. Basil Orchard, a psychiatrist and author of the acclaimed book *The Defense of Insanity*; Dr. Robert Hill, a psychiatrist and former director of the Forensic Inpatient Service of the Clarke Institute of Psychiatry in Toronto; Dr. Graham Glancy, chief psychiatrist, Forensic Service, at the same institution; Dr. Graham Turrall, psychologist and former chief psychologist of the Clarke's Forensic Service; and Drs. Ruth Bray and Andrew Malcolm, who had testified about Helmuth's behaviour at the trial.

Ruby instructed each of them to examine his client to decide if he fit the legal definition of insanity during the time that Hanna's murder was arranged and committed; that is, did Helmuth "know" that it was wrong to murder his wife, and was he sufficiently cogent to form the "intent" to arrange her death? Before testing Helmuth, each of the experts was given extensive medical and police reports on the inmate, as well as a statement of facts in the case that Ruby told them to assume was correct.

One by one, the doctors' reports made their way across the lawyer's desk, each with the same emphatic conclusion: Helmuth Buxbaum should have been found not guilty of his wife's murder by reason of insanity.

Dr. Frank Ervin reported that in order to make sense of Hanna Buxbaum's gruesome murder, it was necessary to focus on "a single, dominant datum," the extensive frontal lobe damage to his brain Helmuth had suffered in the wake of his 1982 stroke. Citing his striking personality change, emotional shallowness, inappropriate impulsiveness, ostentatious sexuality, and grossly impaired social judgement, Ervin concluded that Helmuth was suffering from a very well known disease of the mind – Frontal Lobe Dysfunction or Organic Personality Syndrome.

"The list of impairments is not limited to Buxbaum. It is characteristic of patients with this disorder. It is instructive to review the descriptions of Phineas Gage [1868], the first well-documented case of a traumatic lesion quite similar to that of the appellant. By 1921, Browning, in reviewing the field, spoke of the right frontal lobe as a promoral centre. We no longer think of centres for such abstract functions as morality, but all observers before and after have called attention to the loss of social inhibitions and lack of awareness of moral and legal concepts of right and wrong in these cases."

Ervin observed that Helmuth had lost his ability to know the difference between right and wrong and could not have formed the intent to murder his wife, "even though he could respond to initiatives from others about a murder plan." The ability to form concepts and anticipate the natural consequences of a particular action were also impaired by his particular type of brain damage.

"The deficits described are profound, irreversible, and predictable. I am surprised that they were not presented to the family in 1982 and a recommendation made for guardianship or other control over money and business decision-making . . . Buxbaum entered 1983 with all the impulsivity [sic] and amorality of a two and a half year old child . . . Helmuth Buxbaum was (and is) suffering from a disease of the mind . . . As a consequence of his disease of the mind, he did not know that it was wrong to murder his wife."

Like Ervin, Dr. Robert Hill was struck by the clear post-stroke neurological damage supported by radiological imaging in both the right frontal and right parietal lobes of Helmuth Buxbaum's brain. Although he used what he called a more precise diagnostic label to describe the inmate's condition – 'pseudopsychopathic' rather than 'organic personality' – it denoted the same deficiencies: "a pattern of thinking, feeling, and behaviour similar to psychopaths, but in which the basic cause is brain damage . . . There were reported changes in attitude and function – lack of sense of responsibility, lack of control over impulses, lack of moral sense, self-centred, poor judgment, and inability to foresee consequences of behaviour – classical of the psychopath, but in this case, coming after the CVA [cerebrovascular accident: the stroke] are in my opinion the direct result of brain damage. This means that the changes were not because he *didn't* care, but because he *couldn't*; his ability to show normal functioning was grossly impaired as a result of the disease."

Hill observed that Helmuth's brain damage, exacerbated by heavy cocaine use, had imprisoned him in a perpetual present, an infantile rut in which future possibilities or consequences could no longer modify his behaviour. "More tragically," the psychiatrist reported, "he doesn't see events in the future as real: only the here and now is operative upon him. Impairments of time have been well documented as occurring in [cases of others with] lesions such as sustained by Mr. Buxbaum."

Painting the picture of a man who had become morally weightless, floating from day to day oblivious to the consequences of his actions because his damaged brain couldn't relate them to concepts of punishment, societal norms, or simple conscience, Dr. Hill forcefully concluded that Helmuth Buxbaum had been insane at the time of his offence: "In my opinion, the evidence is overwhelming that he has and had Organic

Brain Disease . . . Whether something was legal, right or wrong, was not something which his brain could address."

Dr. Basil Orchard offered the diagnosis of Organic Personality Syndrome that he believed effectively created a new personality for the convicted murderer, very different from his premorbid self. Orchard even attributed Helmuth's voracious and hopelessly indiscreet sexual appetite to a physical cause: clearly visible damage to the basal ganglia of the frontal lobe. As for Helmuth's ability to appreciate the nature of his part in Hanna's murder (during his meeting with the psychiatrist, Helmuth giggled and became teary-eyed for no apparent reason), Orchard left no doubt about where he stood as a clinician: "This disease of the mind would also render him incapable of appreciating the nature and quality of his action such that he could not conceive that Hanna would be finally dead and personally gone and unable to be with him."

The chief psychiatrist of Forensic Services at the Clarke Institute also came down with a diagnosis of Organic Personality Syndrome. Assuming that Robert Barrett's description of Hanna's murder was accurate, Dr. Graham Glancy concluded that Helmuth's brain pathology "creates a reasonable doubt whether his capacity to know and intend these things existed . . . In this context also the subtlety of the syndrome needs to be taken into account."

Glancy explained that if, at the time of Hanna's execution, Helmuth had been asked if he understood the physical consequences of having his wife shot, he would have acknowledged that a bullet would inflict serious damage and even death. While a layman would use that response to argue that Helmuth was therefore responsible for Hanna's murder because he appreciated the nature of what he was doing at the time, the forensic psychiatrist made it the springboard for an exotic professional distinction:

"Even in this scenario, however, such knowledge of the physical consequences of his actions ignores the subtlety of the frontal lobe syndrome. In this syndrome, it is well documented that subjects sometimes act out utterly inappropriate or harmful actions, despite being told this and understanding it, because they are unable to appreciate the consequences of the act . . . When told how to solve a puzzle correctly, the subject with this disorder will be able to demonstrate that they know the correct method of solution, but will again and again persist in doing it wrongly because they do not realize that the consequence of doing it wrongly will be a failure to 'solve' the puzzle."

After conducting three days of clinical interviews and putting his subject through a battery of fifteen psychological tests in the sweltering July heat at Kingston penitentiary, Dr. Graham Turrall concluded that Helmuth Buxbaum suffered from a "major mental illness," which he described as Organic Personality Disorder. As a result of his 1982 stroke, Helmuth had undergone "significant intellectual, emotional, personality and behavioral changes," he reported.

When Turrall administered the Wechsler Memory Scale test, he discovered a striking feature of the subject's response pattern: when Helmuth Buxbaum's memory failed him, he simply "confabulated," or made up an answer. His ability to shift cognitive focus – to plan, problem-solve, or self-correct in new situations – was three full standard deviations below the expected norm for his age, a finding that indicated to Turrall "severe" neuropsychological deficits in the right cerebral hemisphere. His subject's responses were sometimes stunningly inadequate. When Turrall presented Helmuth with a series of blocks he was to put together to solve a problem, he had simply piled them one on top of the other. "I had never seen that response before in nearly twenty years of testing," Turrall said.

On the crucial issue of Buxbaum's mental condition at the time of Hanna's murder, Dr. Turrall was unequivocal: damage from his 1982 stroke had been so great, and his consumption of cocaine so heavy, that he neither appreciated the nature and quality of the conspiracy he had been involved in nor comprehended that what he did was legally wrong. As a result of his disease of the mind, Helmuth Buxbaum was legally insane.

Of the seven experts retained by Ruby, Dr. Ruth Bray was one of only two who had examined the inmate both before and after his conviction. At Eddie Greenspan's request, she had spent six hours interviewing Helmuth at the Niagara Regional Detention Centre on September 12 and 24, 1985. She had also arranged for five hours of self-administered psychological tests at the same time. Now, three years later, after spending another five hours with Helmuth the convict, the eminent psychologist had not changed her mind:

"Helmuth can be seen as fitting the legal criteria for insanity . . . My opinion in 1985 was, and remains, that many of Helmuth Buxbaum's behaviours are out of his rational control; he can be expected to have a conscious set of values which are not in line with his primitive response pattern . . . The tests which I gave support the idea that he could espouse and believe one set of things when with Hanna, his family, and his 'straight' acquaintances, and respond with clearly different thinking and behaviour when with 'rounders' or street people."

Bray also found that Helmuth clearly suffered from delusional think-ing, as evidenced by his insistence that his six children had maintained a very close and supportive relationship with him. In fact, virtually all of the Buxbaum children had privately rejected their father shortly after his con-viction and refused for many years thereafter to visit him in prison.

Bray advised that Buxbaum's unreliable recollections of what had hap-pened were the result of the inevitable memory lapses and distortions associated with Organic Personality Syndrome. "I doubt if he is aware of the 'truth or fiction' of what has happened, and his re-construction of events relies on those around him. While it is difficult for persons of a normal mentality to comprehend the type of disconnected and even para-doxical thinking of individuals with Helmuth Buxbaum's particular handicap, it is my contention that he would not appreciate that the plans he might have discussed with Robert Barrett would actually result in the loss of Hanna; he could be described as unable to comprehend the conse-quences of that planning would be her death."

Interestingly, Bray reported that Helmuth's own assessment of his bizarre and ultimately criminal behaviour of 1984 was that he was experiencing a mid-life crisis, or alternately, that his immoral behaviour had prompted God to send "evil" to him in the form of Robert Barrett. As the psychiatrist soon found out, Helmuth himself had some very defi-nite ideas on his mental condition, views that were jarringly at odds with the medical experts.

"I suggested to him that there was overwhelming evidence to indicate that he was implicated in a plot to take his wife's life and that his difficulty in thinking clearly about this made a plea of insanity more logical than his insistence on a plea of not guilty. Mr. Buxbaum protested vehemently at the idea that anyone would question his sanity. He stated with some anger that if his lawyer went against his belief that he should be acquitted that he would fire him and change lawyers. The type of amnesia that he shows for his involvement can be seen as consistent with the neurological impair-ment which has been documented and reinforced by the cocaine use."

Like Dr. Bray, Dr. Andrew Malcolm had examined Helmuth on sev-eral occasions before his trial, conducting a psychiatric assessment at the behest of Eddie Greenspan. In Malcolm's opinion, both at the time of Helmuth's trial, and now at his appeal, the single most important fact in the tragic case was the brain damage Helmuth had suffered in 1982, a calamity the doctor believed had left him with irrefutable mental deficits according to the medical evidence of the day: "In London University

Hospital various diagnostic tests were carried out and these clearly indicated left-sided weakness, partial thrombosis of the proximal right middle
cerebral artery and an early right frontal lobe infarct . . . Mr. Buxbaum
suffered several cerebral infarcts on April 17, 1982."

It was, according to the doctor, the great watershed in Helmuth Buxbaum's life. The driven businessman who had worked so hard to build
Treugott Management into a multimillion-dollar empire began to lead a
"vegetative existence," spending no more than sixteen hours per month
on his business affairs. Helmuth also lost much of his "adult tact" and
displayed striking examples of post-stroke lechery and lewdness. His
descent to the level of a primitive child was reinforced by his preoccupation with the temporary impotence following his stroke: "He became
impulsive, careless, childish, and self-centred. He withdrew his interest in
church affairs and began, for the first time in his life, to use coarse language. He became unpredictable and capricious. He became preoccupied
with the need to overcome his sexual disability and his efforts in this
regard resulted in unrestrained promiscuity."

Cocaine, Malcolm reported, had made the problem much worse.
Consuming more than two thousand dollars' worth a week of the power-
fully reinforcing drug, Helmuth had begun to exhibit even more psycho-
pathic behaviour, immersing himself in the hedonistic world of Kelly's
Bar and surrendering to the control of his pimp and drug supplier,
Robert Barrett. As time went on, Helmuth exchanged his former world
of home, business, and church for the "orgasmic intoxication" of cocaine.
And it was in this disinhibited and irresponsible state, befriending people
who would have horrified him in the years immediately before his stroke,
that he began to talk about killing his wife.

Malcolm wrote, "It is my opinion that at such times his mind was not
operating in any way that I could consider normal. I do not believe he
could measure and foresee the consequences of telling such a man as
Robert Barrett that he would like to put an end to his wife's interference
with his life . . . Mr. Buxbaum was a mentally compromised man and he
suffered from a major and measurable loss of cerebral integrity . . . His
thinking lacked flexibility and the capacity to abstract. It was significantly
concrete, simple and immediate. His judgment was impaired . . . Indeed,
he may have talked loosely with Barrett about some ill-defined solution to
guarantee himself a life entirely free of any restraining influence, but if
he did so, he was speaking in the magical manner of a child and without
any appreciation of the manifold consequences of such a plan. He was not

being the careful, prudent and mentally organized creator of successful enterprises. He was clearly indicating that he had regressed to a quite primitive level of mental organization; that he was, in fact, so altered from his preexisting self as to be definable as insane . . . From a neurological point of view, the damage to Mr. Buxbaum's brain is real and demonstrable. From a psychiatric point of view, the impairment is so severe that it warrants a diagnosis of an Organic Brain Syndrome. It will be interesting to see whether, on appeal, the court will conclude that this degree of impairment constitutes insanity in the legal sense as well."

If the doctors were right, the justice system had not tried and punished a criminal, but abused a man whose mental illness, and his crime, had been triggered by a dissected cerebral artery. Eddie Greenspan had been charged with the daunting task of making the elephant of his client's guilt disappear; Clayton Ruby now had a task that was nearly as difficult: to produce the other elephant, the strange and persistent insanity that may have turned Helmuth Buxbaum into an unwitting killer.

19

JUDGEMENT DAY REVISITED

*"This is probably the only forensic case that I've been
involved in where I felt the physical evidence was
compelling, as opposed to just the psychological evidence . . .
a clear-cut case of actual brain damage which would affect
judgement . . . You've got an incompetent individual . . .
That's what we tried."*
— Forensic psychologist Dr. Ruth Bray on Helmuth Buxbaum

As convinced as he was by the medical evidence that his client was insane,
Clayton Ruby was under no delusions about his chances of winning Helmuth a new trial or an acquittal on the grounds of a belated Section 16
defence. Judges are no more immune than the general public to the view
that the insanity argument has become a kind of gimmick of last resort, a
legal parlour trick performed by ingenious "experts" and adroit lawyers
that often leads to the most heinous crimes going unpunished.

The very nature of Helmuth's mental disorder made Ruby's task even
more difficult. Most cerebrovascular disease involves the deep structures
of the brain. Accordingly, firm data about frontal lobe dysfunction is minimal compared to what is known about other areas of the brain. In fact,
the study of frontal lobe impairment is a quagmire for researchers for a
variety of reasons unique to the disease, including the peculiar trait that it
rarely respects anatomical boundaries.

Nor is it easy to separate post-stroke frontal lobe behaviour from a
patient's "premorbid" state — mental illnesses he may have been suffering
from before the stroke. Even the most sophisticated medical technology is
not of much help; CAT-scans and EEGs are simply not sufficiently sensitive
to pinpoint the exact location and extent of any pathology that may result
from a stroke. Even the size of the lesion on the brain doesn't seem to
affect the potential for personality change. Compounding the problem,
most neuropsychological tests are not able to measure adequately the

extent of frontal lobe deficits in brain-damaged patients. In layman's terms, there are simply very few reliable tests that deal with human emotion and personality.

What *is* known about frontal lobe function remains tantalizingly general. From clinical observation, researchers believe that the right side of the brain plays the lead role in human emotional behaviour. They have noticed, for example, that aneurysms and arteriovenous malformations that bleed into the frontal lobe often produce behavioural changes. They have also found that the ability to predict the consequence of a chosen behaviour and to come up with alternative plans if those consequences are inappropriate appears to be a frontal lobe function. Based on that insight, they have theorized that damage to this "anticipatory selection process" may, in fact, underlie some of the personality changes frontal lobe patients experience.

But at a practical level, what brain researchers actually know about frontal lobe damage is a little like astrophysics: one part fact to nine parts grasping at straws. In the absence of definitive research, what the medical world is left with is a composite picture of how frontal lobe patients behave, a pathological self-portrait sketched on the canvas of their post-stroke daily life.

Such patients are often poorly motivated, apathetic, and oddly uninhibited. Although they may still have a normal IQ, there is often a striking impairment of intellectual functioning – a lack of insight, diminished capacity to plan, and decreased initiative. One of their most common traits is an indifference to the past and future in favour of an all-consuming preoccupation with a hedonistic and often amoral present. "Confabulation" – having false or bizarre responses to routine questions – is another characteristic of the disease, as are the patients' flat denials that they are suffering from brain damage – a characteristic that may arise from memory disturbances caused by the condition.

But again, the evidence isn't hard and fast; similar traits are also observed in patients suffering from other psychiatric disorders, including mania, sociopathy, and schizophrenia. To truly understand this cognitive disorder of the brain's ability to judge, regulate, and plan, medical experts agree that more research is needed. To be more reliable, such research would have to be based on a broad spectrum of data, including the subject's premorbid personality, response to testing, clinical syndromes, and neuro-anatomical profile. Interestingly, all of that material was available in Helmuth's case, placing him on the cutting edge of the medical study of frontal lobe damage – exactly where you don't want to be when your fate is being decided in a forum that relies on precedent to make its judgements.

But the medical complexity of Buxbaum's case was the least of Clayton Ruby's worries. He knew only too well that every profession that comes before the court has to lie down on the Procrustean bed of the law; psychiatric medicine was no exception. Seven eminent doctors may have been ready to say that Helmuth Buxbaum was medically insane, but the only experts who really mattered were men who had never been to medical school. Ultimately, a troika of judges would make up its mind not on the basis of psychiatric testimony, medical tomes, or the classic frontal lobe profile of Phineas Gage, but on the precepts of the Criminal Code and sober judicial practice and precedent.

Helmuth Buxbaum's fate was in the hands of those lofty, medical amateurs who presided over the Court of Appeal for Ontario.

Under Canadian law, every accused person is presumed to be, and to have been, sane, unless they prove otherwise on a balance of probabilities – a reverse onus that sets this statute apart from most others. Section 16 of the Criminal Code as it was at the time of Buxbaum's trial made clear that simple delusions were not enough to win an acquittal; an insanity defence could only succeed when a person was either in a state of "natural imbecility" (congenital defect or natural decay) or when they were suffering from a "disease of the mind" that renders them incapable of "appreciating" the nature and quality of an act or omission, as opposed to merely "knowing" that it is wrong.

Since Helmuth's appeal on the grounds of insanity would be made under subsection 2 of Section 16, the various legal concepts embodied in that part of the Code were crucial to Ruby's task. According to the Criminal Code, the term "disease of the mind" includes any illness, disorder, or abnormal condition which impairs the human mind and its functioning. Whether the condition is well understood by medical science or not, it is a disease of the mind if it prevents a person from comprehending what he is doing. Such a mental disorder may also qualify as a disease of the mind even if it is not likely to recur – hence the defence of temporary insanity. Personality disorders are explicitly included as possible diseases of the mind, although the insanity defence is not made out when an accused merely lacks the appropriate feelings for his victim or fails to show remorse or guilt as a result of his mental disorder. "Transient disturbances," the so-called normal stresses of life which may lead to a fleeting malfunction of the mind are clearly excluded, as are self-induced incoherent states caused by alcohol or drugs.

On the nice distinction between "knowing" and "appreciating" that a particular act or omission is wrong, the general provisions of Section 16 make a legal rather than a moral judgement. For a court to find that an accused person *understands* the nature of what he's been charged with, simple knowledge of what he's done is not enough; the accused must also "appreciate" the consequences of his act – a further step of rational analysis that marks the legal divide between a sane and an insane person.

As demanding – and subjective – as the Code's insanity provisions are, Ruby was fairly certain that a strong case could be made for his client's insanity on the basis of Organic Personality Syndrome. But before he could argue that in the court of appeal, there was a formidable procedural hurdle to be cleared. Since the defence of insanity had not been raised at Helmuth's trial, Ruby could only introduce it on appeal by putting fresh evidence before the court. And that put him squarely up against a daunting test, the so-called due diligence rule.

The essence of this evidentiary rule is simple: if, through the exercise of due diligence, an accused and his counsel could have produced in the lower court the evidence they wish to bring forward on appeal, it is generally not admitted by the higher court. Since Malcolm and Bray could have testified on the insanity issue at Helmuth's original trial, it would be difficult for Ruby to convince the appeal court that anything the doctors now had to say could qualify as fresh evidence.

Even more detrimental to the appeal was the fact that both Malcolm and Bray readily admitted that their testimony at Helmuth's trial provided much of the basis for what lawyers routinely refer to as "a Section 16." It was just that Eddie Greenspan hadn't advanced that defence, a state of affairs that could, depending on Greenspan's reasons, have dread consequences for Helmuth's appeal.

It was a trap of process rather than fact. When an accused person represented by a competent counsel refrains from calling evidence at his trial for "tactical" reasons, subsection 686 (1) (a) of the Code generally precludes raising it on appeal. The rationale is essentially practical. Since much of a court's power flows from the finality of its decisions, the working integrity of the judicial system would be undermined if an accused could, in effect, discard an unsuccessful defence and replace it with a new one on appeal.

Despite encouraging a practice founded more on bureaucratic policy considerations than on justice issues *per se*, the Criminal Code does allow for exceptions to the due diligence rule, particularly in criminal cases where its application is somewhat relaxed. If, for example, an appellant can satisfactorily explain why particular evidence was not brought forward at trial, he may be permitted to advance it on appeal. If the new evidence is also decisively relevant, credible, and likely to have affected the earlier judicial result, it will then be admitted. Since the medical evidence in Helmuth's case fit all three of these other criteria, the only real question for the court to consider was whether it ought to be admitted. In other words, Ruby would have to explain satisfactorily to the court why Eddie Greenspan hadn't raised a Section 16 defence at Helmuth's trial. If he couldn't, the odds were good that his alternate defence of insanity would be struck down by the due diligence rule and Helmuth's appeal under Section 16 would fail.

The experienced counsel was about to stray into an area of the law greyer than a winter sky before the snow falls.

There were three replies to the question Ruby needed to answer, none in harmony with the others. When it came to Buxbaum and Greenspan, the discord was hardly surprising; their bitter fee dispute had poisoned the waters between them, and Greenspan hadn't helped matters with a remark attributed to him in the *Toronto Star*: "As for Buxbaum, I tried to make my fees so high – lawyers call it a get lost fee – that he wouldn't go for it. But he did."

Helmuth's anger over the quip at his expense (he complained to Law Society of Upper Canada about it) may have coloured his recollection of how Greenspan had approached the insanity defence at the time of the trial. He maintained, "The question of [an] insanity defence was never raised because Mr. Greenspan was so sure that he would win the case hands down. But even if he considered it, he would not deign to lower himself to discuss legal matters of this magnitude with an earthling like myself."

Greenspan remembered it differently and insisted that the chief reason insanity had never been raised at trial was his own client's emphatic instruction. Greenspan told Ruby that both he and his associates, students-at-law Arthur Fish and Robert Sheppard, had repeatedly explained the nature of the insanity defence to Helmuth, who never wavered from his original direction not to raise it.

Although Greenspan had hired psychiatrists and psychologists to assess Helmuth's mental condition and to testify about possible causes for his bizarre behaviour in the period before his wife's murder, he insisted that "no expert retained by the defence ever offered the slightest suggestion that the Appellant [Buxbaum] was insane within the meaning of a s. 16 of the Criminal Code."

But when Ruby first contacted two of Greenspan's key expert witnesses, Dr. Ruth Bray and Dr. Andrew Malcolm, he discovered that their recollections did not jibe with those of the man who had hired them. Dr. Malcolm said that after twice assessing Helmuth in the months before his trial, he felt "quite clearly" that the accused had a potential defence of insanity. He said that it was "likely" that he had discussed his feelings about a Section 16 defence with Greenspan personally, but he had no doubt that he had passed that opinion along to other counsel assisting Greenspan on the case: "I am certain that lawyers assisting Mr. Greenspan were aware that it was my opinion that Mr. Buxbaum was insane at the time of the offence and could have this defence available to him."

Dr. Ruth Bray was even more categorical in her rejection of Greenspan's recollection of events. After examining Helmuth twice in September 1985, she remembered telling both Greenspan and his associate, Chris Buhr, that the accused had a defence under Section 16. "During the course of our discussions I clearly expressed the view that the defence of insanity was available in Mr. Buxbaum's case. I believe I also indicated some surprise that this defence was not being raised," she swore in an affidavit. "Mr. Buhr made it clear to me that the matter of insanity was not at issue."

After Bray held a number of conversations with Andrew Malcolm in which both doctors expressed concern about Helmuth's mental state at the time of his wife's murder, she then remembered speaking directly to Greenspan about the possibility of raising an insanity defence on Helmuth's behalf. According to Bray, Greenspan informed her that such a defence was inappropriate. "My understanding," she now wrote, "was that there were two prime reasons: firstly, since his [Greenspan's] client was fit to stand trial, proclaimed his innocence, and was clear that he would not entertain a defence of insanity, that this could not be pursued; and secondly, that the evidence available supported a different explanation as to the motivation and culpability of Mr. Buxbaum."

In an interview with one of Ruby's law students during the preparation for Helmuth's appeal, Dr. Bray said that she would have told anyone who inquired that Helmuth Buxbaum had been insane at the time of his wife's murder. The trouble was, Bray claimed, no one on the defence team had ever asked her. Greenspan later confirmed her contention, admitting that he had never sought an opinion from his psychiatric experts, either orally or in writing, on Helmuth's fitness to stand trial or the possibility of raising an insanity defence on his behalf.

Complicating the picture even further was the $250,000 bonus clause in Greenspan's contract with Helmuth, monies that were to be paid above and beyond the lawyer's $1.3 million bill for fees and disbursements, but only in the event that the accused man was "ultimately acquitted of all charges."

Ruby, who thought the bonus clause "unprecedented and inappropriate," mulled over the possibility that it may also have put Greenspan in a conflict of interest with his own client. If, for example, a defence of not guilty by reason of insanity didn't qualify as a clean acquittal (leading as it would to incarceration in a mental institution under a Lieutenant-Governor's warrant, rather than to freedom), the bonus clause would not be activated, providing Greenspan with a possible reason for pleading the case the way he did at his client's expense.

But what Ruby didn't know was if the bonus would have been payable even if an insanity defence had been successfully led, a circumstance that would then have absolved Greenspan of any professional conflict of interest. Although Ruby was fairly certain that Helmuth, at least, believed that the extra quarter-million dollars was, in fact, for a clean acquittal, there was nothing in his contract with Greenspan that explicitly confirmed that impression.

Assuming that doctors Bray and Malcolm had told Greenspan about the availability of the insanity defence before Helmuth's trial, using that information on appeal would mean alleging the defence counsel was incompetent. Ruby knew that such a tactic would put him up against two solid obstacles: Greenspan's considerable reputation as the finest criminal lawyer in the land, and the principle of solicitor-client privilege, one of the foundations of the legal system. And while he was prepared to argue that even Wayne Gretzky occasionally scored on his own net, Ruby knew that Greenspan was keenly aware of exactly what was expected of a lawyer when acting on behalf of his client – even if that client was insane.

Solicitor-client privilege is viewed by most law societies as absolute. It is for counsel and the accused alone to decide what plea to enter and what evidence to call, and for the court to judge the facts that are brought before it. The deliberations between an accused and his counsel are secret by design and there is no obligation on a lawyer to apprise the court of anything a client might say. If anything, the onus works in the opposite direction. Assuming that an accused is fit to stand trial and to instruct counsel, his lawyer is bound to follow instructions in accordance with the dictates of solicitor-client privilege.

The insanity defence lays bare without removing it a ticklish problem inherent in the principle of solicitor-client privilege. What, for example, should a lawyer do when confronted by strong evidence of insanity in a client who instructs him not to raise a Section 16 defence? The common practice in the legal profession is to follow the instructions of the client, bearing in mind that there is absolutely no sanction for the lawyer to breach privilege with an accused who is fit to instruct counsel. And while that path can lead to judicial disaster – the criminal conviction of an insane accused – it will never lead to trouble for the lawyer who observes the letter of solicitor-client privilege. He is merely performing his role according to the best traditions of the bar – just as Eddie Greenspan had done in representing Helmuth Buxbaum.

Clayton Ruby had viewed the terrain of solicitor-client privilege from both sides of the fence on the insanity issue. He had once followed an insane client's instruction not to raise a Section 16 defence, only to see her convicted of murdering her infant child. The convicted woman gave the same instructions to her appeal lawyer, who, in turn, didn't raise insanity before the appellate court. Her conviction was upheld, but fortunately for justice, the appeal judges sensed insanity in the case and ordered a psychiatric assessment over the objections of the appellant and her counsel. When the results came back, the court of appeal quashed the woman's conviction, once again over the appellant's objections, and substituted a verdict of not guilty by reason of insanity.

The case had been a personal turning point for Ruby. "I resolved that I would never again take instructions from a client not to raise insanity where I had substantial evidence of insanity. There is nothing morally wrong with it. Lots of lawyers would have no problem with it. It was just the wrong way to do it for me."

Ruby subsequently found himself representing a man charged with a serious criminal offence who gave every indication of madness, including the fact that he wore spoons in his shoes to ground himself from the electrical rays that "they" were beaming in on him. Once again under instructions from his client not to raise the insanity defence, he complied.

But Ruby also privately alerted the presiding judge that there was strong evidence of insanity in the case. Notwithstanding the accused's instructions to counsel, the judge instructed Ruby to call the insanity evidence. The man was acquitted under the provisions of Section 16, but to Ruby the lesson was anything but clear. "It was one judge's view. I breached privilege when I did that. I talked about a client's instructions and our discussions of evidence. I felt justified in doing it and [the judge] agreed. Many judges would say, 'Why are you telling me this? You are a disgrace!' It's a real trap. The Law Society rules don't allow for breaching privilege."

In the end, Ruby and his colleagues decided that advancing Eddie Greenspan's incompetence to account for the fact that an insanity defence hadn't been raised at Helmuth's trial would be a rocky road that probably led over a cliff. At best, the discrepancies between Greenspan's recollection of pretrial conversations about Helmuth's mental condition and those of doctors Malcolm and Bray would lead to a mudslinging contest that would prove impossible to resolve. It was the same with the bonus clause, with the exception that if a court had to choose between the credibility of the eminent lawyer and the convicted murderer, it would inevitably choose Eddie Greenspan.

Ruby decided to rely on the only clean argument he had: the medical evidence that Helmuth Buxbaum had been insane at the time he instructed counsel not to raise an insanity defence. Ruby would argue that Helmuth's choice of a plea was in no way a "tactical" decision not to lead the best evidence he had to defend himself, but rather an extension of the mental illness he was suffering from. As Dr. Andrew Malcolm put it: "The situation that arose in the Buxbaum case is one which in my experience can occur where an accused person refuses to raise insanity as a defence . . . In these cases when counsel follows the instructions of their client and the Crown does not raise the defence and the trial judge does not leave the defence to the jury, there is a real risk that a person who was insane at the time of the commission of the offence will be convicted. Obviously this situation requires some guidelines on everyone's behalf."

The question was, would the Ontario Court of Appeal decide to make law in the Buxbaum case or simply enforce the Code as it existed?

In the months leading up to the appeal, Helmuth registered a kind of Pyrrhic victory over those friends and family members who had wanted to have him declared legally dead in order to wrest his wife's estate from her sole beneficiary. First, the Supreme Court of Ontario had reserved judgement on a motion to have Helmuth "disentitled" until the courts finished hearing all appeals of his 1986 murder conviction. Then the court quashed another attempt by the Buxbaum children to seize full control of the family assets.

The legal battle had begun in June 1987 when Paul Buxbaum sent two bitter letters to his imprisoned father, telling Helmuth that he couldn't "stomach" watching the family businesses stagnate for want of decisive leadership and outlining a plan to invest the family fortune in Florida real estate in partnership with his brother Mark. After all that had happened, though, Helmuth was not wanted on the entrepreneurial voyage. "Any relationship that flourishes must be based upon trust," Paul wrote. "To be frank, trust is in short supply . . . Because of your geographic location, you will have to trust us (Mark and me) with working out the details in regards to future operations. If you demand to know the details of each investment project, or operational decision, the bureaucratic hell would create frustration which I am not willing to live with."

Helmuth, who had spent twenty years investing conservatively, was aghast at his sons' plan to fritter away his millions on risky investments without so much as consulting him. He immediately petitioned the court to prevent Paul and Mark from seizing control of the Buxbaum fortune. His opposition was passionate.

"These proposals were totally unacceptable to me and I was never consulted with respect to these matters. I am vehemently opposed to these schemes suggested by my sons Paul and Mark . . . As a businessman who has amassed these monies with my wife, Hanna, through hard work and attention to detail, I am concerned and verily believe the monies of the estate and my own monies will be improperly handled in light of my sons' recent proposals. I want to avoid any possible problems that may result from the speculative forms of investment that my sons in their youthful exuberance may be inclined to get involved with."

Eleven months later, in June 1988, the Supreme Court of Ontario sided with the imprisoned millionaire. Paul Buxbaum, Doug Dakin, and Howard Johnson were relieved as administrators of Hanna Buxbaum's estate, and Royal Trust was appointed in their place to manage the dwindling Buxbaum fortune.

Helmuth's victory was costly; within six months, Phillip Buxbaum, the last child to stand by his father, bitterly renounced him. Before their feud, Phillip had actively worked to advance his father's appeal, even though his siblings were pressuring him to cut all ties with Helmuth. But the young man's bond with his father began disintegrating in September 1988. In a letter to Clayton Ruby, Helmuth explained what had led to the break: "Liza just visited me. I had asked Mr. Coon from Bracebridge, our security contractor, to change the locks on my cottage in Huntsville and change the security lock as well. Phillip and his wife apparently went to the cottage, and without permission from anyone, broke in, setting off the alarm. The OPP arrived but did not charge Phillip or Nikki.

"Please write a letter to Phillip with a copy to me and another to the OPP in Huntsville, advising him that any entry into the cottage without express permission from me will result in charges of B/E and we will hold him responsible for damages to the cottage. (Phillip practically destroyed our security system in his rage!)

"Liza tells me that there were indications in the cottage that someone had been living there, that parties took place with the use of drugs and that the cottage is in a deplorable, filthy condition. Apparently, Phillip has the delusion that the cottage belongs to his mother's estate, which is not correct."

The rift between father and son had serious consequences for Helmuth's appeal. Before their falling out, Phillip had submitted an affidavit swearing that his father had indeed undergone the kind of behavioural changes that were consistent with Organic Personality Syndrome. The young man's first-hand observations provided a crucial evidentiary bridge to the formal diagnosis given by the seven psychiatrists and psychologists who supported Helmuth's appeal on the grounds of insanity.

But on November 11, 1988, Phillip Buxbaum called Clayton Ruby to say that he had changed his mind about co-operating with the appeal and wanted to rescind and retract the statement he had given in his affidavit – information that was crucial for Ruby's application to adduce fresh evidence. Ruby quickly wrote a letter to Helmuth to inform him of what had happened and to advise him that the last of his children had apparently forsaken him:

"He [Phillip] thinks that you don't really love your family, that you are too much in the thrall of [Liza] Dikih, and he is particularly angry about you changing the lock on the cottage which caused him some upset one weekend.

"Though I have not yet advised him of what our position will be, it will be that he cannot have his affidavit back and that we intend to use it and him as we see appropriate, and if necessary, we will subpoena him to give evidence.

"You should know, however, that he is now firmly with the rest of the family and is not interested in helping you at all."

Helmuth Buxbaum's appeal of his conviction for conspiring to murder his wife began at 10 A.M. on Monday, February 6, 1989 – Clayton Ruby's forty-seventh birthday. The eminent lawyer had filed a total of sixty-two grounds for quashing the conviction against his client, but dealt with only twenty-nine of them in his factum. In making oral arguments, Ruby reduced the number even further, offering oral submissions on only twelve of the remaining grounds and abandoning all other points of his original notice of appeal.

As a secondary argument, he made a motion to introduce fresh evidence to support an insanity plea based on seven identical affidavits from the doctors who had examined Helmuth for the appeal. Ruby's two-pronged strategy had clear objectives: if successful on the merits, he wanted a new trial in which he would argue that Helmuth ought to be acquitted on the grounds that his psychiatric condition and drug use had rendered him incapable of forming the necessary *mens rea*, or criminal intent, to murder his wife. If successful on the insanity argument, he wanted the court to quash Helmuth's murder conviction and replace it with a verdict of not guilty by reason of insanity.

From Ruby's earliest contact with the Crown, he knew that he would face stiff opposition on both arguments. Not only was Crown attorney John Pearson anxious to contest every ground of Helmuth's appeal on the merits, he was also prepared to mount a strong challenge to Ruby's attempt to introduce the medical affidavits as fresh evidence. Helmuth Buxbaum's original conviction for first degree murder was one of the most celebrated cases in Canadian jurisprudence, and Pearson wasn't prepared to cede an inch of that hard-won turf to his famous opponent without a fight.

With Insp. Ron Piers watching quietly from the public gallery (Helmuth did not attend the court proceedings), Ruby made the arguments on the merits that he hoped would convince the judges to grant his client a new trial. He alleged that Helmuth did not have the necessary *mens rea* to participate in Hanna's murder, and accused the trial judge, Mr. Justice John O'Driscoll, of clearly favouring the Crown's case in his charge to the jury. He also argued that the learned judge had interfered in the cross-examination of Robert Barrett and had failed to instruct the jury on the lesser offence of second degree murder – a plausible criticism given Helmuth's brain damage and cocaine use, even though, technically speaking, there is no lesser offence on the charge of arranging a murder. Claiming that the Crown had blackened his client as well as prosecuted him, he took issue with Michael Martin's use of testimony on Helmuth's sexual activities and drug use, which he claimed was irrelevant to the murder charge and had greatly prejudiced the jury and the press against the accused.

When Ruby finished, the judges asked the Crown to respond to seven of his twelve arguments. After Pearson's detailed rebuttal, the stage was set for the court to address the appellant's motion to adduce fresh evidence on the secondary argument that Helmuth had been insane at the time of his wife's murder. They had no idea of how opposed to such a defence Helmuth was, or that Ruby had only gotten him to agree to raising it at all by making it a secondary argument. After opening the sealed affidavits from the seven psychiatrists and psychologists, the court asked the Crown to make arguments on their admissibility.

Pearson took the view that Ruby's motion was not really an application to adduce fresh evidence at all, but a thinly veiled attempt to repudiate the position Helmuth had taken in the lower court. To the Crown team, it was far from certain that an appellant could even raise insanity on appeal for the first time. Compounding the procedural low blow from Pearson's point of view was the fact that Ruby wanted to replace Helmuth's failed defence with a position Eddie Greenspan had expressly disavowed at trial. As Pearson put it in the Crown factum, "To permit an Appellant to raise on appeal a defence deliberately disclaimed at trial would be to allow an abuse of process."

Pearson also argued that the affidavits themselves amounted to no more than "hearsay" about how Helmuth and Greenspan had resolved the insanity issue at the time of the original trial. Until the court heard from the two men most directly involved, Greenspan and Buxbaum, there would be no way of knowing if the expert opinions were based on fact or strategic fancy.

Mr. Justice John Brooke agreed; unless Ruby backed up the medical affidavits with supporting evidence from the principals, the court wouldn't accept the expert opinion into evidence. When Ruby tried to explain what had happened at Helmuth's original trial, Brooke cut him off with a bolt from the bench: "*You* can't give evidence." There was only one route left: to find out why insanity hadn't been raised at Helmuth's trial from the one man who could best answer that question, Eddie Greenspan.

The prospect left Ruby cold. During preparation for the appeal, he had asked Greenspan about the insanity defence and gotten much more than he'd bargained for. Fully aware that questions about defence strategy at Helmuth's trial could easily lead to the accusation of incompetence of counsel, Greenspan provided Ruby with a detailed and very damaging picture of his relationship with Buxbaum both before and during the murder trial. His candour was as understandable as it was self-interested: if Helmuth wanted to waive solicitor-client privilege to bring out information helpful to his appeal, then Greenspan was going to tell the whole truth, not just the part that might be construed as an indictment of how he had handled the original trial.

"Generally speaking," Greenspan later wrote, "what a client says to his lawyer in seeking or obtaining legal advice is privileged, and neither the client nor the lawyer can be compelled to disclose it. The client may, however, waive the privilege by voluntarily offering his testimony, or that of the lawyer, concerning the communication. The client may also be deemed to have waived the privilege by, for example, attacking his lawyer's conduct of the case in such a way that to defend himself the lawyer must disclose the communication."

And disclose he did. Included in Greenspan's March 10, 1988, letter to Ruby was the devastating information about Helmuth's mid-trial confession to his lawyers that he had recognized Pat Allen when he stopped behind the disabled Chevy Nova on the morning of his wife's murder, and that Allen had told him to get in touch with Barrett at the Westbury Hotel.

In now asking for an affidavit from Greenspan to satisfy the court's request for first-hand information about how Helmuth's defence had been conducted, Ruby knew that he was running the risk that his flamboyant colleague might justifiably repeat the information he had included in this letter. If he did, Ruby's primary argument on appeal would be devastated, and he would be left with an insanity defence to which the court had so far reacted with singular coolness. His only option was to ask Greenspan very precise questions and hope that he restricted his answers to those matters and those matters alone.

In a February 15, 1989, fax to Greenspan, Ruby requested a reply to five specific questions, including Helmuth's instructions to his former counsel concerning the insanity defence. In making his request, Ruby emphasized that he would be getting a qualified waiver from Helmuth releasing Greenspan from the normal obligations of solicitor-client privilege concerning the matters queried.

Before returning his affidavit, Greenspan sent a disquieting note to Ruby in which he said he would respond to all of his questions, but that "matters outside the scope of the five points" might well come up in the course of cross-examination in the event he were called as a witness. The implication was clear; Greenspan had no intention of becoming the fall guy in Helmuth Buxbaum's appeal; if his former client waived privilege in some matters, then he had better be prepared to have the whole truth come out.

Three days after his note to Ruby, Greenspan returned a lengthy affidavit that included the compromising information he had described in his earlier letter. Ruby made one last attempt to remove the damaging material, writing to Greenspan that portions of his affidavit were clear breaches of solicitor-client privilege expressly not covered by Helmuth's qualified waiver. He suggested a new wording that would make clear that insanity had been raised within the defence ranks during the trial, but without making reference to Helmuth's dramatic disclosure about his roadside conversation with Pat Allen on the morning of July 5. But Greenspan was not about to have another lawyer, however celebrated, put words in his mouth; his affidavit came back with answers to a few more of Ruby's questions, but with the offending material untouched. Ruby never filed the affidavit with the court.

Tuesday, March 6, the day set aside for further examination of the insanity issue, was used instead for closing arguments. The court reserved its judgement and the eight-day appeal hearing was over.

While the court wrestled with its decision during the next five weeks, Helmuth Buxbaum made an important decision of his own. On February 17, 1989, he married Liza Dikih, the woman who had been visiting him regularly in various Ontario jails and penitentiaries for several years now. The simple ceremony was conducted by a justice of the peace in a trailer at Kingston penitentiary. After he'd gone, the newlyweds toasted themselves with vodka the bride had smuggled into the prison in a douche. Once again, the media pressed its nose to the glass of Helmuth's private life: "The couple will honeymoon in a private visiting trailer inside prison grounds until Monday afternoon," wrote the *Toronto Star*, "but Buxbaum must stick his head out the window at noon, 4 p.m. and 11 p.m. for a head count."

The new bride insisted that Helmuth's money played no part in her decision to marry a man serving a twenty-five-year sentence for murdering his wife, her only thoughts were of their future life together. In an earlier interview with writer Sidney Katz for *Chatelaine* (Clayton Ruby was given a complete veto over the article's editorial content as a condition of granting the interview), Dikih explained that she and Helmuth planned to move to Florida or Europe if he were successful with his appeal. But if he was forced to remain in prison until 2009 (his earliest possible parole date), she was also ready to stand by her man: "That doesn't frighten me. I'll move near the prison where I can visit Helmuth regularly and have occasional conjugal visits. What can be better than being near the man you adore?"

While the press waited for the outcome of Helmuth's appeal, it found another reason to get his name back into print. Hoping to raise $100,000 for the only professional orchestra in southwestern Ontario, Orchestra London decided to stage a month-long interior design exhibition in the former Buxbaum residence at Komoka. The fundraising promotion was immediately attacked by the guardian of the Buxbaum children as tasteless and insensitive. Citing the extreme discomfort the event would cause the convicted murderer's family, Doug Dakin urged people to boycott the event.

Few took the Baptist minister's advice to heart. When the *London Free Press* published news of the coming event, complete with directions to Helmuth and Hanna's former dream home, curiosity seekers showed up in droves, choking Komoka with bumper-to-bumper traffic. When the event actually took place, 500 people a day paid eight dollars apiece to inspect the mansion's twenty-eight rooms. In a scoffing article in *Saturday Night*, illustrated with a skeleton standing in one of Komoka's closets, journalist Eve Drobot quoted one paying customer who had lost his bearings in the labyrinth: "Hell, he didn't have to kill her. He could have just gotten her lost down here."

On April 13, 1989, the newlyweds received an unwelcome gift from the Ontario Court of Appeal. In a unanimous decision, the court dismissed Helmuth's appeal, rejecting every argument Clayton Ruby had advanced to get his client a new trial. Although the judges agreed that Buxbaum's original trial had been flawed by a number of legal and technical errors, they were deemed to be minor.

The court also rejected Ruby's bid to raise a defence of insanity. Devoting most of their twenty-five-page judgement to that single issue, the court ruled that the new evidence Ruby sought to introduce on Helmuth's mental condition at the time of his wife's murder "could have been discovered before the trial." Ruling that the medical affidavits were therefore inadmissible, the court ordered them resealed without ever effectively testing their contents.

They wrote, "We must do what we believe is in the interests of justice. Here, the defence of insanity is not the primary defence. It was not at trial and it still is not. The appellant's defence is that he was not guilty because he did not do the things he is accused of doing. He seeks to rely on the defence of insanity only if his other defences fail."

Unhappy with the rationale behind the court's decision, and convinced more than ever that his insane client was the victim of a miscarriage of justice, Ruby vowed to take the fight to the Supreme Court of Canada. But soon after the appeal court decision, he began to have serious doubts about Helmuth's ability to give competent advice to counsel, doubts that he expressed in a note to his personal file on the Buxbaum case.

"I spoke with Helmuth this morning (Wednesday)," he wrote, "and he told me that he very recently has been suffering mentally in a way in which he had not before. In particular, he was having very bad headaches on a very frequent basis and his short-term memory was 'shot to hell' . . . He said that five minutes after he got off the phone with me, he would not be able to remember that we had agreed that he would call me back at 3:30 P.M. the next day. This strikes me as a very dangerous problem and I want to think about it."

A few weeks later, Ruby was confronted with independent proof that Helmuth was indeed suffering from bouts of memory loss and a distorted sense of time – tell-tale signs of the condition psychiatrists had sworn he was suffering from. On May 16, 1989, he penned a note to file to record the incident: "I spoke with Liza Buxbaum on May 8, 1989 and I explored the question of ability to give instructions. She spends much more time with him than I do and says that his memory loss comes and goes. There are times where she speaks to him when he simply does not appreciate or hear what she is saying, even though they are face to face. He will pick up one or two words in a sentence and make up his own meaning . . . However, on other occasions, he seems quite lucid and competent and can remember things she said weeks ago. Unfortunately, he thinks some of the things that were said weeks ago were said recently (as in the last few minutes). This strikes me as a very dangerous problem and I want to think about it."

Despite his misgivings, Ruby was persuaded by Liza Buxbaum that Helmuth at least understood the nature of the litigation he was involved in, and on that basis proceeded to take the case to the highest court in the land. In a half-day submission to the Supreme Court of Canada on October 2, 1989, Ruby argued that Helmuth's appeal had been dismissed on the basis of a legal error, namely, that the Ontario Court of Appeal should have accepted the medical affidavits attesting to his client's insanity. Three days later, the Supreme Court justices sided with their provincial cousins and rejected Ruby's arguments. Once again, the press was there to record the moment. "The long legal saga surrounding Helmuth Buxbaum, the millionaire Baptist who turned to drugs and prostitutes and drove his wife Hanna to the scene of her death, is over," the *Globe and Mail* observed.

Helmuth was shocked by the failure of his appeal and predicted that, in future years, when brain damage from strokes was better understood, the judges would look back and see how wrong they had been. But only days later, he excitedly reported to Clayton Ruby that Robert Barrett and Pat Allen were in custody in Calgary, Alberta, a fact gleaned from the ever-whirring prison rumour mill. Convinced that his accusers were about to change their stories, he instructed Ruby to make contact:

"Check to see what they have been charged with; what there is, if anything, you could do for them, if they are willing to be interviewed by you and your partner . . . If you show them that I am concerned that they have proper legal counsel, they (particularly Barrett) will switch sides and tell you the truth. If they would be willing to give you a taped interview . . . then you have the bombshell you are looking for! Should you or any of your agents be killed during this action, I will disavow any knowledge of you or your operation."

20

REMEMBRANCE OF
THINGS PAST

"You know, darling, that I have always loved you, and I still
do, and your sudden death was the most shocking experience
of my life. It hurt me so badly, at times, I thought I was losing
my mind."

– *Helmuth Buxbaum to his deceased wife, Hanna, January 1991*

Like the weathered poster of a circus that has come and gone, the dread
celebrity of murder fades and cracks with time.

After the Supreme Court of Canada dismissed his appeal, Helmuth
Buxbaum sank from public view behind the limestone walls of Kingston
penitentiary, a balding and overweight lifer who washed underwear in the
prison laundry while contemplating the prospect of growing old inside.

Occasionally, as in the demise of his shortlived marriage to Liza
Dikih, or his 1990 jailbreak attempt with Don "Mad Dog" Kelly, Helmuth's own actions put him back in the news, complete with the standard paragraph summarizing the salient details of his grisly crime. More
frequently, though, he was trotted out in the media as a freak, one of the
country's ten most notorious murderers on a list compiled by weary editors looking for a good summer feature. As the whole man became more
ghostly with each passing year, the public persona of inmate 929455B
grew more inhuman – an icon of infamy forever defined by his gaudy
passage through the courts.

Of the various alumni of Kelly's Bar who had graduated from petty
crime to murder, Pat Allen experienced a complete sea-change, earning
full parole on May 30, 1988, just four years after he conspired to execute
Hanna Buxbaum. A year and a day later, it was Robert Barrett's turn to be
released. Both had used their prison time judiciously: Allen was treated
for a learning disability and went on to acquire the rudiments of the

formal education that had eluded him on the outside; after receiving help for his drug addiction, Barrett took up computer programming. The men who had testified against Helmuth Buxbaum in return for lesser charges and lighter sentences began their lives over again, Allen in British Columbia, and Barrett, ironically, in southwestern Ontario, not far from where the Buxbaums once lived.

It was a different story for Gary Foshay and Terry Armes. Like Helmuth, the dread highwaymen of the Buxbaum murder are still in prison serving lengthy sentences with no possibility of parole – fifteen years for Foshay and twelve for Armes. Armes remains convinced that his principal mistake was his failure to strike a timely deal with the prosecution. Like many prisoners, the man who was convicted of putting the fatal bullet in Hanna Buxbaum's head has become a born-again Christian. For Gary Foshay, seeing the light has finally extended to admitting that he was at the murder scene on that muggy July night in 1984, although he now swears that Pat Allen was Hanna's executioner. In May 1994, his appeal to have his second degree murder conviction reduced to manslaughter was summarily rejected, a turn of events that hasn't sweetened his thoughts towards his quicker-witted, and now free, accomplices.

Like their European forbears, who were driven half-way around the world by forces beyond their control, the Buxbaum family has been scattered to the four winds – precisely the Diaspora Helmuth had predicted if the Komoka homestead were sold. Paul Buxbaum got an M.A. in business administration in San Francisco and moved to Colorado, where he upheld a family tradition by going to work in the nursing home business. Phillip and Mark sunk roots in Florida, where Mark attended university in Tampa and Phillip landed a job as an employment consultant, later starting his own business. To smooth the dogged business of beginning afresh, all of the Buxbaum sons have changed their names. After taking nursing courses, Esther Buxbaum married Scott Dakin, the son of her guardian, Pastor Doug Dakin, setting up house in London and eventually starting a family. With future plans to become a missionary (her young husband is a graduate of the Moody Bible Institute in Chicago), Esther wanted to stay in Ontario until her youngest brother, Danny, finished university in nearby Waterloo.

For the obvious but never-spoken reason, the estrangement between father and children went on for many years. Helmuth's refusal to finance his sons' business plans, his anger at Esther for not seeking his approval before choosing a husband, and his own, unpopular marriage to Liza

Dikih only made matters worse. But when he agreed to a deal with the Christian Mutual Life Insurance company that paid $750,000 U.S. to his children in settlement of Hanna's million-dollar life insurance policy (a portion was held back to pay Helmuth's associated legal costs), there was an accommodation of sorts.

At Christmas, and on the occasional birthday, all of the children except Paul and Ruth have passed through Kingston's enormous wooden gates, stowed their personal belongings in the tiny wall lockers just inside, and proceeded through three security doors to the visiting and correspondence room, where the man who used to be their father awaited them. The pleasure of seeing one another again seemed always to be overwhelmed by the fact that the reunion was taking place in a federal penitentiary; the awkwardness is visible in a group picture the prison photographer took to commemorate Helmuth's rare visits. Something in the Buxbaum family was given the death penalty after Hanna's murder.

Almost out of legal options, Clayton Ruby nevertheless continued the fight to redress what he considers to be one of the worst miscarriages of Canadian justice – the apparently proper conviction of an insane man without the evidence for that insanity ever being tested in a court of law Having run out of tribunals to make that case, the lawyer who represented Donald Marshall at the Royal Commission into the country's most infamous miscarriage of justice appealed directly to the federal justice minister in 1990 under Section 690 of the Criminal Code. A year later, future prime minister Kim Campbell turned down his application for the Mercy of the Crown, declaring that Ruby's plea on behalf of Helmuth had "fallen short" of the high standard required to send the case back to trial or to the appeal courts. The eminent lawyer was disturbed: "The system was protected, so the trial's appearance of fairness was not in any way shattered by the notion that there was important evidence that wasn't raised, but the individual got crushed. It bothers me a lot. No lawyer likes to be associated with a miscarriage of justice because it leaves you with a terrible taste in your mouth forever. You don't ever get over it."

The law itself took on a new shape in the years following Helmuth's conviction. In May 1991, the Supreme Court of Canada made a landmark ruling in *Regina v. Swain* that created a new common law rule concerning the defence of insanity. Although the case arose over the issue of a person's right to control his own defence (the court enhanced that right by setting stricter limits on the circumstances under which the Crown could bring out insanity evidence over the objections of an accused), there were some ironic implications for the Buxbaum case.

"Society's interest in ensuring that persons who are not criminally responsible are not convicted cannot override the right of an accused to control his own defences and to forego [sic] the defence of insanity if this is in his interests," then Supreme Court Justice Bertha Wilson wrote.

In the wake of Swain, an accused is now entitled to the trial of two issues: his guilt or innocence on the merits, and if convicted, a separate determination on the insanity defence without the pejorative impression that he was somehow trying to cheat justice. What Ontario's Court of Appeal had rejected in Buxbaum's case was now the law of the land. As Antonio Lamer, Chief Justice of the Supreme Court of Canada, put it, "This new common law rule would give an accused the option of waiting until the Crown had discharged its full burden of proof to raise the insanity issue, without removing the existing right of an accused to raise evidence of his or her mental condition during the course of the trial."

Making the irony bittersweet was the fact that Clayton Ruby's law firm argued *Swain*.

"The values that we expressed to the Court of Appeal in Buxbaum were precisely the ones that we later presented to the Supreme Court of Canada in Swain and they accepted those values. It was exactly the same rationale and it was accepted because they were a better court. They felt freer to create law that would allow those values full play and the Court of Appeal didn't share those values one whit," Ruby said later.

For Ruby the issue was no longer just that Helmuth Buxbaum was not guilty by reason of insanity (although he believed that to be true), but that by the standards of the *Swain* ruling he had had only half a trial. But Ruby had no illusions. Unlike the astonishing case of David Milgaard, where the Supreme Court of Canada ordered a new trial for the convicted murderer based on retroactively applying the law as it exists today to a trial that in the court's opinion had otherwise been sound (Saskatchewan prosecutors subsequently decided not to retry Milgaard), Ruby knew that there would be no demonstrations on the lawns of Parliament demanding the same treatment for Helmuth. Public scepticism about whether a convict had actually committed a crime was one thing; doubt about an inmate's responsibility for a heinous murder because of insanity was quite another.

Having exhausted all conventional legal remedies, Ruby took his client's case to the United Nations Human Rights Committee of the Centre for Human Rights in Geneva. On April 23, 1993, Ruby asked the commissioners to consider the Buxbaum case under the optional protocol to the international covenant on civil and political rights to which Canada is a signatory.

In a written submission, he argued that Helmuth had been deprived of his rights under Article 14 of the protocol that guarantees everyone convicted of a crime the right to have the conviction reviewed by a higher tribunal according to the law. By resealing the expert evidence on his client's mental condition without forming an opinion about it or admitting it into evidence, the Court of Appeal for Ontario had "failed to give fair hearing to the evidence of insanity adduced before it," as required by Section 686(1) of the Criminal Code. Ruby included affidavits from Dr. Ruth Bray and Dr. Andrew Malcolm attesting to the fact that they had advised Helmuth's original defence team of the availability of a Section 16 defence before he stood trial. But his fight was clearly with the Canadian courts, not Eddie Greenspan and associates.

"It cannot be in the interests of justice to incarcerate an individual for the commission of a crime when that person was clearly insane at the relevant time. This principle is one which has been upheld numerous times in the Canadian Criminal justice system. The Court of Appeal for Ontario refused to acknowledge these over-riding interests by giving more importance to the supposed tactics of defence counsel than to the interests of a person for whom there is abundant evidence of insanity."

Although the United Nations commissioners have no power to reverse the decision of a domestic tribunal, Ruby knew that a finding in Helmuth's favour would have impact. In the handful of cases that have made their way to the UN forum in Geneva, Canada has always reacted swiftly when found in breach of its international treaty obligations. Ruby hoped that case No. 534/1993 would be one of them. It was not. On October 19, 1993, the United Nations court ignored the substance of Ruby's submission and ruled that Helmuth's case was "inadmissible" for procedural reasons.

It was not quite the end of the legal trail. In the ongoing civil action against Helmuth by his nephew Roy Buxbaum, lawyer J. Gregory Richards intends to argue that Buxbaum isn't liable for any psychological trauma Roy may have experienced as a result of witnessing Hanna's murder because his uncle had been (and remains) insane. If the jury agrees with Richards, it will establish Helmuth's insanity as a matter of judicial record and cast serious doubt on the criminal court that found him guilty of murder and the appeal court that upheld that conviction without testing the medical evidence. Armed with irrefutable proof of Helmuth's organic brain damage that predates Hanna's murder, as well as the unanimous opinion of several experts who make a prima facie case for Helmuth's insanity, Richards, like Ruby, believes that something profoundly important is at stake for both Helmuth and the legal system when the case is heard.

The law officers who handled the celebrated case have undergone metamorphoses of their own in the years since Helmuth's conviction. Crown prosecutor Michael Martin has been elevated to the bench, and several police investigators have also been promoted. As Deputy Commissioner of the OPP, Ron Piers is now one of the most powerful policemen in the country. Mel Getty is a staff sergeant in charge of a field detachment in Norfolk, Ontario, and Paul Edwards is an inspector with the Criminal Investigation Branch in Orillia.

As a group, the police and prosecutors remain convinced that Helmuth Buxbaum was dealt with properly under the law. Although Judge Martin admits today that the Crown was never able to come up with a firm total for the murder money paid by Buxbaum to Barrett, he has no doubt that the right people were punished for Hanna Buxbaum's murder. As for the deal with Barrett and Allen, the Crown team holds to the opinion that it expressed at the time of the trial: in order to guarantee the convictions of the man who had arranged and paid for Hanna's murder, and the man who had actually pulled the trigger, a plea bargain was a necessary evil they could live with in the circumstances. Regarding the insanity defence raised on appeal by Clayton Ruby, Buxbaum's prosecutors make no bones about the fact that had such a defence been raised at trial, it would have been vigorously contested.

Of all the law officers associated with the case, no one has followed its legal twists and turns as closely as Ron Piers. He is proud of the work of the OPP in solving Hanna Buxbaum's murder, and it was clearly the high point of his police career as an inspector. The first accomplishment listed under the heading of "Investigations" on his extensive curriculum vitae is the Buxbaum case. He sat through all of Helmuth's trials, including the Ontario Supreme Court appeal, where Ruby tried to raise the insanity defence. Piers, too, thinks that justice was served. Carefully prefacing his reflections on the case with the assertion that he is not an expert in the field of psychiatry, Piers says, "I have been around the courts long enough to know that if an accused can find seven doctors to say that he is insane, the Crown can find seven more to say that he isn't. As far as I'm concerned, the affidavits saying that Buxbaum is insane are in the same league as the affidavits Greenspan produced at the bail hearing attesting to his good character."

After so many years in prison, Helmuth Buxbaum candidly admits that he has become institutionalized. He has grown accustomed to his tiny cell, the bad food, and the loneliness. The incessant noise no longer keeps him awake at night, and he has made his peace with guards he once viewed as sadistic dullards. Seen by other inmates as a "straight john," the avuncular inmate is only infrequently bothered by con men looking for a piece of his dwindling fortune. Instead, he goes about his new job as assistant to the chaplain with a measure of respect. He edits the chaplaincy newsletter and sings in the prison choir, having rediscovered the devotional zeal of his youth and early middle age. If he can manage to retrieve it from the basement of his cottage in Huntsville, he would even like to resume his childhood study of the violin. Once appalled by Kingston penitentiary, he has since turned down transfers to lower security institutions, resigned to his anonymous place in the steel thickets of the country's prison system.

But his private war for justice continues. Although he once wrote to Clayton Ruby that "after four years it is rather difficult to remember if I subconsciously encouraged Barrett to do what he did," Helmuth quickly resumed his efforts to prove his complete innocence after the failure of his 1989 appeals. He retained private investigator Chuck Graham, a retired RCMP officer who was initially hired to find out if Liza Buxbaum was engaging in adulterous affairs, but who soon found himself carrying out other assignments. "If you have someone working in the London area," Helmuth wrote him, "I have reasonable assurance that my late wife, Hanna Buxbaum, carried on an affair with a jeweller from Mount Brydges . . . Perhaps your investigator could check my suspicion out in London when he is there."

In time, Graham's investigative efforts came to be exclusively focused on proving Helmuth's innocence. Acting on his client's instructions, and often relying on his facts, Graham proceeded to gather affidavits from sources who claimed to have information exonerating Helmuth of any responsibility in his wife's death. In 1991, for example, James Clifford signed a statement swearing that he had heard Pat Allen admit to shooting Hanna Buxbaum. Unfortunately, Clifford, a lifelong criminal, happened to be serving time in Kingston penitentiary for break and enter when he was seized with the urge to set the record straight.

Although others would simply add Clifford's name to the long list of killers and thieves from Peter McDonald to Peter Demeter who claimed to have information proving Buxbaum's innocence, Helmuth smoothly assimilated the report from his private investigator into a new theory of his wife's murder. Pat Allen, not Gary Foshay, had actually shot Hanna; since the Crown had missed that central fact, it was easy to see how they had wrongfully convicted Helmuth of arranging his wife's murder. Helmuth even experienced a traumatic flashback to July 5, 1984, in which he now remembered that Gary Foshay had fired a bullet in his direction when he had tried to come to the assistance of his doomed wife.

Untroubled by the conundrums of logic, and ever contemptuous of what he took to be the secular lunacies of justice gone awry, Helmuth began to wonder if the earthquake that had struck the courtroom during Eddie Greenspan's summation might not supply the key to undoing his wrongful conviction. "There was a time when the breaking of the hanging rope during a hanging was interpreted as God's intervention and the condemned man's life was spared. Such a supernatural earthquake could also be interpreted in similar terms. Is there an old law on the books dealing with supernatural intervention?" he asked his lawyer.

Eventually, Helmuth's thoughts turned to Hanna. First he prepared her Victim Impact Statement, which he duly sent to Ron Fainstein in the federal Justice Department. Almost all of the one-and-a-half-page document dealt with the injustice of Helmuth's conviction, but the last line was devoted to its ostensible subject: "Remembering Hanna well, I would conclude by stating that Hanna's last, fleeting prayer probably was: 'Father forgive them, for they know not what they do!' I agree! – Reflections from prison. I. M. Innocent!"

A week later, Helmuth wrote directly to the woman he stood convicted of having murdered:

"Dearest Hanna,

"Soon it will be seven years since you left this world, your children and me to answer the call of the Lord to come home. I still miss you, especially during my devotional times because it reminds me [of] when we experienced such close intimacy spiritually through our common bond with our Saviour, the Lord Jesus Christ.

"I wonder sometimes what you are doing, if you can see everything that is happening on earth, especially your children and me. I am sure that by now you have met my parents, my sister Musja [Maria] and my sister Elizabeth who died many years ago and, yes, I am sure you welcomed your mother last year when she was called home at the Tabor Manor in St. Catharines. You know, one of the seven accused men, Terry Kline, told me that he was praying to you at Elgin-Middlesex Detention Centre but I told him not to do that; that Scripturally we are forbidden to pray to angels or men or women. The chaplain at the prison was praying for your soul during a chapel service and, again, I don't understand why highly educated people cannot read and understand the instructions clearly found in the Word of God.

"You don't know how many times I have wished that the gunmen (I know now that there were at least two men with guns), would have shot us both on Highway 402 on July 5, 1984. But God in His wisdom wanted me to stay behind and possibly help our children during their teenage years when they particularly need the love [of] their parents. This was made extremely difficult since the Canadian prisons discourage the public's interest in their prisoners and often hinder the relatives to visit with their caged ones.

"However, I am physically well; you know that I have hardly any headaches anymore and have put on an extra 50 pounds which I would like to lose; and I will, once I have been exonerated and acquitted of all these false accusations and get a chance to exercise again. You know, darling, that I have always loved you and I still do and your sudden death was the most shocking experience of my life; it hurt me so badly, at times, I thought that I was losing my mind . . .

"However, I can report that you can be proud of your children . . . You would really be surprised at Phillip, mother Hanna, or should I say Grandmother Hanna? You have a grandson. Phillip got married to a beautiful girl whose name is Nicholle (Nikki for short) and supports his own family by hiring more educated people than himself to place them in well paying positions around the world . . .

"I know from scripture that the redeemed remember, can see and speak, and sometimes I think how wonderful it must be to meet and speak with Samuel, David, Elijah, Solomon, Paul or Esther, Hanna or Moses or Abraham. But then, of course, I don't know if everybody has access to all others.

"You probably know that most born-again believers believe that the Lord's second-coming to rapture His church could be any day now. So, I try to watch and be ready; have some oil in my lamp and be ready to leave. I think that it will be in the next 7 years, since I think Israel must rebuild the temple before the Antichrist appears. Can you imagine how much suffering awaits those unprepared for the wrath of God when the world (minus the church) must go through 7 years of suffering such as the world has not seen? So I will be there soon honey, and so will almost all of your family! Soon you will see your youngest son Danny and Esther, Ruth and even your grandson Tyler-John! How much joy there will be! . . .

"You know a lot more now about why and when God answers prayer, but you know [the] biggest answer to your prayer – "Lord, save Robert Barrett" – came only after your death. And you know, the first thing he did is that he wrote an affidavit confessing his perjury and voluntarily submitted this to my criminal lawyer, Clayton Ruby. In case you wonder why I am still in prison, let me tell you that psychiatrists have been able to convince my lawyer that I am crazy, and so I will probably have to stay in prison until I die, or until the Lord raptures me right out of prison. But don't worry about that . . . I have turned my life over to the Lord and it is perfectly fine with me to stay put and hold still until He sees fit to change my circumstances.

"I do worry about our children from time to time: you know all the teaching we did about forgiving so that God can forgive us likewise (The Lord's Prayer) seems to be lost. Some children are still caught up in the root of bitterness, not realizing that they hurt themselves the most if they persist in staying bitter. How wonderfully relieving it is when we forgive; how it takes the burdens from our shoulders!

"Do you remember all the hours we spent planning the lives of our children? Well, you know, it does not work that way. Even with the best intentions, parents can only influence their children for so many years and then they decide things for themselves and must learn their own lessons from their own mistakes!

"But I don't want to ramble. The purpose of this letter is basically to tell you that all your children still love you, want to do what is right, and that your motherly and diligent work with them was not in vain! I wish I could see them now, but perhaps you see them better and more often than I do!

"Honey, writing this letter has been a refreshing and uplifting experience for me. I will write again. Thanks for your unconditional love and patience for me and our children! You are in a much better place now than we are because where you are, 'there is no more death, neither sorrow, nor crying, neither is there any more pain: for the former things have passed away.'

In the years since the murder, London has remained much as it was when Helmuth and Hanna made their business headquarters here and the Buxbaums were regulars at the Swiss Chalet every Sunday after church. The Thames River still snakes through the city, a feature more permanent even than the sturdy buildings that house London Life and the other insurance companies that lend the place its air of solid prosperity. Beyond its immediate environs, the city exacts tribute from the thriving farming communities in its commercial orbit: Strathroy, Tillsonburg, Lucan, Exeter, and Forest. Even the announced closure of the local military base, clouding the future of London's General Motors plant, which makes vehicles for the army, has done little to shake the confidence of the city's 300,000 inhabitants.

For all its underlying immutability, the place has undergone the thousand subtler transformations occasioned by the changing fortunes of its private citizens, their voyages up and down, and their passages. Kelly's Bar and the Wellington Tavern have disappeared, one already levelled in the name of urban renewal, and the other, an empty shell awaiting the wrecker's ball. The two-storey office building with its chocolate-coloured bricks where Helmuth used to start every work day with a religious service is still there, but Treugott Management has long since ceased to be its prize tenant. Directly across Wonderland Road, West Park Baptist Church squats on its prime piece of real estate, its impressive bulk facing Helmuth's former nursing home headquarters. It has a new pastor now, Rev. Paul Fawcett having left the church and returned to the United States not long after his star parishioner's conviction. Despite Helmuth's beseeching letters, the church's Board of Elders stubbornly refuses to practise what it preaches; the sinner remains unforgiven by the custodians of the flock of which he was once so prominent a member.

Just outside the city, the good earth dwarfs all merely human concerns.

The trees that the Buxbaums religiously planted every spring at their Komoka estate are bigger now, affording shade in the hot summer afternoons, and a leafy serenade when the wind comes up. The nursing home that set the hard-working immigrants on the road to a fortune beyond their wildest imaginings is now three times as large and operates under the name Country Terrace. Just behind it, another family has taken up residence in the sprawling Buxbaum mansion. It looks much as it did in old photographs, except that the words "God is Love," which Helmuth had inscribed on the pillars at the head of the driveway, have been sandblasted away by the new owners.

The curious, it seems, need no encouragement.

Sunbaked and barren, Campbell Cemetery sits behind a green, wrought-iron fence and a ragged stand of stunted cedars – a field of bones squeezed by the unceasing industry of the living. On the day that Hanna was buried beside Helmuth's parents, Otto and Luise, you could still see the Buxbaums' dream house from her gravesite; since then, a few buildings and a windmill have popped up to spoil the view. Hanna's dust, reposing in a grave with a double headstone to accommodate her husband of twenty-three years when the time comes, doesn't seem to mind. A plastic bouquet propped against her black marble monument nearly obscures the epitaph from Revelations: "Their works do follow them."

It hardly matters. There is usually no one here to read it, or to see the late afternoon sun glinting off her cold stone, or to hear the thrush, deep in its cornfield, singing.